MEDIA AND SOCIETY AFTER TECHNOLOGICAL DISRUPTION

The internet has reshaped the media landscape and the social institutions built upon it. Competition from online media sources has decimated local journalism and diminished the twentieth century's established journalistic gatekeepers. Social media puts individual users front and center in the creation of the content that they consume. Harmful speech can spread further and faster, and the institutions responsible for policing that speech – Facebook, TikTok, YouTube, and the like – lack any clear twentieth-century analog. The law is still working to catch up to the world these changes have wrought.

This volume gathers sixteen scholars in law, media, technology, and history to consider these changes. Chapters explore the breakdown of trust in the media, changes in the law of defamation and privacy, challenges of online content moderation, and financial viability for journalistic enterprises in the internet age. This title is also available as Open Access on Cambridge Core.

Kyle Langvardt is an Assistant Professor of Law at the University of Nebraska College of Law. He has written extensively on technology regulation and the First Amendment, with a special focus on issues relating to content moderation and consumer protection.

Gus Hurwitz is Senior Fellow and Academic Director of the Center for Technology, Innovation, and Competition at the University of Pennsylvania. He is also the Director of Law & Economics Programs at the International Center for Law & Economics, and was previously a professor of law and founding director of the Governance & Technology Center at the University of Nebraska. His teaching and research blends law, technology, and business to study the benefits of costs and technological change.

Media and Society After Technological Disruption

Edited by

KYLE LANGVARDT

University of Nebraska

GUS HURWITZ

University of Pennsylvania

CAMBRIDGE
UNIVERSITY PRESS

CAMBRIDGE
UNIVERSITY PRESS

Shaftesbury Road, Cambridge CB2 8EA, United Kingdom

One Liberty Plaza, 20th Floor, New York, NY 10006, USA

477 Williamstown Road, Port Melbourne, VIC 3207, Australia

314–321, 3rd Floor, Plot 3, Splendor Forum, Jasola District Centre, New Delhi – 110025, India

103 Penang Road, #05–06/07, Visioncrest Commercial, Singapore 238467

Cambridge University Press is part of Cambridge University Press & Assessment, a department of the University of Cambridge.

We share the University's mission to contribute to society through the pursuit of education, learning and research at the highest international levels of excellence.

www.cambridge.org
Information on this title: www.cambridge.org/9781009174428

DOI: 10.1017/9781009174411

First published 2024

A catalogue record for this publication is available from the British Library

A Cataloging-in-Publication data record for this book is available from the Library of Congress

ISBN 978-1-009-17442-8 Hardback

For my family

Kyle Langvardt

With gratitude to Kyle and Elana, who took a gamble on an iconoclast and without whom this book would not have happened

Gus Hurwitz

Contents

Contributors

Jane Bambauer, Dorothy H. and Lewis Rosenstiel Distinguished Professor of Law, James E. Rogers College of Law, University of Arizona

Ashutosh Bhagwat, Distinguished Professor and Boochever and Bird Endowed Chair for the Study and Teaching of Freedom and Equality, UC Davis School of Law

Erin C. Carroll, Professor of Law, Legal Practice, Georgetown University Law Center

Laura Edelson, Assistant Professor, Northeastern University

Amy Gajda, Professor of Law, Tulane University

Gus Hurwitz, Senior Fellow and Academic Director, Center for Technology, Innovation, and Competition, University of Pennsylvania; Director of Law & Economics Programs, International Center for Law & Economics

RonNell Andersen Jones, University Distinguished Professor and the Teitelbaum Chair, University of Utah S.J. Quinney College of Law; Affiliated Fellow, Yale Law School Information Society Project

Thomas E. Kadri, Assistant Professor, University of Georgia School of Law; Affiliate Faculty, University of Georgia Institute for Women's Studies; Legislative & Policy Director, Clinic to End Tech Abuse at Cornell University

Kyle Langvardt, Assistant Professor of Law, University of Nebraska College of Law

Laurie Thomas Lee, Professor, University of Nebraska-Lincoln, College of Journalism and Mass Communications

Lyrissa Lidsky, Raymond & Miriam Ehrlich Chair in U.S. Constitutional Law, University of Florida Levin College of Law

Paul Matzko, Research Fellow, Cato Institute

Helen Norton, University Distinguished Professor and Rothgerber Chair in Constitutional Law, University of Colorado School of Law

Alan Z. Rozenshtein, Associate Professor of Law, University of Minnesota Law School

Eugene Volokh, Gary T. Schwartz Distinguished Professor of Law, UCLA School of Law; Visiting Fellow (Senior Fellow starting May 2024), Hoover Institution, Stanford University

Ramsi A. Woodcock, Wyatt, Tarrant & Combs Associate Professor of Law, University of Kentucky College of Law, Secondary Appointment, Department of Management, University of Kentucky Gatton College of Business & Economics

Acknowledgments

This has been an ambitious, complex project, and it would not have been possible without the substantial financial support that the Nebraska Governance and Technology Center received from the John S. and James L. Knight Foundation. Nor would it have been possible without the institutional support of the University of Nebraska and its College of Law, which housed the Nebraska Governance and Technology Center.

We also thank our colleague Elana Zeide for her early help in shaping the project's direction and recruiting contributors. Woody Barfield provided invaluable advice on what it takes to get a book like this published. And several student editors also helped get these chapters ready for print: McKinley Brock, Lauren Bruning, Anthony Budell, Robert Drust, Jeff Owusu-Ansah, Paige Ross, and Emma Schlenker. Finally, we thank Sarah Burns, the late-stage editor who consolidated these essays into a single work and whose thousands of small, sharp edits elevated the material in so many ways.

Introduction

Gus Hurwitz and Kyle Langvardt

The internet has remade both the media and the social institutions that surround the media. Speech was not cheap in the twentieth century. News organizations had to buy newsprint, paper, distribution networks, transmitters, spectrum licenses – all kinds of things that cost much more than a Facebook page – if they wished to reach an audience. But the few news organizations that *could* cover these costs held a safe market position, and from this perch, they wielded a great deal of epistemic and moral authority in their communities. They became "gatekeepers" with the power and the responsibility to decide what information, and what claims, were fit to print. Much of media law, and particularly First Amendment law, seems to have developed around the assumption that news organizations could and would play this gatekeeping role, and that the government should therefore rarely need to.

That world is gone. Competition from the internet and social media has decimated the business model that underwrote the twentieth century's gatekeepers. And those twentieth-century media institutions that have survived disruption – institutions such as the *New York Times* or the major television networks – are in no position to *play* gatekeeper. News consumers mostly get whatever flavor of "news" they wish, and individual speakers mostly decide what kind of speech is fit to post. There are gatekeepers in this environment, but they are institutions like Facebook, TikTok, or YouTube that bear little resemblance to yesterday's news giants and that wield their power in ways that lack any clear twentieth-century analog. The law is only beginning to catch up.

This project gathers sixteen scholars in law, media, technology, and history to consider these changes together. We divided these sixteen scholars into four groups of four, with each group considering one broad facet of the situation.

PART I: TRUSTED COMMUNICATORS

We asked the first group of authors to write on the decline in trust that traditional media institutions have suffered in recent years. Authors reflected on the implications of this decline in trust for media's ability to shape and convene public discourse. They also considered the causes of this loss in trust, and what might be done to get it back.

PART II: DEFAMATION AND PRIVACY

The second group of authors wrote on the law's role in policing communications that inflict privacy and reputational harms. This group paid particular attention to the role of technological development in driving a proliferation of harmful speech, and also to the law's emergent response.

PART III: PLATFORM GOVERNANCE

We assigned the third group to write on tech platforms and the role they play as private regulators of the content they host. Authors wrote on how this regulation plays out in practice, and more generally, on its costs, benefits, and risks. The group also considered changes to regulatory or technical architecture that may improve the systems of content moderation that is in place today.

PART IV: SUSTAINING JOURNALISTIC INSTITUTIONS

This final group wrote on traditional media institutions' struggle to maintain financial solvency in the twenty-first century. Authors compared the failure of some models (newspapers) with the successes of others (television, social media), and considered various regulatory proposals to stanch the losses.

PART I

Trusted Communicators

1

Introduction

Trusted Communicators

Kyle Langvardt

Trust in media institutions has declined more or less apace with trust in every other kind of major institution in public life. Or perhaps it is more correct, as Ashutosh Bhagwat observes in his contribution to this project, to say that trust has declined in the *types* of media institutions, the proverbial Walter Cronkites, that dominated "the media" during the twentieth-century period when modern American ideals around free speech and journalistic value were still taking form.

Today much of the trust that mainstream media institutions once enjoyed has migrated, in a fragmented way, toward attention merchants of various shapes and scales that treat the news as a mere opportunity to juice engagement by serving identity-affirming content to targeted market segments. And though some of the major mainstream media institutions survive and continue to produce top-quality factual reporting (the *New York Times*, for example), even these outlets must play the identity-affirmation game at some level. There is no way in such an environment for America's trusted media communicators to play the consensus-building role that they once did. Instead, the trust dynamic between Americans and their many news sources today works to accelerate polarization and exacerbate their seeming inability to agree on the facts.

All of the authors in this research cluster agree that the collapse in media trust (or diffusion of media trust, however you want to view it) stems, at least in part, from technological changes that have expanded competition among news producers and created a "buyer's market" for news. Within these constraints, what can worthy, fact-based media institutions do to restore the trust they have lost?

In Chapter 2, "Getting to Trustworthiness (but Not Necessarily to Trust)," Helen Norton opens the discussion by backing up a step: What does it mean for a news outlet to be *worthy* of trust? The question invites two observations. First, an institution may misappropriate the trust of many readers, or something functionally similar to trust, by pandering to them, manipulating them, or engaging in a range of other similar practices that make an institution *less* worthy of trust rather than more. But second, it may also be possible for an institution to gain a degree of public trust by demonstrating its trustworthiness in noticeable ways – and if done skillfully, this second approach may provide at least a partial path toward aligning economic viability with ethical reporting. Professor Norton's chapter takes some initial steps on this path, identifying a working index of trustworthy and non-trustworthy media behaviors and offering some ways to elevate trustworthy behaviors. But she acknowledges that this high road will be hard and uncertain.

In Chapter 3, "Sober and Self-Guided Newsgathering," Jane Bambauer discusses one particularly insidious form of untrustworthy reporting: dramatic coverage of facts that are accurate but nevertheless misleading because they are statistically unrepresentative. Such reporting, which often plays on identity-driven fears or hostilities, causes harm by inspiring news consumers to approach life, and each other, with overcaution and hostility. But as Professor Bambauer argues, media institutions trying to compete in a fragmented market face intense pressure to produce just this kind of content. Audiences demand it because they are victims of heuristic biases that make them crave identity affirmation. Professor Bambauer therefore proposes a bit of very difficult jujitsu: If news producers cannot get out from under reader demands in a buyers' market, then they should try to reshape reader demands by retraining them to put facts in better perspective – or at least to invest their trust more intelligently in institutions that do. But this maneuver – as Professor Bambauer concedes – will take a very long time to execute.

In Chapter 4, "The New Gatekeepers? Social Media and the 'Search for Truth'," Ashutosh Bhagwat questions whether it is even appropriate to hope that some new generation of gatekeepers can pick up the Walter Cronkite mantle. As he argues, the whole notion that a select few should play gatekeeper based on their status as elite "trusted communicators" chafes against the "marketplace of ideas" theory that conventionally motivates First Amendment thought. Or perhaps more to the point, a market clustered around trusted communicators looks less like the bazaar that Oliver Wendell Holmes envisioned and more like a *real* market, with heavy concentrations of power that tend to draw from accidental circumstances and endowment effects rather than some ideal of consumer rationality. On this view, Cronkite had the public's trust because there was only enough spectrum for a few networks; Google has the public's trust because it is the gateway to the internet. Yet we have looked to these gatekeepers to set terms for public discourse and the democratic process – an odd result given that neither gatekeeper secured its position by actually persuading the public.

Finally, in Chapter 5, "Beyond the Watchdog: Using Law to Build Trust in the Press," Erin Carroll argues that the various problems of media trust may appear less intractable if the law would update its sense of the role journalists should play in a democratic society. For more than half a century, an adversarial "watchdog" ethic of journalism provides the near-exclusive metric for journalistic prestige in the United States. This same view of the press shapes the most memorable press-freedom rhetoric from the Supreme Court and animates most portrayals of journalists doing good work in movies and TV. But the watchdog role, as Professor Carroll observes, can exacerbate partisan dynamics while narrowing a news institution's base of trust in the community. So while the watchdog ethic provides invaluable benefits to democratic governance, it can also *frustrate* democratic governance and impair trust in media if news institutions lean exclusively into it. Instead, Professor Carroll urges news institutions to rediscover the largely forgotten idea that news institutions should aspire to act as *facilitators* and *fora* for citizen discourse in a democratic community. Such a role does not lend itself so much to the segmented identity-affirmation dynamic that undermines public consensus and solidarity and motivates untrustworthy coverage. And as a mode of speech governance, this is a role that would ideally advance public discourse rather than control it.

2

Getting to Trustworthiness (but Not Necessarily to Trust)

*Helen Norton**

2.1 INTRODUCTION

Political scientist and ethicist Russell Hardin observed that "trust depends on two quite different dimensions: the motivation of the potentially trusted person to attend to the truster's interests and his or her competence to do so."[1] Our willingness to trust an actor thus generally turns on inductive reasoning: our perceptions of that actor's motives and competence, based on our own experiences with that actor.[2] Trust and distrust are also both episodic and comparative concepts, as whether we trust a particular actor depends in part on when we are asked – and to whom we are comparing them.[3] And depending on our experience, distrust is sometimes wise: "[D]istrust is sometimes the only credible implication of the evidence. Indeed, distrust is sometimes not merely a rational assessment but it is also benign, in that it protects against harms rather than causing them."[4]

* Thanks to Erin Carroll, Ash Bhagwat, and Jane Bambauer for thoughtful comments and questions, and to Kyle Langvardt for leading this effort.

1 Russell Hardin, *Distrust: Manifestations and Management*, *in* DISTRUST 8 (Russell Hardin ed., 2004); *see also* RUSSELL HARDIN, TRUST & TRUSTWORTHINESS 1 (2002) ("To say that I trust you in some context means that I think you are or will be trustworthy toward me in that context.").

2 *See* HARDIN, TRUST & TRUSTWORTHINESS, *supra* note 1, at 89 ("If the evidence sometimes leads to trust, then it can also sometimes lead to distrust. Indeed, on the cognitive account of trust as a category of knowledge, we can go further to say the following: If, on your own knowledge, I seem to be trustworthy to some degree with respect to some matter, then you do trust me with respect to that matter. Similarly, if I seem to be untrustworthy, then you do distrust me. There is no act of choosing to trust or distrust, your knowledge or beliefs about me constitute your degree of trust or distrust of me.").

3 *See* Vincent Blasi, *Toward a Theory of Prior Restraint: The Central Linkage*, 66 MINN. L. REV. 11, 73–74 (1981) (describing distrust as "a comparative notion").

4 HARDIN, TRUST & TRUSTWORTHINESS, *supra* note 1, at 89.

Actors and institutions thus cannot control whether others trust them.[5] So in this chapter, I focus not on how to encourage the public to trust the media, but instead on how to encourage the media to do what it *can* control – in other words, to behave in ways that demonstrate its trustworthy motives and competence.[6]

To be sure, different communities find different behaviors indicative of trustworthiness, and thus the media's choice to behave in ways that some communities find trustworthy may simultaneously inspire other communities' distrust. For example, as demonstrated by an exhaustive study conducted by information and technology scholars Yochai Benkler, Robert Faris, and Hal Roberts, some contemporary media cultures value, and thus trust, media institutions that privilege truth-seeking – while others trust those that simply confirm identity:

> Media and politicians have the option to serve their audiences and followers by exclusively delivering messages that confirm the prior inclinations of their constituents, or by also including true but disconfirming news when the actual state of the world does not conform to partisan beliefs. For media, this is the key distinction between partisan media and objective media.[7]

In other words, different media ecosystems confer, and receive, trust for different behaviors and different end goals.[8]

This chapter addresses media behaviors that are likely considered trustworthy in media cultures that reward truth-seeking rather than identity confirmation.[9] It thus

[5] *See id.* at 9 ("A central problem with trust and distrust is that they are essentially cognitive assessments of the trustworthiness of the other party and may therefore be mistaken."); Deborah Welch Larson, *Distrust: Prudent, If Not Always Wise*, *in* DISTRUST, *supra* note 1, at 34 (same).

[6] In using the term "media," I acknowledge (but do not resolve) the important and difficult problem of whether and when to characterize social media as part of the "press," or news media. *See* PETER COE, MEDIA FREEDOM IN THE AGE OF CITIZEN JOURNALISM 60 (2021) ("In addition to changing the way in which we consume news, whether some social media platforms have altered the media ecology and disrupted the paradigm in another way – by becoming media companies in their own right, and therefore subject to the enhanced right to media freedom and the obligations and responsibilities that this brings – is the source of ongoing debate."); Erin Carroll, A *Free Press without Democracy*, 56 U.C. DAVIS L. REV. 289, 304 (2022) (distinguishing "a truth-based, free press" from a broader concept of the "media" that includes those broadcasters and publishers less focused on truth).

[7] YOCHAI BENKLER, ROBERT FARIS & HAL ROBERTS, NETWORK PROPAGANDA: MANIPULATION, DISINFORMATION, AND RADICALIZATION IN AMERICAN POLITICS 76–77 (2018).

[8] *See id.* at 78 (describing some media outlets' strategy of "emphasizing partisan-confirming news over truth and helping segments of the public reduce their discomfort by telling them that the outlets providing disconfirming news are not trustworthy" and describing outlets that "compete by policing each other for deviance from identity confirmation, not truth").

[9] *See id.* at 80 ("[A] media ecosystem that operates under the reality-check dynamic will tend to be more robust to disinformation operation because each outlet in this system gains from exposing the untruth and loses by being caught in the lie or error. Its audiences are less likely to trust any media source in particular, and more likely to check across different media to see whether a story is, in fact, true."); *id.* at 359 ("The good news is that the mainstream media continues to perform an enormously important role for most Americans" – that is, those outside the 25–30 percent that rely on identity-confirming media).

leaves aside the even more difficult problem of how to encourage other ecosystems to reward truth-seeking even when truth disconfirms identity.[10]

To start, consider how the media's self-interest and incompetence (both real and perceived) create barriers to its trustworthiness. More specifically, self-interest is among the motives that trigger distrust: We find it hard to trust self-interested actors to act in ways attentive to our own interests.[11] The media's potential for self-interest thus often fuels the public's distrust, just as governmental actors' self-interest also often triggers the public's distrust.

When I speak of the media's potential for self-interest, I refer to the media's need to do whatever it takes to survive financially, especially in today's destabilized media environment. Concerns about the media's motives include perceptions that it is all too willing to invade privacy, oversensationalize, or cater to advertisers' preferences for self-gain – in other words, to exploit others to capture users' attention and engagement to protect its economic bottom line.[12]

Self-interested (and thus untrustworthy) media behaviors include the deployment of platform designs and interfaces that collect, aggregate, and analyze data about us in ways that enable them to influence our choices.[13] To be sure, sometimes such designs and interfaces give us more of what we want. But too often they manipulate us – in other words, they influence our behavior in ways that we would resist if we were aware of these efforts. Nobody wants to be manipulated, especially when we understand manipulation (as a number of ethicists do[14]) to mean a hidden effort to target and exploit our vulnerabilities. Yet the contemporary speech environment enables that sort of manipulation in unprecedented ways.[15] The news media is by no means immune, as press law scholar Erin Carroll has documented the substantial extent to which news organizations collect – and allow others to collect – data about

[10] *See id.* at 387 ("Breathing new life into the truth-seeking institutions that operate on reason and evidence would require a revival of the idea that science, scholarship, journalism, law, and professionalism more generally offer real constraints on what one can say and do, and that they are not all simply modes of legitimating power.... The former is unlikely without the latter. These political and cultural developments will have to overcome not only right-wing propaganda, but also decades of left-wing criticism of objectivity and truth-seeking institutions. Developing such a framework without falling into high modernist nostalgia is the real answer to the threat of a post-truth era.").

[11] *See* Hardin, *Distrust*, *supra* note 1, at 8 (explaining trust as depending in great part on "the motivation of the potentially trusted person to attend to the truster's interests" rather than simply to her own interests).

[12] *See* Carroll, *supra* note 6, at 339 (describing the press's growing "tendency to preference the commercial imperative of satisfying consumer desire over the mission of promoting democracy").

[13] *See* Helen Norton, *Manipulation and the First Amendment*, 30 WM. & MARY BILL RTS. J. 221, 221–30 (2021).

[14] *See* Daniel Susser, Beate Roessler & Helen Nissenbaum, *Online Manipulation: Hidden Influences in a Digital World*, 4 GEO. L. TECH. REV. 1, 26 (2019) (defining manipulation).

[15] *See* Norton, *supra* note 13, at 224–30.

their online readers.[16] Indeed, some news organizations "are even trying to predict how a particular piece of news might make a reader feel and to target advertising accordingly."[17]

These manipulative technologies also enable microtargeting that increases the likelihood that certain speech will cause harm, because "it is not subject to regulatory scrutiny, not subject to meaningful widespread public scrutiny and because [] false claims in such political ads are likely to be spread farther, faster, deeper, and more broadly than true claims in political ads."[18] So too does the amplification enabled by new technologies increase the likelihood that falsehoods or similarly destructive expressive choices will spread farther, faster, and more effectively.[19]

The media's failure to demonstrate "respect for and knowledge of their readers and communities" also triggers suspicion of its motives and competence.[20] Consider, for instance, how public perceptions (accurate or not) that the media is arrogant toward, or disinterested in, its audience cast doubt on its willingness and ability to invest in and engage with that audience.[21] Those who are less powerful cannot afford to trust those who are more powerful without meaningful constraints in place. (To be sure, those perceived as more powerful do not always perceive themselves as such; nevertheless, perceptions of relative power contribute to dynamics of trust and distrust.)

What does it mean for an actor to behave in trustworthy ways? Constitutional law often asks this question with respect to *the government*, devising doctrinal rules more suspicious of the government in contexts where courts perceive the government as untrustworthy.[22] In the First Amendment context, for instance, experience suggests that the government is least likely to behave in trustworthy ways in settings where it may be self-interested, intolerant, or clumsy (as can be the case where it draws

16 Erin C. Carroll, *News as Surveillance*, 59 WASHBURN L.J. 431, 431 (2020).

17 *Id.* at 432.

18 Dawn Carla Nunziato, *Misinformation Mayhem: Social Media Platforms' Efforts to Combat Medical and Political Information*, 19 FIRST AMEND. L. REV. 32, 60–61 (2020).

19 *See* Soroush Vosoughi, Deb Roy & Sinan Aral, *The Spread of True and False News Online*, 359 SCIENCE 1146 (2018) (concluding that online falsehoods spread farther and faster than truth); *see also* DANIEL KAHNEMAN, THINKING, FAST AND SLOW 62 (2011) (summarizing cognitive psychology findings that repeating a falsehood is an effective way to get listeners to believe it).

20 ROY L. MOORE, MICHAEL D. MURRAY & KYU HO YOUM, MEDIA LAW AND ETHICS 55 (6th ed. 2022).

21 *See* Doron Taussig & Anthony M. Nadler, *Conservatives Feel Blamed, Shamed and Ostracized by the Media*, THE CONVERSATION (Apr. 13, 2022) (describing a study that found that conservatives distrusted the mainstream media because they found it "disdainful of conservatives and their communities").

22 *See* JAMAL GREENE, HOW RIGHTS WENT WRONG: WHY OUR OBSESSION WITH RIGHTS IS TEARING AMERICA APART 66 (2021) ("In Professor John Hart Ely's later influential description of this standard, the Court would resort to heightened review when it found that the political process was undeserving of trust.").

malleable lines absent adequate information or expertise).[23] Conversely, the government is more likely to behave in trustworthy ways in settings where its discretion is limited, where we do not see evidence of a self-interested or intolerant motive, or where the setting leaves us even more distrustful of powerful and unrestrained private actors than we are of the government.[24]

This may also be the case for the media. The remainder of this chapter seeks to spur additional thinking about what it means for the media to behave in trustworthy ways. In so doing, it flags a handful of possibilities for checking the media's potential to act in its own self-interest and for demonstrating its competence – sketching a menu of options (rather than detailing or exhausting them) that variously rely on markets, norms and architecture, and law.[25]

2.2 ENCOURAGING TRUSTWORTHY MEDIA BEHAVIOR THROUGH ALTERNATE FINANCING AND BUSINESS MODELS

Proposals for new financial models seek to relieve the economic pressure on media to capture eyeballs at the expense of truth. Along these lines, some thoughtful commentators urge the government to provide financial support for news media through taxes on digital advertising and on platforms' collection of user data.[26] Others emphasize the value of citizen journalists who are beholden neither to media owners' nor to advertisers' preferences and pressures.[27] Either way, the objective is to reduce or remove media's financial dependence on satisfying others' tastes and agendas, thus freeing it to choose more trustworthy behaviors.

2.3 DEMONSTRATING TRUSTWORTHY MEDIA BEHAVIOR THROUGH NORMS AND DESIGN

The media can also demonstrate trustworthiness by rejecting manipulation, microtargeting, and similarly self-interested practices (to be sure, it's easier to make such

[23] *See* Helen Norton, *Distrust, Negative First Amendment Theory, and the Regulation of Lies*, Knight First Amend. Inst. (Oct. 19, 2022), https://perma.cc/RJA9-X454.

[24] *Id.*

[25] *See* Lawrence Lessig, *The New Chicago School*, 27 J. Legal Stud. 661, 662–64 (1998) (describing how law, social norms, markets, and architecture provide different means of regulating human behavior).

[26] *See, e.g.*, Am. Acad. of Arts & Sci., Comm'n on the Practice of Democratic Citizenship, Our Common Purpose: Reinventing American Democracy for the 21st Century 53 (2020) (proposing "a tax on digital advertising that could be deployed in a public media fund that would support experimental approaches to public social media platforms as well as local and regional investigative journalism"); Martha Minow, Saving the News: Why the Constitution Calls for Government Action to Preserve Freedom of Speech 103 (2021) (proposing that government tax platforms' use of our data, and then amplify and support various local, regional, and national public interest news sources).

[27] Coe, *supra* note 6, at 90.

choices when accompanied by the sorts of changes in financial models discussed in Section 2.2).[28] More specifically, the media can choose designs, interfaces, and practices that encourage and enable curiosity (and thus truth-seeking) over those that manipulate user attention and engagement through outrage and identity confirmation.

Along these lines, Taylor Dotson, who studies the culture and politics of science and technology, recommends that the press offer not only fact-checks but "disagreement checks ... that highlight the complicated sub-issues involved."[29] In support, Dotson describes studies concluding that difficult conversations "aren't constructive when participants think of them in terms of truth and falsehood or pro and con positions, which tend to spur feelings of contempt.... Simply reading an essay highlighting the contradictions and ambiguities in an issue leads people to argue less and converse more."[30]

Similarly, organizational psychologist Adam Grant recommends "complexifying: showcasing the range of perspectives on a given topic."[31] The related technique of motivational interviewing asks interviewees not only what they think, but how they came to think that and to identify their values; in other words, motivational interviewing focuses first on "finding out what someone knows and cares about rather than trying to convince them about something."[32]

And when journalistic practices themselves pose barriers to the media's trustworthiness, trustworthy behavior includes reforming or abandoning those practices. As one illustration, the media can choose not to amplify, and thus reward, destructive behavior. Media scholars Joan Donovan and danah boyd recommend that the

28 *See* MINOW, *supra* note 26, at 24 (describing users' vulnerability to frauds and hoaxes "enabled by 'dark posts' – ads that are invisible to all but those targeted and that do not reveal who paid for or is behind them," and to "'[c]lickbait' – arresting headlines and attention-drawing ads – [that] enables a surprising amount of disinformation").

29 Taylor Dotson, *Fact-Checking May Be Important, but It Won't Help Americans Learn to Disagree Better*, THE CONVERSATION (Jan. 18, 2022), https://perma.cc/XUM9-ZYFS.

30 *Id.*; *see also* Elizabeth F. Emens, *On Trust, Law, and Expecting the Worst*, 133 HARV. L. REV. 1963, 1997 (2020) ("[T]he overarching rubric of epistemic curiosity, like cognitive distrust, suggests an orientation toward learning rather than assuming."); *id.* at 2002 ("[A] knowledge gap that appears more difficult or impossible to resolve may lead to anxiety and diminished curiosity. Making information more readily available may not only enable, but also enhance, curiosity.").

31 ADAM GRANT, THINK AGAIN: THE POWER OF KNOWING WHAT YOU DO NOT KNOW 164–65 (2021) ("A dose of complexity can disrupt overconfidence cycles and spur rethinking cycles. It gives us more humility about our knowledge and more doubts about our opinions, and it can make us curious enough to discover information we were lacking."); *see also id.* at 171 ("New research suggests that when journalists acknowledge the uncertainties around facts on complex issues like climate change and immigration, it does not undermine their readers' trust. And multiple experiments have shown that when experts express doubt, they become more persuasive. When someone knowledgeable admits uncertainty, it surprises people, and they end up paying more attention to the substance of the argument.").

32 SARA E. GORMAN & JACK M. GORMAN, DENYING TO THE GRAVE: WHY WE IGNORE THE FACTS THAT WILL SAVE US 264 (2017).

media intentionally engage in "strategic amplification," urging the media to recognize "that amplifying information is never neutral" and thus to consider amplification's costs along with any benefit it provides.[33] This means that news media at times should engage in strategic silence by declining to amplify coverage of certain behaviors, like high-profile suicides.[34]

Relatedly, the media can choose to privilege truth over neutrality. Concluding that professional journalists "are subject to a persistent propaganda campaign trying to lure them into amplifying and accrediting propaganda,"[35] Benkler, Faris, and Roberts urge that journalists privilege "transparent, accountable verifiability" over "demonstrative neutrality" by providing enhanced public access to its underlying materials and sources and by encouraging sources' independent verification.[36]

Trustworthy behavior also includes demonstrated humility. This includes acknowledging one's own limitations and one's potential to harm others.[37] It also demands sensitivity to and empathy for our human cognitive and emotional frailties:[38] "[U]ndergirding our efforts to reach people should always be understanding and composure. No one is immune from bias, heuristics, or emotional decisionmaking."[39] Demonstrated humility thus embraces the need for feedback, scrutiny, and (where appropriate) correction.[40] So too does the media's demonstrated humility require its ongoing commitment to education and improvement. For instance, public-health experts Sara Gorman and Jack Gorman urge members of the media to invest in self-education about the nature of the scientific process (including what scientific evidence is and is not contestable) along with the cognitive science

33 Joan Donovan & danah boyd, *Stop the Presses? Moving from Strategic Silence to Strategic Amplification in a Networked Media Ecosystem*, 65 Am. Behav. Scientist 333, 346, 333–34 (2021).

34 *Id.* at 343–44 ("In cases of extremism and suicide, it is imperative for journalists and news organizations to be silent until they can be strategic, speaking only when raising the issue is in the public interest. This is not a departure from current best practices so much as an update to meet the challenges of networked media.").

35 Benkler, Faris & Roberts, *supra* note 7, at 358; *see also id.* at 359 ("As long as the media ecosystem is highly asymmetric structurally and in its flow of propaganda, balance and neutrality amplify disinformation rather than combat it.").

36 *Id.* at 357.

37 *See* Sophia Rosenfeld, Democracy and Truth: A Short History 31 (2018) ("Just as ordinary citizens have to have confidence in experts as well as one another to a considerable degree, believing these authorities to be honestly conveying the most accurate and objective information they have available, experts need to show themselves to be responsive to public feedback, abiding by popular mandates and subjecting themselves to scrutiny, for the whole system to work.").

38 Gorman & Gorman, *supra* note 32, at 262.

39 *Id.* at 256–64; *see also id.* at 8 ("[B]elittling people who come to believe in false conspiracy theories as ignorant or mean-spirited is perhaps the surest route to reinforcing an anti-science position.").

40 *See* Jonathan Rauch, The Constitution of Knowledge: A Defense of Truth 109 (2021) (recommending that truth-seeking institutions subject themselves to scrutiny and the possibility of self-correction).

illuminating the challenges in communicating about these matters to a public uncomfortable with uncertainty.[41]

2.4 ENCOURAGING TRUSTWORTHY BEHAVIOR THROUGH LAW

As legal scholar, Martha Minow observes, law sometimes enables the media's untrustworthy behavior.[42] Indeed, Professor Minow identifies the government's passivity as an additional barrier to a healthy news environment: "The critical and ongoing role of government in American media exposes as false any claim that the First Amendment bars government action now. The disruptive dimensions of the digital revolution are distinctive only in the relative passivity of government in attending to effects on markets, quality, and democracy."[43]

Just as law can be a barrier to trustworthy behavior, so too can law encourage – and even require – trustworthy behavior. As I've discussed elsewhere, differences in power and information sometimes matter to First Amendment law, allowing the government's interventions that protect comparatively vulnerable listeners from comparatively powerful speakers.[44] The same can – and, in my view, should – be true of the government's interventions in certain settings to protect listeners from speakers' manipulative efforts (i.e., speakers' efforts to target and exploit users' vulnerabilities in ways hidden from those users).[45]

More specifically, law can empower and protect audiences by requiring the media's (and other powerful actors') transparency about the data they collect from us and what they do with it.[46] Minow, for instance, urges courts to adopt an "awareness doctrine" to "improve users' knowledge of the sources and nature of what they receive and also the patterns of their own engagement" – for example, by "involv[ing] content distributors in devising labels to distinguish news reports from opinion or unverified claims."[47] Others propose that constitutional and other legal advantages be made available only to media actors that commit to behave in trustworthy ways. Along these lines, Peter Coe suggests that constitutional

[41] GORMAN & GORMAN, *supra* note 32, at 257–58.

[42] MINOW, *supra* note 26, at 23 (observing that social media is not mediated by "the norms of professional journalists [to] test and filter out misinformation and propaganda. How much does the insulation for civil liability that is presently afforded to digital platforms lead to insufficient precautions against such exploitation and misuse?"); *see also* Julie E. Cohen, *Tailoring Election Regulation: The Platform Is the Frame*, 4 GEO. L. TECH. REV. 641, 655 (2020) ("In the context of platform-based, massively intermediated environments, the legal system should be . . . more concerned with a deliberate design orientation that privileges automatic, habitual response and reflexive amplification.").

[43] MINOW, *supra* note 26, at 37.

[44] *See* Norton, *supra* note 13, at 230–31.

[45] *See id.* at 232–42 (discussing possible interventions and their constitutionality).

[46] *See* Carroll, *supra* note 16, at 442 ("To the extent the press continues to surveil, it should be clearer that it is doing so.").

[47] MINOW, *supra* note 26, at 126.

protections from the government's interference with newsgathering activities should be available to media that "act[] ethically and in good faith and publish[] or broadcast[] material that is based on reasonable research to verify the provenance of it and its sources."[48]

2.5 CONCLUSION

The elephant in the room, of course, is that the media's choice to engage in some of these trustworthy behaviors may undermine its ability to survive financially in a twenty-first-century speech environment rife with competition for listeners' increasingly scarce time and attention. By "trustworthy behaviors," I mean rejecting microtargeting, manipulation, and other profit-maximizing yet destructive practices. Declining to amplify destructive behavior. Disclosing data sources, evidence sets, the personal data that the media collects from its users and what it does with it. Demonstrating epistemic humility. Seeking out and responding to public feedback and scrutiny. Investing in self-education about scientific and other technical matters.

Indeed, our own oh-so-human cognitive and emotional vulnerabilities (that are themselves so often truth-resisting) contribute to the public's distrust of the media in ways that are difficult for the media to address. For a variety of cognitive, social, and biological reasons, we often prefer the succor of identity confirmation over the discomfort of complexity and truth.[49] These frailties, in turn, may threaten the financial survival of media that refuse to cater to them.[50]

In other words, as Guy-Uriel Charles explains, we have not only a supply-side problem when it comes to media outputs, but also a demand-side problem when we

[48] Coe, *supra* note 6, at 168; *see also id.* at 174 (describing socially responsible media behaviors as acknowledging "the inherent flaws in our nature" and our vulnerability "to sensationalized stories, false news and its regurgitation, entrenchment of views by virtue of preconceived schemas, the fact that we are often unable to assess the veracity of anonymous and pseudonymous speakers and that we are largely unaware of the machinations of online platforms, and, as a result of all of this, our inability to rationally assess the marketplace"). Perhaps more trustworthy media behavior might lead to greater legal protections for the media through more robust application of the Press Clause. *See* RonNell Andersen Jones & Sonja R. West, *Presuming Trustworthiness*, Knight First Amend. Inst. (Nov. 18, 2022), https://perma.cc/3HJ8-BHVG (reporting on their empirical findings that the Supreme Court has largely abandoned its traditional presumption that press speakers are trustworthy).

[49] *See* Gorman & Gorman, *supra* note 32, at 246 ("[T]he ability to understand facts is not the driving force. Rather, the need to belong to a group that maintains its identity no matter what facts are presented is the fuel for these contradictory beliefs. This need is characteristic of people from every race, income level, intellectual capacity, and country."); *id.* at 252 ("Science demands that we be open to changing our minds constantly, but human biology and psychology insist that we hold onto our beliefs with as much conviction as we possibly can. This conflict is fundamental to our reluctance to accept new scientific findings.").

[50] *See* Coe, *supra* note 6, at 1 ("These pressures encourage journalists operating within this structure to publish content that appeals to mass audiences and attracts advertisers, rather than engage in high-quality, yet expensive and time-consuming, diverse public interest journalism.").

are reluctant to reward the media's truth-seeking outputs.[51] Even so, Erin Carroll focuses on the supply side when she calls on the press to develop new "practices of freedom."[52] And I too focus on the supply side in asking what it means for the media to behave in ways that demonstrate trustworthy motives and competence.

Easier said than done, I know.

[51] *See* Guy-Uriel Charles, *Giving the People What They Want: Supplying the Demand for Disinformation*, BALKINIZATION (Apr. 13, 2022), https://perma.cc/4TLR-9EH2 ("If the problem of misinformation presents a demand-side problem, or to the extent that there is both a demand-side and supply-side problem, supply-side only solutions are not likely to resolve the problem.").

[52] Carroll, *supra* note 6 ("Just as our form of government impacts our degree of press freedom, press freedom impacts how we are governed. Consequently, press action will protect far more than just the press."); *see also* MOORE, MURRAY & YOUM, *supra* note 20, at 71–72 (describing media's other-regarding responsibilities to include the responsibility to be accurate, competent, just, fair, and humane – that is, attentive to one' effects on, including one's potential to harm, others).

3

Sober and Self-Guided Newsgathering

Jane Bambauer

3.1 INTRODUCTION

This chapter addresses an underappreciated source of epistemic dysfunction in today's media environment: true-but-unrepresentative information. Because media organizations are under tremendous competitive pressure to craft news that is in harmony with their audience's preexisting beliefs, they have an incentive to accurately report on events and incidents that are selected, consciously or not, to support an impression that is exaggerated or ideologically convenient. Moreover, these organizations *have to* engage in this practice in order to survive in a hypercompetitive news environment.[1]

To help correct the problem, this chapter outlines new forms of newsgathering tools that leverage digital information to provide a sense of how representative (or not) any particular event may be. This contextualizes the news and leads to more *sober* – that is, less hyperbolic and reactive – interpretations of it. Newsgathering institutions can also become much more interactive so that a participant has the ability to easily find facts that they are confident will not be tainted from the strategic selection or cherry-picking of a news authority or intermediary. These tools will make newsgathering more *self-guided*.

3.2 THE PROLIFERATION OF TRUE-BUT-MISLEADING NEWS

Many beliefs circulating through American discourse at any given time are in some sense corrosive – to society, to personal health and safety, or to some other part of

1 The economic pressure is sometimes referred to as "audience capture," and it was on dramatic display in the publicly released text messages between Tucker Carlson and other Fox employees which revealed that the network needed to produce favorable coverage of Donald Trump in order to maintain their audience. Yassine Meskhout, *Fox News' Audience Capture Problem* (Mar. 6, 2023), https://ymeskhout.substack.com/p/fox-news-audience-capture-problem.

life. The path to these corrosive beliefs is tiled with true-but-misleading information. Although the American news landscape is marred by some wholly made-up stories (that the COVID vaccine includes trackers, for example), these falsities make up a relatively small set of corrosive beliefs. Most corrosive beliefs have some factual corroboration – some true anecdotes that undergird the beliefs. But the factually true anecdotes imply something larger that is not supported by more representative data.[2]

For example, vaccines are "dangerous" in the absolute sense. There are examples of side effects and even death caused by the COVID vaccines.[3] But on a relative scale they are safe – that is, they are much less dangerous than the risks from not vaccinating (for most people).[4] Thus, the distorted beliefs that tend to emerge on the political right are the result of exaggerating the likelihood of vaccine risk or undervaluing the likelihood of severe illness and death from COVID among the unvaccinated, or both. The same criticism can and should be levied on the political left, too, based on the perceived risk of COVID to children. Children can, of course, contract and even die from COVID, but these risks are lower than the risks from other viruses like RSV that we have implicitly chosen to tolerate as a background risk.[5] An unvaccinated child is at much lower risk of contracting COVID than a fully vaccinated adult.[6] When the news focuses on child mortality from COVID or on vaccine danger, it does damage to the full truth.[7] Beliefs about terrorism and police violence tend to suffer from a similar lack of scale and proportionality.

[2] This problem, which I'm summarizing as a proportionality problem, is similar to Barry Glassner's diagnosis of journalism problems in BARRY GLASSNER, THE CULTURE OF FEAR xiv–xvii, 26–29 (1999).

[3] *Selected Adverse Events Reported after COVID-19 Vaccination*, CTRS. DISEASE CONTROL, https://perma.cc/DJ4X-URSJ.

[4] *Id.*; Stanley Xu et al., *COVID-19 Vaccination and Non-COVID-19 Mortality Risk – Seven Integrated Health Care Organizations, United States, December 14, 2020 – July 31, 2021*, 70 MMWR MORB. & MORTAL. WKLY. REP. 1520 (2021). When combining the risk of death from COVID *and* non-COVID causes, the vaccinated group has much lower mortality across all age ranges. *See* CTRS. FOR DISEASE CONTROL & PREVENTION, RATES OF COVID-19 CASES OR DEATHS BY AGE GROUP AND VACCINATION STATUS, https://data.cdc.gov/Public-Health-Surveillance/Rates-of-COVID-19-Cases-or-Deaths-by-Age-Group-and/3rge-nu2a.

[5] Meike Meyer et al., *Morbidity of Respiratory Syncytial Virus (RSV) Infections: RSV Compared with Severe Acute Respiratory Syndrome Coronavirus 2 Infections in Children Aged 0–4 Years in Cologne, Germany*, 226 J. INFECTIOUS DISEASES 2050 (2022).

[6] PUBLIC HEALTH ENGLAND, COVID-19 VACCINE SURVEILLANCE REPORT: WEEK 36 at 15 (Sept. 9, 2021).

[7] *See, e.g.*, Edmund DeMarche, *New Zealand Links 26-Year-Old's Death to Pfizer's COVID-19 Vaccine, Reports Say*, FOX NEWS (Dec. 20, 2021), https://perma.cc/U8P5-KPE3; Noah Weiland & Erin Schaff, *At a Children's Hospital, a Wave of Young Patients Struggling to Breathe*, N.Y. TIMES (Aug. 27, 2021). One note: I use "news" throughout this chapter in an expansive and entirely descriptive way: it is whatever the news industry produces, as well as whatever individuals consume that they think is "news." Thank you to Erin Carroll for pointing out that scholars who study the news often use a narrower definition that would require a certain amount of contextual accuracy.

This is not a new phenomenon. Ashutosh Bhagwat's chapter provides a reminder that the newspaper and broadcast gatekeepers in the 1990s were already shedding the journalism ethic of maintaining even the perception of a "view from nowhere." Yochai Benkler and his coauthors provide some empirical evidence that news organizations that cater to a more conservative audience began to drift further to the ideological right when talk radio provided alternative channels for news and discourse for an audience that was alienated by the mainstream news.[8] Twenty-four-hour cable news provided even more opportunity for alternative content. Increased competition gave each news organization increased economic incentive to highlight facts that are consistent with, or at least not offensive to, their audience's worldview. Given that any audience is only human and susceptible to political tribalism, the problem of unrepresentative and cherry-picked facts is utterly unsurprising.

When there were only a few gatekeepers, there were fewer incentives to cater to political tribalism in this way.[9] Even if the two newspapers in a town had traditionally catered to different political audiences, *both* papers had an incentive to stay close to the median audience member so that they might win over readers from the other paper. Without serious competition on the far-left or -right that could outflank the paper, catering to the middle had no economic disadvantages. But when more news organizations compete for audience, the economic strategy changes.[10] Facts will predictably be picked to match the interests and priors of more fractured, niche audiences.

Quite understandably, news organizations of longstanding status like the *New York Times* are defending their turf and claiming identity as a uniquely trustworthy source for truth without reckoning with the fact that their survival depends on supplying facts that cater to the short-term preferences of their readers. Breitbart is just as understandably trying to discredit the *New York Times* and establish itself as a better, more legitimate gatekeeper for facts. Breitbart's insurgency is carried out without acknowledging that *its survival, too,* depends on supplying facts that cater to its audience (which demands a desecration of established, elite gatekeepers). These two sources of news are not at all equivalent, but that says more about the beliefs and demands of the audiences that each has been able to attract than it does about an enduring commitment to delivering facts that accurately represent reality.

Modern journalism fails to meet a duty of proportionality. Proportionality would require that the decision to report about a threat and the manner in which it is

[8] Yochai Benkler et al., Network Propaganda 313–29 (2018).

[9] This is consistent with the "Hotelling theory" that explains why it makes sense for multiple competitive producers to sometimes make very similar products. Harold Hotelling, *Stability in Competition*, 39 J. Econ. 41 (1929).

[10] Matthew Gentzkow & Jesse M. Shapiro, *Competition and Truth in the Market for News*, 22 J. Econ. Perspectives 133 (2008); Andrea Blasco & Francesco Sobbrio, *Competition and Commercial Media Bias*, 36 Telecomm. Pol'y 434 (2012); Matthew Gentzkow et al., *Media Bias in the Marketplace: Theory*, Nat'l Bureau of Economic Res. Working Paper 19880 (2014).

reported are informed by how risky it is relative to other widely known and understood threats. Proportionality goes to subtext – whether a particular story is worthy of a reader's attention given other concerns that might deserve the reader's focus. *The Elements of Journalism* devotes a chapter to making the news "Comprehensive and Proportional,"[11] but this element is in direct tension with the economic viability of the modern newsroom.

The Society of Professional Journalist's Code of Ethics does not even require proportionality in its list of duties for seeking truth. Instead, the search for truth is described in narrow terms of factual accuracy as well as more abstract terms like being "vigilant and courageous about holding those with power accountable" and "boldly tell[ing] the story of the diversity and magnitude of the human experience."[12] These objectives actually exacerbate the problem by pushing journalists to prioritize the unusual or anti-authority stories. They are in tension with the sort of corrective I will propose here – encouraging the use of tools that allow readers to understand in a statistical way whether an event is an aberration or not.

3.3 MORE ACCESS TO TRUE-BUT-MISLEADING NEWS IN THE INTERNET AGE

The internet generally and social media specifically has increased the prevalence of true-but-misleading news dissemination. This is so for several reasons:

(1) **Source material.** The internet provides abundant information from which events (especially bad events) can be selected. Moreover, the search costs for any particular type of (bad) event are also much lower. A person who proactively searches for cases where a child died of COVID or where an adult died from the vaccine will find them, and find them easily. Thus, the costs of gathering selective evidence are dramatically lower. To be sure, even in the era of the industrialized media, the facts that people encountered were nonrandom and were selected based on a number of factors and constraints, but it was *more random* than an information environment that is all but defined by self-selection through functionality like search and tailored news feeds.[13]

(2) **Even more competition between news producers.** Talk radio and the diversified array of channels on cable television may have begun the process of splintering the news industry, but the low costs of

[11] Bill Covach & Tom Rosenstiel, Elements of Journalism 282 (2021).

[12] Soc'y of Prof. Journalists, SPJ Code of Ethics (Sept. 6, 2014), https://perma.cc/6DC6-U65K. The *Elements of Journalism* also emphasizes emphasizing the voice of the less powerful, which could be a de-biasing force to ensure that proportional threats to marginalized groups are fairly reported, but it could just as well serve as a biasing force that overemphasizes a sense of threat that comes from the powerful.

[13] Thanks to Kyle Langvardt for crystalizing this point for me in the course of editing.

information distribution brought an explosion of online news producers that have intensified the competition and the pathologies that come along with news-as-a-consumable-good.

(3) **Targeted news feeds.** Just as the search costs for finding evidence have declined, the costs of matching news to listeners has also been dramatically reduced by technology. This is especially true on social media, where news feeds wind up functioning as a sort of news aggregator for each individual. A social-media user's selection of friends and their history of clicks and reading time allow platforms to predict which types of stories the user is likely to read in the future. This is what Facebook does when it optimizes for "engagement." This is, in some ways, just a reiteration of point 2 – intensified competition. Data-driven news feeds allow platforms to infinitely stratify the market and create niches the size of a single consumer.[14] This optimization has been characterized by the *Wall Street Journal* and other news outlets as a needlessly sinister manipulation of its users,[15] but it can be explained just as easily by competitive pressure: Facebook, too, needs to give users an experience that is engaging enough to keep them from switching to another activity or competitor.[16]

(4) **Social pressure.** Social media also breeds epistemic conformity within groups and subcultures. A user who sees her friends posting news stories or anecdotes will naturally feel some social pressure to stay willfully blind to facts or context that contradict the tenor and political valence of the conversation she is seeing among friends.[17] In other words, social media will sometimes pose a tension between a user's epistemic goals and her social ones, and the latter will sometimes win.

It is worth noting what is *not* on this list – the popular misdiagnoses. Algorithms do not override users' preferences and push them toward more extreme content. Empirical evidence consistently finds that the users' selection of friends and their responsive behavior, rather than algorithmic manipulation, explain what content is

[14] News organizations engage in hypertargeting too. For a full account of how automated bots are useful both as a sort of focus group tester at scale as well as for gathering new information that can become source material for a news story, *see* Nicholas Diakopoulos, Automating the News: How Algorithms Are Rewriting the Media (2019).

[15] Keach Hagey & Jeff Horwitz, *Facebook Tried to Make Its Platform a Healthier Place: It Got Angrier Instead*, Wall St. J. (Sept. 15, 2021).

[16] After all, Facebook's source of revenue is from advertising. If it loses eyeballs to *anything else* – *not* just to another social media site, but even to a different form of entertainment or leisure – it loses money. Thus, it is in a cut-throat competitive environment as well, in at least some respects.

[17] Jane R. Bambauer, Saura Masconale & Simone M. Sepe, *Cheap Friendship*, 54 U.C. Davis L. Rev. 2341 (2021).

served and consumed.[18] Nor are lightning-rod figures like Donald Trump, Alex Jones, and Tucker Carlson the ultimate causes of the current state of the news. They are symptoms and by-products of a news market that rewards true-but-misleading information. Finally, American free speech jurisprudence is also not a major contributing factor, as the problems described here are to a great extent global phenomena. As Gilad Abiri recently said at the Yale Free Expression Scholars Conference, "the epistemic divide is everywhere [around the world.] Fox News is not. And the First Amendment is not."[19]

Thus, the nuisance of selective evidence gathering and true-but-misleading news is structural: It is generated easily in the digital information environment, and it is demanded by the listener and platform user in a hypercompetitive tournament for attention.

3.4 A NEW HUMAN EXPERIENCE: EVERY BAD THING ALL AT ONCE

My grandmother worked for the Food & Drug Administration shortly after it was created. Although she had a chemistry degree, most of her skills were underutilized and she spent her time inspecting for bug parts in canned food. When I was young, I asked my grandmother whether she was turned off of canned food since she knew how many bugs are accidentally included in them. She explained that it had the opposite effect – that she knows bug parts are rare and that in any case, they almost never cause any harm. I realized that the fear of eating bugs for her was similar to the fear of getting in a car accident for me. She saw bugs, but she saw many, many more cans. So she ate canned beans happily while I, haunted by the stories she told involving severed cockroach carcasses, approached every can with dread.

Consuming news on the internet puts us in this sort of state with respect to nearly every type of mishap, misfortune, and failing. As a result, the internet's effect may be even greater than a linear progression in media competition would suggest on its own. Humans are hard-wired with high sensitivity to threats, and with heightened concern about small numbers of bad, unfamiliar outcomes.[20] The internet provides access to *all* of the bad, unfamiliar outcomes.

18 Eytan Bakshy, Solomon Messing & Lada A. Adamic, *Exposure to Ideologically Diverse News and Opinion on Facebook*, 348 SCI. 1130, 1130 (2015); Mark Ledwich & Anna Zaitsev, *Algorithmic Extremism: Examining YouTube's Rabbit Hole of Radicalization* (2019), https://perma.cc/KZ4G-3CE5; Annie Y. Chen et al., *Subscriptions and External Links Help Drive Resentful Users to Alternative and Extremist YouTube Videos* (2022), https://perma.cc/AK4A-WFLK.

19 Gilad Abiri, Comments at the Free Expression Scholars Conference at Yale University (Apr. 30, 2022).

20 Dean Mobbs et al., *The Ecology of Human Fear: Survival Optimization and the Nervous System*, 9 FRONTIERS NEUROSCI. 55 (2015).

Humans are not good at putting bad news into proportional perspective when they do not have direct experience of the baseline or background risk.[21] In the internet age, wisdom will require some means of acquiring that skill.

On this aspect of my formulation of the modern news problem, Martin Gurri's book *The Revolt of the Public* has been exceedingly influential. Gurri explains that the high visibility given to every bureaucratic mistake or negative outcome has caused social-media users to lose trust in institutions and to demand a reckoning.[22] Elites then fuel the fire by insisting that actually they *do* live up to superhuman standards rather than attempting to defend their performance based on realistic assessments: "The fiction of extraordinary ambition and mastery has persisted, without irony, in our political language."[23] The large gap between the rhetoric of excellence and the selective but highly salient evidence of failure revs up the instinct of the public to tear down the establishment. This instinct gets filtered through political tribalism, of course, with the Republican base setting their sights on expert agencies while the Democratic base focuses on institutions like law enforcement. But both camps stumble on a similar lack of awareness about trend lines, proportions, counterfactuals, and the limits on performance that constrain every institution.

News organizations have failed to provide the sort of information that would contextualize news and opinions for some topics like police violence, crime, COVID risks, and elections. They have no economic incentive to do so. But even if they wanted to provide context, traditional newsgathering practices cannot keep up with the sort of data that would offer proportionality and nuance on *every* topic, let alone do so consistently. Likewise, consumers of news do not yet have the appetite and skills to digest this sort of content even if it were available.[24]

This leaves us in a pretty dark place. And yet, against this bleak backdrop, I believe there is reason for optimism. Every shock to the communications environment, from writing to the printing press to broadcast, has come with a tumultuous period

[21] Amos Tversky & Daniel Kahneman, *Judgment under Uncertainty: Heuristics and Biases*, 185 Sci. 1124, 1127 (1974) (discussing availability and salience heuristics).

[22] Martin Gurri, The Revolt of the Public and the Crisis of Authority in the New Millennium 27–32 (2019).

[23] *Id.* at 226. On the other hand, a similar argument was made by Deborah Tannen in the 1990s, when the mechanism for cynicism and the destruction of institutions could not have been social media. *See* Deborah Tannen, The Argument Culture: Stopping America's War of Words 77 (1998). However, there is a way to reconcile Tannen's observations and Gurri's. Tannen believes that one-way communication (in other words, broadcast) breeds contempt. *Id.* at 240. However, even writing in the early phase of the internet, she did not see communications innovations like email changing the dynamic of contempt. Email, and eventually blog comments and social media, may be more analogous to a quick succession of broadcasts than they are to face-to-face conversation.

[24] Erik Brynjolfsson & Andrew McAfee, Race against the Machine: How the Digital Revolution Is Accelerating Innovation, Driving Productivity, and Irreversibly Transforming Employment and the Economy 7 (2012).

of confusion, conflict, and – eventually – a new equilibrium.[25] Those new equilibria have often put demands on culture and education that in retrospect seem impossible. Imagine living shortly after the printing press had been invented and observing a population with nearly universal illiteracy. If you said, "We really need to teach everyone to read so that, in a few centuries, everyone will have a job and social life that depends on the sort of knowledge transmission that can really only happen through text," you would be the town loony.

What comes next are some recommendations from a town loony.

3.5 PREDICTIONS AND SOLUTIONS (GRADE ME IN 200 YEARS, PLEASE)

Free speech luminaries like Oliver Wendell Holmes used the scientific method as an analogy to First Amendment theory.[26] If everyone has a chance to propose a hypothesis, the best ideas, that have the closest relationship to reality, will win out. They will replicate more often when listeners test them. This process, even when it is working, is filled with error. Scientists generally understand this and tolerate the sort of errors that lead down a messy and indirect path toward progress.

The comparison between free speech and the scientific method is aspirational, of course, and even scientists will occasionally abandon their loyalty to the methods when political, social, and psychological factors predominate.[27] Nevertheless, the very fact that a growing proportion of the population – a larger one than ever before in history – work in fields that require training in science and statistics suggests that facility in statistical reasoning may become as widespread and commonplace as reading is today. And even if our work does not require it, the sheer ubiquity of data may cause news consumers to prefer a different sort of news: one that situates a particular event into a larger trend or distribution in order to make sense of it.

We should not be interested in rebuilding the sort of news institutions that were profitable and powerful in the twentieth century. It would be a fool's errand to even attempt such a task, since consumers with democratized access to information about sensational events will not tolerate a gatekeeping organization that tries to control

[25] BRIN, *infra* note 37, at 5; RAY DALIO, PRINCIPLES FOR DEALING WITH THE CHANGING WORLD ORDER: WHY NATIONS SUCCEED AND FAIL 3 (2021) (describing the "big cycle" of peaceful and prosperous periods followed by depressions and revolutionary periods).

[26] Thomas Healy, *Holmes's Other Metaphor*, 51 SETON HALL L. REV. 1 (2020); Joseph Blocher, *Free Speech and Justified True Belief*, 133 HARV. L. REV. 440 (2019); Gary L. Francione, *Experimentation and the Marketplace Theory of the First Amendment*, 136 U. PENN. L. REV. 417, 422 (1987).

[27] THOMAS KUHN, THE STRUCTURE OF SCIENTIFIC REVOLUTIONS (1962); Dan M. Kahan, *Ideology, Motivated Reasoning, and Cognitive Reflection*, 8 JUDGMENT & DECISION MAKING 407 (2013).

attention.[28] Cheap access to an ocean of information, such as that which we have now, calls for a different form of newsgathering: one that gives consumers the autonomy to choose which topics and phenomena to explore, but also provides information and incentives to pursue those inquiries in a manner that avoids exaggeration and sensationalism. Newsgathering of the future should be democratized, and it should also be sober.

To some extent, the major internet platforms have already created the means to democratize newsgathering by creating tools for users to actively (e.g., Google Search) or passively (e.g., Facebook's Feed) engage with information that is most relevant to their interests. However, even these platforms, significant as they are, do not provide easy access to raw data or representative information, even to those who proactively want to find it. They do not provide proportionality at the micro level – that is, within a given topic of interest, they do not provide enough means to contextualize the information we see to understand whether the information is representative of real trends. For example, a user who wants to check their beliefs about the minimum wage and, as a first cut, wants to know whether the trend in creation of jobs in a particular state changed after the passage of a minimum-wage law would have a difficult time finding these figures. Try it yourself. In my case (searching for Arizona), the most relevant information I could find came in the form of highly mediated opinion pieces that use some evidence to corroborate their point of view, but not the sort of raw data I was looking for. Thus, despite the seismic shift in access to information that companies like Google have created, easy access to the *right* information is still lacking.

In terms of the sobriety of the news, internet intermediaries have done little to lower the temperature of debates or to incentivize more nuanced and proportionate reactions to events. Doing so would put the intermediary at a competitive disadvantage in the short run, and possibly in the medium and long run as well.

Thus, there is an opportunity and a need for government, academic, and nonprofit institutions to create better newsgathering tools that can interoperate with news organizations and eventually discipline them.

3.6 TOOLS FOR SOBER, SELF-GUIDED NEWSGATHERING

A complex society cannot function without intermediaries and interpreters. But the intermediaries who win the competition for user trust will be picked by a public that, right now, is exceedingly skeptical and time-strapped. Intermediaries of the future must prioritize ease of use and tamp down resistance from political bias.

[28] Thus, I disagree with Martha Minow's recommendation to rebuild local journalism. *See* Martha Minow, Saving the News: Why the Constitution Calls for Government Action to Preserve Freedom of Speech 101–44 (2021). Even if local journalism is a good source of information (which it may not be, relative to the sort of journalism that could be developed through big data), consumers will not be interested.

Consumers want something else, too: They want to win arguments, or at least feel like they have a chance of having a fair argument, with friends and family. This, too, should be taken into account in a responsible newsgathering model as well.

The most promising tools for renovating the newsgathering process are those that create frequent feedback loops so that beliefs are constantly tested and adjusted.[29] The news should use interactive or gamified elements to draw readers into sober, self-guided newsgathering practices. What follows is a nonexhaustive list of self-directed newsgathering mechanisms that have at least some empirical support for their value.

3.6.1 *Confronting Assumptions*

What proportion of U.S. residents are immigrants? And what proportion of those immigrants are *undocumented* immigrants?[30]

While it is possible to have a productive conversation and debate about U.S. immigration policy without knowing the answers to those questions (as well as many others), the political beliefs that currently drive the terms of debate implicitly rely on an assumption about the answers to them. The belief that most Mexican-Americans entered the country illegally, for example, or that undocumented immigrants are a major source of job loss, might be undermined by the statistics.

Interactive news media can begin a session by asking readers basic questions like these related to a topic, and can also provide a user interface that crowdsources proposed intro questions from users. *The New York Times* already uses some gamified news quizzes along these lines that challenges readers to see how much they know about, for example, the human reproductive system as a gateway to better understanding news about the overturning of *Roe v. Wade*.[31]

Tools that guide a user to make their factual assumptions explicit (and to correct them, where they are wrong) are valuable for two reasons. First, they provide a baseline to contextualize news stories. Second, research on the phenomenon known as "the illusion of explanatory depth" suggests that this sort of exercise primes news consumers to be more cautious about their own expertise and less confident in their

[29] Erin Carroll's chapter in this collection describes community journalism, a promising mechanism for feedback loops that differs from the more atomistic solutions I propose here. *See* Erin Carroll, *Beyond the Watchdog: Using Law to Build Trust in the Press*, 3 J. FREE SPEECH L. 57 (2023).

[30] Out of 324 million U.S. residents, 46 million are immigrants. *Table 1.1: Population by Sex, Age, Nativity, and U.S. Citizenship Status*, U.S. CENSUS BUREAU, FOREIGN BORN: 2019 CURRENT POPULATION SURVEY DETAILED TABLES (2019), https://perma.cc/TJB8-U6LK. 11.4 million of the immigrants are undocumented. DEP'T OF HOMELAND SECURITY, ESTIMATES OF THE UNAUTHORIZED IMMIGRANT POPULATION RESIDING IN THE UNITED STATES: JANUARY 2015–JANUARY 2018 (2021), https://perma.cc/K7GA-4WW2. Thus, the answers are 14% and 24%, respectively. And only 3.5% of U.S. residents are undocumented immigrants.

[31] *Can You Answer These Sex Ed Questions? A Post-Roe Quiz*, N.Y. TIMES (July 7, 2022).

political convictions.[32] Of course, the preparatory-quiz questions can be exploited to solidify factual understandings that help one side of a debate without solidifying the facts that are most useful to the other side of it, so the crafting and curation of the questions will require a credible mechanism for neutrality or input from the reader about what facts they think are most important in order to come to an opinion on the topic.

3.6.2 *Defining Mind-Switching Facts*

Consider your belief about whether access to charter schools is, on balance, good or bad for a community. Once you have your position in mind, do the following exercise:

Write out three facts (or sets of facts) any one of which, if true, would cause you to change your mind about this topic (assuming everything else stays the same).

This exercise is useful for three reasons: First, it focuses the user's attention on the assumptions that are necessary for sustaining their belief, and therefore points to subsequent questions that would help them either corroborate or abandon those beliefs. Second, it pre-commits the user to the adage "If the facts change, I change my mind. Do not you?" If, down the road, credible reporting finds that one of the mind-switching conditions is met, there would be a cost on a user (in cognitive dissonance, at least, if not reputation) who stubbornly insists on keeping their position anyways. Third, the exercise will almost always lead the user to think about the big picture rather than anecdotes. In other words, a person who is generally against charter schools will not say "I'll change my mind if there is a single example of an underprivileged child attending a charter school and then doing well in life," nor will he say "I will change my mind if there is an example of a public teachers union that helps a bad teacher keep his job." Focusing on the big picture will allow the user to tell a debate partner to not bother with the anecdotes because anecdotes do not require a concession. At the same time, the user will become aware that for the same reasons, an example of a single poorly run charter school with bad outcomes will not move the needle for a debate partner who is generally in favor of charter-school programs.

3.6.2.1 Graded Predictions and Wagers

What probability would you give each of the following events?:

- Democrats will win the presidency and will win or retain majorities in both the U.S. House and Senate in November 2024: ___%
- Inflation in the U.S. will average under 3% in 2023 per the PCE price index: ___%

[32] Leonid Rozenblit & Frank Keil, *The Misunderstood Limits of Folk Science: An Illusion of Explanatory Depth*, 26 COGNITIVE SCI. 521 (2002).

- China's GDP growth will be above 5% for the year 2023: ___%
- 20% of U.S. adults will receive a vaccination or booster against COVID at some point during the calendar year 2024: ___%
- The WHO will designate another virus or variant of concern by the end of 2024: ___%
- A peace agreement between Ukraine and Russia will be in place by the end of 2024: ___%

Many blogs and news outlets are designing annual-predictions lists of this sort. Most of the categories here, for example, were borrowed from a list published on *Vox*.[33] Grading, which can be done by the user or by the news venue, is necessarily crude since the nonoccurrence of an event that a user assigned a high probability to is not necessarily an indication of error. Short lists like this one are typically graded by converting the predictions to binary predictions (treating predictions above 50% as a 1 and below 50% as 0) and then comparing them to outcomes. Longer lists can be graded by dividing predictions into tranches (e.g., 0–20%, 21–40%, 41–60%, 61–80%, and 81–100%) and then evaluating whether the items in each tranche occurred close to (10%, 30%, 50%, 70%, and 90%) of the time, respectively.[34]

The benefits of a periodic prediction exercise are similar to the benefits of the "confronting assumptions" tool because users can see that some beliefs – previously strongly held ones – turned out to be unfounded. But also, the exercise unearths for users the need to foster dispassion and to think in longer time horizons.

Closely related to predictions are wagers, where individuals place bets about what is true or what will happen. Prediction markets like PredictIt allow individuals to place bets on certain social and political predictions. Their predictions outperform many pollster and pundit predictions because they aggregate knowledge across multiple people who have skin in the game.[35] That makes their reported odds a good source of aggregated news in and of itself. But participating in the prediction markets can create feedback loops that train users to become better at prediction by aligning their beliefs with the most valid evidence. With appropriate limits on how large a wager can be or how much any person can expose themselves to financial risk, prediction markets may be a form of betting that governments should actively encourage.

In addition to centralized prediction markets, which are already well on their way to becoming established institutions, wagers may have a role to play in decentralized

[33] Dylan Matthews et al., *22 Things We Think Will Happen in 2022*, Vox (Jan. 1, 2022), https://perma.cc/WL5J-FGTQ.

[34] This grading technique is adopted in the book *The Scout Mindset*. Julia Galef, The Scout Mindset: Why Some People See Things Clearly and Others Do not 73–90 (2021).

[35] Thomas Heath, *These Gamblers Are Putting Money on the Outcome of the Impeachment Inquiry*, Wash. Post (Nov. 13, 2019); Eli Dourado, *Let Us Become a Nation of Bettors: How Prediction Markets Can Make the World More Rational*, Ctr. for Growth & Opportunity (Aug. 21, 2020), https://perma.cc/BE4A-4SH9.

contexts as well. For example, imagine if in the first months of the COVID pandemic, an X (formerly Twitter) user could have responded to a tweet that said "COVID is not any more deadly than the flu" by pressing a "friendly wager" button. This would allow the user to define terms for a counterprediction (e.g., "By the end of the year 2020, the CDC will attribute more deaths to COVID than the average annual death count from flu from 2014–2019" and with a resolution date set for January 15, 2021). If the author of the original tweet accepted the friendly wager (either for a small amount of money or simply for public bragging rights), the results would be resolved on January 15. If the author of the original tweet provides an alternative wager (e.g., one that offers similar terms but with a different source of authority or a different resolution date), the wagerer will have the opportunity to take or reject the alternative. If the author neither accepts nor counters the wager proposal, the fact that there was a wager left hanging would be publicly visible.

This style of decentralized wager runs some risks. It could amp up the sort of black-and-white thinking and humiliation-style argumentation that already pervades online culture. On the other hand, as David Brin has argued, the impulse for machismo and shouting down "enemies" shows no sign of receding, and even-keeled fact-checking exercises have been futile. (Indeed, fact-checkers are often another target of ridicule and contempt.[36]) Wagering helps turn aggressive culture against itself and gives a way for "fact people" to win on an ideologue's own turf.[37]

3.6.2.2 Simulations

If you visit Shinyapps.io, you can find a COVID policy simulator that allows users to select a geographic area, choose a COVID variant, select a vaccine effectiveness, and then select from four interventions (e.g., stay-at-home orders) for variable time periods. The simulator will then provide estimates of the trends in deaths, cases, hospital beds available, and several other COVID-related health outcomes. Unfortunately, the simulator does *not* provide estimates of the economic and health impact of the selected interventions, and does not provide an option to alter the creator's choice of R-value or type of behavioral precautions. This example shows that the bias of a simulator's design team can easily diminish the simulator's potential to be a convincing teaching tool. But if simulators were a major part of news consumption, different organizations and groups would compete to create the best – the most widely accepted – simulator, and that one would have to provide a more complete set of inputs, rules, and predicted outputs.

[36] Ben Lyons et al., *How Politics Shape Views toward Fact-Checking: Evidence from Six European Countries*, 25 Int'l J. Press/Pol. 469 (2020); Jonathan Walter et al., *Fact-Checking: A Meta-Analysis of What Works and for Whom*, 37 Pol. Commc'n 350 (2020).

[37] David Brin, Polemical Judo: Memes for Our Political Knife-Fight 56–57, 248–53 (2019) (discussing fact people and use of wagers, respectively).

Interactive media that allow the user to set certain starting facts and define the rules of cause-and-effect can discover that even *their own beliefs* lead to implications that are different from what they had assumed. For example, in the case of the COVID precautions game, users who play around with the simulator will discover through trial and error that there is an inescapable trade-off between costs of COVID and costs of the precautions.[38] Players (and governments) can do worse than the pareto frontier, but they cannot do better. This is a valuable realization because it injects realism into the meaning of government success and failure. That is, neither a decline in GDP *nor* a high COVID death count are evidence, in and of themselves, that the government has been incompetent.

3.7 DATA REPOSITORIES AND DIGITAL ALMANACS: AN INFRASTRUCTURE FOR SOBER AND SELF-GUIDED NEWSGATHERING

Journalism during the industrial era typically relied on reporters to collect facts and synthesize them into a digestible story or account. But it is not necessary, and in fact not ideal, to have the same institution perform both of these tasks. To the contrary, institutions set up to collect information could be more trustworthy if they were independent from the individuals and groups that synthesize the information into news items.

The tools I have described above facilitate a democratic form of newsgathering of a particular sort – the kind that synthesizes and contextualizes information from a large number of events. Generating the raw data for these tools is an entirely different sort of newsgathering – the building and maintaining of data repositories. All of the synthesizing tools described above will depend on data sources that are trusted by a large majority of individuals to be acceptably accurate.

Thus, while existing media organizations should supplement the news reporting that they offer with the interactive tools I have described, it will be increasingly important to create new institutions that simply collect and collate data about nearly every topic. These data repositories can also publish "almanacs" that present the data through a series of tables and graphs that are most likely to be of interest to users. They can also create query systems or user interfaces that provide access to deidentified microdata.

Some such organizations exist already. The Census Bureau, the Bureau of Justice Statistics, and the Bureau of Labor Statistics all serve the core purpose of providing multiuse data that can shed light on a wide variety of questions, and they provide almanacs on various topics. Nongovernment repositories, such as NORC or Our

[38] Jan Kulveit, *On the Dilemma between Lives and Economy: What Can Be Illustrated in the Pandemic Simulation Covidgame.info*, Boundedly Rational Notes on Complex Systems (July 8, 2021), https://perma.cc/W9PM-8UFN.

World in Data, also provide models for the sorts of data resources that will be necessary to encourage and satisfy a statistically literate population. Google and other for-profit companies occasionally enable public access to some data too.[39] But extant organizations offering public access to data are quite limited in several ways. First, compared to the richness of data that large corporations and the government have access to, they are poor in quality. Attempts to make them more rich and more accessible are mired in controversy around the potential risk that people described by the data may be reidentified or harmed. The Census Bureau, for example, currently takes a zero-tolerance approach to these risks, and as a result sacrifices a lot of public benefit that could result from greater access to Census statistical data.[40] To capture the value of pooled data, data repositories need to be encouraged to use a combination of technical and legal protections to keep risk low, and policymakers and the public need to accept some risk in exchange for the benefits of a data commons.

Another problem is a lack of trust in data repositories that are in fact trustworthy.[41] While federal statistical agencies and large research-data aggregators have not yet been doused in the cynical acid that has scarred many other institutions, they could be once they are used to refute a major talking point by Team Red or Team Blue. However, this may be avoidable if the data repository is expansive enough to contain data that support statistics that *both* sides of the spectrum would want to cite.[42] Neither side will want to tarnish a data source that could help them score points in the next argument. Also, in theory, accusations about the unreliability or corruption of a data source could be subjected to independent audits by a source that most individuals trust (including crowd-sourcing).[43]

3.8 IF YOU BUILD IT, WILL ANYONE COME?

I confess this chapter has a contradiction. I started by explaining that traditional news media and internet platforms serve sensational, nonrepresentative information because people are not interested in sober, representative news. If this is so, why

[39] GOOGLE TRENDS, http://trends.google.com; META TRANSPARENCY REPORTS, https://transparency.fb.com/data/.

[40] Timothy B. Lee, *Why the 2020 Census Has 9 Fake People in a Single House*, FULL STACK ECON. (Mar. 7, 2022), https://perma.cc/3RSF-9256.

[41] GURRI, *supra* note 22, at 390; BRIN, *supra* note 37, at 249 (this is the "Sez You" problem).

[42] For example, the same Bureau of Justice Statistics provide evidence that hate crimes are up and crimes against peace officers are down (useful for Team Blue when showing that there is no reason for an uptick in use of force by police officers against black and minority communities), but it also shows that a disproportionate share of violent crimes are committed by black men (useful for Team Red when arguing that differences in the rates of arrest or uses of force by race might be attributable to differences in the baseline risk of violence for each group). *See* BUREAU OF JUST. STAT., LAW ENFORCEMENT OFFICERS KILLED AND ASSAULTED, 2019 – TABLES (2020), https://perma.cc/6R5Y-A4DT.

[43] ASHUTOSH BHAGWAT, OUR DEMOCRATIC FIRST AMENDMENT 112–18 (2020).

would I expect anybody to use the newsgathering and sense-making tools I've described? Am I not fighting against human nature?

I have three tentative responses, and they may all be wrong: First, some of the tools (like wagers) are designed to tap into the rhetorical food fight and steer the combatants – us, basically – towards a more fact-based battle.

Second, an untapped demand for these newsgathering tools may arise if the tools were easier to use and free of charge. It may be that these sorts of resources do not exist because they are expensive to build and maintain, and cannot be expected to capture the benefits. After all, a data repository loses a lot of its value as a tool for public discourse if it requires each user to pay a subscription cost, because then those users cannot direct others to the resource for verification. In other words, the new newsgathering tools I've described here may have the economic qualities of a classic public good, and will therefore need money and energy from the government or from foundations in order to get off the ground.

Third, there may be something to the controversial theory that the increased supply of a product can cause an increase in the demand for it: If democratic, sober newsgathering is made available, people may over time develop a taste for it and value it highly enough to actually pay for it even if they would not do so right now.

3.9 CONCLUSION

The New York Times recently won a Pulitzer Prize for its reporting on "a disturbing pattern of fatal traffic stops by police."[44] The anchor story for the series described the last moments of fatal encounters with police during traffic stops. It then explained that "over the past five years, a *New York Times* investigation found, police officers have killed more than 400 drivers or passengers who were not wielding a gun or a knife" during pursuits that began with routine traffic stops.[45] More than 300 of these involved stops that progressed to a suspect flight or car chase.[46] The article rejects the claim that police officers involved in these traffic stops had any reason to fear risk to their own life or safety. "Of the roughly 280 officers killed on duty since late 2016, about 60 died – mostly by gunfire – at the hands of motorists who had been pulled over.... In fact, because the police pull over so many cars and trucks – tens of millions each year – an officer's chances of being killed at any vehicle stop are less than 1 in 3.6 million" – a risk that the article goes on to call "statistically negligible."[47]

Personally, I agree that the risk of officer safety is small enough that in a typical traffic-stop scenario, the police should harbor no concern for their personal safety.

44 The 2022 Pulitzer Prize Winner in National Reporting, https://perma.cc/K92F-D9DS.

45 David D. Kirkpatrick et al., *Why Many Police Traffic Stops Turn Deadly*, N.Y. Times (Nov. 30, 2021).

46 *Id.*

47 *Id.*

Police should not be trained to think that every traffic stop is a risky encounter. But news consumers who watch Fox will notice that the risk to unarmed drivers is as "statistically negligible" as the risk to armed police if that term is applied consistently. After all, the numbers of unarmed drivers killed by police are within the same order of magnitude as the numbers of police killed by drivers.[48] Thus, the implication of the article – that every traffic stop is a vector for danger and police abuse – is also misleading. The credibility of the paper (and the Pulitzer for that matter) will remain low among the Fox audience as long as news stories appear to be aggregated in a way designed to fit a particular worldview and to avoid information that could undermine that view. And it goes without saying, I suspect, that Fox News and other news media catering to a conservative viewpoint have the same flaw.

Newsgathering tools developed today should look nothing like the tools of the past. News in the twentieth century was riddled with true-but-unrepresentative stories that provided fertile ground for paranoia, distrust, nihilism, and political dogma. These problems metastasized on the internet, but the flaw is foundational. That flaw is the over-reliance on stories that provide a misleading sense of real trends.

In an information-scarce environment, every true anecdote about a tragedy or mistake was helpful for assessing risk and making plans. Even noisy information was better than the alternative. But in an information-rich environment, when nearly every possible claim has some true-but-misrepresentative examples as support, the ultimate objective of knowledge must be separated from the anecdote-driven facts that have constituted "the news" for centuries. Fact-checking a story is a necessary but insufficient requirement for a news system that will help the public converge on accuracy. The twenty-first century and beyond will need news institutions that give users autonomy in their explorations of the news and the context to form beliefs and argue with each other in a statistically valid manner.

[48] Moreover, readers who are not inclined to believe that police officers pose a high risk to residents are also likely to see trends that run against the narrative of the article, since police-caused killings have remained steady while homicides targeting the police have increased. *Compare Fatal Force*, WASH. POST, https://perma.cc/RHE7-9BXZ, *with* Emma Tucker & Priya Krishnakumar, *Intentional Killings of Law Enforcement Officers Reach 20-Year High, FBI Says*, CNN (Jan. 13, 2022), https://perma.cc/NY7C-QPQJ. It is also not clear that the denominator chosen (*all* traffic stops) is appropriate since the risk, to both police officers and drivers, is much higher under conditions where a driver refuses to pull over, for example. These cases also involve greater risk to the general public.

4

The New Gatekeepers?

Social Media and the "Search for Truth"

*Ashutosh Bhagwat**

4.1 INTRODUCTION

What is the role of "trusted communicators" in disseminating knowledge to the public? The trigger for this question, which is the topic of this set of chapters, is the widely shared belief that one of the most notable, and noted, consequences of the spread of the internet and social media is the collapse of sources of information that are broadly trusted across society, because the internet has eliminated the power of the traditional gatekeepers[1] who identified and created trusted communicators for the public. Many commentators argue this is a troubling development because trusted communicators are needed for our society to create and maintain a common base of facts, accepted by the broader public, that is essential to a system of democratic self-governance. Absent such a common base or factual consensus, democratic politics will tend to collapse into polarized camps that cannot accept the possibility of electoral defeat (as they arguably have in recent years in the United States). I aim here to examine recent proposals to resurrect a set of trusted communicators and the gatekeeper function, and to critique them from both practical and theoretical perspectives. But before we can discuss possible "solutions" to the lack of gatekeepers and trusted communicators in the modern era, it is important to understand how those functions arose in the pre-internet era.

* Thanks to Jane Bambauer, Joseph Blocher, Erin Carroll, Helen Norton, Alex Tsesis, and participants at the Freedom of Expression Scholars Conference for extremely helpful comments; and to Gus Hurwitz, Kyle Langvardt, and Elana Zeide for organizing this larger project. Finally, thanks to Christine Hanon for exemplary research assistance.

1 By gatekeepers, I mean entities and/or institutions who control what information and what sources of information the general public is exposed to without great effort on the audience's part.

4.2 THE OLD GATEKEEPERS

Underlying the concept of trusted communicators is the question of "Who to trust?" But underlying *that* question is yet another, more foundational one: "Who *decides* who to trust?" Ultimately, of course, each person must decide for themselves who to trust. But for a societal consensus on this question to emerge, some common source of authority must exist. If there is one lesson that can be drawn from the modern era of social media, it is that robust, public discourse alone cannot be expected to generate an automatic consensus on who can be trusted (or on trustworthy facts). The quest for trusted communicators, then, is in truth a quest for authoritative sources of trust – which is to say, a quest for authority. In the internet era, centralized control over information flows has fragmented and, consequently, so too has the authority to identify trusted communicators. Before seeking to recreate such authority, however, it is important to understand how and why such authoritative sources of information emerged in the pre-internet era, when modern expectations about trust and a factual consensus developed – which is to say, during the first six or seven decades of the twentieth century.

Who were the creators and designators of trust during this period? In short, it was the institutional media. Moreover, through most of the twentieth century, institutional media acted as the gatekeepers of knowledge and news as well. Just who constituted the institutional media gatekeepers, however, changed over time. During the first part of the century, perhaps the crucial period in the development of gatekeepers and trusted communicators, it was major daily newspapers, especially those associated with William Randolph Hearst and Joseph Pulitzer, as well as Adolph Ochs's *New York Times*. As we shall discuss in more detail, in many ways it was cultural clashes between Hearst and Pulitzer on one side and Ochs on the other that generated the dominant gatekeeper/trusted-communicator model.[2]

After World War I, while newspapers certainly maintained their importance, commercial radio broadcasters emerged as another crucial – and soon more popularly accessible – media institution. The first commercial radio station began broadcasting in 1920 in Pittsburgh, Pennsylvania. Four years later, 600 commercial radio stations were broadcasting in the United States. In 1926, the first national radio network, NBC, was formed.[3] As evidenced by President Franklin Delano Roosevelt's fireside chats during the Great Depression, radio quickly emerged as a widely available, popular means for institutional media – and those trusted communicators to whom they provided airtime, such as FDR – to reach mass public audiences.

Finally, around the mid-century, at the beginning of what many considered the Golden Age of the institutional media, television broadcasters began to complement

[2] *See generally* W. Joseph Campbell, The Year That Defined American Journalism: 1897 and the Clash of Paradigms (2006).

[3] *KDKA Begins to Broadcast: 1920*, PBS (1998).

and eventually supplant radio (and newspapers) as the key institutional media. The Federal Communications Commission (FCC) first authorized commercial television broadcasts in 1941, but because of World War II, commercial television broadcasts did not begin in earnest until 1947.[4] And then the industry exploded. From 1946 to 1951, the number of television sets in use rose from 6,000 to 12 million. By 1955, half of American households owned television sets.[5] Moreover, during the 1940s, the three iconic national television networks – the National Broadcasting Company (NBC) (evolved from the first radio network), the Columbia Broadcasting System (CBS) (evolved from a competing radio network), and the American Broadcasting Company (ABC) (spun off from NBC by order of the FCC) – had also emerged.[6] Finally, with the creation in 1956 of NBC's *The Huntley-Brinkley Report* (the first television news broadcast), television's dominance as the primary source of news for most Americans (and the concomitant decline in the influence of newspapers) began.[7]

The rise of broadcasting also led to the rise of the quintessential trusted communicators of this era, the network reporter and, later, anchorman. Coincidentally, the figures that epitomize both roles were affiliated with CBS. Edward R. Murrow first rose to prominence during the radio era through his revolutionary reporting on Hitler's *Anschluss* of Austria in 1938, and he became a household name by reporting live from London during the London Blitz in the early 1940s. He then moved to television and demonstrated continuing enormous influence through broadcasts, including a pathbreaking one in 1954 criticizing Senator Joseph McCarthy's witch-hunt against Communists, which contributed to McCarthy's downfall.[8]

The other, even more important trusted communicator of the broadcast era was of course Walter Cronkite. Cronkite first became prominent (among other things, as the first designated "anchorman") during CBS's coverage of the 1952 presidential nominating conventions. But it was with the launch of *The CBS Evening News with Walter Cronkite* in 1962 that Cronkite's central role as *the* trusted communicator emerged.[9] Cronkite's influence was most famously demonstrated when his critical coverage of the Vietnam War in 1968 led to an important swing in public opinion against the war and contributed to President Lyndon Johnson's decision not to run for re-election. Cronkite's status is illustrated by the fact that a 1972 poll named him "the most trusted man in America."[10] The institutional media and its key figures,

[4] Mitchell Stephens, *History of Television*, Grolier Encyclopedia, https://perma.cc/G8MT-6JPP.

[5] *Id.*

[6] *Id.*

[7] *Id.*

[8] David Mindich, *For Journalists Covering Trump, A Murrow Moment*, Colum. Journalism Rev. (July 15, 2016), https://perma.cc/Z77V-NGBC.

[9] Stephens, *supra* note 4.

[10] *Walter Cronkite: American Journalist*, Britannica (Mar. 7, 2022), https://perma.cc/AAM9-A4N5.

epitomized by Murrow and Cronkite, were thus *the* trusted communicators of this era.

Even though their technology and reach varied, the gatekeepers/trusted communicators described above shared some basic characteristics. First, they were relatively scarce. The economics of newspapers meant that during most of this period, metropolitan areas could only support one or a handful of newspapers.[11] With respect to the broadcast medium, the number of radio and television stations in any particular locality that actually produced original content (as opposed to playing music or broadcasting reruns of sitcoms) was limited by the same economic factors (essentially economies of scale) as newspapers. In addition, the fact that the number of possible broadcast frequencies was physically limited – electromagnetic spectrum, as the Supreme Court put it, is a "scarce resource"[12] – necessarily limited the number of outlets in any particular market. Indeed, in practice, the broadcast-television market, especially in its role as disseminator of national news and general knowledge, was completely dominated by the three major networks (NBC, CBS, and ABC) until the launch of the Fox network in 1986 – and that only added one additional player. This situation only changed with the spread of cable television in the 1980s (and thus the end of spectrum scarcity because of the large channel capacity of cable systems), resulting in the launch of cable-only CNN in 1980 and then of Fox News in 1996.

The second shared characteristic between different types of gatekeepers and trusted communicators was that these gatekeepers sought to construct an "objective," nonpartisan image. The roots of this development, which has become an essential element of modern journalistic ethics,[13] can be found in the conflict between the sensationalist journalism championed by newspaper tycoons William Randolph Hearst and Joseph Pulitzer, and the "counteractivist," nonpartisan model of Adolph S. Och's *New York Times* (which he purchased in 1896[14]). While the Hearst/Pulitzer model was dominant in the late nineteenth and early twentieth centuries, Ochs's commitment "to give the news impartially, without fear or favor, regardless of party, sect, or interests involved" – a commitment Ochs announced on his first day of ownership of the *Times*[15] – eventually won out.[16] By 1920, this norm of objectivity[17]

[11] *See* Miami Herald Pub'g Co. v. Tornillo, 418 U.S. 241, 249–50 & n.13 (1974).

[12] Red Lion Broad. Co. v. FCC, 395 U.S. 367, 391 (1969).

[13] *See SPJ Code of Ethics*, Soc'y Prof. Journalists, https://perma.cc/K48S-5YWR ("Ethical journalism should be accurate and fair").

[14] Bill Kovach & Tom Rosenstiel, The Elements of Journalism: What Newspeople Should Know and the Public Should Expect 76 (4th ed. 2021).

[15] *Id.*

[16] *See generally* Campbell, *supra* note 2; *Invisible Men: The Future of Journalism*, Economist 67–68 (July 18, 2020).

[17] Andrew Porwancher, *Objectivity's Prophet: Adolph S. Ochs and the New York Times*, 36 Journalism Hist. 186, 187 (2011), https://perma.cc/UJ6T-6N5Y.

(which had previously gone by the name of "realism"[18]) was becoming the dominant paradigm of journalism, as reflected by the fact that the Society of Professional Journalists' first Code of Ethics, adopted in 1926, calls for journalistic "impartiality," meaning that "[n]ews reports should be free from opinion or bias of any kind."[19]

It is important to note, however, that this goal of objectivity was a historical anomaly. Prior to the early twentieth century, newspapers and publishers did not pretend to be objective – to the contrary, they were explicitly partisan. Important historical examples include *The Aurora*, the newspaper edited by Benjamin Franklin Bache (Ben Franklin's grandson) in the late 1790s, which was tied to the Democratic Republican party of Jefferson and Madison (Bache and other Jeffersonian newspaper editors were prosecuted by the Adams Administration for sedition),[20] and Horace Greeley's *New York Tribune*, which was closely associated with the Republican Party before and during the Civil War.[21] Needless to say, these newspapers were *not* viewed as trustworthy by their political opponents (as demonstrated by Bache's prosecution). After World War I, however, economic pressures led to the consolidation of newspapers and a notable decrease in the number of daily newspapers – as epitomized by the merger in 1924 of the old rivals the *New York Herald* (which, though allegedly nonpartisan, often supported Democratic Party policies during the Civil War) and Greeley's *New York Tribune*.[22] As a consequence, newspapers began to seek broader (and so bipartisan) audiences, which required them to abandon their partisan affiliations. Not coincidentally, journalistic ethics during this period also embraced objectivity as a desirable norm, as noted above.

The trend toward objectivity continued as newspapers were gradually supplanted by broadcast: first radio, then (even more dominantly) television. For television broadcasting in particular, the push for objectivity was driven by similar economic motivations to maximize audience share because of the effective monopoly on national news held by the three national networks. In addition, the FCC's Fairness Doctrine, in effect from 1949 to 1987, strongly incentivized objectivity on the part of both radio and television broadcasters by requiring them to present opposing views on public issues, and by creating a right of reply on the part of individuals subject to a "personal attack" during broadcast programming.[23] Facially objective news coverage avoided triggering either requirement.[24]

[18] Walter Dean, *The Lost Meaning of "Objectivity"*, AM. PRESS INST., https://perma.cc/6CRR-EWWL.

[19] *Sigma Delta Chi's New Code of Ethics*, SOC'Y PROF. JOURNALISTS, https://perma.cc/5CMS-BSUZ.

[20] For a good discussion of this episode, *see* GEOFFREY R. STONE, PERILOUS TIMES: FREE SPEECH DURING WARTIME 35 (2004).

[21] JAMES M. MCPHERSON, BATTLE CRY OF FREEDOM: THE CIVIL WAR ERA 251–52 (1988).

[22] *New York Herald: American Newspaper*, BRITANNICA, https://perma.cc/FLE8-YWJV.

[23] Red Lion Broad. Co. v. FCC, 395 U.S. 367, 375–79 (1969); Matt Stefon, *Fairness Doctrine*, BRITANNICA, https://perma.cc/HYP3-JNUE.

[24] *Id.*

This performed objectivity, playing out in a highly concentrated broadcast market, enabled a small set of individuals and institutions to emerge as "trusted communicators" in the eyes of a broad swath of the American public. We might call this the Murrow–Cronkite Effect. Furthermore, this institutional structure permitted trusted media figures to extend public trust to elite, designated "experts" *outside* the media by giving those experts the gatekeepers' imprimatur in the form of interviews and airtime (as an example, consider Edward R. Murrow's famous 1955 interview of Jonas Salk, the inventor of the polio vaccine[25]). As a consequence, during this "golden era," most of American society obtained news and knowledge from a few common and generally trusted sources.

What engendered this broad-based trust,[26] which in today's world seems inconceivable? I would argue that the answer, in short, was a lack of alternative voices. The public trusted media gatekeepers because they had no choice – there were no significant opposing voices to question or undermine that trust because of concentration within the institutional media. It was precisely these factors – concentration and lack of choice – that made the institutional media, especially the three television networks, gatekeepers who exercised effective control over the flow of information into almost every American household. Indeed, it is hard to imagine how a media institution could play gatekeeper without this kind of option scarcity.

Furthermore, for economic reasons discussed above, these gatekeepers adopted an "objectivity" that overwhelmingly tended to reflect the views of the political center in order to maximize their potential audience. As a consequence, there were simply no opportunities for the public to question consensus facts, or to become aware of what the institutional media was not telling them (such as President Kennedy's philandering, or the CIA's secret coups during President Eisenhower's administration). I am not insinuating that Murrow and Cronkite did not earn the public's trust – I have no doubt that they did, through ethical and insightful journalism. But that trust ultimately depended on a lack of choice or alternative, nonmainstream voices.

4.3 THE COLLAPSE OF THE OLD GATEKEEPERS

Eventually, of course, this system of institutional concentration and consensus collapsed. The first developments along these lines are probably traceable to the FCC's repeal of the Fairness Doctrine in 1987,[27] which in turn led to the rise of

[25] Michael Hiltzik, *On Jonas Salk's 100th Birthday, a Celebration of His Polio Vaccine*, L.A. Times (Oct. 28, 2014), https://perma.cc/JE3A-XAMP.

[26] To be fair, it is far from clear that the trust I am describing here extended to minority communities, but that is another story.... Thanks to Helen Norton and Erin Carroll for (independently) pointing this out to me.

[27] Stefon, *supra* note 23.

right-wing talk radio, a medium which did not pretend or aspire to objectivity.[28] In addition, the explosion of the cable-television medium during the 1980s ended the era of television concentration because television no longer required scarce spectrum,[29] which in turn permitted the launch of the overtly partisan Fox News in 1996,[30] at the very dawn of the internet era. But while these developments began undermining the era of (supposed) media objectivity and the media's gatekeeper function, there can be little doubt that the internet, and especially the rise of social media, put a final end to the institutional media's control over public discourse. These, however, are relatively recent events. X was founded in 2006,[31] the same year that Facebook became available to the general public.[32] But at first, these were relatively obscure platforms. It was not until the availability and widespread adoption of smartphones – the first iPhone was not released until 2007,[33] and smartphones did not come into common use for several years after then – that social media became mobile and easily usable, leading to its exponential growth.[34]

By the 2010s, the importance of social media in displacing traditional media as the primary engine of public discourse was evident – so much so that by 2017, that most hidebound of American institutions, the United States Supreme Court, recognized social media as "the most important places ... for the exchange of views."[35] Every citizen became a potential publisher and people suddenly possessed a plethora of choices regarding what voices to pay attention to, ending once and for all the gatekeeper function of the institutional media. And for the same reason, the range of opinions expressed publicly became massively more diverse, ending the media's role in creating consensus around a common set of facts and beliefs. The Murrow–Cronkite Effect had vanished.

With the collapse of the gatekeeper function also came the collapse of trusted communicators. There are no Edward Murrows or Walter Cronkites in the social-media/Fox News era; instead we have Tucker Carlsons and Robert F. Kennedy,

[28] It is no coincidence that *The Rush Limbaugh Show* was launched nationally in 1988. *America's Anchorman*, RUSH LIMBAUGH SHOW, https://perma.cc/KF4Y-5E74.

[29] During the 1980s, the number of cable networks exploded from 28 to 79, and cable penetration in American households enjoyed similar growth. *See* Brad Adgate, *The Rise and Fall of Cable Television*, FORBES (Nov. 2, 2020), https://perma.cc/ZD29-R4KZ.

[30] Michael Ray, *Fox News Channel*, BRITANNICA (Mar. 2, 2022), https://perma.cc/8Y5G-VQMS.

[31] Jack Meyer, *History of Twitter: Jack Dorsey and the Social Media Giant*, THESTREET (Jan. 2, 2020), https://perma.cc/L8V2-94LY.

[32] *Who We Are*, META, https://perma.cc/686G-8AUA.

[33] *Apple Reinvents the Phone with iPhone*, APPLE (Jan. 9, 2007), https://perma.cc/5A8B-HCRT.

[34] As an illustration, from 2008 to 2012, the number of Facebook users grew from 100 million to 1 billion – the latter being greater than the combined populations of the United States and the European Union. Kurt Wagner & Rani Molla, *Facebook's First 15 Years Were Defined By User Growth*, VOX (Feb. 5, 2019), https://perma.cc/85JZ-895C.

[35] Packingham v. North Carolina, 137 S. Ct. 1730, 1735 (2017).

Jr.s (Mr. Kennedy, the son of Bobby Kennedy, is an active anti-vaccine propogandist[36]). This development is frankly unsurprising if one accepts, as I argued above, that much of the public's trust during the Murrow–Cronkite era was a product of the institutional media's gatekeeper function. No more gatekeepers, no more trust.

To be fair, the elimination of gatekeepers is not the only development that has contributed to the loss of trusted communicators. Most obviously, political polarization has also played an important role. As many people have drifted into more radicalized political positions, they inevitably cease to trust the traditional trusted communicators of the center (or, more honestly, the center-left) that made up the institutional media. Individuals whose views sit in the far-right or far-left have no reason to trust institutional speakers such as *The New York Times* or CNN. But here, too, the loss of gatekeepers plays an important causal role. During the peak of the gatekeeper era, most people had no access or exposure to radical voices unless they actively sought them out – and such voices were, as a result, quite rare. Today, social media and other internet forums provide easy access to a vast range of viewpoints, permitting individuals to trust whomever they please – usually voices that reinforce and intensify their existing views. Of course, there have always been radical movements and conspiracy theories, but the rapid spread and sheer scope of the QAnon conspiracy theory, for example, would not have been possible in the pre-internet era; its ideas would never have gotten past the gatekeepers.

4.4 THE NEW GATEKEEPERS?

The loss of faith in institutional elites, including the institutional media, and the resulting collapse of consensus has had profound consequences. One impact has been to further exacerbate political polarization – though it should be noted that the internet did not create modern polarization, which can be traced back at least to Newt Gingrich's 1994 "Contract with America" and the bloody political battles of the 1990s. More fundamentally, however, the loss of gatekeepers and trusted communicators has either threatened or eliminated the possibility of an ideology-free consensus on even basic facts. For individual media consumers, ideology seems to play a heavy role in shaping factual perceptions, regardless of objective reality. As an example, consider the fact that in 2016, 72 percent of Republicans expressed doubts about Obama's birthplace, despite his Hawaiian birth certificate being in the public record.[37]

This loss of what one might call "consensus reality" has created an intellectual atmosphere of existential angst in some elements of American society. This is most

[36] Adam Nagourney, *A Kennedy's Crusade against Covid Vaccines Anguishes Family and Friends*, N.Y. Times (Feb. 26, 2022).

[37] Josh Clinton & Carrie Roush, *Poll: Persistent Partisan Divide over "Birther" Question*, NBC News (Aug. 10, 2016), https://perma.cc/2EBV-QR3F.

evident within the mainstream media (perhaps unsurprisingly), but it is also an important part of the dialogue in politics (mainly on the left) and in academia (almost definitionally the left). To be clear, there is no question that a lack of factual consensus has had negative social consequences. It has made compromise – or even dialogue – across partisan lines far more difficult. And as the United States' experience with COVID-19 demonstrates, it can lead to deeply irrational policy choices (both on the left and right, to be clear). But the intellectual angst that I describe is often expressed in an existential manner, as fear for the very survival of our society (caused by such factors as the false belief among many Republicans, fostered by President Trump and elements of the conservative media, that the 2020 presidential election was stolen from Trump[38]).

The practical ways in which these elements of society have operationalized their angst has been to place enormous amounts of pressure on social-media platforms such as Facebook, X, and YouTube to actively block (among other things) online falsehoods in order to recreate a consensus reality. Not a day goes by, seemingly, without another thundering op-ed published in *The New York Times*[39] or *The Washington Post*[40] decrying misinformation and "fake news" and blaming social-media platforms for failing to suppress it. Meanwhile, Democratic members of Congress such as Amy Klobuchar and Elizabeth Warren have been pushing aggressively for legislation that would force social media to suppress mis- and disinformation.[41]

In short, these critics want social-media platforms to become the *new* gatekeepers, replicating the role of the twentieth-century institutional media in deciding what information and sources of information the public should be exposed to. Their logic appears to be that, because a small number of social-media platforms now host such a large portion of public discourse, the owners and controllers of those platforms should therefore ensure that the flow of information to individuals is accurate and "clean," just as the twentieth-century institutional media did when it held a similar bottleneck position. And in fact, given their dominant market positions, the "big four" owners of the key social-media platforms on which political discourse occurs – essentially Meta (which owns Facebook and Instagram), X, Alphabet (formerly

38 *See, e.g.*, Zachary Ross, *The Five Biggest Threats Our Democracy Faces*, BRENNAN CTR. FOR JUST. (Dec. 15, 2020), https://perma.cc/6F6R-FJY2.

39 *See, e.g.*, Richard L. Hasen, *How to Keep the Rising Tide of Fake News from Drowning Our Democracy*, N.Y. TIMES (Mar. 7, 2022); Greg Bensinger, *How Twitter Can Fix Itself*, N.Y. TIMES (Dec. 1, 2021); Andrew Higgins, Adam Satariano & Jane Arraf, *How Fake News on Facebook Helped Fuel a Border Crisis in Europe*, N.Y. TIMES (Nov. 22, 2021).

40 Jennifer Rubin, *It's Time to Stand Up to Facebook*, WASH. POST (Oct. 4, 2021); Joe Scarborough, *Zuckerberg Says He's "Disgusted" by Trump's Rhetoric. It's Just Crocodile Tears*, WASH. POST (June 18, 2020).

41 *See, e.g.*, Health Misinformation Act of 2021 (S.2448), https://perma.cc/Z7F9-4PQD; Cecelia Kang & Thomas Kaplan, *Warren Dares Facebook with Intentionally False Political Ad*, N.Y. TIMES (Oct. 12, 2019).

Google, which owns YouTube), and ByteDance (which owns TikTok) – might well jointly possess the power to shape discourse akin to the three broadcast television networks of the twentieth century. But should they?[42]

I have argued elsewhere that any *legal* requirements forcing internet platforms to suppress "fake news" would almost certainly violate the First Amendment.[43] The question I am raising here is whether, leaving aside the (dubious) constitutionality of regulation, it is even a good idea for social-media firms to act as gatekeepers (and for critics to push them to do so). In other words, *should* social-media firms be in the business of screening out false information and determining who is and is not a trusted communicator? Leaving aside the question of whether this is even possible (does anyone believe that Mark Zuckerberg can replace Walter Cronkite as "the most trusted man in America"?), I believe that they should not.

There are several reasons why social-media firms are ill-suited to be effective gatekeepers (or, as Mark Zuckerberg would have it, "arbiters of truth"[44]). First and foremost, they have no economic incentives to do so. The traditional institutional media emphasized their objectivity and sought to develop reputations as trusted gatekeepers because it was in their economic interest to do so. Objectivity and trust increased viewership and market share. The same is not true with social media. Social-media algorithms emphasize relevance, not truth. That is what increases engagement, and so profits. Asking for-profit companies to take on roles that they have no economic incentive to adopt strikes me as both dubious policy and likely futile.

Second, social-media firms have absolutely no expertise or training that would enable them to be either effective gatekeepers or effective identifiers of trusted communicators. As a practical matter, while social-media algorithms are quite effective at sorting by relevance and interest, I am doubtful that they can be designed to identify "truth" or its opposite, given the tenuous and disputed nature of truth. More fundamentally, the people who work for the large tech firms are unlikely to be effective at the gatekeeper function. They are, after all, software engineers, not journalists or trained experts on subject matters such as science, history, or economics, and it seems unlikely, given the culture of Silicon Valley, that they will become so. Training the Mark Zuckerbergs of the world to be journalists is likely to be about as successful as it would have been to train Walter Cronkite to code. Furthermore, social-media platforms do not themselves generate content, unlike many traditional experts (though those experts, as noted below, have themselves had a spotty record in identifying "truth"), which significantly reduces the incentives for these firms to develop serious in-house expertise (or for highly qualified experts to want to work for

[42] *See* Eugene Volokh, *The Reverse Spider-Man Principle: With Great Responsibility Comes Great Power*, 3 J. FREE SPEECH L. 197 (2023).

[43] Ashutosh Bhagwat, *The Law of Facebook*, 54 U.C. DAVIS L. REV. 2353, 2393–94 (2021).

[44] Yael Halon, *Zuckerberg Knows Twitter for Fact-Checking Trump, Says Private Companies Shouldn't Be "The Arbiter of Truth"*, FOX NEWS (May 27, 2020), https://perma.cc/AUM3-3UJY.

them – fact-checking is boring compared to content creation). Moreover, recent history suggests that when social-media firms do rely on "expert" elites to identify misinformation, the results can be dicey – as illustrated by the fiascos of labeling the lab-leak theory of COVID's origins as misinformation,[45] or the decision to suppress a negative story about Hunter Biden on the eve of the 2020 presidential election.[46] Indeed, social-media critics are notably vague about how exactly social-media firms are to identify "truth" (or its opposite, misinformation) going forward . . . other than, that is, strongly suggesting that misinformation is whatever they themselves – the political and media elites – deem it to be.

Finally, I would question whether *any* gatekeepers of information and/or "trusted communicators" are ultimately beneficial to society or consistent with principles of free expression. First, it is important to acknowledge that truth, especially ideologically tinged truth, is a slippery thing.[47] While I do not deny the existence of objective facts (e.g., COVID-19 is real, and vaccines do work and do not cause autism), that sort of objectivity falls apart very soon after one gets beyond simple, provable facts. Certainly, COVID-19 is a real and dangerous disease, but where did it originate? Maybe a lab in Wuhan, maybe not – we may never know. Was closing primary schools for lengthy periods of time necessary to combat the spread of COVID-19? Teachers and parents may have different answers. Is it necessary or wise to vaccinate young children against COVID-19, given their low risk of severe illness? The expert-provided answers to these questions are, in truth, guesswork or opinions (albeit informed ones) dressed up as objective fact (or "science"). Should disagreement with these experts be suppressed or labeled as misinformation?

The more fundamental question, once we get beyond a very narrow range of objective facts, is whether gatekeepers and deference to designated "experts" (i.e., trusted communicators) really offer the best way to identify "truth" and, conversely, misinformation. Those who favor gatekeepers, including social-media gatekeepers, assume that gatekeepers and experts are necessary to hold back the tide of fake news. But there is a deep tension between this institutional approach and basic theories of free speech, as most famously encapsulated by Justice Oliver Wendell Holmes's foundational metaphor of the "marketplace of ideas": "that the best test of truth is the power of the thought to get itself accepted in the competition of the market."[48] Nor is it consistent with Justice Louis Brandeis's equally fundamental adage that, when faced with false or dangerous speech, "the remedy to be applied is more speech, not enforced silence."[49]

45 *See* Brett Stephens, *Media Groupthink and the Lab-Leak Theory*, N.Y. Times (May 31, 2021).

46 Andrew Prokop, *The Return of Hunter Biden's Laptop*, Vox (Mar. 25, 2022), https://perma.cc/7XGK-BPRU.

47 For a thoughtful, extended discussion of this problem, *see* Jane Bambauer, *Snake Oil Speech*, 93 Wash. L. Rev. 73 (2018).

48 Abrams v. United States, 250 U.S. 616, 630 (1919) (Holmes, J., dissenting).

49 Whitney v. California, 274 U.S. 357, 377 (1927) (Brandeis, J., concurring).

Both Holmes's and Brandeis's theories of free speech, while differing in details, are premised on the assumption that citizens should be permitted to freely engage in political debate, to the point even of advocating lawless behavior. This is because, according to Holmes, only then can truth emerge, and, according to Brandeis only then can citizens fully engage in our democracy. The concept of gatekeepers is simply inconsistent with both these visions. Gatekeepers are anathema to competition, and they are also quintessential silencers rather than enablers of "more speech."

4.5 CONCLUSION

In short, perhaps the collapse of gatekeepers and trusted communicators is not such a terrible thing after all. None of this is to assert that the truth will necessarily emerge from the competition of the market. Markets are often flawed, and even though the internet and social media have removed the barriers to entry that plagued twentieth-century public discourse, there are other problems, often rooted in our political polarization, that continue to interfere with the free exchange of ideas – an obvious example being social media's tendency to create speech silos. Nor is it to claim that citizens, given the opportunity, will engage in honest and civil democratic deliberation. Human nature being what it is (and the desire for ideological self-reinforcement being what it is), we know today that Holmes's and Brandeis's shared optimism about the results of open discourse was probably not justified. But the gatekeeper solution, whereby a handful of elite actors control public discourse, is not consistent with either principles of free expression or the role of citizens in our democracy. Instead of trying to recreate a bygone (and, frankly, deeply flawed) era, perhaps we should be thinking about how to reinvigorate a marketplace of ideas and encourage genuine democratic deliberation that both surmount political polarization. How we might attempt to do so is beyond the reach of this chapter,[50] but such an effort, rather than creating new gatekeepers, seems to me the best hope for curing the ills of our public discourse and of our democracy.

[50] I have advanced some preliminary thoughts on this question elsewhere. *See* Ashutosh Bhagwat, Our Democratic First Amendment 112–17 (2020) (arguing for greater reliance on crowd-sourcing, similar to the Wikipedia model, to work towards more factual consensus); *see also* Joseph Blocher, *Institutions in the Marketplace of Ideas*, 57 Duke L.J. 821 (2008) (explaining the role that institutions such as universities and schools can play in reducing transaction costs within the marketplace of ideas).

5

Beyond the Watchdog

Using Law to Build Trust in the Press

*Erin C. Carroll**

5.1 INTRODUCTION

It was 1971 and *Los Angeles Times* editor Nick Williams had what he called a "terribly uneasy feeling." In a letter to one of the paper's Washington correspondents, he wrote of his suspicion that journalism had "lost credibility ... with an alarming percentage of the people." If the plummet continued, Williams fretted, journalists will have "destroyed or weakened a keystone of our Constitution."[1]

Williams's assessment was not entirely wrong. Polling data from 1971 confirmed that a dismal 18 percent of Americans had a "great deal of confidence" in the press.[2]

But he also wasn't quite right. Far from undermining American government's democratic foundations, the press was likely shoring them up, having already entered what has been called its "Glory Days."[3] This era was brought about, in part, by the press's performance of its watchdog role, exposing political corruption and government cover-ups. It was also brought about by something else: law. The Supreme Court and legislatures boosted the press by celebrating this watchdog role and granting it tools to enhance this work.[4]

Today, 1971 feels familiar. Polls again register dreadfully low levels of trust in the media. "Terribly uneasy" may be a generous description of how journalists feel

* I am grateful to Ashutosh Bhagwat, Jane Bambauer, and Helen Norton for their insightful feedback on this chapter. Many thanks also to Gus Hurwitz, Kyle Langvardt, and Elana Zeide for spearheading this project. And, finally, special thanks to Tom Rosenstiel for conversations that informed this work. All errors are mine.

1 Matthew Pressman, On Press: The Liberal Values that Shaped the News 59 (2018).

2 *Id.* at 58.

3 RonNell Andersen Jones, *What the Supreme Court Thinks of the Press and Why It Matters*, 66 Ala. L. Rev. 253, 255–56 (2014).

4 *See generally* New York Times Co. v. United States, 403 U.S. 713 (1971) (The Pentagon Papers Case); Sheppard v. Maxwell, 384 U.S. 333 (1966); Neb. Press Ass'n. v. Stuart, 427 U.S. 539 (1976).

about the public's perception of them and the press's ability to continue playing its democratic role.

Are we again on the verge of a reinvigorated and newly effective press, or is trust headed deeper into the abyss? Institutions, including the press, are at an inflection point. History gives press advocates a basis for optimism. Yet, history provides no failsafe template.

Today, if journalists were to double down on their still-vital watchdog role as a way of building trust, such an effort might backfire. There is a risk that in our hyper-polarized society, citizens would recoil, finding this aggressive brand of journalism too cynical, negative, and politicized. A new approach is needed.

A promising approach would be to embrace another key journalistic function, one that has received far less attention and adulation from judges, legislators, and legal scholars than the press's watchdog role: the press's role as a convener and facilitator of the public square. As Bill Kovach and Tom Rosenstiel write in their journalism classic, *The Elements of Journalism*, a key function of journalism is to "provide a forum for public criticism and compromise."[5] Of late, journalists themselves are embracing this role as they develop what has alternately been called "community-centered journalism," "social journalism," and "engaged journalism."

This journalism movement envisions the relationship between journalists and citizens very differently than watchdog journalism does. In watchdog journalism – true to the metaphor – journalists are protectors of the public. As watchdogs, they use their professional expertise and privileged position as members of the Fourth Estate to expose government wrongdoing. In this way, the press exercises a position of power over citizens. The intent is to wield power benevolently and in the public interest, but it is a hierarchical relationship nonetheless.

In contrast, community-centered journalism intentionally seeks to minimize that power differential. It brings citizens into the news-making process – from deciding what to cover, to assisting with information-gathering, to providing post-publication feedback – creating what Tom Rosenstiel has called a "virtuous circle of learning."[6] Some community-centered journalists have gone so far as to say that the movement's primary aim is not necessarily the creation of news; it is building trusting and healthy communities. News is a by-product.

[5] Bill Kovach & Tom Rosenstiel, The Elements of Journalism: What Newspeople Should Know and the Public Should Expect xxvii (4th ed. 2021). The Harvard-based *Nieman Reports* has said of the book, "Since its publication in 2001, '*The Elements of Journalism*' has been the industry-standard text on the ethics and practice of journalism." Bill Kovach & Tom Rosenstiel, *In Praise of Digital: An Excerpt from the New Edition of "The Elements of Journalism,"* Nieman Reports (July 17, 2014) (describing the book in an introduction to an article by the book's authors).

[6] Mónica Guzmán, *What Exactly Is Engagement and What Difference Does It Make?*, Am. Press Inst. (May 2, 2016), https://perma.cc/WP7M-EBVY (quoting Tom Rosenstiel, *News As Collaborative Intelligence: Correcting the Myths About News in the Digital Age*, Ctr. for Effective Pub. Mgmt. at Brookings 3 (June 2015), https://perma.cc/7S47-65KU).

Judges, legislators, and legal scholars should take note of this shifting journalistic landscape. Just as law helped to build and maintain public trust in the watchdog press in the 1960s and 1970s, it likewise has a part to play now. The legal system can solidify the role of the press not only as a watchdog (still a necessary function) but also as a facilitator and convener, as exemplified by the community-centered press movement. And it can do so using methods drawn from the Glory Days: positive rhetoric about the press and legislation that eases the press's ability to fulfill its democratic functions. Legislation could be as straightforward as allocating funds for local meeting spaces and training for journalists. By creating a legal framework for the press that is richer and more reflective of diverse journalistic practices, law would strengthen the "virtuous circle" Rosenstiel describes.[7] Greater public trust in the press could be a by-product.

5.2 TRUST, THE WATCHDOG PRESS, AND THE SUPREME COURT: A VERY BRIEF HISTORY

To the extent that something as intangible as trust can be measured, pollsters have tried to do so. For at least sixty years, they have asked American citizens to rate the strength of their trust in the mass media, including newspapers, TV, and radio.[8] That trust was at a nadir in 1971 when the *Los Angeles Times*'s Nick Williams was expressing alarm.[9] Yet, in the next handful of years, trust soared. By 1976, in a Gallup poll, 72 percent of Americans expressed a "great deal" or "a fair amount" of trust in the media to report "the news fully, accurately and fairly."[10] This was a high point; in the nearly fifty years since, Gallup has recorded a steady decline in this trust. It dipped to 32 percent in 2016 – the lowest number on record for the poll (which began in 1972).[11] It has hovered around this level ever since.[12]

What shifted? Trying to pinpoint causes for the deterioration of trust is difficult; they are numerous and intertwined. One especially tempting explanation – blaming the internet and social media – is simplistic and wrong-headed. Trust was declining long before the internet was widely used.

At least a few threads can be pulled from the tangle of possibilities and identified with some confidence. First, Americans' declining trust in the press (in the late 1960s and today) came at times of national upheaval and uncertainty. In the 1960s this included the Vietnam War, a racial reckoning, and high-profile assassinations. Today, we face a racial reckoning anew, intense political polarization, growing

7 *See id.*
8 PRESSMAN, *supra* note 1, at 58.
9 *Id.*
10 Megan Brenan, *Americans' Trust in Media Dips to Second Lowest on Record*, GALLUP (Oct. 7, 2021), https://news.gallup.com/poll/355526/americans-trust-media-dips-second-lowest-record.aspx; Art Swift, *Americans' Trust in Mass Media Sinks to New Low*, GALLUP (Sept. 14, 2016), https://perma.cc/Z3LD-J697.
11 Swift, *supra* note 10.
12 Brenan, *supra* note 10.

wealth inequality, global democratic regression, and a pandemic. Second, both deep dips in press trust track the public's declining trust in institutions generally.[13]

Beyond social, economic, and political conditions, the press shares in the blame. As Kenneth Newton and Pippa Norris's "institutional performance model" holds, the public's trust in institutions falters when those institutions perform poorly.[14] There is plenty we could critique about the press's performance both in the 1960s and today. This could include reporter bias, a lack of diversity, and too thin a wall between the business and journalism sides of many news organizations.

But if the press is partially responsible for the southward turn in trust, then it should also take some credit for the mid-1970s spike. The numbers indicate that, at that time, the public believed the press was doing something right. A strong candidate for that something right: watchdog reporting. More generically called investigative reporting or accountability reporting, this is the brand of journalism that focuses on exposing government malfeasance and corruption. Watchdog reporting gained public recognition in the early to mid-1970s.

In 1971, both *The New York Times* and *The Washington Post* began publishing excerpts of and writing about the Pentagon Papers, secret government documents detailing the United States' involvement in the Vietnam War.[15] In 1972, *The Washington Post* helped to expose that a burglary at the Watergate was part of broad spying and sabotage effort aimed at re-electing President Richard Nixon.[16] The fallout prompted Nixon's resignation in 1974.

Of course, despite its impressive shoe-leather reporting, the press did not boost its own image single-handedly. Credit is also due to other institutions that lionized the press at this time, the U.S. Supreme Court and Congress. Law – whether judge-made or statutory – was essential in amplifying the way in which the press already performed its democratic roles and in providing tools and inspiration for the press to continue to play those roles.[17]

[13] *See* Ethan Zuckerman, *Mistrust, Efficacy and the New Civics: Understanding the Deep Roots of the Crisis of Faith in Journalism*, Aspen Inst. (2017), https://perma.cc/U6QC-NQZK. By "the press," I mean an institution comprised of journalists and others (editors, designers, data scientists, etc.) regardless of publishing medium who are committed to the mission of providing the public with the information that it needs to engage in democracy. *See* Kovach & Rosenstiel, *supra* note 5, at 7 ("The primary purpose of journalism is to provide citizens with the information they need to be free and self-governing.").

[14] *See* Kenneth Newton & Pippa Norris, *Confidence in Public Institutions: Faith, Culture, or Performance?*, *in* Disaffected Democracies: What's Troubling Trilateral Countries 61 (Susan J. Pharr & Robert D. Putnam eds., 2000); Zuckerman, *supra* note 13 (theorizing that the institutional performance model helps explain the current lack of trust in institutions).

[15] *The Watergate Story: Timeline*, Wash. Post (Jan. 18, 2023), https://perma.cc/W8CE-AQ9T.

[16] Carl Bernstein & Bob Woodward, *FBI Finds Nixon Aides Sabotaged Democrats*, Wash. Post (Oct. 10, 1972), https://perma.cc/K6J2-5HDF.

[17] *Cf.* Jones, *supra* note 3, at 255–56; RonNell Andersen Jones & Sonja R. West, *The U.S. Supreme Court's Characterizations of the Press: An Empirical Study*, 100 N.C. L. Rev. 375, 378–79 (2022).

First, with respect to the U.S. Supreme Court, from the late 1960s and through the early 1980s, the Court decided nearly all the cases that now comprise the press law canon. In these opinions, the Court laid rhetorical and legal groundwork for public trust in the press. As a group, these opinions are so laudatory of the press, this era has been referred to by legal scholars as the press's "Glory Days."[18] Many of these cases focus on the press's watchdog role. For example, in *New York Times Co. v. United States*[19] (known as the Pentagon Papers Case), Justice Black wrote that under the First Amendment, "[t]he press was protected so that it could bare the secrets of government and inform the people. Only a free and unrestrained press can effectively expose deception in government."[20]

The Pentagon Papers Case, as well as other cases that discuss the press's role as a watchdog, evince the deep trust that the Court had for what it seemed to view as a sister institution. For example, in the 1966 case of *Sheppard v. Maxwell*,[21] the Court built up the press by calling it a "handmaiden of effective judicial administration" through "guard[ing] against the miscarriage of justice by subjecting the police, prosecutors, and judicial processes to extensive public scrutiny and criticism."[22] It is hard to imagine a demonstration of deeper trust than this – an expression by the Court that it needed the press to do its own job effectively.

A decade later, in *Nebraska Press Association v. Stuart*,[23] the Court reaffirmed its trust in the press and perhaps reflected the public's newfound surge in trust. In invalidating a bar on the press publishing accounts of confessions in a criminal trial, Justice Brennan's concurrence, joined by Justices Stewart and Marshall, spoke again of the importance of the press serving as a check on the judiciary. He wrote, "[F]ree and robust reporting, criticism, and debate can contribute to public understanding of the rule of law and to comprehension of the functioning of the entire criminal justice system, as well as improve the quality of that system by subjecting it to the cleansing effects of exposure and public accountability."[24]

During these Glory Days at the Supreme Court, Congress was also laying groundwork for the press-trust bump. In 1966, Congress passed the Freedom of Information Act, which allows any person to request government agency records on any topic.[25] Newspapers were the driving force behind the law, and its key congressional sponsor cited the needs of a free press when urging its passage.[26] Despite

[18] Jones, *supra* note 3, at 255–56.
[19] 403 U.S. 713 (1971).
[20] *Id.* at 717 (Black, J., concurring).
[21] 384 U.S. 333 (1966).
[22] *Id.* at 350.
[23] 427 U.S. 539 (1976).
[24] *Id.* at 587.
[25] 5 U.S.C. § 552.
[26] John E. Moss, *Clarifying and Protecting the Right of the Public to Information* (June 20, 1966), https://perma.cc/4SK7-E7DM (quoting statement by Honorable John E. Moss from the June 20, 1966 Congressional Record).

criticism of its implementation by agencies, FOIA remains more than a half-century later a key tool for watchdog reporting.[27] Moreover, FOIA spawned transparency laws in state legislatures across the country.[28] All fifty states now have sunshine laws modeled on FOIA.[29]

None of this is intended to be a claim that courts or legislators single-handedly resurrected public trust in the press during the 1970s. Even proving that they moved the needle is difficult. Yet, it can be shown that watchdog journalism thrived toward the end of the press's Glory Days in the Court and after Congress's passage of FOIA.[30] Because the shift in journalistic practice towards a watchdog role surged post-Watergate, this suggests the press felt buoyed by positive rhetoric from the Supreme Court as well as by the tools granted to it legislatively. Given the potential of courts and legislatures to contribute to such a shift, it is worth asking how law can assist anew.

5.3 TRUST, AND THE PRESS AS FACILITATOR OF DELIBERATION IN PUBLIC SQUARES

As a starting point, it helps to return to journalistic first principles and consider whether any are apt to spark renewed trust and are also aligned with the press's democracy-enhancing role. In the 1960s and 1970s, the Supreme Court and legislatures homed in on the press as a watchdog. This role required trust in the institutional press's authority, particularly its role as a Fourth Estate and a check on the three branches of government.

It might be appealing to simply revisit the watchdog role and look for ways that law can reinvigorate the press's watchdog efforts. These efforts would likely be welcomed by journalists and press advocates. The press's watchdog role continues to be central to its self-image as well as its democratic function, especially in our current era of burgeoning autocracy.[31]

Yet, polling suggests that doubling down on watchdog journalism is likely not the best way to win public trust today. One recent study by Gallup and the Knight Foundation on trust in local news sources concluded that even though the press has a "mandate to help democracy flourish," "more aggressive coverage of social and political issues could further polarize views – and possibly lead to an erosion of trust" at least at the local news level.[32] A separate poll, published in 2021 by the Associated

[27] *See* Erin C. Carroll, *Protecting the Watchdog: Using the Freedom of Information Act to Preference the Press*, 2016 Utah L. Rev. 193, 210–15 (2016).

[28] *See Issue Brief: State Freedom of Information Laws*, Society Am. Archivists (May 2015), https://perma.cc/MGQ9-RZ9F.

[29] *See id.*

[30] Daniel C. Hallin, *The Media, the War in Vietnam, and Political Support: A Critique of the Thesis of an Oppositional Media*, 46 J. Pol. 1, 13 (1984).

[31] *See* Erin C. Carroll, *A Free Press without Democracy*, 56 U.C. Davis L. Rev. 289, 313 (2022).

[32] Knight Found. & Gallup, State of Public Trust in Local News 1 (2019), https://perma.cc/8VSP-CZLM.

Press-NORC Center for Public Affairs Research and the American Press Institute, suggested that conservatives are less likely to see the value in watchdog reporting. Examining the relationship between people's "moral values" and the "core values" of journalism, the study found that those "who most value loyalty and authority are much less likely than others to endorse the idea that there should be a watchdog over those in power."[33] About 86 percent of those in the study who valued loyalty and authority identified themselves as conservative or moderate.[34] The report, which used trust as a way of thinking about how the press can appeal to a broader audience, concluded that "[t]o woo subscribers, the media will need to vary its messaging beyond traditional appeals about journalism being a watchdog."[35]

In keeping with this suggestion, another tack is to look to innovations in today's press – and those particularly aimed at journalism's democracy-enhancing mission – for guidance. In the late 1960s and 1970s, watchdog reporting was a focus for newsrooms and was coming into its own journalistically. It made sense for the Supreme Court and legislatures to amplify and celebrate this press role. Looking at journalistic practice today, at a time of significant institutional challenge and change, another press role is coming to the fore. That is the role of the press as a convener and facilitator of community conversation and deliberation. It is this role that helps build the shared epistemic foundations central for democracy.[36] In this way, it is a fundamental press role deserving of protection.

In one sense, journalists have recognized this convening role as a press function for decades. *The Elements of Journalism* lists as one of its ten elements of journalism that journalism "must provide a forum for public criticism and compromise."[37] In doing so, it references the 1947 Hutchins Commission report "A Free and Responsible Press," which stated that "[t]he great agencies of mass communication should regard themselves as common carriers of public discussion."[38] *Elements* authors Kovach and Rosenstiel stress that this forum must have two qualities. First, it "should adhere to all the other journalistic principles," including a dedication to "truthfulness, facts, and verification."[39] In addition, "it should relate directly to Madison's recognition of the central role of compromise in democratic society."[40]

33 Associated Press-NORC Ctr. for Pub. Affs. Rsch. & Am. Press Inst., A New Way of Looking at Trust in Media: Do Americans Share Journalism's Core Values 1 (Apr. 2021), https://perma.cc/33VJ-BLEM.

34 *Id.* at 4. The study found that liberals tended to especially value care and fairness. *Id.* at 5.

35 *Id.*

36 *See* Aziz Huq & Tom Ginsberg, *How to Lose a Constitutional Democracy*, 65 UCLA L. Rev. 78, 130 (2018) ("The practical operation of liberal democracy requires a shared epistemic foundation.").

37 Kovach & Rosenstiel, *supra* note 5, at xxvii.

38 *Id.* at 226.

39 *Id.* at 232, 247.

40 *Id.* at 247.

Of late, as journalists seek to rebuild lost trust, they have embraced this role in the form of "community-centered journalism." Community-centered journalism – along with engaged and social journalism – seeks to involve the community more directly in the news-making process as a means of strengthening those communities. As one researcher describes engaged journalism, it is "an inclusive practice that prioritizes the information needs and wants of the community members it serves, creates collaborative space for the audience in all aspects of the journalistic process, and is dedicated to building and preserving trusting relationships between journalists and the public."[41]

To do this, community-centered journalism shifts the power dynamic between journalist and citizen from one that has long been hierarchical and transactional to one that is more collaborative.[42] Rather than the press dictating what issues are important and so serving a gatekeeping function, engaged journalists look to the community to help assess needs and interests. For example, in her book *Community-Centered Journalism*, journalism scholar Andrea Wenzel features *Curious City*, "an ongoing news experiment" in which Chicago radio station WBEZ asks its listeners to submit questions that journalists can help answer. She notes that this approach marks a shift from the "traditional story cycle" in which the public only becomes involved at the time of publication, to a "public-powered story cycle," in which it plays a role far earlier.[43] In an effort to build community and trust, and to be sure they reached all corners of the community, WBEZ journalists began driving around the city to solicit questions. They also partnered with community organizations, brewpubs, and libraries to build a stronger network.[44]

In this way, engagement journalism produces what one would expect – news – but its advocates say it does more: It builds and reinforces community. Speaking of a *Seattle Times* engagement-journalism project called the Education Lab, the project's editor Sharon Chan said: "The discrete product . . . was the relationship."[45] As with many engaged-journalism efforts, the Education Lab began with a "listening tour" aimed at hearing what issues teachers, students, parents, and other community leaders thought should be covered. To keep the community involved in the process, reporters "asked questions on social media, published guest columns by community members, held live Q&As with reporters about their stories and hosted events and even workshops to deepen conversations and make it easier for people to act."[46] In presenting the project with an inaugural prize for community engagement, judges

[41] Andrea Wenzel, Community-Centered Journalism: Engaging People, Exploring Solutions, and Building Trust 11 (2020) (quoting Lindsay Green-Barber, *Towards a Useful Typology of Engaged Journalism*, Medium (Oct. 18, 2018), https://perma.cc/6ZP8-CQHK).

[42] *See id.* at 12.

[43] *Id.* at 51.

[44] *Id.* at 63.

[45] Guzmán, *supra* note 6.

[46] *Id.*

for the Associated Press Media Editors Awards said that "[t]he newspaper helped to turn often angry rhetoric into constructive dialogue that parents, educators, and community members craved."[47]

Although the level of attention being paid to engaged journalism is new, the seeds of this method have been germinating for decades. Wenzel cites James Carey's ritual view of communication – dating from the early 1990s – as an intellectual precursor. She writes that "[i]n Carey's ideal . . . the value of the press comes from creating a space for the public to understand information through public discourse and by 'encouraging the conversation of its culture.'"[48] She also credits Jay Rosen as a "founding proponent" of a "public or civic journalism movement of the 1990s" that, in Rosen's words, called for journalists to "address people as citizens, potential participants in public affairs, rather than victims or spectators" as well as to "improve the climate of public discussion, rather than simply watching it deteriorate."[49]

As this movement has bloomed, the broader journalism world has taken notice. The *Columbia Journalism Review*, a key industry publication, has featured engaged-journalism leaders and practices on its pages.[50] The Solutions Journalism Network, which advocates for a type of community-centered journalism, has grown from its two founding *New York Times* reporters in 2013 to an organization that has worked with more than 500 news outlets and 20,000 journalists.[51] The concept of community-centered journalism has also attracted philanthropic funding. The Democracy Fund, for example, runs "The Engaged Journalism Lab," which is focused on "building trusted, inclusive, and audience-driven journalism."[52] And the graduate journalism school at the City University of New York has a master's program focused on "social journalism."[53]

This recognition and support suggest that community-centered journalism is becoming a key journalistic practice. As Rosen wrote in 2019, "Engagement journalism, solutions journalism, less extractive journalism, a more agile, iterative newsroom. Nothing I have seen while watching these emerge suggests they are

[47] *Id.*

[48] WENZEL, *supra* note 41, at 14 (quoting James Carey, *A Republic If You Can Keep It: Liberty and Public Life in the Age of Glasnost, in* JAMES CAREY: A CRITICAL READER 220 (Eve Stryker Munson & Catherin A. Warren eds., 1997)).

[49] *Id.* at 10 (quoting Jay Rosen, *The Challenge of Public Journalism, in* THE IDEA OF PUBLIC JOURNALISM 44 (Theodore Glasser ed., 1999)).

[50] *See, e.g.*, Darryl Holliday, *Journalism Is a Public Good. Let the Public Make It*, COLUM. JOURNALISM REV. (Dec. 15, 2021), https://perma.cc/2PQU-QQWJ; Lauren Harris, *Community-Engaged Journalism Is Both an End and a Means to Survival*, COLUM. JOURNALISM REV. (Aug. 26, 2020), https://perma.cc/3YPM-8U39; Andrea Wenzel & Letrell Deshan Crittenden, *Covering Germantown: The Road to Community Engagement*, COLUM. JOURNALISM REV. (Jan. 17, 2020), https://perma.cc/FL3Y-HJ8G.

[51] *Mission*, SOLUTIONS JOURNALISM NETWORK, https://perma.cc/6A6Q-6HEQ.

[52] *About*, ENGAGED JOURNALISM LAB, https://perma.cc/7FP3-B73L.

[53] *See* Carrie Brown, *Engaged Journalism: It's Finally Happening*, NIEMAN LAB: PREDICTIONS FOR JOURNALISM 2020, https://perma.cc/7SDX-DNDY.

going away soon. The shocks to the system have been so many that the culture of the press is evolving."[54]

Those running engaged-journalism projects are still discerning how best to measure their impact; data about their effect on citizens' trust specifically is difficult to come by.[55] Yet, its scholars and practitioners believe it is indeed building trust. Andrea Wenzel argues that engaged-journalism projects "can contribute to a communication environment with greater trust between media, community members, and organizations, where residents feel more connected and invested."[56]

Scholarship in other disciplines also suggests that engagement journalism has the potential to foment trust and is desperately needed. For example, philosopher Robert B. Talisse argues in his book *Overdoing Democracy* that for democracy to work, we need to invest in "civic friendship."[57] In a world oversaturated with politics, this friendship is based on bringing community members – even those who "staunchly object" to one another's values – together to build relationships through activities and conversation that are apolitical.[58] It is by building trust through civic friendship that we can start to rebuild a working democracy, argues Talisse.[59] Community-centered journalism is poised to do this by serving as a facilitator and convener, and law can help.

5.4 THE ROLE FOR LAW IN PRESS TRUST-BUILDING

In some senses, law has already recognized the press's facilitative role. The Supreme Court has understood the press to serve as a facilitator of the public square. In *Mills v. Alabama*,[60] the Supreme Court said that the Constitution "specifically selected" the press "to play an important role in the discussion of public affairs."[61] Press law scholar RonNell Andersen Jones cites *Mills*, *Miami Herald Publishing Co. v. Tornillo*,[62] and other cases in arguing that the Court's "Glory Days characterizations also positively portray the press as a dialogue builder – a critically important distiller of societal information and shaper of community conversations through the application of editorial insight and journalistic acumen."[63]

In *Tornillo*, in which the Court struck down a Florida "right-of-reply" statute, the Court indicated that the metaphorical space in which the press serves as a dialogue

54 Jay Rosen (@jayrosen_nyu), TWITTER (Nov. 16, 2019, 3:05 PM), https://perma.cc/5BL7-JLJN.
55 WENZEL, *supra* note 41, at 152–53.
56 *Id.* at 4.
57 ROBERT B. TALISSE, OVERDOING DEMOCRACY 150 (2021).
58 *Id.* at 147, 163, 170; ASHUTOSH BHAGWAT, OUR DEMOCRATIC FIRST AMENDMENT 134–39 (2020) (arguing for a revival of civic association that is not focused on politics).
59 TALISSE, *supra* note 57, at 35–36.
60 384 U.S. 214 (1966) (invalidating under the First Amendment a state criminal law banning election day newspaper editorials urging people to vote a certain way).
61 *Id.* at 219.
62 418 U.S. 241 (1974).
63 Jones, *supra* note 3, at 257.

builder is "the marketplace of ideas."[64] That marketplace, said the Court, quoting *New York Times v. Sullivan*,[65] is a place where "debate on public issues should be uninhibited, robust, and wide-open."[66] The *Sullivan* Court described a marketplace that was freewheeling and even inhospitable. It said the marketplace "may well include vehement, caustic, and sometimes unpleasantly sharp attacks on government and public officials."[67]

Together, these cases describe an information ecosystem in which the press, exercising its editorial discretion, serves as a gatekeeper and agenda-setter for public discussion.[68] In this ecosystem, the relationship between press and citizen is hierarchical and unidirectional. The Court envisions the press as dictating the terms of the discussion that citizens take up with each other. It does not seem to envision press involvement in that conversation or even press listening. Exchanges are in the form of a "debate" rather than a conversation, collaboration, or deliberation. That debate is "caustic"; it is not for the faint of heart.

This vision of the press as gatekeeper of a marketplace characterized by robust and uninhibited verbal sparring squares well with the press's role as a watchdog. The watchdog role is, by its very nature, an adversarial one. It involves the press serving as a check on government. In doing this, the press acts as a defender and protector of the public.

The Court's vision of the press as a gatekeeper of the public square and marketplace of ideas does not square quite as well, however, with the convener and facilitator role for journalism – what Kovach and Rosenstiel described as "provid[ing] a forum for public criticism and compromise."[69] And it arguably squares even less well with the way in which community-centered journalism views the role of the press – as a co-creator of news with the public. In fact, the gatekeeper role and marketplace metaphor seem quite hostile to this vision.

Beyond being out of step with journalism's evolving conception of its democratic role and its more recent innovations, the Court's description of the press is also dated in another significant way. It is simply no longer true that the mainstream media is the major gatekeeper of the public square or marketplace of ideas. That role has largely been taken over by technology platforms, as the Court itself has recognized. In *Packingham v. North Carolina*,[70] the Court described social-media platforms as "the modern public square" and said that "[t]hese websites can provide perhaps the most powerful mechanisms available to a private citizen to make his or her voice heard."[71]

[64] *Tornillo*, 418 U.S. at 251.

[65] 376 U.S. 254 (1964) (setting the actual malice standard for defamation of a public official).

[66] *Tornillo*, 418 U.S. at 252.

[67] *Sullivan*, 376 U.S. at 270.

[68] Another case that depicts the same model is Columbia Broad. System, Inc. v. Democratic Nat'l Comm., 412 U.S. 94, 187–88 (1973) (Brennan, J., dissenting).

[69] Kovach & Rosenstiel, *supra* note 5, at xxvii.

[70] 137 S. Ct. 1730 (2017).

[71] *Id.* at 1737.

Law's first step then in generating more trust in the press, as it was in the press's Glory Days, is to recognize the ways in which today's press is promoting democracy and the promising directions in which it is headed. The Supreme Court's vision needs updating – both as to what the press is and does, as well as the space in which it operates. As the Court has long recognized, the press is and should remain a watchdog. But the press's role in perpetuating a functioning democracy is much broader than the Court's key press decisions – now decades old – have described.

The press is and should continue to be a facilitator and convener of community conversations. In so doing, the press builds trust between citizens and weaves the fabric of community. This role is not predominantly characterized by a hierarchy with the press sitting atop citizens. And it is not one dominated by aggression or opposition. Rather, it is one in which the press and citizens co-create the boundaries and substance of the space in which they operate. These are not spaces in which journalists or the press necessarily cede expertise, but instead spaces in which they recognize that they are not the only holders of it. Community members also bring wisdom and skills.

The spaces in which these conversations occur can be described not as one "public square" or "marketplace" but as public fora – a multiplicity of locales for community deliberation and collaboration. These press-facilitated or press-convened public fora could look and feel different from the marketplace and public squares that the Court has conjured in the past. They could also be different from one another. They could be physical, but they could also be virtual. They could be typified by speaking and conversation, but they could also include silence, listening, and even collaborative doing. As described, the press is already creating these spaces, and it should be encouraged to expand and embroider upon what it has started.

The Supreme Court could help. As noted, it could begin by updating its understanding of the press. In theory, this would not be difficult. It would not entail granting the press any special rights (something the Court has steadfastly avoided). As it was during the Glory Days, it could largely be a matter of rhetoric. As the Court celebrated the role of the press as a watchdog then, it could likewise laud the role of the press as a convener and facilitator today. To do so, it would not even need to take up a case involving the press as a party. One could imagine a discussion of this vital press role in any case in which the Court took account of public sentiment (reached through discourse and collaboration) or any case in which the Court exercised judicial restraint and deference to the political process (which could then involve citizens – with the help of the press – working through issues of public concern).

Admittedly, the U.S. Supreme Court revisiting and updating its conception of the press (at least in any press-favorable way) seems as elusive a proposition today as building trust is. As press scholars RonNell Andersen Jones and Sonja R. West have shown, the Supreme Court's characterizations of the press have plummeted in quantity and favorability.[72] Jones and West have written: "Our data suggest that any hopes that the judiciary can be trusted to be a savior of press freedom in America might be misplaced."[73] Yet, this need not be an insurmountable obstacle. It may mean that press advocates need to lean more heavily on lower courts and legislatures. Lower courts can just as easily engage in pro-press rhetoric as the Supreme Court. Legislatures too can do so not only through legislation, but through hearings, committee reports, floor statements, and the like. And even though being anti-press sometimes seems like part of the Republican platform, Congress has occasionally shown signs of press friendliness.[74]

Plus, there are fifty state legislatures that can also take up this call – not simply to engage in pro-press rhetoric, but to help create the conditions in which the press can best serve as a facilitator and convener. New Jersey has shown its willingness to participate in such efforts by creating the Civic Information Consortium aimed at "strengthening local news coverage and boosting civil engagement."[75] And given that states can be more protective of press rights than the federal government is, bolstering the press at the local level makes sense. This goal is also aligned with community-centered journalism and its concern with assessing community wants and needs.

Proposals to boost the press's role as facilitator and convener could be broad. They might involve providing public facilities for the press to use for gathering the public. This could range from subsidizing journalists' use of existing spaces to building new community information hubs that could bring together journalists, librarians, historians, and other community information specialists. Other proposals might be aimed at creating and supporting programs that teach community-centered journalism practices to students and citizens. Proposals could also include loan-forgiveness programs for aspiring journalists interested in this work.

Both press advocates and press skeptics might rightfully ask whether the press is the best institution to play this role of community facilitator and convener. Perhaps community glue would be stickier if produced by religious organizations, book clubs, civic associations, or even facets of the legal system like juries and mediators. But the press has already tasked itself with this work and a growing movement of journalists is invested in it. Moreover, journalists' skill set – interviewing, listening, and storytelling – is well-aligned with the facilitator and convener role. Journalists are capable, committed, and already playing this role.

72 Jones & West, *supra* note 17, at 378–79.

73 *Id.* at 380.

74 *See* Meredith Conroy, *Why Being 'Anti-Media' Is Now Part of the GOP Identity*, FiveThirtyEight (Apr. 5, 2021), https://perma.cc/QHR6-YQD4; Erin C. Carroll, *Obstruction of Journalism: A New Way to Combat Violence against Journalists*, Colum. Journalism Rev. (Jan. 13, 2022), https://perma.cc/N9UA-D2M3 (describing bipartisan support for the Fall Journalists Memorial Act).

75 *See* Mike Rispoli, *Why the Civic Information Consortium Is Such a Huge Deal*, Free Press (Mar. 24, 2022), https://perma.cc/XLZ4-QGT9.

5.5 CONCLUSION

By promoting community-centered journalism in these ways, journalists, judges, and legislators would be taking up the call from legal scholar Mary Anne Franks to move past the conventional wisdom of the internet as a "modern public square" and "quintessential site of democratic deliberation."[76] To avoid recreating the hierarchies that have existed in our public square, Franks says "we can envision the flourishing of multiple spaces – online and off, public and private – that provide the conditions necessary for free expression and democratic deliberation."[77] She cites as examples "homes, schools, workplaces, bookstores, hair salons, and clubs."[78] Spaces created by community-based journalism could serve the same goals – these could be in newsrooms, but they could also be in restaurants, libraries, community halls, parks, community information hubs, and any number of other spots. They also need not be limited to physical spaces. Journalists could also convene online communities. Yet, as long as democracy has a geographic component, it will be important for some conversation and compromise to occur between people in physical community with one another.[79]

Yes, this vision expands the parameters of what the law (and even journalism) has imagined journalists and the press to be. That means that both journalism and law will need to engage in what sociologist Thomas Gieryn calls "boundary-work." As Andrea Wenzel explains, this approach "looks at how groups compete in ever changing contexts to define what falls inside and outside a social boundary."[80] Journalists – especially community-centered journalists – are already redefining these boundaries.[81] The law needs to join them. Judges, legislators, and legal scholars need to reflect on what our press is and what we need it to be. The press's role as a convener and facilitator of public fora aligns with its role of providing citizens with the information that they need to participate in government.[82] If we use law to support this role, we could move ever closer to a more ideal democracy.

76 Mary Anne Franks, *Beyond the Public Square: Imagining Digital Democracy*, 131 YALE L.J. F. 427, 427 (Nov. 16, 2021).

77 *Id.* at 429.

78 *Id.* at 428.

79 *See* NIKKI USHER, NEWS FOR THE RICH, WHITE, AND BLUE x–xi (2021) (describing the dominance of national journalism and noting that because "American political power is tied to geography, this [dominance] presents a serious problem for democratic life").

80 WENZEL, *supra* note 41, at 13.

81 *Id.*

82 *See* KOVACH & ROSENSTIEL, *supra* note 5, at 7 ("The primary purpose of journalism is to provide citizens with the information they need to be free and self-governing.").

PART II

Defamation and Privacy

6

Defamation and Privacy

What You Can't Say about Me

Gus Hurwitz

The laws of defamation and privacy are at once similar and dissimilar. Falsity is the hallmark of defamation – the sharing of untrue information that tends to harm the subject's standing in their community. Truth is the hallmark of privacy – the disclosure of facts about an individual who would prefer those facts to be private. Publication of true information cannot be defamatory; spreading of false information cannot violate an individual's privacy. Scholars of either field could surely add epicycles to that characterization – but it does useful work as a starting point of comparison.

Yet both defamation and privacy law look similar in relief. Purported information about an individual – be it true or not – is shared with others, and through that sharing the individual experiences (subjective or objective) harm. In both, the subject of speech by one party appeals to the courts for relief from perceived harm resulting from that speech.

Speech has greater potential to be perceived as harmful today than it did at any point during the twentieth century – the century during which the contours of both defamation and privacy law were principally defined. Today we live in an era of "cheap speech and big speech." The cost of producing and publishing speech has never been lower and the scale of the audience for that speech has never been larger. At the individual level, idle speech about other people (e.g., gossip, rumors) has migrated from locker rooms and water coolers to X – words whose impact was historically limited in terms of private reach and duration have become public and persistent. At the public level, competition between media outlets – once limited to a few established media outlets but now including potentially anyone with an X account and an appeal to the political or prurient – creates a race to publish anything deemed newsworthy. And by virtue of coverage, the once minor, trivial, or private can be thrust into the public spotlight, at least for limited public purposes.

Contingent facts, those most likely to be made subject to public scrutiny through either process, are not likely to be clearly true or false. Rather, the process of their publication is more likely relevant to how we, as a society, ought to evaluate the propriety and harmfulness of their publication. The chapters that follow explore both defamation and privacy law in this new era of cheap speech and big speech.

Lyrissa Lidsky leads things off with Chapter 7, "Cheap Speech and the Gordian Knot of Defamation Reform." In her contribution, Professor Lidsky traces the development of defamation law alongside technology from the Restatement (Second) of Torts in 1977. As she says, "A lot has changed since 1977." Lidsky tells us that "Today's conversation is animated by concerns about the effects of cheap speech on the information ecosystem, with the critics asking if the constitutional strands of current defamation law tilt the scales too sharply in favor of free expression." In particular, Lidsky assesses criticisms that Justices Thomas and Gorsuch have leveled at the First Amendment law of defamation – and she expresses skepticism about the reforms these Justices seemingly propose. But she also expresses sympathy for the idea that reform is needed, calling for "new remedies to better vindicate reputation and set the record straight, construct new incentives for journalists of all stripes to adhere to professionally developed standards for getting the facts right, and establish new deterrents to libel bullying." In focusing on the reputational aspect of the defamation harm, Lidsky implicitly calls attention to the relationship between defamation and privacy harms.

In Chapter 8, "Defamation, Disinformation, and the Press Function," RonNell Anderson Jones takes a deeper look at Justice Gorsuch's suggestion that the Supreme Court reconsider *New York Times v. Sullivan*, "the foundational First Amendment precedent in defamation law." In so doing she sounds a cautionary note. In the era of cheap speech it is easy to find criticism of institutional media publishing what amounts to disinformation. But the reality, Jones tells us, is more complicated: The institutional media are not our primary disinformation generators and distributors. To the contrary, they work hard to get things right and compete in terms of their ability to do so. Jones argues that overruling *Sullivan* would threaten media institutions' ability to perform this costly and important function.

The next two chapters turn from defamation to privacy. Privacy harms differ from defamation harms because they typically stem from accurate but intrusive communications rather than false ones. But the emergence of cheap, platform-driven online speech has amplified privacy and defamation harms in a parallel way.

In her contribution, Professor Amy Gajda looks at the publication and changing uses of police mug shots. Mug shots, she explains, were based on a policy that "the public should know who'd been arrested and on what grounds and how they looked at the time of arrest in order to ensure that police had not battered them." Historically, the local press might publish those mug shots they considered newsworthy. Today, a global audience can pick up digitized mug shots from public records websites. Gajda tracks recent developments in both state law and journalistic practice that attempt to narrow these photographs' public circulation. She suggests that the trend toward privacy is likely to continue, and that "one's entire criminal past, including one's older mugshot, could one day come to be even more strongly protected on privacy grounds." Contextualizing this alongside the discussion of privacy, it is remarkable to observe heightened restrictions on the publication of speech that is both factual and based in government activity.

Where Gajda's chapter focuses on facts and speech created by the state, Professor Thomas Kadri's chapter considers privately compiled information, focusing on harms facilitated by data brokers. In the era of cheap speech, it is far easier to collect, process, and bundle information about people – and there is a surprisingly vibrant market for this information. Indeed, the data brokers who make up this market further lower the cost of obtaining information about individuals by scouring various sources – public and sometimes private – for published information. Kadri documents specific instances of harm that such availability of information can facilitate (including the murder of a stalking victim). His greater point, however, is the privacy harm that this inflicts generally by robbing us of the obscurity that we all implicitly and explicitly rely on in our day-to-day lives. The data broker business model is built on taking the possibility of obscurity – the general presumption that our day-to-day activities will be unobserved by others – away from us, at least without each of us undertaking concerted efforts to maintain it. As with the other chapters in this part, Kadri's contribution raises difficult questions about what rights individuals have to control the ways that information about them is used by others.

7

Cheap Speech and the Gordian Knot of Defamation Reform

*Lyrissa Lidsky**

7.1 INTRODUCTION

Dean John Wade, who replaced the great torts scholar William Prosser on the Restatement (Second) of Torts, put the finishing touches on the defamation sections in 1977.[1] Apple Computer had been founded a year before, and Microsoft two, but relatively few people owned computers yet. The twenty-four-hour news cycle was not yet a thing, and most Americans still trusted the press.[2]

A lot has changed since 1977. Billions of people now publish their most profound, trivial, or scurrilous thoughts – unexpurgated – to mass audiences. Trying to compete with "cheap speech" has economically devastated large swaths of the news industry, stripping talent and expertise from newsrooms. Meanwhile, and perhaps unsurprisingly, public trust in news media has eroded dramatically.[3] These developments pose the biggest challenge for defamation law since the invention of the printing press. Yet they have not inspired dramatic reform to the common law of defamation.[4] Or at least not yet. As the American Law Institute begins a new Restatement of Defamation Law, it is important to consider what a successful program of reform might look like.

* I would like to thank Kyle Langvardt, Lili Levi, Jake Linford, and Robert Post for their comments on an earlier draft of this work.

1 RESTATEMENT (SECOND) OF TORTS §§ 558–623 (1977).

2 Darren K. Carlson, *Trust in Media*, GALLUP (Sept. 17, 2002), https://perma.cc/X4T6-JNJA.

3 Jeffrey Gottfried, *Republicans Less Likely to Trust Their Main News Source If They See It as "Mainstream"; Democrats More Likely*, PEW RSCH. CTR. (July 1, 2021), https://perma.cc/G3LR-CRRA ("About two-in-ten adults (18%) express a great deal of trust in the accuracy of the political news they get from national news organizations (though a majority – 64% – have at least *some* trust).").

4 RonNell Andersen Jones & Lyrissa Lidsky, *Of Reasonable Readers and Unreasonable Speakers: Libel Law in a Networked World*, 23 VA. J. SOC. POL'Y & L. 155 (2016).

In this chapter, I examine some of the most important "reforms" to defamation law since 1977 and speculate about why those reforms have been predominantly constitutional and statutory, with common-law developments playing a less important role. I then evaluate recent critiques of defamation law's constitutional dimensions by two U.S. Supreme Court Justices, paying special attention to Justice Neil Gorsuch's argument that changed circumstances related to cheap speech justify reconsidering and perhaps eliminating some First Amendment constraints on the common law of defamation. I tally defamation law's scorecard in vindicating reputation and deterring disinformation, which leads me to concur with some of Justice Gorsuch's critiques. I nonetheless question his prescription. Merely rolling back constitutional protections will not deliver the proper balance between protecting individual reputation and safeguarding the types of speech that contribute to informed democratic decision-making, because powerful people will increasingly use defamation law to punish their critics. To achieve a proper balance, a more comprehensive approach to reform is needed. I offer the outlines of such an approach for untangling (rather than cutting) the inseverable interweaving of tort, constitutional, and statutory law.

7.2 DEFAMATION LAW REFORM: 1977–PRESENT

In its long history, defamation has been a sin, a crime, and a tort. In the United States, it now exists as a complex body of doctrine comprised of common law, constitutional law, and statutory law. The most important changes to defamation law since 1977 were constitutional and statutory rather than common-law changes. In 1977, the U.S. Supreme Court was still in the process of "constitutionalizing" defamation law. That process began with the Court's seminal decision in *New York Times v. Sullivan* in 1964.[5] There, for the first time, the Court interpreted the First and Fourteenth Amendments to set limits on state common law in defamation cases involving public officials; the Court held that these limits were necessary to prevent state tort law from chilling uninhibited, robust, and wide-open commentary about government officials acting in their official capacity. Famously, *Sullivan* held that these officials could not recover for defamation absent proof that the person who allegedly defamed them knowingly or recklessly disregarded the falsity of the defamatory statement. But *Sullivan* was just the beginning. The Court later interpreted the First and Fourteenth Amendments to limit the common law in ways that reshaped practically every element of the defamation tort, particularly in cases involving litigants who were public officials, public figures, or ordinary people involved in matters of public concern – that is to say, almost all cases! The effect of the Court's defamation jurisprudence was to impose a labyrinthine set of constitutional doctrines on the tort of defamation. It also imposed on lower courts the

[5] 376 U.S. 254 (1964).

burden of interpreting these doctrines in novel situations and deciding whether to do so narrowly or, as they did in the case of deciding which plaintiffs qualified as public figures, expansively. Nonetheless, the Supreme Court's constitutional doctrines fundamentally recalibrated the balance between reputation and free expression in defamation law: The common law could provide more protection for free expression than these doctrines required, but it could not provide less.

The Supreme Court's constitutional doctrines did not foreclose common-law creativity in adapting to changing circumstances, but in the decades following the Court's last major defamation decision in the early 1990s, legislators – not courts – played the leading role in enacting pro-defendant reforms. In the 1980s and early 1990s, scholars called for defamation reform in order to respond to a "dramatic proliferation of highly publicized libel actions brought by well-known figures who seek, and often receive, staggering sums of money."[6] These calls for comprehensive reform had little traction in state courts, but starting in the 1990s and continuing to the present, states passed legislation to respond to the perceived problem of powerful actors weaponizing libel actions against ordinary citizens. The original impetus for such laws was the work of Professors George Pring and Penelope Canan. Pring and Canan documented the rise of a type of suit they branded Strategic Lawsuits Against Public Participation, or SLAPPs; they used this term to describe frivolous defamation suits brought by powerful local actors such as real-estate developers to stifle the criticisms and civic participation of ordinary citizens in forums such as zoning board meetings.[7] Their influential work, which culminated in a 1996 book, detailed how such suits invade not just First Amendment rights to free expression but also the right of citizens to petition their governments for redress of grievances. Pring and Canan brought public attention to the weaponization of defamation law by the powerful against the relatively powerless, and their work inspired more than half of all state legislatures to pass laws establishing procedures to allow defendants to obtain early dismissals of meritless libel suits; the laws sometimes enabled defendants to collect attorneys' fees as well.[8] Where such anti-SLAPP laws exist, and especially in jurisdictions adopting them in their stronger forms, they have dramatic

[6] Rodney A. Smolla, *Let the Author Beware: The Rejuvenation of the American Law of Libel*, 132 U. Pa. L. Rev. 1, 1 (1983). *See generally* David A. Anderson, *Is Libel Law Worth Reforming?*, 140 U. Pa. L. Rev. 487 (1991); Randall P. Bezanson, *The Libel Tort Today*, 45 Wash. & Lee L. Rev. 535 (1988); C. Thomas Dienes, *Libel Reform: An Appraisal*, 23 U. Mich. J.L. Reform 1 (1989); Paul A. LeBel, *Special Issue: Defamation and the First Amendment: New Perspectives*, 25 Wm. & Mary L. Rev. 779 (1984).

[7] Their 1996 book documents their work on this topic going back to the 1980s. *See* George W. Pring & Penelope Canan, SLAPPs: Getting Sued for Speaking Out 3 (1996). For an excellent critique of their book by one of my former students, see Joseph W. Beatty, *The Legal Literature on SLAPPs: A Look behind the Smoke Nine Years after Professors Pring and Canan First Yelled "Fire!"*, 9 U. Fla. J.L. & Pub. Pol'y 85 (1997).

[8] The Public Participation Project maintains a website with a list of states that have adopted anti-SLAPP laws. *See State Anti-SLAPP Laws*, Pub. Participation Project, https://perma.cc/8RR7–8EJW.

effects on libel litigation – and not just on cases that fit Pring and Canan's original paradigm.

As important as anti-SLAPP legislation is, the most dramatic defamation reform of the last forty or so years took place in 1996, with the passage of Section 230 of the Communications Decency Act. It is not a stretch to say that this statutory defamation reform helped propel the Cheap Speech Revolution. Section 230(c) immunized internet service providers and website operators from liability for defamatory communications posted by their users. Congress granted this immunity to the actors we would later come to call platforms and, more recently, Big Tech.[9] Congress's legislative efforts stemmed from dissatisfaction with common law's attempt to apply traditional defamation law principles to internet service providers. Prior to the passage of Section 230, two influential district-court decisions held that internet service providers who exercised editorial control by editing or taking down user-generated content would be liable for defamatory content posted by their users, just as newspapers are liable for defamatory content they publish in letters to the editor; internet service providers who eschewed editorial control, however, would be liable only upon receiving notice of users' defamatory content and subsequently failing to remove it, just as – ostensibly[10] – bookstores and other content "distributors" are.[11]

[9] 47 U.S.C. § 230 (Supp. III 1999). The CDA is Title V (§§ 501–09) of the Telecommunications Act of 1996. *See* Act of Feb. 8, 1996, Pub. L. No. 104-104, 110 Stat. 133 (codified as amended in scattered sections of 18 U.S.C. and 47 U.S.C.).

[10] Professor Benjamin Zipursky has questioned whether the Restatement (Second) provisions concerning distributor liability accurately stated the law, given that the cases it cited were "overwhelmingly prior to the Restatement (First)." Benjamin Zipursky, *The Monsanto Lecture: Online Defamation, Legal Concepts, and the Good Samaritan*, 51 Valparaiso U.L. Rev. 1, 21 (2016).

[11] *See* Stratton Oakmont, Inc. v. Prodigy Servs. Co., 1995 WL 323710 (N.Y. Sup. Ct. May 24, 1995). The key issue in *Stratton Oakmont*, which was decided on a motion for partial summary judgment, was whether the internet service provider Prodigy was a "publisher" or a "distributor" for purposes of defamation liability. *See Stratton Oakmont*, 1995 WL 323710 at *1. A second issue was whether its bulletin-board moderator, who was also a defendant in the suit, was its agent for purposes of defamation liability. *See id.* "Publisher" and "distributor" are terms of art in defamation law. At common law, a publisher would be strictly liable not only for originating a defamatory statement but also for repeating or otherwise republishing a third party's defamatory statements. *See* Restatement (Second) of Torts § 578 (1977). A distributor, on the other hand, would be liable only for "distributing" the defamatory communications of third parties if the distributor knew or had reason to know of the defamatory content. *See id.* at § 581 ("[O]ne who only delivers or transmits defamatory matter published by a third person is subject to liability if, but only if, he knows or has reason to know of its defamatory character."). The reason for the distinction was simple. Publishers, like newspapers and broadcasters, have complete editorial control over the material they publish, and therefore it is fair to hold them liable for it. Distributors, such as bookstores, libraries, and newsstands, have no practical ability to monitor every publication they distribute, and it is therefore unfair to impose liability absent notice of defamatory content and some type of fault. *See generally id.* § 581 cmts. d–g. Because the facts of *Stratton Oakmont* suggested at most negligence on the part of Prodigy, the plaintiff needed the court to treat Prodigy as a publisher in order to have any hope of recovery. Internet service providers do not fit neatly into defamation's traditional categories. The *Stratton*

These decisions disincentivized internet service providers from taking down problematic content to avoid being treated like traditional media "publishers."

Yet, instead of merely insulating internet service providers from liability akin to that of traditional publishers, the broad language of Section 230's immunity insulated ISPs from distributor – or notice-and-takedown – liability as well, ostensibly to fuel the growth of the internet as an economic engine. Whether this was necessary is arguable, since most of the world imposes notice-and-takedown liability on Google, Facebook, and other Big Tech actors. Nonetheless, the effect of Section 230 has been to foreclose U.S. victims defamed online or in social media from accessing the deep pockets of Big Tech. Only the person posting the defamatory statement may be sued, regardless of whether that person can even be found or has resources to litigate or satisfy a defamation judgment. Section 230's effect on the development of defamation law over the last quarter of a century cannot be overstated. Absent Section 230, suits against online intermediaries would be much more common than they are today, and common-law courts would certainly bear more responsibility for adapting defamation principles to Big Tech practices – shaping those practices in the process. If the Supreme Court narrows the scope of immunity under Section 230, we can once again expect a dramatic reshaping of Big Tech practices.

To say that constitutional and statutory developments were the biggest news of defamation law over the last forty-five years is not to say that the common law has not responded at all to some of the novel issues cheap speech poses. For example, courts have had to decide whether an internet post is slander or libel, whether a person who provides a hyperlink to an article has "published" it for defamation purposes, and what to do about defamation cases based on reviews or rankings determined by algorithms.[12] New issues continue to arise, and as they do, courts tend to adapt common-law doctrines by analogizing new communications formats to old ones,

Oakmont court nonetheless examined the degree of editorial control exercised by Prodigy and held that Prodigy should be treated as a publisher rather than as a distributor. *See Stratton Oakmont*, 1995 WL 323710 at *5. The court therefore suggested that, although internet service providers should normally be categorized as distributors, Prodigy's "own policies, technology and staffing decisions … have altered the scenario and mandated the finding that it is a publisher." *Id.* A contemporaneous internet defamation opinion also looked at the degree of editorial control exercised by an internet service provider in concluding that it should be treated as a distributor instead. Cubby, Inc. v. CompuServe, Inc., 776 F. Supp. 135, 140–41 (S.D.N.Y. 1991). This created the seemingly paradoxical result that internet service providers who allowed more problematic content on their sites received more favorable liability treatment than those who tried to moderate problematic content. Section 230 of the Communications Decency Act was enacted to overturn this common law experiment to give at least as favorable treatment to service providers who exercised editorial control as those who eschewed all control. *See* H.R. Conf. Rep. No. 104-458, at 194 (1996), *reprinted in* 1996 U.S.S.C.A.N. 124, 207–08 (suggesting that Communications Decency Act was meant to overturn the Stratton Oakmont decision).

12 *See* Jones & Lidsky, *supra* note 4 (discussing these and other adaptations).

though they sometimes resort to creatively using equitable doctrines, such as libel injunctions, to deter those who might not be deterred by orders to pay money damages.[13]

Even so, common law's creativity in responding to cheap speech has been stymied by its inherent incrementalism and respect for precedent: Even now, only a minority of states have eradicated the outmoded distinctions between libel and slander, which arose from a jurisdictional battle between ecclesiastical and seigneurial courts in England and which commentators have decried for hundreds of years.[14] But an even bigger obstacle to comprehensive common-law reform is the Supreme Court's pervasive constitutionalization of the underlying tort. Having tilted the scales toward the First Amendment in most defamation cases, the Supreme Court left little leeway for states to add reputational protections for their citizens and, for much of this time, the substantive and procedural constitutional protections seemed more than sufficient to protect free expression, especially when coupled with statutes allowing for early dismissals of frivolous actions. The effect has been a sort of practical pre-emption of common law rebalancing reputation versus expression. Now, however, there is growing discontent with our information ecosystem: Is defamation-law reform the answer?

7.3 DEFAMATION LAW'S NEW CRITICS

Today's public conversation about defamation-law reform is being galvanized by a spate of high-profile lawsuits and critiques of the law offered by a president and two Supreme Court Justices. Today's conversation is animated by concerns about the effects of cheap speech on the information ecosystem, with the critics asking if the constitutional strands of current defamation law tilt the scales too sharply in favor of free expression.

The Media Law Resource Center's data confirm the popular impression that more defamation lawsuits have been brought in the last few years than previously. Moreover, the ones that have been brought seem to be more visible. High-profile

[13] Eugene Volokh, *Anti-Libel Injunctions*, 168 U. PA. L. REV. 73 (2019).

[14] PAUL MITCHELL, THE MAKING OF THE MODERN LAW OF DEFAMATION 4 (2005). Eight states have explicitly abandoned the distinction, and Louisiana never adopted it. *See* Mehau v. Gannett Pac. Corp., 658 P.2d 312, 320 (Haw. 1983); Bryson v. News Am. Publ'ns, Inc., 672 N.E.2d 1207, 1215 (Ill. 1996); Toler v. Süd-Chemie, Inc., 458 S.W.3d 276, 281 n.7 (Ky. 2014), as corrected (2015); Newberry v. Allied Stores, Inc., 773 P.2d 1231, 1236 (N.M. 1989); West v. Thomson Newspapers, 872 P.2d 999, 1008 n.12 (Utah 1994); Schaecher v. Bouffault, 772 S.E.2d 589, 594 (Va. 2015); Grein v. LaPoma, 340 P.2d 766, 769 (Wash. 1959); Butts v. Royal Vendors, Inc., 504 S.E.2d 911, 916 (W. Va. 1998); *see also* Wattigny v. Lambert, 408 So. 2d 1126, 1134 (La. 1981) (holding that there is no distinction between slander and libel actions in Louisiana, citing a treatise that references the lack of the split in the French civil-law tradition upon which Louisiana law is based).

plaintiffs appear to have multiplied,[15] with household names such as Sarah Palin, Devin Nunes, Roy Moore, and Donald Trump all suing for defamation.[16] Other recent lawsuits are noteworthy because they involve high-profile defendants and important societal issues. Notable in this regard are:

- the many lawsuits by women who were called liars after alleging sexual harassment by Donald Trump;
- the lawsuits brought by parents accused of being "crisis actors" after their children were murdered at Sandy Hook, which have now resulted in judgments of more than a billion dollars against internet personality Alex Jones;
- the lawsuits, now settled or dismissed, by a Kentucky teen whose perplexity was misreported by many media sources as racism based on a viral video that contained its own refutation;
- the lawsuit, currently on appeal, brought and won by actor Johnny Depp against his former wife Amber Heard for accusing him of sexual violence, and her countersuit, also won in part and also on appeal, for his accusations that she fabricated evidence to further her defamatory accusations;
- the lawsuits, now settled, by Georgia poll workers accused of tampering with the results of the 2020 presidential election; and
- the lawsuits, ongoing, by the providers of electronic voting machines alleged by prominent Trump partisans and conservative news networks to have fraudulently delivered the 2020 election to President Biden.

Like high-profile defamation lawsuits of past eras, these involve high-profile political figures, celebrities, and reputable media. Unlike their high-profile predecessors, they also involve fringe media outlets, a president – as both defendant and plaintiff – and even individuals posting to social media through pseudonymous parody accounts, such as @DevinNunesCow.

More interesting than the number of recent libel lawsuits is the prominence of libel law's recent critics. While running for president, Donald Trump promised to

[15] There is data, however, suggesting that suits against mainstream media have declined from their high in the 1980s. Justice Neil Gorsuch cited statistics in his dissent in Berisha v. Lawson, 141 S. Ct. 2424, 2428 (2021) suggesting that "the number of trials involving defamation, privacy, and related claims based on media publications has declined dramatically over the past few decades."

[16] *See, e.g.*, Palin v. N.Y. Times Co., 933 F.3d 160 (2d Cir. 2019); Nunes v. Cable News Network, 2023 WL 2468646 (M.D. Fla. 2023) (granting CNN's motion to dismiss); Nunes v. NBCUniversal Media, LLC, 2022 WL 17251981 (S.D.N.Y. 2022) (holding Nunes alleged prima facie case of defamation regarding one of several factual allegations about him made by NBC); Carroll v. Trump, 2023 WL 2669790 (S.D.N.Y. 2023) (denying Trump's motion for partial summary judgment in defamation action); Moore v. Cecil, 488 F.Supp.3d 1144 (N.D. Ala. 2021) (holding Roy Moore stated a claim for defamation and defamation by implication against the sponsor of a television advertisement about him). Susan E. Seagar, *Trump Is a Libel Bully but Also a Libel Loser*, 32 Commc'ns Law. 1 (2016), https://perma.cc/44ZK-RRPC.

"open up" libel laws. Critics derided Trump's promise, noting – correctly – that presidents control neither state common law nor the interpretation of the First Amendment.[17] Yet, though Trump's promise to change libel law may not have amounted to much in the short term, Justices Clarence Thomas and Neil Gorsuch may have begun playing a long game to galvanize constitutional reform. Justice Thomas began calling for reconsideration of *New York Times v. Sullivan* in his concurrence in the Court's denial of certiorari in *McKee v. Cosby* in 2019, which was a defamation case brought by a woman against the former actor Bill Cosby. Cosby had accused her of lying about him sexually assaulting her. Although Justice Thomas's opinion in that case seemed quixotic at the time, he subsequently has asked the Supreme Court to consider rolling back or eliminating the constitutional protections grafted onto libel law in two more libel cases in which the Court denied certiorari. Justice Gorsuch has written separately in one of these cases, *Berisha v. Lawson*, to echo Thomas's call for reconsideration – though on different grounds.[18] The latest of these cases was relisted repeatedly before the Court denied certiorari, and in light of the recent activism of the Supreme Court in overturning settled constitutional precedents, court prognosticators suspect the Court may take a case revisiting its defamation jurisprudence soon.

So far, Justice Clarence Thomas has grounded his critique of the Court's defamation jurisprudence largely in originalism concerns, calling *New York Times v. Sullivan* and the subsequent Supreme Court cases extending it "policy-driven decisions masquerading as constitutional law" that lack any relation to the "text, history, or structure of the Constitution."[19] Justice Thomas asserts that the Court should inquire "whether either the First or Fourteenth Amendment, as originally understood, encompasses an actual-malice standard for public figures or otherwise displaces vast swaths of state defamation law."[20] He indicates this inquiry would reveal that the Court's defamation jurisprudence is supported by "little historical evidence" and should be overruled.[21] Scholar Matthew Schafer has already cast

[17] Hadas Gold, *Donald Trump: We're Going to 'Open Up' Libel Laws*, Politico (Feb. 26, 2016), https://perma.cc/T29X-S3ZS.

[18] U.S. Supreme Court Associate Justice Clarence Thomas called for reconsideration of New York Times v. Sullivan in 2019 in three recent opinions: McKee v. Cosby, 139 S. Ct. 675 (2019) (Thomas, J., concurring in denial of certiorari); Berisha v. Lawson, 141 S. Ct. 2424 (2021) (Thomas, J., dissenting from denial of certiorari); Coral Ridge Ministries Media v. S. Poverty L. Ctr., 142 S. Ct. 2453 (2022) (Thomas, J., dissenting from denial of certiorari). Federal appeals court judge Lawrence Silberman subsequently echoed Justice Thomas's criticisms in Tah v. Glob. Witness Publ'g, Inc., 991 F.3d 231, 251 (D.C. Cir. 2021) (Silberman, J., dissenting). Justice Neil Gorsuch also called for reconsideration of Sullivan in his own dissent from the grant of cert in *Berisha*, 141 S. Ct. 2424. Thomas's originalist arguments are addressed and refuted in a Media Law Resource Center White Paper titled *New York Times v. Sullivan: The Case for Preserving an Essential Precedent*, https://perma.cc/A4WN-25BS.

[19] *Coral Ridge Ministries*, 142 S. Ct. at 2455.

[20] *McKee*, 139 S. Ct. at 680.

[21] *Id.* at 682.

doubt on Thomas's historical evidence concerning the original meaning of the First Amendment,[22] and the Justice's reliance on *scandalum magnatum*, a disavowed action by which British monarchs and "great men of the realm" (i.e., members of the peerage) criminally punished their critics, is singularly unpersuasive and even embarrassing.[23] Be that as it may, however, the originalist portion of Thomas's argument, even if he were correct in his historical analysis, is likely to convince only those who believe that the First Amendment should protect no more speech today than it did in 1791 (or perhaps in 1868, when the Fourteenth Amendment was ratified).

Justice Thomas's policy arguments are more persuasive. These focus on the "real-world" negative effects of the Court's constitutionalization of defamation law.[24] He asserts that the Court's defamation jurisprudence has "allowed media organizations and interest groups 'to cast false aspersions on public figures with near impunity.'"[25] His boldest claim, however, is that the actual-malice standard fosters lies in public discourse by "insulat[ing] those who perpetrate [them] from traditional remedies like libel suits."[26] He cites examples of conspiracy theories, hoaxes, and campaigns of online character assassination as evidence for the proposition that "lies impose real harm." Although he does not fully connect the premises of his argument to his conclusion, he seems to assert that the common law of libel, left to its own devices, could deter viral lies and other pernicious disinformation.[27] Beyond that, he does not elaborate on how unshackling the common law from First Amendment constraints would deter the proliferation of lies, and he does not ground the need for this deterrent fully in "cheap speech" concerns.

Justice Gorsuch, on the other hand, spotlights changes in the communication environment since 1964 as a basis for the reconsideration of *Sullivan*, and he claims that these changes undermine the rationales of the Court's actual-malice standard and public-figure doctrine. If Justice Gorsuch is correct in his criticisms, his call for reform should resonate even with those who have no truck with originalism. It is therefore useful to evaluate Gorsuch's concerns and determine what types of reforms might ameliorate them.

In an opinion dissenting from the denial of certiorari in *Berisha v. Lawson*, Justice Gorsuch postulates that the Framers understood the importance of press freedom to the healthy functioning of democracy.[28] Nonetheless, he writes, "like most rights, [freedom of the press] comes with corresponding duties."[29] One of those duties is

22 Matthew L. Schafer, *In Defense: New York Times v. Sullivan*, 82 LA. L. REV. 81 (2021).
23 *Id.* at 145–46.
24 Berisha v. Lawson, 141 S. Ct. 2424, 2425 (2021) (Thomas, J., dissenting).
25 Coral Ridge Ministries Media v. S. Poverty L. Ctr., 142 S. Ct. 2453, 2455 (2022) (Thomas, J., dissenting).
26 *Id.*
27 *Berisha*, 141 S. Ct. at 2424.
28 *Id.* at 2425.
29 *Id.* at 2426.

the duty "to try to get the facts right – or, like anyone else, answer in tort for the injuries they cause."[30] The implicit message of his dissent is that the press once tried to get the facts right, but this may no longer be the case.

Although Justice Gorsuch criticizes *Sullivan* as "overturning 200 years of libel law," his chief lament is not an originalist one.[31] Instead, his chief argument is that changes in "our Nation's media landscape" since 1964 have undermined *Sullivan*'s logic.[32] According to Justice Gorsuch, "revolutions in technology" have allowed "virtually anyone in this country" to "publish virtually anything for immediate consumption virtually anywhere in the world."[33] Justice Gorsuch concedes that "this new media world has many virtues," such as enhancing individuals' access to information and opportunities to debate, but he appears to believe social media's virtues are outweighed by negative effects on information quality.[34] According to Gorsuch, the social-media revolution has undermined the economic model that once gave newspapers and broadcasters professional and economic incentives to strive for accuracy and the ability to invest in the reporters, editors, and fact-checkers necessary to deliver it. He also blames the "new media environment"[35] for the spread of disinformation, which financially rewards its creators, "costs almost nothing to generate,"[36] and spreads more effectively than real news.

Gorsuch suggests that these changes undermine the justifications for *Sullivan*'s actual-malice standard. For example, he questions the need for actual malice to play a role in protecting "critical voices" from defamation liability, implying that the sheer quantity of people who possess an electronic "soapbox" is sufficient to guarantee a diversity of views.[37] He further indicates that while the actual-malice rule may have made sense in a media environment that had "other safeguards" against "defamatory falsehoods and misinformation," it no longer makes sense once those safeguards – such as the media's professional and economic incentives to deliver accurate information – have (or so he claims) evaporated.[38]

In the meantime, Gorsuch criticizes the evolution of the actual-malice standard "from a high bar to recovery into an effective immunity from liability."[39] Perplexingly, he contends that actual malice now creates a legal incentive for "publishing *without* investigation, fact-checking, or editing," a contention with

30 *Id.*
31 *Id.* (citing Dun & Bradstreet, Inc. v. Greenmoss Builders, Inc., 472 U.S. 749, 766 (1985)).
32 *Id.*
33 *Id.* at 2427.
34 *Id.*
35 *Id.*
36 *Id.* (citing David A. Logan, *Rescuing Our Democracy by Rethinking* New York Times Co. v. Sullivan, 81 Ohio St. L.J. 759, 800 (2020)).
37 *Id.*
38 *Id.* at 2427 (citing Logan, *supra* note 36, at 794–95).
39 *Id.* at 2428.

which many media lawyers would surely disagree.[40] Defendants win cases, after all, by negating fault. But for Justice Gorsuch, the actual-malice standard "has evolved into an ironclad subsidy for the publication of falsehoods by means and on a scale previously unimaginable."[41] Thus, he concludes, the actual-malice standard now thwarts, rather than bolsters, the "informed democratic debate" that First Amendment theory envisions.[42]

He also decries the fact that "today's world," with its "highly segmented media," casts more and more citizens as "public figures" for defamation purposes, leaving "far more people without redress than anyone [in 1964] could have predicted."[43] The effect, he speculates, may be to deter "people of goodwill" from entering "public life" or engaging "in democratic self-governance."[44] Again he suggests that *Sullivan*'s original justifications may be thwarted rather than advanced by the expansion of the public-figure doctrine in the social-media era, and he asks the Supreme Court as a whole to "return[] its attention" to the limits that its jurisprudence has placed on the common law of defamation.[45]

7.4 DEFAMATION'S SCORECARD

Between them, Justices Thomas and Gorsuch lay the fault for the unfortunate state of public discourse at the feet of today's defamation law, with Justice Gorsuch specifically faulting the law's inability to address the dangers of "cheap speech" because of the actual-malice and public-figure doctrines. He further suggests that revisiting the constitutional limits on defamation law might help bolster the declining quality of journalism, combat the rise of disinformation and lies, deter campaigns of character assassination, and foster "informed democratic debate."[46] Is he correct?

First, it is important to note that the common law of defamation was famously complex even prior to the intervention of constitutional law in 1964, and nothing has happened since then to significantly reduce that complexity. Defamation law comes by its complications honestly: Laws protecting reputation appeared in Anglo-Saxon law before the Norman Conquest, and at least as early as the thirteenth century, defamation was a spiritual offense, punishable by excommunication in ecclesiastical courts. Later, ecclesiastical and seigneurial courts divided jurisdiction between them for different kinds of defamation, and in the later Middle Ages and into the sixteenth and seventeenth centuries, the Crown punished "disgraceful words and speeches

40 *Id.*
41 *Id.*
42 *Id.*
43 *Id.* at 2429.
44 *Id.*
45 *Id.* at 2430.
46 *Id.* at 2428.

against eminent persons," known as *scandalum magnatum*.[47] Each of these historical developments contributed to the anomalies and absurdities of the common law of defamation,[48] and that was *before* the Supreme Court effectively froze these complexities into place and began adding many more in the thirty years following 1964.

Taking these complexities into account, it is fair to judge defamation law by how well it protects the values it purports to protect. The tort side of defamation is meant to protect individual reputation, a value no "civilized society" can "refuse to protect."[49] The tort reflects society's "basic concept of the essential dignity and worth of every human being."[50] The tort exists not only to safeguard and vindicate reputational injury but also to compensate injured individuals for dignitary, relational, and economic harms that flow from reputational injury. Moreover, the tort exists to exert a civilizing influence on public discourse: It not only gives society a means for announcing that certain speech violates our norms of propriety but also helps set a necessary anchor in truth. Yet the interests protected by defamation law are not the only interests implicated by the tort's operations, and the purpose of the "constitutional" parts of defamation law are to make sure the public continues to receive information necessary for democratic self-governance and informed individual decision-making. Further, the Constitution protects citizens' rights to participate in forming public opinion and, in turn, shaping public policy. Statutory modifications, such as anti-SLAPP laws and the immunity provided to internet service providers by the Communications Decency Act, also attempt to prevent the tort from unduly chilling valuable social activity. Given the complex balancing performed by the constitutionalized and statutorily modified tort of defamation, how does the law score in achieving its various purposes?

Let us start with the good news. One value that today's defamation law attempts to serve is to encourage media to perform their watchdog role by providing robust coverage of public officials and public figures. By that standard, media in the United States, including our newspapers and broadcasters, have more scope and license to cover and criticize public figures and public officials than any other media in the world. We can see the effects of these robust First Amendment protections in the intense coverage of presidents, congressional leaders, judges, and other influential public officials. It occasionally seems as though no personal predilection of our public officials is too inconsequential to escape notice. It is especially remarkable that the media continue to intensively cover now-former president Trump, despite

[47] John C. Lassiter, *Defamation of Peers: The Rise and Decline of the Action for* Scandalum Magnatum, 1497–1773, 22 AM. J. LEGAL HIST. (1978).

[48] W. PAGE KEETON & WILLIAM LLOYD PROSSER, PROSSER AND KEETON ON THE LAW OF TORTS § 111, 771 (5th ed. 1984) ("There is a great deal of the law of defamation which makes no sense.").

[49] Anderson, *supra* note 6, at 490.

[50] Rosenblatt v. Baer, 383 U.S. 75 (1966).

his long-standing propensity to bring defamation lawsuits against those who criticize him. We also see the effects of First Amendment doctrines that protect newsworthy information about public figures in the spotlight the media shine on celebrities, businesspeople, and other so-called "influencers." Concededly, coverage is less robust at local levels, but that appears to be a product of economics, not law. Even so, whether *Sullivan*'s actual-malice rule is essential to enabling the press to play their watchdog role is hard to know, but it stands to reason that being absolved of liability for inevitable human error and simple negligence might aid the vigor with which the press pursues the powerful.

That said, *Sullivan*'s protective mantle for journalistic errors is not the only variable to consider in evaluating the incentive structure of today's defamation laws. For publishers subject to it, the potential chilling effect that defamation law exerts on free expression flows not just from the likelihood that a jury or judge will hold a publisher liable; the chilling effect also flows from the high cost of defending against even meritless suits and the unpredictable extent of damages, both of which are exacerbated by common law's famous complexities and anomalous doctrines such as presumed damages, as well as those of constitutional law. Legal complexity contributes to the high costs of libel defense, and the unpredictability of damages that may be "presumed" when plaintiffs do prevail exert a degree of chill on coverage. This chill would be fine, even desirable, if only meritorious plaintiffs recovered and recoveries were predictably related to actual reputational harms suffered. Yet a survey of the libel landscape reveals lottery-like windfalls for a select few that are only marginally connected to their injuries.

Contrary to Justice Gorsuch's assertion, some of these recoveries are by plaintiffs who are public figures. Although verdicts for plaintiffs are rare, plaintiffs who do win sometimes obtain verdicts in the millions (or a billion now, as in the Alex Jones cases). Other recent wins include the recent libel verdict against actor Amber Heard procured by her ex-husband Johnny Depp based on allegations of spousal abuse, and the verdict against Oberlin College by a bakery falsely accused of racist acts.[51] Settlements, too, may reach into the millions, as attested recently by those obtained by Kentucky teen Nicholas Sandmann against *The Washington Post* and other media organizations that falsely accused him of bigoted misconduct. (Other *Sandmann* cases were recently dismissed.) Moreover, in the cases that Smartmatic and Dominion Voting Systems have brought against Fox News and others, the plaintiffs seek damages in the billions with a straight face.[52] Although these verdicts, settlements, and claims may not deter the judgment-proof, nor those ignorant of the law, any media organization must take into account the unpredictable risk of being

[51] Complaint, Gibson Bros. v. Oberlin College, 2017 WL 11249640 (Ohio Com. Pl. Nov. 7, 2017).

[52] Complaint, Dominion Voting Sys., Inc. v. Herring Networks (OAN), No. 2021–2130 (D.D.C. Nov. 7, 2022); Complaint, Dominion Voting Sys., Inc. v. Newsmax Media, Inc., No. N21C-08-063 EMD (Del. Super. Ct. Aug. 10, 2021).

sued and found liable, even if the Supreme Court's First Amendment jurisprudence has stacked the constitutional deck in favor of free expression.

Even if defamation law may incentivize robust coverage of society's influencers for some, it does a relatively poor job of vindicating wrongfully tarnished reputations.[53] Gorsuch's diagnosis of the constitutional difficulties that make defamation cases seem impossible for public figures and public officials are real, primarily because lower courts have expanded the public-figure category to include almost anyone who is involved in public life in any way. And even those clearly categorized as public figures may choose to prove actual malice in order to seek punitive damages.

A recent case illustrates why some might believe the actual-malice standard prevents the media from being held responsible for getting the facts wrong. Former vice-presidential candidate Sarah Palin sued *The New York Times* for libel based on an erroneous editorial blaming a Palin political website for inciting a mass shooting. Palin's website had featured crosshairs over an Arizona congressional district, and the site "targeted" congressperson Gabrielle Giffords for electoral defeat. After Giffords and others were shot by a deranged gunman in 2011, a controversy arose over what had inspired the gunman, but a contemporaneous police report made clear that the gunman was not motivated by politics. Nonetheless, in 2017, the *Times* brought up the previously discredited theory about Palin's website, claiming that "the link to the political incitement was clear."[54] The *Times* quickly discovered the error and issued a correction hours after it was published. When the case went to trial, the focus was on whether the error was an "honest mistake" or instead deliberate or reckless.[55] The evidence focused on the rush to finish the piece before its deadline, the editors' erroneous correction to the work of the writer, the subsequent request for the writer to double-check the piece, and the error made by the fact-checker.[56] Although Palin testified about the alleged harms she'd suffered, the trial focused more on the *Times*' journalistic process than

53 *See* Gertz v. Robert Welch, Inc., 418 U.S. 323 (1974) (discussing plaintiff's interest in vindication). In traditional libel suits, plaintiffs' primary goals in bringing suit include restoring reputation, correcting what plaintiffs view as falsity, and exacting vengeance. *See* Randall P. Bezanson, *Libel Law and the Realities of Libel Litigation: Setting the Record Straight*, 71 Iowa L. Rev. 226, 227 (1985). Defamation suits are often driven by "emotion, rather than money," since defamation actions may be the only avenue available to vindicate a plaintiff's damaged reputation. Bruce W. Sanford, Libel and Privacy 609 (2d ed. 1991); Marc A. Franklin, *Winners and Losers and Why: A Study of Defamation Litigation*, 1980 Am. B. Found. Res. J. 455, 462 ("The defendant's solvency is probably not central to the decision to sue because the plaintiff's reputation is at issue and thus an apology or a small recovery may vindicate the plaintiff.").

54 Ben Feuerherd, *NYT Fact-Checker Missed Assertion about Palin in 2017 Editorial*, N.Y. Post (Feb. 7, 2022), https://perma.cc/HN64-ZG95.

55 Ben Feuerherd, *Sarah Palin Error in Editorial Was 'Honest Mistake,' New York Times Lawyer Claims*, N.Y. Post (Feb. 11, 2022), https://perma.cc/B5SS-3J9R.

56 *Id.*

the wrong to Palin. And Palin lost based on the latter issue: The jury found no liability, and the trial judge openly stated that he would have found Palin's evidence insufficient to prove the *Times*' error was deliberate or reckless had the jury found differently. Thus, Palin received vindication – if that is what she was seeking – only to the extent of bringing publicity to the *Times*' error, which the trial judge called a product of "unfortunate editorializing."[57]

Based on Palin's verdict, Justice Gorsuch could be forgiven for thinking that the actual-malice standard is an insurmountable barrier to plaintiffs' recoveries. This is a common and long-standing misimpression. In fact, thirty years ago, distinguished defamation scholar David Anderson complained that high-profile mistakes by the press created an "exaggerated impression in the minds of some potential plaintiffs and lawyers that the press is impervious to public-plaintiff libel suits" when in fact, that is not the truth, as the verdicts, settlements, and costly litigation already discussed above reveal.[58] But Palin's suit also highlights a more significant flaw in today's defamation law: Many plaintiffs would like the libel trial to act as an authoritative public declaration that they were wronged by a defendant's accusation, but this is not a result the libel trial is designed to give.

What of Truth? Justice Gorsuch laid the blame at the feet of defamation law for failing to combat disinformation and misinformation in the social-media era, and he even theorized that more defamation actions would enhance press credibility. Certainly, Gorsuch is not alone in decrying the rise of misinformation and disinformation, though critics cast blame for the situation in different quarters: The Trump White House famously fought a rhetorical war against "fake news" in the press, and the Biden White House proposed, briefly, a Disinformation Governance Board to counter misinformation affecting national security, though the proposal was withdrawn after public outcry. Many critics blame Big Tech platforms for not doing more to eradicate false information, while others fault them for doing too much censorship along partisan lines. Meanwhile, the purveyors of false information include state actors exploiting the power of social networks to undermine social stability or pursue other political ends; rogue actors creating fake news for profit; people using social media to voice their delusional conspiracy theories; partisans primed to believe only the information they want to believe and pass it along to others; lawyers determined to represent clients using whatever "facts" are expedient, ethics rules be damned; and, finally, journalists who fail to adequately investigate, edit, or verify the information they publish – perhaps because of preexisting biases.

Even aside from the fact that defamation law can only address lies that affect individual reputation, only some of the purveyors of misinformation or

[57] Dominick Mastrangelo, *Judge to Throw Out Sarah Palin's Lawsuit Against New York Times*, HILL (Feb. 14, 2022), https://perma.cc/5SWV-DN2K; *see also* Allie Griffin, *Sarah Palin's Attempt to Disqualify Judge Jed Rakoff from NY Times Defamation Trial Fails*, N.Y. POST (June 1, 2022), https://perma.cc/P7F7-M4ZJ.

[58] Anderson, *supra* note 6, at 523.

disinformation are even capable of being deterred by the prospect of a U.S. defamation lawsuit. Moreover, those who *can* be deterred are probably the smallest contributors to the disinformation crisis. Sloppy journalism might be deterred at the margins by changes in defamation law, though it is unlikely that the inevitable human errors that occur in the rush to meet deadlines will cease, and changes to make it easier to sue for negligent or even innocent mistakes run the risk of deterring coverage of those with the resources (and propensity) to sue.

More to the point, the actual-malice standard already allows plaintiffs to target lies and recklessly spread falsehoods, and a couple of recent lawsuits are setting out to prove it. Smartmatic and Dominion Voting Systems supplied electronic voting machinery for the 2020 presidential election. They became targets of President Trump's partisans, who alleged that the companies' machines had assisted in stealing the election from Trump through fraud. Smartmatic and Dominion Voting Systems separately filed defamation cases against various purveyors of this so-called Big Lie, and these lawsuits have become test cases for whether defamation lawsuits can be used to combat hyper-partisan disinformation. But they are also test cases for whether certain news networks have gone too far in embracing such disinformation and lending their credibility to lies and reckless falsehoods.

The defendants in these suits include lawyers who formerly represented President Trump; supporters of President Trump; news networks Newsmax, One America News, and Fox News; and several journalist-news hosts, including Lou Dobbs and Maria Bartiromo.[59] In its 285-page complaint against Fox, Smartmatic seeks $2.7 billion in damages. Dominion's suit against Fox seeks $1.6 billion. In both cases, defamation law's failure to insist on only compensating for actual harms means that plaintiffs can claim damages completely untethered to any objective reality.

Nonetheless, the lawsuits make damning allegations, suggesting that the news networks named in the case promoted the Big Lie to stoke ratings – despite having

[59] *See, e.g.*, Complaint, U.S. Dominion, Inc. v. Herring Networks, Inc., 2021 WL 3522347 (D.D.C. 2021) (trial pleading); Complaint, Smartmatic USA Corp. v. Lindell, 2022 WL 168592 (D. Minn. 2022) (trial pleading); U.S. Dominion, Inc. v. Byrne, 600 F. Supp. 3d 24, 2022 WL 1165935 (D.D.C. 2022) (denying motion of Patrick Byrne, CEO of Overstock.com, to dismiss Dominion's defamation suit); U.S. Dominion, Inc. v. Powell, 554 F. Supp. 3d 42, 56 (D.D.C. 2021) (denying motion to dismiss Dominion's defamation claims against Trump lawyers Sidney Powell, Rudy Guiliani, and MyPillow CEO Mike Lindell); U.S. Dominion, Inc. v. MyPillow, Inc., No. 21-7103, 2022 WL 774080 (D.C. Cir. Jan. 20, 2022); U.S. Dominion, Inc. v. MyPillow, Inc., 2022 WL 1597420 (D.D.C. 2022) (granting motions to dismiss counterclaims made by MyPillow's CEO against Smartmatic and Dominion Voting Systems and granting, in part, Smartmatic's motion for sanctions against Lindell for filing frivolous claims); Smartmatic USA Corp. v. Herring Networks, Inc., 2022 WL 2208913 (D.D.C. 2022) (denying motion to dismiss claim against Herring Networks (One American News Network) for lack of personal jurisdiction). For the actions against Fox, *see* Smartmatic USA Corp. v. Fox Corp., No. 151136/2021 (Sup. Ct. N.Y. Cnty.); U.S. Dominion, Inc. v. Fox News Network, LLC, No. N21C-03-257-EMD, 2022 WL 100820, at *3–4 (Del. Super. Ct. Jan. 10, 2022) (noting that Dominion "stated a defamation claim under any pleading standard, including New York's anti-SLAPP clear and convincing evidence standard").

evidence that the allegations of fraud made by network hosts and their guests were false. Judges have so far refused to dismiss the voting-machine companies' claims.[60] Should these cases go to trial, they will put a powerful spotlight on the editorial choices of the news networks, and there is some indication they have already led Fox to fire some of the news hosts who were most instrumental in trumpeting the voting-fraud allegations. Whether lawsuits such as this will result in more media responsibility and credibility overall seems dubious, however, especially since the facts are distinctly atypical. Nonetheless, plaintiff victories could potentially bankrupt some of these news networks, sending a klaxon signal warning that the actual-malice standard is not, after all, a free pass for falsehoods.

7.5 FIRST DO NO HARM

As detailed above, Justice Gorsuch is simply wrong to assume that actual malice is an insurmountable barrier to recovery for defamation. Nonetheless, some of Gorsuch's skepticism regarding the current state of defamation law seems justified: Defamation law inadequately vindicates reputation, and it only combats disinformation at the margins – though, contrary to his assertions, it does do that! But whether defamation law would perform these tasks better if *Sullivan* and its progeny were to be repealed is by no means clear, especially since most of the purveyors of disinformation seem to be beyond the reach of defamation law. While allowing a wider swath of plaintiffs to bring suit by proving negligence rather than actual malice might lead to more plaintiffs achieving vindication, it seems unlikely that it would significantly bolster the quality of journalism in a way that leads to more "informed democratic debate."[61]

Gorsuch's prescription ignores the problem that *Sullivan*'s holding was trying to solve, namely, the use of defamation lawsuits as a tool that the powerful use to delegitimize and defang their critics. In *Sullivan*, Southern officials sued civil-rights leaders and a Northern newspaper, *The New York Times*, for publishing an advertisement decrying the repeated arrests and harassment of Dr. Martin Luther King. The advertisement contained minor inaccuracies, the kind that newspapers inevitably make even when trying to get the facts right. These minor errors were enough to justify the Alabama jury in awarding the police commissioner $3 million from the *Times* and the other defendants. At this time, this was the biggest libel verdict in U.S. history,[62] and the jury made the award despite the fact that the commissioner had

[60] U.S. Dominion, Inc. v. Fox News Network, LLC, No. N21C-11-082-EMD-CCLD, 2022 WL 100820 (Del. Super. Ct. June 21, 2022).

[61] Berisha v. Lawson, 141 S. Ct. 2424, 2428 (2021) (Gorsuch, J., dissenting).

[62] *See* ANTHONY LEWIS, MAKE NO LAW: THE SULLIVAN CASE AND THE FIRST AMENDMENT 14 (1991). By the time the Supreme Court decided the case, libel actions threatened to silence media reporting on the Civil Rights Movement. *See* Sullivan, 376 U.S. at 277–78 (noting that state libel actions could bring newspapers such large judgments that "those who would give

"made no effort to prove that he suffered actual pecuniary loss."[63] Had the verdict been allowed to stand, the South would have continued to use libel law to hamstring the Civil Rights Movement and to punish newspapers for making minor factual errors while performing their watchdog role. Had it been allowed to stand, papers like the *Times* would have faced the choice between their economic survival and ceasing to cover the most important news stories of the era.

To prevent this result, the Supreme Court famously held that public officials could not use the law of torts to punish their critics: They did so by beginning the conversion of the defamation law from a no-fault regime to a largely fault-based regime, as well as one that requires plaintiffs suing for stories involving matters of public concern to prove falsity. The constitutional standards protect merely negligent defamatory falsehoods, giving journalists and citizens "breathing space" to report and opine about the doings of public officials.

Justice Gorsuch fails to appreciate that this breathing space is still needed. Rich people still sue their critics for defamation because they can: It's a relatively easy way to inflict pain on one's critics and to make would-be critics think twice, even if the defendant ultimately "wins." Politicians still sue the relatively powerless to punish them for their temerity in speaking out. The media, while not the only targets of weaponized defamation suits, still deserve protection not only because they are repeat players but also because, as Justice Gorsuch recognized, they have played a special role in producing an informed citizenry since the country's founding. Overturning *Sullivan* would subject an economically weakened and unpopular press to even more variable defamation laws, making them easier targets for those who despise them and their roles. If the goal is to ensure that informed democratic debate does not suffer, it is hard to see how jettisoning the actual-malice standard accomplishes it, unless it is replaced by a series of complex doctrinal reforms.

7.6 A PRESCRIPTION FOR REFORM

Even so, Justice Gorsuch is clearly right about one thing: Defamation law needs reform. Ideally, that reform would look comprehensively at the various common-law, constitutional, and statutory components, and study how they work together. It would bring simplicity and clarity to the "doctrinal intricacy" of current law. It would consider whether doctrines such as libel, slander, and presumed damages have outlived their usefulness. It would also develop new remedies to better vindicate reputation and set the record straight, construct new incentives for journalists of all stripes to adhere to professionally developed

voice to public criticism" would be effectively silenced). *Sullivan* also involved several non-media defendants in addition to *The New York Times*, and the logic of the decision applied equally to them all. *See id.* at 279–80.

63 *Id.* at 260.

standards for getting the facts right, and establish new deterrents to libel bullying, including a reduction of the availability of lottery-like windfalls obtainable only by the fortunate few. While reform is needed, however, simply cutting the constitutional strands of the Gordian Knot of defamation law risks unraveling protections for expression without enhancing the other goals the law is supposed to advance.

8

Defamation, Disinformation, and the Press Function

RonNell Andersen Jones

8.1 INTRODUCTION

Coordinated campaigns of falsehoods are poisoning public discourse.[1] Amidst a torrent of social-media conspiracy theories and lies – on topics as central to the nation's wellbeing as elections and public health – scholars and jurists are turning their attention to the causes of this disinformation crisis and the potential solutions to it.

Justice Neil Gorsuch recently suggested that, in response to this challenge, the U.S. Supreme Court should take a case to reconsider *New York Times v. Sullivan*, the foundational First Amendment precedent in defamation law.[2] A major premise of Justice Gorsuch's critique of *Sullivan* is that the changing social-media dynamics – and the disinformation crisis that has accompanied them – threaten the nation's democracy. He argues this changed terrain may call for less stringent constitutional protections in defamation actions. This chapter explores and challenges that critique. Justice Gorsuch is correct that rampant social-media disinformation poses a grave risk to our political and social stability, but there is a troubling disconnect between the anti-disinformation and pro-democracy concerns he articulates and the doctrinal revisions he considers. When the interrelationships between disinformation, defamation, and democracy are interrogated – and especially, when they are situated within the constitutional value of the press function that served as the backdrop for *Sullivan* – it becomes clear that unwinding the *Sullivan* doctrine would not be a productive tool for remedying the problem of rampant social-media

[1] *See* Janna Anderson & Lee Rainie, *The Future of Truth and Misinformation Online*, Pew Rsch. Ctr. (Oct. 19, 2017), https://perma.cc/4DNE-2XUY; *During This Coronavirus Pandemic, "Fake News" Is Putting Lives at Risk: UNESCO*, U.N. News (Apr. 13, 2020), https://perma.cc/4PZJ-72XH (discussing the "contamination" of information exchange caused by orchestrated campaigns that repeat and amplify disinformation).

[2] Berisha v. Lawson, 141 S. Ct. 2424, 2424 (2021).

lies. Indeed, doing so carries the very real risk of exacerbating the problem. Abandoning the *Sullivan* line of protections would impair those valuable press speakers who are actively prioritizing trustworthy newsgathering and corrective reporting, and it would do so with no meaningful payoff in solving the online-disinformation problem that seems to be driving this proposed reconsideration.

This inquiry matters. *Sullivan* is not exclusively a press-freedom case, but at this critical juncture, it is a centerpiece of protection for some core press functions (performed by both legacy media and others) that are crucial to healthy public discourse. A *Sullivan* scaleback harms those entities that are incentivized to get information right, to invest in careful newsgathering, and to engage in important journalistic investigations exposing those who peddle disinformation. At a moment of declining newsroom and press-litigation resources and of increased willingness of public people to weaponize defamation as a tool for silencing and deterring critics, the risks of self-censorship voiced by the unanimous *Sullivan* Court are especially grave.

Representative democracy needs the press function to survive and flourish. There is every reason to believe that a rollback of *Sullivan* would compound rather than alleviate the disinformation problem and would further imperil the fragile democracy.

8.2 THE SULLIVAN DOCTRINE

New York Times v. Sullivan came to the Supreme Court at another moment of intense focus on the need for vibrant dialogue in American democracy. As the Civil Rights Movement pressed across the Deep South, its story was carried through the nation by way of prominent Northern newspapers, especially *The New York Times*.[3] The case arose out of a full-page editorial advertisement that the *Times* published, which criticized the way that police had used violence and illegal tactics to try to quell the peaceful protests in Montgomery, Alabama.[4] The basic thrust of the charges contained in the advertisement was true, but the advertisement contained minor factual errors.[5] Sullivan, the Montgomery police commissioner, sued for defamation, and Alabama common law did not require that he prove either falsity or fault. The trial judge instructed that the statements were libelous per se and that general damages could be presumed. A jury

[3] New York Times Co. v. Sullivan, 376 U.S. 254, 256–57 (1964).

[4] *Id.* at 257–58.

[5] *Id.* at 257–59. For example, the advertisement said that protestors sang "My Country 'Tis of Thee," when they in fact sang "The Star-Spangled Banner." Under Alabama law, a publication was libelous per se if the words tended to injure a person's reputation, and Sullivan successfully argued that the words were "of and concerning" him by reflecting poorly on the performance of the government agency he oversaw. "Once 'libel per se' ha[d] been established, the defendant ha[d] no defense as to stated facts unless he [could] persuade the jury that they were true in all their particulars." *Id.* at 267.

awarded a half-million-dollar verdict against the newspaper, which was upheld by the Alabama Supreme Court.[6] The suit – one of eleven filed by Alabama officials alleging libelous reporting of local events and seeking a total of more than five and a half million dollars in damages – was a clear effort to wield defamation law as a silencing mechanism, and it worked. The newspaper pulled correspondents out of the state for a year in response.[7]

In a unanimous opinion that centered on the intersection of democratic self-governance and free speech, the Supreme Court held that the Constitution imposes limitations on defamation liability.[8] The First Amendment, the Court said, prevents "a public official from recovering damages for a defamatory falsehood relating to his official conduct unless he proves that the statement was made with 'actual malice' – that is, with knowledge that it was false or with reckless disregard of whether it was false or not."[9] The deliberately demanding standard operates "against the background of a profound national commitment to the principle that debate on public issues should be uninhibited, robust, and wide-open, and that it may well include vehement, caustic, and sometimes unpleasantly sharp attacks on government and public officials."[10] Criticism of the powerful – and the conversations that emerge out of this criticism – are at the core of the First Amendment's purpose and value to us as a citizenry.[11] The doctrinal incentives should spur and support those conversations. The *Sullivan* fact pattern demonstrated the chilling effect posed by the threat of staggeringly expensive litigation and damages. The standard that the Court developed in *Sullivan* offered protection to some false statements, which the Court deemed "inevitable in free debate," as a way of ensuring that true statements would have "the breathing space" that they need to survive.[12] After *Sullivan*, a set of cases extended this actual-malice standard to so-called public figures[13] – those who have achieved either broad fame or have become central to some specific conversation on a matter of public concern.[14] *Sullivan* is not a press-specific case – its standard applies anytime a public plaintiff brings a defamation action – but in the last six decades, it has been relied upon heavily by those performing the press function.

6 *Id.* at 256.

7 Walter Dellinger, *The Right to Be Wrong*, N.Y. TIMES (Sept. 1, 1991), https://perma.cc/54EG-LRF5.

8 *Sullivan*, 376 U.S. at 286.

9 *Id.* at 279–80.

10 *Id.* at 270.

11 *Id.* at 272.

12 *Id.* at 271–72.

13 Curtis Publ'g Co. v. Butts, 388 U.S. 130, 155 (1967); Gertz v. Robert Welch, Inc., 418 U.S. 323, 323 (1974).

14 Separately, Justice Gorsuch's dissent from denial of certiorari in *Berisha* raised the question of whether the new social media landscape also changes the scope and contours of public figuredom.

8.3 JUSTICE GORSUCH'S CRITIQUE

In his dissent from denial of certiorari in *Berisha v. Lawson*,[15] Justice Gorsuch argued that, in light of the new media landscape and the disinformation crisis that it has enabled, the Court should reconsider the *Sullivan* framework.[16]

The libel plaintiff in *Berisha*, the son of a former president and prime minister of Albania, contended that a book defamed him by implicating him in an arms-dealing scandal.[17] Justice Gorsuch maintained that his colleagues on the Court should have taken the case. He argued that a "new media environment" that "facilitates the spread of disinformation" requires reevaluation of the constitutional standard.[18] Pointing to the rapid spread of social-media conspiracy theories and other online lies, he suggested that "the deck seems stacked ... in favor of those who can disseminate the most sensational information as efficiently as possible without any particular concern for truth."[19] Indeed, he noted, "the distribution of disinformation" – which "costs almost nothing to generate" – has become a "profitable" business while "the economic model that supported reporters, fact-checking, and editorial oversight" has "deeply erod[ed]."[20] Justice Gorsuch suggested that the justification undergirding the *Sullivan* standard may have less force "in a world in which everyone carries a soapbox in their hands"[21] and where there are fewer "safeguards ... to deter the dissemination of defamatory falsehoods and misinformation."[22] Social-media lies are so fast and so appealing, Gorsuch wrote, that "falsehood and rumor dominate[] truth."[23] Importantly, then, the factual foundation for Justice Gorsuch's concern appears to be rooted in dissemination and spread – concerns about the way that modern social-media technology amplifies untruths and the way that propaganda outpaces truthful information from the trustworthy professional newsgatherers that may have predominated the communication landscape as understood by the Justices who decided *Sullivan*.

15 Berisha v. Lawson, 141 S. Ct. 2424, 2425 (2021) (Gorsuch, J., dissenting from denial of certiorari).

16 With his *Berisha* opinion, Gorsuch became the second Justice to suggest a rethinking of *Sullivan*. Justice Thomas, who also dissented from denial of certiorari in *Berisha*, had already taken this position two years earlier, rooting his argument primarily in a view of First Amendment originalism. McKee v. Cosby, 139 S. Ct. 675, 676 (2019) (Thomas, J., concurring); *see also* Coral Ridge Ministries Media, Inc. v. S. Poverty L. Ctr., 142 S. Ct. 2453 (2022) (Thomas, J., dissenting from denial of certiorari) (arguing for reconsideration of *Sullivan*).

17 *Berisha*, 141 S. Ct. at 2424 (The 2016 Jonah Hill movie *War Dogs* is loosely based on this true story of young Floridians who convinced the Pentagon to award them a $300 million contract to arm America's allies in Afghanistan.).

18 *Id.* at 2427.

19 *Id.* at 2428.

20 *Id.* at 2427.

21 *Id.*

22 *Id.*

23 *Id.* ("A study of one social network reportedly found that 'falsehood and rumor dominated truth by every metric, reaching more people, penetrating deeper ... and doing so more quickly than accurate statements'.").

Today, the thinking goes, the best way to curb these viral, coordinated falsehoods is to make it easier to bring defamation actions. In Justice Gorsuch's view, lowering the barrier to doing so would serve anti-disinformation and pro-democracy aims.

8.4 A POOR TOOL FOR THE CRISIS

Upon closer consideration, however, it seems the doctrinal revision Justice Gorsuch has in mind would have the exact opposite effect. As a practical, legal, and structural matter, it would advance neither the goal of curbing disinformation nor the interest in fostering a healthy democratic public sphere.

As an important starting matter, much of the most-problematic disinformation at the core of the crisis is not itself defamation. Huge swaths of the rampant lies that have caused the gravest concern in recent years – falsehoods about medical treatments,[24] vaccination,[25] elections,[26] climate change,[27] and a wide variety of other social and political issues – are not attacks on the reputation of any individual or entity. They lie, to be sure. But they do not defame. When a widely shared social-media post claims broadly that an election was stolen or a vaccine is a deep-state plot, there is no obvious reputational attack at issue and thus no basis for a libel suit.

[24] *See* Davey Alba, *Facebook Groups Promoting Ivermectin as a Covid-19 Treatment Continue to Flourish*, N.Y. TIMES (Sept. 28, 2021), https://perma.cc/8748-A5UF (highlighting the role of Facebook groups in spreading disinformation about ivermectin as a treatment for COVID-19); Jennifer Nilsen, *Cord Blood and Medical Misinformation: The Big Business of Unproven Stem Cell Treatments*, MEDIA MANIPULATION CASEBOOK (Nov. 1, 2021), https://perma.cc/S59X-E4NH (tracking the origin and spread of disinformation related to unproven stem cell treatments as a "near cure-all" for any ailment).

[25] *See* Linda Qiu, *No, Covid-19 Vaccines Are Not Killing More People than the Virus Itself*, N.Y. TIMES (May 7, 2021), https://perma.cc/7928-YT25 (reporting on popular social media claims asserting that COVID-19 vaccinations have caused more deaths than the virus itself); Reuters Fact Check, *Fact Check-VAERS Data Does Not Prove Thousands Died from Receiving Covid-19 Vaccines*, REUTERS (Apr. 2, 2021, 8:35 AM), https://perma.cc/E9FA-TBDT (fact-checking a widely viewed Facebook video claiming the COVID-19 vaccine killed thousands of people); Katherine J. Wu, *No, There Are No Microchips in Coronavirus Vaccines*, N.Y. TIMES (Dec. 17, 2020), https://perma.cc/7928-YT25 (debunking popular online claims that Pfizer's coronavirus vaccine contains a tracking microchip planted by the government); Sarah Evanega et al., *Coronavirus Misinformation: Quantifying Sources and Themes in the COVID-19 'Infodemic'*, CORNELL (July 23, 2020), https://perma.cc/BF54-4R6J (tracking common COVID conspiracies, including miracle cures, "deep state" conspiracies, and assertions about population control).

[26] *See* Davey Alba, *These Two Rumors Are Going Viral Ahead of California's Recall Election*, N.Y. TIMES (Sept. 15, 2021), https://perma.cc/M4TX-M2MH (explaining the rumor preceding California's gubernatorial recall election that holes in ballot envelopes were being used to screen votes); Linda Qiu, *The Election Is Over, but Ron Johnson Keeps Promoting False Claims of Fraud*, N.Y. TIMES (Mar. 21, 2021), https://perma.cc/B9U5-QU8X (tracking the continued spread of disinformation regarding a fraudulent presidential election, despite claims having been addressed and debunked by government cybersecurity leaders).

[27] *See* Jeffrey Pierre & Scott Neuman, *How Decades of Disinformation about Fossil Fuels Halted U.S. Climate Policy*, NPR (Oct. 27, 2021), https://perma.cc/YEN5-YW6L (tracking the oil industry's coordinated efforts to undermine data showing the effects of climate change).

Justice Gorsuch's stated concerns are about falsehoods more generally, and he is not wrong that these fast-spreading lies are polluting public discourse and inflicting harm. However, the harm inflicted is a harm against public sensibility that stems from an assault on facts, not a harm against a potential defamation plaintiff that stems from an assault on reputation.[28] While defamation law aims to ensure that our public discourse has an anchor in truth, it only concerns itself with one quite-specific anchor, and it is not the one with which Justice Gorsuch seems most concerned. Adjustment of the *Sullivan* standard simply does not do the major anti-disinformation and pro-democracy work that needs to be done.

Occasionally, of course, the two overlap – for example, when disinformation is not merely a generic lie about a stolen election but a lie about a particular postmaster backdating mail-in ballots,[29] or particular election workers tampering with votes,[30] or a particular voting-machine company rigging an outcome[31] – and defamation litigation might then be a useful, pro-democratic tool in the ways Gorsuch apparently envisions. Some conspiracy theories spread falsehood that is reputation-harming.[32] But there is no reason to believe that disinformation as a wider phenomenon is going to serve itself up in a way that merits a defamation claim.

Indeed, significant research in this area suggests that it often does not. Much social-media disinformation is generated by a very small number of initial producers for money or political gain and then disseminated broadly on platforms by armies of others who make broad claims that are false but not harmful to any individual reputation. A powerful recent illustration is the so-called Disinformation Dozen, a

[28] Bente Birkeland, *Election Defamation Lawsuits Open New Front in Fight against Defamation*, NPR (Mar. 27, 2021, 7:00 AM), https://perma.cc/AS9L-4D99 ("Many conspiracy theories do not target a specific person or company, so there's no one to file a lawsuit against."); John Cook, Ullrich Ecker & Stephan Lewandowsky, *Misinformation and How to Correct It*, *in* Emerging Trends in the Social and Behavioral Sciences 1, 3 (Robert A. Scott, Stephen M. Kosslyn & Marlis Buchmann eds., 2015) (noting the ways that anti-science campaigns "misinform the public on issues that have achieved consensus among the scientific community, such as biological evolution, and the human influence on climate change").

[29] Complaint at 10, Weisenbach v. Project Veritas, No. 10819-21 (Pa. Ct. Com. Pl. Aug. 13, 2021); *Project Democracy Joins Defamation Suit Against Project Veritas: Group Maliciously Lied About a PA Postmaster in the Aftermath of 2020 Election*, Protect Democracy (Aug. 16, 2021), https://perma.cc/4TB5-UUQR.

[30] Complaint, Freeman v. Hoft, No. 4:21-cv-0 1424 (E.D. Mo. Dec. 5, 2021); Betsy Woodruff Swan, Kyle Cheney & Josh Gerstein, *Pa. Voting Official Sues Trump, Giuliani, Others over 2020 Allegations*, Politico (Nov. 2, 2021, 11:05 PM), https://perma.cc/JJ4R-4VWQ.

[31] US Dominion, Inc. v. Fox News Network, LLC, No. N21C-03-257 EMD (Del. Super. Ct. Mar. 26, 2021); Smartmatic USA Corp. v. Fox Corporation, No. 151136/2021 (N.Y. Sup. Ct. Feb. 8, 2021); Smartmatic USA Corp. v. Michael J. Lindell, No. 22-cv-00098-WMW-JFD (D. Minn. Jan. 18, 2022).

[32] *See, e.g.*, Dave Collins, *Alex Jones Ordered to Pay $965 Million for Sandy Hook Lies*, AP News (Oct. 12, 2022), https://perma.cc/7BU4-Q4DS.

group of individuals found to be responsible for almost two-thirds of the anti-vaccine content circulating on social-media platforms.[33] While some of the content produced by the Disinformation Dozen has been leveled at individuals,[34] much of the false and deceptive anti-vaccination content is packaged in the form of misleading data designed to sway opinion rather than target reputation.[35] This is not a *Sullivan* problem, and reconsideration of *Sullivan* is not a solution to it. There is no reason to believe that adjusting constitutional free speech standards in defamation law would be an efficient or effective tool for tackling the core of the issue.

To the extent that the concern here is actively defamatory disinformation campaigns – wholly invented, consciously distributed conspiracy theories that knowingly target an individual's reputation with falsehoods for clicks[36] – this material already falls outside the scope of *Sullivan* protection. A number of important debates are emerging about the purveyors of these falsehoods – including whether even a successful defamation suit can dislodge an audience's belief in these conspiratorial lies or meaningfully impact the incentives of those producing them.[37] But this defamatory material is, by definition, distributed with knowing falsity or reckless disregard for the truth. The *Sullivan* doctrine, as it now stands, envisions liability for these actors, and a reconsideration of the doctrine would, again, be a poor instrument for tackling the concerns that continue to exist.

Moreover, as a practical matter, the online social-media mobs disseminating lies are not natural targets for defamation suits, because there are so many communicators in the amplification process and because so many of them may be

[33] *The Disinformation Dozen*, Ctr. for Countering Digital Hate (Mar. 24, 2021), https://perma.cc/FFQ3-N2VJ; Audrey McNamara, *A Dozen Anti-vaccine Accounts Are Responsible for 65% of Disinformation Shared Online, New Report Finds*, CBS News (Mar. 25, 2021, 10:09 PM), https://perma.cc/FC2K-J3QX (noting that nearly two-thirds of anti-vaccine content that had been shared or posted on Facebook and X more than 812,000 times between February 1 and March 16, 2021, came from twelve accounts).

[34] *The Disinformation Dozen*, *supra* note 33 (describing allegation that Bill Gates had a role in planning the COVID-19 pandemic).

[35] *Id.* at 12–21; Sheera Frenkel, *The Most Influential Spreader of Coronavirus Misinformation Online*, N.Y. Times (Nov. 25, 2022), https://perma.cc/BBG6-X7VK; Davey Alba & Sheera Frenkel, *From Voter Fraud to Vaccine Lies: Misinformation Peddlers Shift Gears*, N.Y. Times (Jan. 7, 2021), https://perma.cc/R4U4-VCNL (discussing campaigns spreading lies about vaccines being delivered with a microchip or being harmful to health).

[36] *See, e.g.*, Terrence McCoy, *Inside a Long Beach Web Operation That Makes Up Stories about Trump and Clinton: What They Do for Clicks and Cash*, L.A. Times (Nov. 22, 2016), https://perma.cc/RD6R-LZB2 (describing the process by which writer Paris Wade found a "totally misleading" photograph to "trick people into treading the news"); Laura Sydell, *We Tracked Down a Fake-News Creator in the Suburbs. Here's What We Learned*, NPR (Nov. 23, 2016, 3;31 PM), https://perma.cc/K986-S564 (describing the rapid spread of a fabricated story about an FBI agent murdered for leaking Hillary Clinton's email).

[37] *See, e.g.*, David Bauder, *Is Alex Jones Verdict the Death of Disinformation? Unlikely*, AP News (Oct. 17, 2022), https://perma.cc/BA3W-FSRV; Zeynep Tufekci, Opinion, *We Should Try to Prevent Another Alex Jones*, N.Y. Times (Oct. 16, 2022), https://perma.cc/2FGD-NKA6.

anonymous.[38] Take, for example, one common disinformation pattern: A lie initiates on an anonymous web platform like 4chan, makes its way through private or semiprivate groups on social media, then gains traction on Reddit or YouTube before finally emerging into mainstream social-media platforms like X, Facebook, and Instagram.[39] Breaking down the networks that power the spread of that disinformation might require thousands of actions against individual users. The ability to target any one user might pose real challenges. It would, as a starting matter, require knowledge of identity. But both inauthentic bots that mimic human behavior through programming and deceptive accounts that strategically adopt personas of individuals from marginalized groups are regularly deployed to amplify messages and shape political discourse.[40] Moreover, real human social-media users may shield their identities through pseudonyms or more sophisticated tactics that obscure a user's IP address or geographic location.[41] Bringing a suit against an unknown defendant is possible but not always practical, and plaintiffs may not be able to justify the expense of such extensive discovery.[42] Additionally, pursuing action against an unknown defendant runs the risk that revealing the defendant's identity may defeat jurisdiction or lead to the conclusion that the individual lacks the personal resources to pay out damages in the event of a successful claim.[43] Individual social-media users are likely not attractive targets for defamation suits because they lack the assets to pay damages,[44] and the platforms themselves are statutorily immune from most defamation suits under Section 230 of the Communications Decency Act.[45] Thus,

[38] *See* Darrell M. West, *How to Combat Fake News and Disinformation*, BROOKINGS (Dec. 18, 2017), https://perma.cc/XNH6-ZDGY (noting the link between disinformation and "the likelihood that people will engage in worse behavior if they believe their actions are anonymous and not likely to be made public").

[39] Claire Wardle, *5 Lessons for Reporting in an Age of Disinformation*, FIRST DRAFT (Dec. 27, 2018), https://perma.cc/9XDG-5VSR; Alice Marwick & Rebecca Lewis, *Media Manipulation and Disinformation Online* 27, DATA & SOC'Y RSCH. INST. (May 15, 2017), https://perma.cc/HCY7-SRYE (noting the disinformation goals of advancing ideology and earning money through advertising revenue).

[40] Brian Friedberg & Joan Donovan, *On the Internet, Nobody Knows You're a Bot: Pseudonymous Influence Operations and Networked Social Movements*, 6 J. DESIGN & SCI. (Aug. 7, 2019), https://perma.cc/98RE-UCCU; Matthew Hindman & Vlad Barash, *Disinformation, 'Fake News' and Influence Campaigns on Twitter* 16, KNIGHT FOUND. (Oct. 2018), https://perma.cc/AB8A-635V (noting the proliferation of academic research documenting the role of bots in promoting fake news).

[41] *See* Friedberg & Donovan, *supra* note 40.

[42] Erik P. Lewis, *Unmasking "Anon12345": Applying an Appropriate Standard When Private Citizens Seek the Identity of Anonymous Internet Defamation Defendants*, 2009 U. ILL. L. REV. 947, 953–54.

[43] *Id.*

[44] Steven Seidenberg, *Lies and Libel: Fake News Lacks Straightforward Cure*, ABA J. (July 1, 2017, 12:15 AM), https://perma.cc/UCQ5-2BDQ (noting that many potential defendants "lack sufficient funds to justify bringing lawsuits against them.").

[45] 47 U.S.C. § 230.

the adjustment to *Sullivan* that Justice Gorsuch floats as an anti-disinformation, pro-democracy tool is unlikely to be effective against many of the key targets. In a wide array of disinformation cases, defamation suits are simply the wrong tool for the job.

8.5 PRESERVING THE PRESS FUNCTION

The actual likely targets of such suits? News organizations, which carry libel insurance and have more assets, and so are much more susceptible to the kind of situation *Sullivan* squarely addresses – defamation suits used by the powerful to intimidate and silence their critics.[46]

Thus, it is not merely the case that an unwinding of *Sullivan* is a poor instrument for addressing the concerns that are at stake in the social-media disinformation crisis. After all, to say that it is not a full solution does not mean that it might not be a partial one worthy of consideration. But weighed against these weak benefits are some staggering costs to the operation of the press function, which has to be a part of the equation if the goal is to reduce disinformation and preserve the discourse central to democracy.

Defamation law is a tool that is not particularly viable against the online mobs of coordinated lies, but that will, without the carefully crafted constitutional buffers from *Sullivan*, increase the burden on those that are financially and professionally invested in providing accurate information to the polity. Removing those protections, then, would not only fail to meaningfully advance Justice Gorsuch's anti-disinformation and pro-democracy goals, but actively harm them.

Performers of the press function are among the rare remaining information producers with information-production models that center on building trust, maintaining professional standards, and serving as a watchdog with an accountability mission. The press function, performed in both its traditional and its evolving structures, is invaluable to democratic self-governance.[47] This is because press communicators are among the most likely to have norms of investigating, verifying, and contextualizing material for audiences[48] and to have reader and viewer

[46] Richard Tofel & Jeremy Kutner, *A Response to Justice Gorsuch, in New York Times v. Sullivan: The Case for Preserving an Essential Precedent* (2022), https://perma.cc/VY3G-LLZ6 ("In the realm of litigation, the 'optimal legal strategy' for publishers who cannot afford to be sued is, and has been, to be less aggressive in coverage. For those who still can afford it, i.e., can afford rapidly rising libel insurance rates and deductibles, the optimal strategy is to practice journalism in a way that minimizes the combined cost of insurance and litigation itself.").

[47] *See* Erin Carroll, *Promoting Journalism as Method*, 12 DREXEL L. REV. 691 (2020).

[48] RonNell Andersen Jones & Lisa Grow Sun, *Freedom of the Press in Post-Truthism America*, 98 WASH. U. L. REV 419 (2020) (describing key components of the constitutional press function); RonNell Andersen Jones, *Press Speakers and the First Amendment Rights of Listeners*, 90 U. COLO. L. REV. 499 (2019) (arguing press speakers engage in special institutional First Amendment activities on behalf of audiences).

relationships that require them to hold themselves accountable and "show their work."[49]

Beyond this, the press has been responsible for some of the most vital fact-checking[50] and falsehood-countering tools of our time, actively *correcting* disinformation about public health,[51] politics,[52] and other topics important to public discourse and democracy.[53] Certainly, our growing understanding of disinformation (and of the audiences that are groomed to believe it) makes clear that simple counter-information and exposure alone are inadequate weapons for this battle. But it remains the case that the press performs those functions Justice Gorsuch highlights as crucial to democracy.[54] In response to the tsunami of lies, news organizations are combatting the spread of disinformation with good journalism. This press function includes investigative work that reveals the organized disinformation efforts that are of such concern to Justice Gorsuch[55] and that exposes the

[49] *See, e.g.*, Christoph Koettl, *Satellite Images and Shadow Analysis: How the Times Verifies Eyewitness Videos*, N.Y. Times (Sept. 4, 2018); *Policies and Standards*, Wash. Post, https://perma.cc/HZ5W-M5AZ; Sarah Matthews et al., *A Reporter's Guide to Pre-Publication Review*, Reps. Comm. for Freedom Press, https://perma.cc/4FK2-WBPM.

[50] The Pulitzer Prize-winning site PolitiFact originated as an effort by the staff of the *Tampa Bay Times* to fact-check claims made in the lead-up to the 2008 election. Angie Drobnic Holan, *The Principles of the Truth-O-Meter: PolitiFact's Methodology for Independent Fact-Checking*, PolitiFact (Apr. 18, 2022), https://perma.cc/P6JY-SKL4. The site now runs as a nonprofit fact-checking engine under the *Time*' parent company, the Poynter Institute, and partners with media outlets across the U.S. to spearhead state-level fact-checking sites. For example, Texas's site is supported by the work of journalists from the *Austin American-Statesman, Houston Chronicle*, and *San Antonio News-Express*; the *Daily Iowan* provides support for its state site; Capital Public Radio for California's; *Buffalo News* for New York; the *Detroit Free Press* for Michigan; and the *Vermont Digger* for Vermont. *Texas*, PolitiFact, https://perma.cc/37FX-RRSX; *Iowa*, PolitiFact, https://perma.cc/VS8L-KJ22; *California*, PolitiFact, https://perma.cc/WY7L-64SV; *New York*, PolitiFact, https://perma.cc/6YNL-ZES3.

[51] *See, e.g.*, Valerie Pavilonis, *Fact Check: Claim About Growing Number of Diseases Exaggerates, Omits Context*, USA Today (Feb. 22, 2022, 1:07 PM), https://perma.cc/FXH3-RQFN; Reuters Fact Check, *Fact Check–No Evidence Some Covid-19 Vaccines Increase Risk of HIV Infection*, Reuters (Feb. 18, 2022, 1:09 PM), https://perma.cc/K6SR-BTGN; Glenn Kessler, *How the Falsehood of Athletes Dying of Coronavirus Vaccines Spread*, Wash. Post (Feb. 1, 2022, 3:00 AM), https://perma.cc/4222-DDSN; Maggie Astor, *No, Other People's Covid Vaccines Cannot Disrupt Your Menstrual Cycle*, N.Y. Times (Sept. 13, 2021), https://perma.cc/VS4T-SCZT.

[52] *See, e.g.*, PolitiFact, https://perma.cc/Y29A-HAQU; Glenn Kessler, *Fact Checker: The Truth behind the Rhetoric*, Wash. Post, https://perma.cc/5WET-3WBP.

[53] *See, e.g.*, Tiffany Hsu, *Tracking Viral Misinformation*, N.Y. Times (Feb. 24, 2022); *Fact Check*, USA Today, https://perma.cc/L2K2-GJTG.

[54] *See* Chip Scanlan, *Writers at Work: The Process Approach to Newswriting*, Poynter. (Aug. 25, 2002), https://perma.cc/4GZ5-4Q3S (describing the general process for newsgathering and writing); *SPJ Code of Ethics*, Soc'y Pro. Journalists (Sept. 6, 2014), https://perma.cc/7VN6-8M4V (describing the ethical standards guiding newswriting).

[55] For example, in 2016, journalists broke the story of a group of Macedonian bloggers responsible for at least 140 U.S.-politics websites propagating false and misleading content, revealed American connections to the network, and exposed a sophisticated strategy to sway public opinion in the lead-up to the 2016 U.S. presidential election. Craig Silverman & Lawrence

origins of conspiracy theories.[56] Americans are aware of the scope and gravity of the risk of disinformation in part because of the operation of this function.[57] A paring back of *Sullivan* protections, making it easier to shut down critical reporting, will make it more difficult for press organizations to do the work necessary to reveal these massive disinformation operations. The press exposes the existence of disinformation and then works to remedy its harm. At its best, the press function includes research and reporting that grapples with widely circulated false information,[58] provides accurate and well-sourced truth, and exposes the harmful consequences of the lies.[59]

This may be the worst possible moment to strip the core protections for those performing this press function. Organizations that are working against disinformation with real newsgathering efforts are already seriously struggling. "[S]uccessive technological and economic assaults have destroyed the for-profit business model that sustained local journalism in this country for two centuries."[60] Critically important democracy-enhancing local news is especially financially imperiled, in ways that have been accelerated by the COVID-19 crisis.[61] Organizations that engage in *reporting* have lost most of their advertising dollars to corporations like Google and Facebook that engage primarily in *repeating* – *including* repeating of disinformation. Citizens in a democracy rely on performers of the press function to help them "stay connected to and informed about what is happening in their backyards – especially in their schools, their governments, and other critical institutions and infrastructures,"[62] and in the absence of this information, streams of disinformation fill the void. Performers of the press function today not only have

Alexander, *How Teens in the Balkans Are Duping Trump Supporters with Fake News*, BUZZFEED NEWS (Nov. 3, 2016, 5:02 PM), https://perma.cc/4FQ2-E6UU; Craig Silverman et al., *Macedonia's Pro-Trump Fake News Industry Had American Links, and Is under Investigation for Possible Russia Ties*, BUZZFEED NEWS (July 18, 2018, 10:24 AM), https://perma.cc/Z3X9-LH5A.

56 Morning Edition, *The Origins of the Seth Rich Conspiracy Theory*, NPR (July 11, 2019, 5:22 AM), https://perma.cc/43KK-NASN.

57 *See, e.g.*, FRONTLINE, *The Plot to Overturn the Election*, PBS (Mar. 29, 2022), https://perma.cc/K8Z4-DX88 (outlining a ProPublica/Frontline project to "trace the sources of misinformation about the 2020 election, demonstrating how a handful of people have had an outsized impact on the current U.S. crisis of democratic legitimacy").

58 David Klepper, *Conspiracy Theories Paint Fraudulent Reality of Jan. 6 Riot*, AP NEWS (Dec. 31, 2021), https://perma.cc/9MGQ-48UH.

59 *See, e.g.*, Vanessa Romo, *Poison Control Centers Are Fielding a Surge of Ivermectin Overdose Calls*, NPR (Sept. 4, 2021, 7:01 AM), https://perma.cc/AB6K-588E.

60 *See* PENELOPE MUSE ABERNATHY, CTR. FOR INNOVATION & SUSTAINABILITY IN LOCAL MEDIA, NEWS DESERTS AND GHOST NEWSPAPERS: WILL LOCAL NEWS SURVIVE? (2020), https://perma.cc/2DWX-ETXX ("In only two decades, successive technological and economic assaults have destroyed the for-profit business model that sustained local journalism in this country for two centuries. Hundreds of news organizations – century-old newspapers as well as nascent digital sites – have vanished.").

61 *Id.*

62 VICTOR PICKARD, DEMOCRACY WITHOUT JOURNALISM: CONFRONTING THE MISINFORMATION SOCIETY (2020).

fewer resources to engage in important coverage of local and national government and other powerful people and organizations,[63] but also face steep rises in libel defense costs that they are no longer well-resourced enough to shoulder. The cost of defending a libel suit can easily wipe out a local news organization.[64]

All of this adds up to exactly the worry the unanimous *Sullivan* Court expressed: that freedom of speech and press would not be exercised, purely because the press speaker was unable to risk the financial consequences. Justice Gorsuch himself noted in *Berisha* that the economic model that supported reporters and newsrooms has eroded. He suggests this should lead to less protection in defamation actions, but he may well have it backwards. This is not the moment to be reconsidering the valuable *Sullivan* protection, if anti-disinformation and pro-democracy goals are taken seriously.

To be sure, press speakers are not uniformly the heroes of the disinformation story. As public confidence in the media hits record lows and the media is increasingly distrusted as overly partisan, its capacity to counter disinformation may be diminished.[65] Indeed, a general decline of public faith in authority, expertise, and the traditional institutions of knowledge and democracy means the role of the press function is itself in a state of flux.[66] Moreover, new scholarship is helping to paint a fuller picture of the interrelationship between some mainstream media outlets and the spread of disinformation. At least some research points to asymmetric political polarization within the media ecosystem that produces a "propaganda feedback loop" far less governed by the reality-check dynamic of professional journalistic norms.[67] Additionally, some have suggested that even more traditional journalistic organizations aiming for neutral, transpartisan newsgathering have become tools for the spread of distorted narratives. Sometimes this happens as traditional journalists, in the name of objectivity, engage in performative neutrality that amplifies disinformation.[68] Sometimes mainstream media outlets spread

[63] *See* Michael Ewens, Arpit Gupta & Sabrina T. Howell, Local Journalism under Private Equity (Oct. 10, 2021) (unpublished manuscript), https://perma.cc/3EW3-HXW3 (tracking the change of news composition away from information about local governance and the resulting decline in participation in local elections).

[64] Meagan Flynn, *A Small-Town Iowa Newspaper Brought Down a Cop. His Failed Lawsuit Has Now Put the Paper in Financial Peril*, WASH. POST (Oct. 10, 2019, 6:41 AM), https://perma.cc/CB8C-LY5H (discussing a local newspaper forced to reduce its publication schedule and engage in fundraising after being sued for defamation for accurately reporting about a police officer).

[65] *See* Megan Brenan, *Media Confidence Ratings at Record Lows*, GALLUP (July 18, 2022), https://perma.cc/CC3S-GYM4.

[66] *See* ASPEN INST., COMM'N ON INFORMATION DISORDER, DECLINE OF TRUST INSTITUTIONS (2021), https://perma.cc/4BPS-Z6NL.

[67] YOCHAI BENKLER, ROBERT FARIS & HAL ROBERTS, NETWORK PROPAGANDA: MANIPULATION, DISINFORMATION, AND RADICALIZATION IN AMERICAN POLITICS (2018) (addressing the ways that the right-wing media is more susceptible to disinformation and the spread of identity-confirming falsehoods).

[68] *See id.*

disinformation into the wider public consciousness merely by telling the potentially newsworthy story of the existence of conspiracy groups and their lies, only to have the coverage itself become a tool for the spread of those lies. Because social-media algorithms rate mainstream journalistic sources as more credible, news stories that in any way reinforce conspiracy theories may be filtered less and have a unique power as a vector for virality.[69] Likewise, because users often read only headlines when scrolling through social-media timelines, researchers are finding that users are sharing journalism from the mainstream media to spread and legitimate disinformation even when the news story itself does not support the lie.[70]

Plainly, there is much work to be done if we are to address all of these issues and advance pro-democracy and anti-disinformation goals. But again, rolling back the *Sullivan* doctrine is no way to do so. Constitutional protection in defamation actions is not some lever that one can pull to address these information-distribution issues. It does not speak to most outrage-media issues, does not solve most matters of propaganda masquerading as news, and is not a useful tool for addressing most confusion and magnification issues. The scope and contours of these harms, as others have noted, "are problems of amplification – amplification by social media platforms and amplification by journalists," and the complex set of norms, regulatory incentives, and laws to address them are going to have to focus on "the architecture of our public square,"[71] not a doctrine that balances reputation and public dialogue.

Justice Gorsuch is right that democracy cannot afford to ignore the imminent crisis of disinformation. But democracy also cannot afford to fruitlessly hamstring the few remaining entities making press-function contributions to its public discourse. The pattern of powerful people attempting to use defamation as a tool to punish and deter critics has not diminished.[72] If anything, recent examples provide forceful evidence that the threat continues to loom large. At this crucial moment, when the preservation of the press function is a matter of immediate concern, the facts on the ground signal that reconsideration of *Sullivan* will not be democracy-enhancing. It will be democracy-threatening.

[69] *See, e.g.*, Orestis Papakyriakopoulos, Juan Carlos Medina Serrano & Simon Hegelich, *The Spread of COVID-19 Conspiracy Theories on Social Media and the Effect of Content Moderation*, Harv. Kennedy Sch. Misinformation Rev. (Aug. 18, 2020), https://perma.cc/CB53-NJKD (finding that mainstream URLs used as evidence for the truthfulness of conspiracy theories are shared up to four times as often as fake-news sites).

[70] *See, e.g.*, Yariv Tsfati et al., *Causes and Consequences of Mainstream Media Dissemination of Fake News: Literature Review and Synthesis*, 44 Annals Int'l Comm. Ass'n 157–73 (2020).

[71] *See* Nabiha Syed, *Sullivan Is Not the Problem*, Knight First Amend. Inst. (Nov. 15, 2021), https://perma.cc/HGV4-AK46.

[72] *See* Justin Wise, *Trump Escalates Fight against Press with Libel Lawsuits*, The Hill (Mar. 8, 2020), https://perma.cc/V7T9-U57X; Trevor Timm, *Trump's Many, Many Threats to Sue the Press since Launching His Campaign*, Colum. Journalism Rev. (Oct. 3, 2016), https://perma.cc/D3QB-G6WA. *See also* J. Clara Chan, *Devin Nunes Sues CNN for $435 Million-Plus in Defamation Suit*, The Wrap (Dec. 3, 2019, 3:38 PM), https://perma.cc/R7FM-GZ5W.

9

Privacy Rights, Internet Mug Shots, and a Right to Be Forgotten

Amy Gajda

9.1 INTRODUCTION

In the spring of 2022, visitors to the Smoking Gun website would find a challenging "game, where [one's] wasted time [was] well spent."[1]

"For today's 'Friday Photo Fun,'" the website explained, "readers must examine five mug shots and match up the respective defendants with the crime for which they were arrested." There appeared five photos of sorry-looking individuals arrested for crimes both serious and not so much. A tattooed white man nabbed by police for narcotics possession; a black woman arrested for speeding; three other individuals arrested for driving while intoxicated, assault and battery, and grand theft, respectively. The match-the-mug-shot-to-the-crime game appeared every Friday.

The Smoking Gun gathered those police booking photos through freedom-of-information laws, statutes designed to give the public access to important governmental information. For a long time in the United States, mug shots have been a part of such governmental openness: The thought was that the public should know who'd been arrested and on what grounds, and how they'd looked at the time of arrest in order to ensure that police had not battered them. Mug shots also helped to avoid mistaken identity, access proponents said. In the past, it was mainly journalists who were those proponents, who would receive the images from police and later assess them for newsworthiness, publishing only those they thought relevant for public view.

Today, it's not only journalists who are interested in mug shots. As the Smoking Gun matching game shows, other types of websites publish the images for reasons beyond news value; some have no focus on news value at all.

This chapter considers mug shots and other once-public information about those arrested by police. It finds that, in direct response to worries about internet-based

[1] Smoking Gun, https://perma.cc/38FV-2B8B.

abuse and online longevity, legislatures and courts have taken action to shield such information from public view. It notes that journalism has shifted to include mug shots in reporting less often and, in some cases, to remove from public databases those mug shots published as a part of older news stories. Given such shifts, this chapter predicts that, soon, most mug shots will no longer be made available through public-records requests and those whose mug shots are published could one day bring a valid publication invasion-of-privacy claim. Finally, given such shifts and potential shifts, it predicts one's *entire* criminal past, including one's older mug shot, could one day be even more strongly protected on privacy grounds.

9.2 TWO SHIFTS IN LAW REGARDING MUG-SHOT PRIVACY

As ubiquitous as mug shots may seem today online and otherwise, at the turn of the twentieth century, courts routinely protected mug shots on privacy grounds. In short, there is support in early case law for a right to privacy in booking photos.

Consider *Joyce v. York*,[2] an 1899 case from New York in which the court suggested even a habitual criminal could have an action against police for including his photograph in a so-called rogue's gallery published for others to view. The court wrote that the "wrong [was] in the nature of a libel,"[3] which back then meant at times that anything either true or false that harmed reputation could lead to liability if published. How one looked at the time of arrest, that court suggested, impacted the way others perceived the person, even if the photograph and the information regarding the arrest were accurate.

In *Itzkovitch v. Whitaker*, too, a decision from 1905, the Louisiana Supreme Court forbade police from circulating an arrestee's booking photograph even though the man was notorious for running a pawn shop and had been arrested several times. "Everyone who does not violate the law can insist upon being let alone (the right of privacy)," the court wrote, and indicated that an individual not yet convicted would be protected from having his booking photograph published to others too.[4] By 1906, the Louisiana court ordered police to return to the not-yet-convicted arrestee all photographic negatives of his mug shot and "to erase and cancel all record entries of the photographs and of the measurement made of the plaintiff" too.[5]

Judges in other states agreed; most courts that had decided lawsuits involving booking photos back then found privacy rights in them,[6] especially – but not

2 People ex rel. Joyce v. York, 27 Misc. 658 (N.Y. Sup. Ct. 1899).

3 *Id.* at 659.

4 Itzkovitch v. Whitaker, 115 La. 479, 481 (La. 1905).

5 Itzkovitch v. Whitaker, 117 La. 708, 709–10 (La. 1905).

6 State *ex rel.* Mavity v. Tyndall, 66 N.E.2d 755, 762 (Ind. 1956) ("Is the placing of appellant's picture in the 'rogues' gallery' described in the complaint so serious a violation of appellant's right to privacy as to justify judicial protection? Most of the cases so hold and we are constrained to follow them.").

exclusively – before the arrestee's conviction. Those states included Indiana,[7] Maryland,[8] Missouri,[9] and New Jersey.[10] Courts were especially concerned about the lasting harm that such images would have on a person's reputation no matter the outcomes of the underlying criminal case. "Upon [an arrestee's] vindication," the New Jersey court wrote in explanation, "the circulation of such information [] could not be undone."[11]

Then, there came a shift in that sort of privacy-protective awareness regarding mug shots. In the 1960s and 1970s, as federal and state governments opened more of their files to the public view as a measure of support for the public's right to know about government matters, mug shots and other arrest information became more accessible, and privacy protections in such information seemed less of a concern. Newspapers back then *wanted* such information so that they might publish news about certain arrests and include, as part of that reporting, the visual images of those charged with particularly noteworthy crimes. They argued it would be best for the public: Community members' minds would be eased if they saw the person who had been placed in custody for a heinous crime, for one. Moreover, as the use of illustrations and thereafter photographs grew more commonplace in newspapers, readers began expecting to see such things. Legislatures and courts came to trust that such ethics-abiding publishers would not make criminal information public unless nearly everyone would agree that it was something the public should know; the personal privacy concerns of those arrested for murder, for example, seemed far less important than the press's freedom to report on such a crime. In short, back then, at a time when the word "publisher" was nearly synonymous with ethics-abiding journalism, the public's right of access trumped any individual's right to privacy.

A good example of that sensibility is the 1996 Sixth Circuit's decision in *Detroit Free Press v. Department of Justice*.[12] There, the *Detroit Free Press* had asked for the mug shots of individuals arrested on federal charges – they were accused of having ties to organized crime – and the appellate court agreed that such access would be appropriate. The judges of the Sixth Circuit, however, first explicitly rejected the argument that the release of such images would be harmful to those arrested even though they had not yet been convicted.[13] Instead, such release could at times be *helpful* to the individuals, the court reasoned, suggesting that published booking images could help reveal mistaken identity or police use of excessive force.[14]

7 State *ex rel.* Mavity v. Tyndall, 66 N.E.2d 755 (Ind. 1956).
8 Downs v. Swann, 73 A. 653 (Md. 1909).
9 State *ex rel.* Reed v. Harris, 153 S.W.2d 834 (Mo. 1941).
10 McGovern v. Van Riper, 43 A.2d 514 (N.J. Ch. Ct. 1945).
11 *Id.* at 525.
12 73 F.3d 93 (6th Cir. 1996).
13 *Id.* at 97.
14 *Id.* at 98.

Second, the court decided, the privacy concerns of the arrestees were of absolutely no concern. They had "already [been] indicted," the court wrote, and "had already made court appearances after their arrests" and, during that process, their names had been made public. Therefore, the court reasoned, the additional release of their mug shots implicated no privacy interests whatsoever because some in the public knew them or knew of them from such coverage already, and at least family and friends knew what they looked like; any release "could not reasonably be expected to constitute an unwarranted invasion of personal privacy" on such facts.[15]

By that point, the Supreme Court had suggested in *Paul v. Davis*[16] that an individual whose mug shot had been included as part of a list of shoplifters had no valid constitutional claim against the police for its release even though he had not been convicted of that or of any crime. It wasn't the perfect parallel because the justices had also suggested that a defamation claim at the state level might be possible, but the rejection of the constitutional claim was noteworthy nonetheless.

The World Wide Web was already hitting the mainstream when the Sixth Circuit's opinion came down. Suddenly, the word "publisher" meant not only an ethics-abiding newspaper, like the *Detroit Free Press*, but anyone with a computer who could publish anything to the world with the click of a mouse.

Those newfangled sorts of publishers eventually recognized that the public had a real interest not only in the more-newsworthy mug shots but in *all* mug shots. Websites appeared that published photos of all arrested; some of those websites suggested that those who wanted the images taken down could pay to make that happen.

Soon, in response to such publications and the clicks that they generated, ethics-abiding newspapers, no doubt feeling they had to keep up, similarly began to publish pages of the images of those arrested with little regard to the news value. Mug shots had become a "game changer," some newspapers reported, "the most popular thing on the website" and therefore a driver of internet traffic to what might otherwise be a news site in economic trouble.[17] Eventually, 40 percent of newspapers that moved online would publish mug-shot galleries.[18]

And so, in 1999, just three years after the Sixth Circuit in *Detroit Free Press* found no privacy interests in mug shots because many already knew what arrestees looked like, a federal court in Louisiana switched gears and suggested that even a public figure – a man who had owned a National Football League team and was known widely for his work in the NFL, a man arrested in conjunction with an investigation into government corruption – would have privacy protections for his mug shot. In its

[15] *Id.*

[16] 424 U.S. 693 (1976).

[17] Corey Hutchins, *Mugshot Galleries Might Be a Web-Traffic Magnet. Does that Justify Publishing Them?*, Colum. Journalism Rev. (Oct. 24, 2018).

[18] Keri Blakinger, *Newsrooms Rethink a Crime Reporting Staple: The Mugshot*, Marshall Project (Feb. 11, 2020), https://perma.cc/47J6-NTU6.

decision in *Times Picayune Publishing Group v. United States Department of Justice*,[19] the court wrote that mug shots were more than just photographs, and for a few reasons: They were linked with the "notorious"; they recorded "unflattering facial expressions"; and "arguably most humiliating of all, a sign under the accused face" with a criminal identification number.[20] "A mug shot preserves in its unique and visually powerful way, the subject individual's brush with the law for posterity," the judge wrote, and its "stigmatizing effect can last well beyond the actual criminal proceedings."[21] Current dissemination could trigger future misuse by rivals, the court reasoned, specifically worrying what might become of the mug shot in future years, "including the reappearance of [a] mug shot in the media," leading to renewed personal embarrassment and discomfort for the depicted individual.[22]

In line with that, in 2016, twenty years after its rejection of privacy in mug shots, the Sixth Circuit sitting en banc changed its mind and overruled its earlier suggestion that there were no privacy rights in booking photos.[23] The court's opinion reflected those same concerns about internet publishers that had been hinted at in the *Times Picayune* decision. These mug shots, these "[e]mbarrassing and humiliating facts," the court wrote, that "connect[ed] individual[s] to criminality," decidedly implicated those individuals' privacy interests.[24] Now, in an internet age, "[a] booking photo cast a long, damaging shadow over the depicted individual."[25] Now, the forever internet meant that arrested individuals might never escape their criminal pasts – meaning that the modern world was far different, the judges wrote, from what existed two decades before:

> In 1996 . . . booking photos appeared on television or in the newspaper and then, for all practical purposes, disappeared. Today, an idle internet search reveals the same booking photo that once would have required a trip to the local library's microfiche collection. In fact, mug-shot websites collect and display booking photos from decades-old arrests [and] [p]otential employers and other acquaintances may easily access booking photos on these websites, hampering the depicted individual's professional and personal prospects.[26]

"In 1996," the Sixth Circuit judges continued, "this court could not have known or expected that a booking photo could haunt the depicted individual for decades."[27] And so, even though the images at issue in 2016 involved police officers who had been arrested for drug crimes and police brutality – a decidedly newsworthy story –

[19] 37 F. Supp. 2d 472 (E.D. La. 1999).
[20] *Id.* at 476.
[21] *Id.*
[22] *Id.* at 479.
[23] Detroit Free Press v. U.S. DOJ, 829 F.3d 478 (6th Cir. 2016).
[24] *Id.* at 481.
[25] *Id.* at 482.
[26] *Id.* at 482–83.
[27] *Id.* at 485.

the court overruled its earlier decision. "The internet and social media," the court wrote, had by then "worked unpredictable changes in the way photographs [were] stored and shared." Mug shots suddenly "no longer ha[d] a shelf life" and the "humiliating, embarrassing [and] painful"[28] images would remain forever accessible even though the individual had changed their ways. The judges decided that those depicted had privacy interests in them after all.

By that point, following the lead of the *Times Picayune* court, two federal appellate courts had similarly ruled in favor of some level of privacy in mug shots.[29] There was also strong language in three key cases from the Supreme Court that reflected those same privacy concerns, language made ever more relevant in an internet age, and some courts deciding mug-shot cases shifted to rely in part on these three cases and not on the breezy mention of mug shots in *Paul v. Davis*.

First, *Doe v. McMillan*,[30] not a mug-shot case but one involving concerns about the long-lasting effects of minors' criminal histories. There, the Supreme Court suggested in 1973 that seventh-grade students named in a congressional report investigating a "troubled school" had privacy interests in their specific instances of "deviant conduct" and their "criminal violations."[31] The justices worried in *McMillan* specifically about potential future harm for those students who would in a few years become adults: With the publication of such material, the justices wrote, the students' "future careers" would be implicated. Therefore, while the Speech and Debate Clause would protect Congress's own publication of the material, the justices reasoned, it would *not* protect "a private republication of documents" containing such information even though the information had been "introduced and made public at a committee hearing" and even though "the hearing was unquestionably part of the legislative process."[32] Such material, though made public, "would ... invite gratuitous injury to citizens for little if any public purpose."[33]

Concurring Justices Douglas, Brennan, and Marshall even more explicitly worried what the public revelation of such information would do to the children in later years. "We all should be painfully aware of the potentially devastating effects" of such government-collected data, they wrote. "Arrests ... [and a]cts of juvenile delinquency are permanently recorded and they and other alleged misdeeds or indiscretions may be devastating to a person in later years when he has outgrown

[28] *Id.* (Cole, J., concurring).
[29] *See* Karantsalis v. U.S. Dep't of Justice, 635 F.3d 497 (11th Cir. 2011); World Publ'g Co. v. U.S. Dep't of Justice, 672 F.3d 825 (10th Cir. 2012).
[30] 412 U.S. 306 (1973).
[31] *Id.* at 308–09 n.1.
[32] *Id.* at 313–14.
[33] *Id.* at 317.

youthful indiscretions and is trying to launch a professional career or move into a position where steadfastness is required."[34]

Second, *Department of the Air Force v. Rose.*[35] There, in 1975, the Court similarly worried that information that had once been released at the Air Force Academy – the names of those convicted of violating Honor Code provisions not to steal, among other things[36] – would lead to harm to the individuals and therefore held that that information should be redacted from any reports turned over to the public. Those who once knew that information "may have wholly forgotten" it, the Court wrote in explanation, and the "risk to the privacy interests" of such an individual, especially one who remained in the military "cannot be rejected as trivial."[37] Such "privacy values" included not only "practical disabilities, such as the loss of employment or friends," but "lifelong embarrassment, perhaps disgrace" as well.[38]

And, finally, *United States Department of Justice v. Reporters Committee for Freedom of the Press.*[39] So-called "rap sheets" containing an individual's "history of arrests, charges, convictions and incarcerations"[40] could be protected on privacy grounds, the Justices decided in 1989, even though the information had once been made public by police and was therefore in effect part of the public record. "The privacy interest in a rap sheet is substantial," the Court wrote, and especially so given the powerful memories in computers that could include information "that would otherwise have surely been forgotten" by people.[41] "Plainly there is a vast difference between the public records that might be found after a diligent search of courthouse files, county archives, and local police stations," the Justices wrote, the more easily accessed "computerized summary located in a single clearinghouse of information."[42] "If a cadet has a privacy interest in past discipline that was once public but may have been 'wholly forgotten,'" the Court wrote, referring to *Rose*, "the ordinary citizen surely has a similar interest in the aspects of his or her criminal history that may have been wholly forgotten."

It's true that all five of those cases – *Detroit Free Press*, *Times Picayune*, *McMillan*, *Rose*, and *Reporters Committee* – *mainly* focused on *access* and on the information about past and present crimes that would be released to the public. But, given such powerfully protective language, a potential right to privacy in mug shots and other arrest information is arguably broader than access. Today, there's also a suggestion that stretches beyond *McMillan*: that the right to privacy in such information could extend to the *publication* of such information as well.

[34] *Id.* at 329–30.
[35] 425 U.S. 352 (1975).
[36] *Id.* at 358–59.
[37] *Id.* at 381.
[38] *Id.* at 376–77 (citing in part the Second Circuit decision in the case, 495 F.2d at 267).
[39] 489 U.S. 749 (1989).
[40] *Id.* at 752.
[41] *Id.* at 771.
[42] *Id.* at 764.

That privacy interest is reflected in the privacy sections of the Second Restatement of Torts, published in 1977. In "Publicity Given to Private Life,"[43] the Restatement authors specifically suggest that one's criminal past may well be protected on privacy grounds, that "a lapse of time" is "a factor to be considered" in such a privacy claim.[44] "Jean Valjean," an example reads, "an ex-convict who was convicted and served a sentence for robbery, has changed his name, concealed his identity, and for twenty years has led an obscure, respectable and useful life in another city far removed."[45] Any newspaper that would ferret out his criminal history and publish it, the Restatement says, could well be liable for invading Valjean's privacy.[46]

Moreover, the Restatement authors suggested that there would also be privacy in some of "a man's . . . past history that he would rather forget."[47]

Such interests – a right to privacy in truth that includes past information about an arrest; what some might consider in a colloquial sense a right to be forgotten – did not come out of the blue. As early as 1884, a court wrote that it would be a "barbarous doctrine" should newspapers be allowed to report anything truthful that they wanted, including "crimes long since forgotten and perhaps expiated by years of remorse and sincere reform."[48] Well more than a century later, the Eleventh Circuit wrote in a related sense that "timeliness . . . boundaries . . . circumscribe the breadth of public scrutiny to [an] incident of public interest" and that, therefore, the nude photographs of a murder victim taken more than twenty years before the crime had no relation to news coverage of it; those photos were not related in time, the court held,[49] and any other holding would "debase[] the very concept of a right to privacy."

This concept made headlines when the European Court of Justice ordered an accurate but ten-year-old newspaper article about a man's debt proceedings de-indexed so that it would be much more difficult to find during an internet search.[50] The court was especially worried about protecting the man's attempt to turn his life around more fully. Besides, it reasoned, the news article was "inadequate," "no longer relevant," and "excessive" in relation to "the light of the time that has elapsed."

Somewhat in line with that, a number of recent court decisions in the United States contain similar concerns about older *criminal* information. In 2021, a federal judge in Pennsylvania ordered the website Mugshots.com to pay $150,000 to a

[43] Restatement (Second) of Torts § 652D (1977).
[44] *Id.* at cmt. k.
[45] *Id.* at cmt. k, illus. 26.
[46] *Id.*
[47] *Id.*
[48] State v. Bienvenu, 36 La. Ann. 378, 382 (La. 1884).
[49] Toffoloni v. LFB Publ'g Grp., 572 F.3d 1201 (11th Cir. 2009).
[50] Case C-131/12, Google Spain SL. v. Agencia Española de Protección de Datos, ECLI:EU:C:2014:317 (May 13, 2014).

former arrestee whose criminal record had been expunged.[51] The website's worldwide use of the man's mug shot from two decades before had significantly harmed his reputation among family and friends, the judge wrote, and instructed that the mug shot be removed.[52] "[I]n an age when it is a widespread practice for employers to conduct an online search on the background of prospective employees," the court reasoned, "any job application by [the man] would most likely entail revelation of the information posted about him online."[53]

In another case from six years before, a state court similarly ordered older criminal information be taken down.[54] Details about the man's criminal past, the court wrote, "are likely not newsworthy twenty-five years after the fact."[55]

Other modern courts have suggested that the release of private individuals' criminal records would be especially forbidden because "there might be little to offset the risk of adverse collateral consequences arising some such disclosure";[56] that police photo arrays should not be made public because "a significant privacy interest warrants protecting the identities of third parties included in the photo lineups" because the images convey the individuals' guilt;[57] that people featured on a website that charged money to have the mug shots removed had valid claims for misappropriation;[58] and that a person arrested on a misdemeanor charge whose booking photo appeared on the internet had a potential privacy claim against the sheriff for making the image public.[59]

And then, in 2018, the Eleventh Circuit found police liable for allowing cameras from the reality show *The First 48* to record images of an arrestee without his consent. The filming and broadcast constituted a seizure of the man's image, the court held, and violated his right to privacy; showing him walking down a police hallway and later being interrogated by police served no legitimate purpose. Thus, the authorities had violated the arrestee's constitutional rights and the court upheld his Section 1983 claim.[60]

In the case involving the sheriff's release of a mug shot, one decided in 2020, the plaintiff had relied in part on what the court said were "several recent federal cases analyzing the issue and determining that arrestees generally have rights to privacy with respect to their booking photos."[61] Those cases helped support the plaintiff's

51 Taha v. Bucks Cnty., 2021 U.S. Dist. Lexis 26961 (E.D. Pa. 2021).

52 *Id.* at *10.

53 *Id.*

54 Hartzell v. Cummings, No. 150103764, 2015 WL 7301962 (Pa. Ct. Com. Pl., Nov. 4, 2015).

55 *Id.* at *11.

56 Boston Globe Media Partners v. Dep't of Crim. Just. Info. Servs., 140 N.E.3d 923, 934 (Mass. 2019).

57 White v. City of Cleveland, 2020 U.S. Dist. Lexis 93919 (N.D. Ohio May 29, 2020).

58 Rogers v. JustMugshots.com, No. BC530194, 2015 WL 5838403 (Cal. Ct. App., Oct. 7, 2015).

59 City of Austin v. Doe, 2020 Tex. App. Lexis 10257 (Dec. 29, 2020).

60 Smart v. City of Miami, 740 Fed. App'x 952 (11th Cir. 2018).

61 *Id.* at *22.

argument that Texas state law prevented the release of mug shots as government information "considered to be confidential by law."[62]

A small number of states today limit access to booking photographs even more clearly. In Illinois, for example, one of the statutory exemptions to the freedom-of-information law says this:

> [A] law enforcement agency may not publish booking photographs, commonly known as "mugshots," on its social networking website in connection with civil offenses, petty offenses, business offenses, Class C misdemeanors, and Class B misdemeanors unless the booking photograph is posted to the social networking website to assist in the search for a missing person or to assist in the search for a fugitive, person of interest, or individual wanted in relation to a crime other than a petty offense, business offense, Class C misdemeanor, or Class B misdemeanor.[63]

If certain mug shots are no longer published online or otherwise, those legislators have reasoned, mocking websites will no longer be able to access them. Other states have passed laws that criminalize the practice of forcing individuals to pay for the removal of their mug shots from websites.[64]

9.3 A SHIFT IN JOURNALISM TOO

In the 2010s, the *Chicago Tribune* would routinely run a feature on its website. It was called "Mugs in the News" and it highlighted 100 people arrested by police throughout the Chicagoland area the day before. The crimes included the sensational, like rape and murder, but also the more mundane, like theft and burglary.[65]

Then, in 2021, the *Tribune* announced a major change, a shift to what it called "compassionate coverage." Not only had it decided not to publish its "Mugs in the News" feature anymore, it had decided to cut back significantly on the use of mug shots in its reporting, period. "Part of this is just plain fairness," editors wrote. "A lot of people" featured in such mug shots "will end up not being convicted," will be found not guilty, or will plead to lesser charges. Moreover, the use of such images "might reinforce racial stereotypes and amount to punitive coverage of people who enter the criminal justice system."[66]

Even more relevant to what might be considered a right for one's criminal past to be forgotten, *Tribune* editors suggested they were working to remove most of the mug shots from old news stories that are now accessible through archival databases. "[W]e have been removing some mug shots from older stories for months now," they

62 *Id.* at *14.
63 5 ILL. COMP. STAT. ANN. 140/2.15.
64 CAL. CIV. CODE § 1798.91.1(b).
65 This information is from Amy Gajda, *Mugshots and the Press-Privacy Dilemma*, 93 TUL. L. REV. 1199 (2019).
66 The information in this paragraph is from Colin McMahon, *How the Chicago Tribune Handles Police Booking Photos*, CHI. TRIB. (Feb. 10, 2021).

wrote, and would continue to "remove many of them as we come upon them." Decisions to publish versus not to publish, to take down or leave up, would be based on "high news value," the editors explained, including high-profile crimes, those involving a public figure, and those with some public-safety purpose.[67]

"The default," editors explained in 2021, was "not to use a mug shot."[68]

The *Chicago Tribune* is not the only newspaper to decide to do such a thing. The Marshall Project, a nonprofit news organization with the criminal justice system as its beat, suggested in 2020 that "faced with questions about the lasting impact of putting these photos on the internet, where they live forever, media outlets are increasingly doing away with the galleries of people on the worse days of their lives."[69]

"Legally, it's public record," one reporter explained, "but legal is not always right."[70]

9.4 THE FUTURE OF MUG SHOTS AND OTHER ONLINE CRIMINAL ARREST INFORMATION

That reporter who suggested in 2020 that mug shots were public records and that, therefore, publishers could publish them without concern for *legal* liability was mostly correct. Today, despite a growing number of court decisions and legislative enactments that hold otherwise in certain cases, in many places and in many situations, a mug shot is indeed a public record, and a news publisher need not worry about the legality of publishing it, especially in a decidedly newsworthy case.

But, given the shift toward some level of privacy in mug shots in law and in journalism, there is a strong likelihood that privacy protections for arrest information including mug shots will continue to increase.

This is for a couple of reasons. The first is that some legislatures and some courts have already put mug-shot-related privacy protections in place. The second reason is that the *law's* definition of privacy responds to *society's* definition of privacy. Consider the language from the Second Restatement of Torts for its "Publicity Given to Private Life," which identifies those times in which certain information is considered too private to be revealed. There, the Restatement provision reads, the "protection afforded to the plaintiff's interest in his privacy must be relative to the customs of the time and place" and to "the habits of his neighbors and fellow citizens."[71] "It is only when the publicity given to him is such that a reasonable

[67] *Id.*

[68] *Chicago Tribune Mug Shot Publication Guidelines*, Chi. Trib. (Feb. 9, 2021), https://perma.cc/PM5K-X65M.

[69] Blakinger, *supra* note 18.

[70] *Id.*

[71] Restatement (Second) of Torts § 652D (1977).

person would feel justified in feeling seriously aggrieved by it" that such an invasion of privacy claim is valid.

Today, it seems that a growing number of judges and journalists agree that such information about one's criminal past or present should be protected. Public sentiment is growing too. In 2020, 85 percent of Americans supported some aspect of a "right to be forgotten" and "more than half (56%) [said] all Americans should have the right to have negative media coverage about themselves removed from public search results." In the meantime, and relatedly, a "smaller share of Americans – though still about four-in-ten (39%) – think the same right should be applied to data collected by law enforcement, such as criminal records or mugshots."[72]

This suggests a growing sensibility that seemingly would protect certain criminal histories, and it means that one day, a reporter who suggests that publishers need not worry about publishing such materials because they are public documents could very well be wrong.

It's true that the Supreme Court's older jurisprudence, including *Florida Star v. B.J.F.*,[73] suggests that it would be unconstitutional to punish the publication of truthful information of public record – but the Justices explained back then that even that jurisprudence has its limits. "We do not hold that truthful publication is automatically constitutionally protected, or that there is no zone of personal privacy within which the State may protect the individual from intrusion by the press, or even that a State may never punish publication of the name of a victim of a sexual offense," the Court wrote in *Florida Star*, because there is "sensitivity and significance" in privacy interests that are as profound as the interest in a free press.

9.5 CONCLUSION

If journalism continues its trend of avoiding the use of mug shots and pushing for the removal of mug shots from its news databases, the only publications making use of mug shots could well be those that use them mostly to mock. If so, additional courts and additional legislatures – and additional members of the public – will surely continue to demand greater protection for mug shots on privacy grounds. And that means that at some point in the future, probably sooner rather than later, there will be no more public release of booking photographs of anyone, except perhaps in those cases in which an arrestee becomes an escapee or is wanted in some other way.

There is additional support in the Second Restatement. The Restatement authors suggest that "if the record is one not open to public inspection . . . it is not public,

[72] The polling data is from Brooke Auxier, *Most Americans Support Right to Have Some Personal Info Removed from Online Searches*, Pew Rsch. Ctr. (Jan. 27, 2020), https://perma.cc/Q35Q-7BYB.

[73] Florida Star v. B.J.F., 491 U.S. 524 (1989).

and there is an invasion of privacy when it is made so." And that means that the society shift toward privacy in mug shots could well expand into liability for *publication* of mug shots too.

All this suggests that those early courts that decided mug-shot cases and protected the privacy of those featured more than the publication had surprisingly modern sensibilities. Today, all the more, as even those early courts suggested, the circulation of mug shots cannot be undone.

10

Brokered Abuse

*Thomas E. Kadri**

10.1 INTRODUCTION

It's accually obsene what you can find out about a person on the internet.[1]

To some, this typo-ridden remark might sound banal. We know that our data drifts around online, with digital flotsam and jetsam washing up sporadically on different websites across the internet. Surveillance has been so normalized that, these days, many people aren't distressed when their information appears in a Google search, even if they sometimes fret about their privacy in other settings.

But this remark is not a throwaway line by a disgruntled netizen. No. It's a boast by a stalker, Liam Youens, who went online to find his victim, Amy Boyer. Youens traced Boyer after buying her work address from a data broker – a company that traffics information about people for profit. Youens documented his search for Boyer's whereabouts on his personal website: "I found an internet site to do that, and to my surprize everything else under the Sun. Most importantly: her current employment."[2] After he asked the broker for more information, he just had to bide his time. "I'm waiting for the results," he wrote ominously, not long before shooting Boyer dead at work.[3]

* Huge thanks to RonNell Andersen Jones, Elettra Bietti, Hannah Bloch-Wehba, Sarah Burns, Ryan Calo, Ignacio Cofone, Julie Cohen, Amy Gajda, Yael Grauer, Nikolas Guggenberger, Woodrow Hartzog, Mike Hintze, Leigh Honeywell, Ido Kilovaty, Anne Klinefelter, Kyle Langvardt, Mark Lemley, Lyrissa Lidsky, Christopher Morten, Paul Ohm, Natália Pires de Vasconcelos, Ani Satz, Evan Selinger, Scott Skinner-Thompson, Eugene Volokh, Rachel Vrabec, Ari Waldman, Rebecca Wexler, Felix Wu, and participants at the Privacy Law Scholars Conference and the UGA-Emory Faculty Workshop. I dedicate this chapter to the clients and volunteers at the Clinic to End Tech Abuse.

1 *Greetings Infidels, I Am Liam Youens*, https://perma.cc/TPY7-JCGA.

2 *Id.*

3 *Id.*; Kaveh Waddell, *How FamilyTreeNow Makes Stalking Easy*, ATLANTIC (Jan. 17, 2017), https://perma.cc/H6AG-CHSE.

Data brokers fuel abuse by sharing people's information and thwarting their obscurity. The value of obscurity, though sometimes overlooked in privacy discourse, rests on the idea that "information is safe – at least to some degree – when it is hard to obtain or understand."[4] Brokers hinder obscurity by making it easier and likelier to find or fathom information about people. This act of foiling obscurity, in turn, facilitates interpersonal abuse. The physical violence suffered by Amy Boyer is but one kind of abuse; people also face stalking, harassment, doxing, defamation, fraud, sextortion, and nonconsensual sharing of their intimate images.[5]

This chapter explores the phenomenon of *brokered abuse*: the ways that data brokerage enables and exacerbates interpersonal abuse. The harms of brokered abuse go beyond the fact that brokers make it easier to surveil people and expose them to physical, psychological, financial, and reputational harms. In addition, people must beg every single broker to conceal their information from thousands of separate databases, over and over again, with little or no legal recourse if brokers reject their efforts to regain some obscurity. Due partly to existing laws, this whack-a-mole burden of repeatedly pleading to obscure data can trigger trauma and distress. Only by grasping this fuller scope of brokered abuse can we begin to regulate it.[6]

This chapter splits into three sections. Section 10.2 introduces the broker industry before Section 10.3 reveals how the law largely fails to address, and is even complicit in, key features of brokered abuse. Section 10.4 then explores the harms stemming from brokered abuse in order to lay some foundations for regulating them.

10.2 DATA BROKERS AS INFORMATION TRAFFICKERS

Data brokerage is a multibillion-dollar industry.[7] Thousands of companies form a sprawling network of brokers that buy, sell, trade, and license gigabytes of human information. Though brokers' business models vary, their power and profit fundamentally stem from trafficking information about people.[8]

4 Evan Selinger & Woodrow Hartzog, *Obscurity and Privacy*, *in* SPACES FOR THE FUTURE: A COMPANION TO PHILOSOPHY OF TECHNOLOGY 119, 119 (Joseph Pitt & Ashley Shew eds., 2018).

5 *See* Danielle Keats Citron, *Sexual Privacy*, 128 YALE L.J. 1870 (2019) (discussing how networked technologies have facilitated various forms of interpersonal abuse).

6 *See* Thomas E. Kadri, *Networks of Empathy*, 2020 UTAH L. REV. 1075, 1075 (urging that "[w]e can neither understand nor address digital abuse unless we view technology in a deeper social context and grapple with how and why digital abuse is harmful").

7 Salome Viljoen, *A Relational Theory of Data Governance*, 131 YALE L.J. 573, 588 n.19 (2021) (observing that "[s]ome evidence pegs the global data-brokerage industry at about $200 billion annually").

8 *See* NEIL RICHARDS, WHY PRIVACY MATTERS 1–11 (2022) (connecting privacy, power, and "human information" and defining privacy as "the degree to which human information is neither known nor used"). For important early scholarship on brokers, *see* Chris J. Hoofnagle, *Big Brother's Little Helpers: How ChoicePoint and Other Commercial Data Brokers Collect and Package Your Data for Law Enforcement*, 29 N.C. J. INT'L L. 595 (2003); Daniel J. Solove &

For the most part, brokers buy information from other companies and gather it from government records and public websites.[9] From there, brokers build profiles including data like a person's name, aliases, photos, gender, birthdate, citizenship, religion, addresses, phone numbers, social-media accounts, email addresses, Social Security number, employers, schools, families, cohabitants, purchases, health conditions, and hobbies. These data dossiers are then sold for a fee or even shared for "free" thanks to the ads adorning broker websites.[10]

There are, to be fair, some benefits tied to the broker industry.[11] Transparency and accessibility come from publicizing information online, including data drawn from public records. Journalists, activists, academics, and the general public can garner insights from this information.[12] Indeed, a person might even evade interpersonal abuse or other ills after discovering an acquaintance's restraining order or criminal record through a broker. Though this kind of data is often accessible in other ways, a Google search is easier, faster, and cheaper than a trip to the county courthouse.[13]

Some people also use brokers to locate heirs or reconnect with long-lost friends and family. Others might rely on brokered data to inform their hiring decisions. Some companies rely on brokers in order to collect debts or discover fraud, corroborating information given to them by a customer or client. And brokers can even assist the legal system, such as when class-action awards are being distributed. These perks cannot be ignored, but we should be wary of their value being exaggerated.

Chris Jay Hoofnagle, *A Model Regime of Privacy Protection*, 2006 U. Ill. L. Rev. 357. For more contemporary reporting, *see* Adi Robertson, *The Long, Weird History of Companies That Put Your Life Online*, Verge (Mar. 21, 2017), https://perma.cc/Z9J8-HU9G; Yael Grauer, *What Are 'Data Brokers,' and Why Are They Scooping Up Information About You?*, Vice (Mar. 27, 2018), https://perma.cc/34YR-A5LN.

9 *See* Margaret B. Kwoka, *FOIA, Inc.*, 65 Duke L.J. 1361, 1376–401 (2016) (detailing how a vast industry of "information resellers" requests federal public records under the Freedom of Information Act (FOIA) and resells them for profit); David E. Pozen, *Transparency's Ideological Drift*, 128 Yale L.J. 100, 125 (2018) (observing that "commercial requesters – including a cottage industry of data brokers and information resellers – submit over two-thirds" of FOIA requests to various federal agencies).

10 *See* Amy Gajda, Seek and Hide: The Tangled History of the Right to Privacy 231–41 (2022) (discussing the extensive data dossiers compiled by brokers and other companies).

11 *See generally* Jennifer Barrett Glasgow, *Data Brokers: Should They Be Reviled or Revered?*, *in* Cambridge Handbook of Consumer Privacy 25 (Evan Selinger, Jules Polonetsky & Omer Tene eds., 2018) (canvassing the apparent benefits that brokers bring to the economy, innovation, and consumers).

12 Thomas E. Kadri, *Platforms as Blackacres*, 68 UCLA L. Rev. 1184, 1184–87 (2022) (discussing how researchers use data to "understand the effects of digital technologies, to oversee the influence that platforms wield, and to hold accountable the private actors that curate our experiences on the internet"); Thomas E. Kadri, *Digital Gatekeepers*, 99 Tex. L. Rev. 951, 977–82 (2021) (detailing how researchers rely on data to provide critical insights to the public).

13 *See generally* Eugene Volokh, *Cheap Speech and What It Will Do*, 104 Yale L.J. 1805 (1995) (predicting that new technologies enabled by the internet will alter information flows by making speech "cheap").

Another set of purported benefits relate to consumers, largely stemming from how businesses use brokered data. In particular, human information fuels the datasets and algorithms that help companies target ads and develop products. The resulting corporate revenue could, at least theoretically, yield cheaper or better services for consumers. I'm skeptical that this species of informational capitalism is in the public's interest,[14] but debunking this defense of data brokerage is not essential. Even if the commercial benefits are substantial, we should not scoff at the serious harms tied to the broker industry.

Though there are many harmful facets of data brokerage, I'll focus here on only one: how brokers enable and exacerbate interpersonal abuse. Most directly, brokers' dossiers can be treasure troves for abusers, who can plunder them for information with just a few clicks and bucks. In Amy Boyer's case, Youens paid a broker $45 for her Social Security number, $30 for her home address, and $109 for her work address.[15] These sums might already seem trifling given the vile result, but many brokers offer much more for far less. In 2013, for instance, a stalker bought Judge Timothy Corrigan's home address for less than $2 and later shot bullets at his house, missing the judge's head by a mere 1.6 inches.[16]

These jarring anecdotes tell part of the story of how brokers enable and exacerbate abuse, but the phenomenon needs more interrogation to show its full scope. To do so, we must unpack how the law can be ineffective and even injurious when responding to brokered abuse.

10.3 THE LAW'S ROLE IN BROKERED ABUSE

There are at least four common regulatory responses to brokered abuse: prohibiting abusive acts, mandating broker transparency, limiting data collection, and restricting data disclosure. Though each measure has some merit, none will suffice. Worse still, recent privacy laws can even inadvertently inflict psychological harms on people seeking to recover from abuse. Let us explore how.

10.3.1 *Prohibiting Abusive Acts*

Regulating abusive acts offers a path to reducing brokered abuse. If we target the underlying abuse, the thought goes, we needn't regulate data brokerage. While this

[14] *See generally* JULIE E. COHEN, BETWEEN TRUTH AND POWER: THE LEGAL CONSTRUCTIONS OF INFORMATIONAL CAPITALISM (2019) (exploring how informational-capitalist discourses have entrenched corporate power); ARI EZRA WALDMAN, INDUSTRY UNBOUND: THE INSIDE STORY OF PRIVACY, DATA, AND CORPORATE POWER (2021) (critiquing the corporate-friendly privacy discourses that shape the legal and technical work sustaining informational capitalism).

[15] Remsburg v. Docusearch, Inc., 816 A.2d 1001, 1005–06 (N.H. 2003). Police also unearthed Youens's plan to find and murder Boyer's family, though he committed suicide before carrying it out. *The Amy Boyer Case*, ELEC. PRIVACY INFO. CTR. (June 15, 2006), https://perma.cc/G6J7-Z8TF.

[16] Hannah Elias Sbaity, *Private Lives at Home and Public Lives in Court: Protecting the Privacy of Federal Judges' Home Addresses*, 28 J. INTELL. PROP. L. 475, 485–86 (2021).

approach is attractive in theory and even viable in certain cases, it's deficient for several reasons.

A host of laws directly regulate abuse, including criminal and tort liability for stalking, harassment, physical violence, doxing, privacy invasions, and voyeurism.[17] But even if these anti-abuse laws retroactively punish harmful acts or vindicate victims' interests in some cases, the continued prevalence of abuse suggests that any prospective deterrence caused by the threat of liability is inadequate. Even when abuse is deterred, these laws do little to lessen people's anxiety when their information is circulating online because they might lack confidence that any deterrence will hold.

To make matters worse, some anti-abuse laws can inadvertently increase people's risks of abuse. For example, when liability depends on an entity intending or knowing that their actions will cause harm, brokers have an incentive to remain ignorant about how brokered data is being used. Consider California's approach to protecting stalking victims who register with the state. A special anti-doxing law prohibits anyone, including brokers, from posting a registered victim's home address, phone number, or image on the internet with the "intent" to "[t]hreaten" the victim or "[i]ncite" a third person to cause "imminent" bodily harm "where the third person is likely to commit this harm."[18] With all these caveats, brokers can comfortably dodge liability by sharing data without asking questions.[19] Indeed, the standard data-brokerage business model – which relies on mass and indiscriminate data disclosures to anyone willing to pay – is incompatible with these kinds of scienter requirements because they implausibly suggest that brokers engage in case-specific deliberation or investigation before sharing data. And yet removing these caveats might pose a different problem because a law that broadly penalizes disclosing information might be vulnerable to constitutional challenges under the First Amendment.[20]

[17] *See, e.g.*, GA. STAT. ANN. § 16–5-90 (criminalizing the offense of "stalking" when a person "follows, places under surveillance, or contacts another person at or about a place or places without the consent of the other person for the purpose of harassing and intimidating the other person"); CAL. PEN. CODE § 653.2 (criminalizing the nonconsensual "electronic distribut[ion]" of "personal identifying information" with "intent to place another person in reasonable fear for his or her safety" and "for the purpose of imminently causing that other person unwanted physical contact, injury, or harassment, by a third party"); *see also* Eugene Volokh, *One-to-One Speech vs. One-to-Many Speech, Criminal Harassment Laws, and "Cyberstalking"*, 107 NW. U. L. REV. 731 (2013) (exploring the scope and constitutionality of stalking and harassment laws).

[18] CAL. GOV. CODE § 6208.1.

[19] Similar challenges arise in holding brokers vicariously liable for helping abusers. Liability for conspiracy or aiding and abetting requires substantial assistance, encouragement, or even a common plan to commit an illegal act. Inadvertently or not, these doctrines reward brokers' willful blindness when a person has dangerous designs with brokered data.

[20] *See* Kadri, *Platforms as Blackacres*, *supra* note 12, at 1234–40. There's no doubt that First Amendment arguments advanced by brokers could chill or weaken regulatory efforts in this space, in part because companies can plausibly argue that doctrine developed in different

Beyond substance, think practicalities. Anti-abuse laws often require a victim's prolonged and active participation in pressing charges or filing lawsuits. There's good reason to empower and involve victims in these legal processes, but the processes themselves can impose burdens that many victims are unable or unwilling to bear. Interacting with police, prosecutors, lawyers, and judges might dissuade some people, while some might also struggle practically or financially to bring civil claims – realities that disproportionately affect those who are already marginalized. Even setting aside these burdens, many people will fret about initiating matters of public record that could further jeopardize their obscurity and safety.[21]

Finally, anti-abuse laws usually will not offer the obscurity remedies that some people will seek. Even if they do (or if such a remedy is eventually negotiated through settlement), legal proceedings move too slowly to address the exigent and immediate dangers that people face. To cap it all off, different brokers are constantly adding to their data stockpiles, so people would need to file new claims against new parties every time new information pops up online.

In short, laws prohibiting abusive acts fail to disturb essential features of brokered abuse. Some regulations might even aggravate matters by encouraging brokers to maintain ignorance when dishing out data, while other legal processes can be too burdensome, risky, or ineffective to be worth a victim's while.

10.3.2 *Mandating Broker Transparency*

Another regulatory tool involves shedding light on data brokerage. While transparency laws can be helpful, they are ultimately insufficient. These laws come in different shapes and sizes, but we can distinguish two types based on their principal goals: administrative transparency that informs regulators and popular transparency that informs individuals. Each has value, but neither meaningfully abates brokered abuse.

Administrative transparency follows a two-step system to educate regulators about the broker industry. Brokers first register with a state agency to create a list of brokers doing business in the jurisdiction, then brokers disclose details about their practices (such as where they obtain data and how they handle complaints). Vermont and

media environments protects their use of information from public records. *See id.* (delving into precedent that limits the government's ability to restrict data flows once information enters the public sphere); *cf.* COHEN, *supra* note 14 (exploring how technology companies have been shielded from legal accountability). This chapter dodges many of these First Amendment questions, leaving them for fuller treatment in the future.

[21] *See* THOMAS E. KADRI, TORT LAW: CASES & CRITIQUE 77–78 (2d ed. 2022) (discussing how this so-called "Streisand Effect" can also be "a *legal* phenomenon" because "suing can garner greater attention, thereby worsening the privacy invasion sought to be remedied by the lawsuit").

California have such laws, and similar themes animate the Data Broker List Act introduced in Congress in 2021.[22]

Popular transparency, by contrast, mainly informs individuals. California, for instance, has passed "right to know" laws that force brokers to reveal details they'd rather conceal: what data they have and whether they have shared it.[23] Similar laws might even oblige brokers to grant people no-cost access to data about themselves, rather than forcing them to pay a fee.

Administrative transparency can help regulators grasp the broker industry and inform future legislation, while popular transparency can help motivated people learn something new about their exposure with particular brokers. But neither approach helps a person facing urgent threats from their information appearing online. There's also no guarantee that transparency will motivate further regulation; if anything, these milquetoast measures might sap political will from stronger proposals.[24] At best, then, transparency laws fiddle with some incentives underlying data brokerage. (Maybe brokers will disclose less data if they have to disclose how they are disclosing data?) At worst, these laws let brokers hide their harmful practices in plain sight while boasting about their regulatory compliance.

10.3.3 *Limiting Data Collection*

A third response to brokered abuse involves curtailing data collection. Again, there are promises and pitfalls to this approach. Laws of this ilk form a privacy mosaic for our information, but there are too many missing pieces to make a pleasing mural.

Longstanding regulations forbid obtaining data through deception, other laws bar intrusive surveillance like hacking, and various legal regimes give companies "gatekeeper rights" to deter data scraping from their websites.[25] These restrictions reach

22 *See* Cal. Civ. Code §§ 1798.99.80 *et seq.*; 9 Vt. Stat. Ann. § 2430; S. 2290, 117th Cong., 1st Sess. (2021), https://perma.cc/C4Z4-QSQF. This approach has also been endorsed by the Federal Trade Commission and forty state attorneys general. *See* Fed. Trade Comm'n, Data Brokers: A Call for Transparency and Accountability (May 2014); Nat'l Ass'n of Attorneys General, *Federal Trade Commission Hearings on Competition and Consumer: Protection in the 21st Century: Public Comments of 43 State Attorneys General* (June 11, 2019), https://perma.cc/U7LD-TF6A. *See generally* Danielle Keats Citron, *The Privacy Policymaking of State Attorneys General*, 92 Notre Dame L. Rev. 747, 747 (2017) (exploring how state attorneys general have been "laboratories of privacy enforcement" and "expanded the frontiers of privacy law").

23 Cal. Civ. Code § 1798.115.

24 *See* Pozen, *supra* note 9, at 135–41 (exploring how soft-touch and targeted transparency mandates in consumer-protection law have "evolved into a stock substitute for more robust and direct regulation"); *cf. id.* at 134 (arguing that reliance on transparency mandates in campaign-finance reform helped to thwart restrictions on election spending).

25 *See, e.g.*, Kadri, *Digital Gatekeepers*, *supra* note 12, at 957–69 (discussing how cyber-trespass laws empower companies to act as "gatekeepers" on their websites); Remsburg v. Docusearch, Inc., 816 A.2d 1001 (N.H. 2003) (endorsing privacy and negligence tort claims if a broker obtains information through deceptive means); 18 U.S.C. § 1039 (making it a federal crime to

only a subset of brokers' activities because gobs of data can be gathered without running afoul of any law.[26] Most importantly, many of these laws do not apply when brokers get data from public records or other publicly accessible sources.[27]

More recently, a new vintage of data-privacy laws has unsettled the broker industry by prohibiting the nonconsensual collection of people's information. But even these stricter rules often contain caveats that let brokers thrive. The California Consumer Privacy Act, for example, provides that the types of "personal information" protected by the law do not include "publicly available information or lawfully obtained, truthful information that is a matter of public concern" – an exception that covers vast troves of brokered data and endorses many broker practices that leave abuse victims vulnerable.[28]

In light of these carveouts for publicly accessible information, one approach to limiting data collection focuses on the state's role in furnishing brokered data.[29] Brokers sustain their services with information from public records like property

fraudulently obtain "confidential phone records information"); 18 U.S.C. § 2511 (making it a federal crime under the Wiretap Act to "intentionally intercept[] ... any wire, oral, or electronic communication"); 18 U.S.C. § 1030(a)(2)(C) (making it a federal crime under the Computer Fraud and Abuse Act to "intentionally access[] a computer without authorization or exceed[] authorized access, and thereby obtain[] ... information from any protected computer"). Whether brokers are liable for scraping and other types of cyber-trespass is a complex matter (and mixture) of criminal, tort, and contract law, but suffice to say that brokers can still collect ample data and steer well clear of these restrictions. *See, e.g.*, Kadri, *Digital Gatekeepers*, *supra* note 12 (discussing liability for scraping under the Computer Fraud and Abuse Act and other cyber-trespass laws); Kadri, *Platforms as Blackacres*, *supra* note 12 (discussing the First Amendment implications of laws regulating scraping).

[26] *See generally* Julie E. Cohen, *The Biopolitical Public Domain: The Legal Construction of the Surveillance Economy*, 31 PHIL. & TECH. 213 (2018) (exploring how law shapes and enables extractive practices of appropriating personal information).

[27] *See, e.g.*, 18 U.S.C. § 2511(2)(g)(i) (providing that "[i]t shall not be unlawful" under the Stored Communications Act, 18 U.S.C. § 2701, to "access an electronic communication made through an electronic communication system that is configured so that such electronic communication is readily accessible to the general public"); hiQ Labs, Inc. v. LinkedIn Corp., 31 F.4th 1180, 1201 (9th Cir. 2022) (holding that the Computer Fraud and Abuse Act, § 1030(a)(2)(C), likely does not apply "when a computer network generally permits public access to its data"); Cox Broad. Corp. v. Cohn, 420 U.S. 469, 471, 473–74, 495–96 (1975) (outlining First Amendment limits on privacy tort claims based on accessing information already in the public domain); Kadri, *Platforms as Blackacres*, *supra* note 12, at 1234–40 (analyzing constitutional doctrine in this area).

[28] *See* CAL. CIV. CODE § 1798.140; *see also* Meg Leta Jones & Margot E. Kaminski, *An American's Guide to the GDPR*, 98 DENV. L. REV. 93, 106, 116–17 (2020) (discussing how brokers are regulated by the European Union's General Data Protection Regulation).

[29] Though this chapter cannot flesh out this point, it's high time to reconsider the state's complicity in supplying brokered data. *See generally* Daniel J. Solove, *Access and Aggregation: Privacy, Public Records, and the Constitution*, 86 MINN. L. REV. 1137 (2002) (urging a rethinking of the regulation of public records in light of new technologies in the Information Age); Danielle Keats Citron, *A New Compact for Sexual Privacy*, 62 WM. & MARY L. REV. 1763, 1818–24 (2021) (advocating for limits on collecting intimate information to protect sexual privacy); Woodrow Hartzog, *The Public Information Fallacy*, 99 B.U. L. REV. 459, 459 (2019) (critiquing how "labeling information as public often functions as a permission slip for

deeds, voter rolls, and marriage licenses. To partially stem this flow, most states have confidentiality programs to allow abuse victims to conceal certain information from state documents.[30] On the plus side, these measures are unlikely to raise First Amendment red flags because nothing forces the government to collect (or publish) the kind of identifying information that most likely endangers people's obscurity.[31] But while limiting government data collection (and publication) brings significant benefits, even the broadest restrictions are insufficient. Public records, after all, are but one source of human information. Most importantly, brokers can still buy data from other companies and gather it from other public websites. Tinkering with public records turns off the cold tap but leaves the hot water flowing.

10.3.4 *Restricting Data Disclosure*

A final way to tackle brokered abuse involves controlling data disclosure. This approach conceivably offers great potential for people seeking to stop brokers publicizing their information online. But the devil is in the details. Many disclosure regulations either do little to thwart abuse or even harm people trying to protect themselves.

Some disclosure rules aren't aimed specifically at either data or brokers, such as tort liability for publicly disclosing certain sensitive information,[32] while other recent

surveillance and personal data practices"); Kirsten Martin & Helen Nissenbaum, *Privacy Interests in Public Records: An Empirical Investigation*, 31 HARV. J.L. & TECH. 111 (2017) (investigating people's privacy interests in public records through an empirical study). The flip side of this symbiotic relationship is also true: we should also reconsider brokers' roles in furnishing the state with data. *See, e.g.*, CMTY. JUST. EXCH., FROM DATA CRIMINALIZATION TO PRISON ABOLITION (2022), https://perma.cc/DQV2-9SS3 (critiquing "data criminalization": "the creation, archiving, theft, resale and analysis of datasets that mark certain people as threats and risks, based on data culled about them from state and commercial sources").

30 *Address Confidentiality Program*, N.Y. STATE, https://perma.cc/V6AK-3MWM (outlining how victims may shield their addresses in some state records by creating a substitute address); *About Safe at Home*, CAL. SEC'Y STATE, https://perma.cc/4AVJ-TDK3 (detailing how victims may seek confidential name changes and voter registration); *see also* DAVIS WRIGHT, ADDRESS CONFIDENTIALITY PROGRAMS: RESOURCE GUIDE (2022) (surveying all fifty states and noting that only Alaska, South Carolina, South Dakota, Utah, and Wyoming lack any form of address-confidentiality program for abuse victims).

31 *See* Neil M. Richards, *Why Data Privacy Law Is (Mostly) Constitutional*, 56 WM. & MARY L. REV. 1501 (2015) (arguing that most laws regulating the collection, use, and disclosure of personal data should survive First Amendment challenges). Though I cover *collection* and *disclosure* here, I omit discussion of *use* restrictions because, at least in the United States, they have offered less promise to restrain brokered abuse. One law frequently touted as relevant to brokers is the Fair Credit Reporting Act (FCRA), 15 U.S.C. § 1681 k, which prohibits employers from using certain data in hiring decisions. Brokers enter the picture because FCRA arguably restricts them from knowingly providing employee-screening data. Even if this contentious interpretation were accepted, such a narrow and consumer-focused law does little to address interpersonal abuse.

32 *See* Robert C. Post, *The Social Foundations of Privacy: Community and Self in the Common Law Tort*, 77 CALIF. L. REV. 957, 978–1008 (1989) (dissecting the privacy tort of public disclosure of private facts).

proposals would make brokers pay for selling people's data or ban them from sharing location and health information. Such constraints meddle with brokerage around the margins, but none brings fundamental reform and some plausibly exempt publicly accessible data.[33]

Given these limitations, let us focus instead on modern laws providing rights to conceal or remove information from broker databases or websites. California offers a rare example in the United States of providing these legally mandated obscurity rights, so we'll use it as a short case study to examine the virtues and vices of such a regulatory regime. Under the state's general "right to opt-out," all Californian consumers may direct businesses not to sell their personal information to third parties, meaning that the company must not disclose their data for profit once a person exercises their obscurity right.[34] But California law also goes one step further. Abuse victims who register with the state's Safe at Home program have more expansive obscurity rights. Of particular note, brokers cannot knowingly display a victim's phone number or home address on the internet. If a victim asserts their reasonable fear related to that information, a broker must conceal the data for four years and could face injunctions, court costs, and attorney's fees for noncompliance. And if anyone, including a broker, displays or sells the information with intent to cause certain harms, victims may seek treble damages and receive a $4,000 fine per violation. To help implement the law's protections, California provides an online opt-out form that victims can use to invoke their obscurity rights.[35]

Though California's goals are laudable, this innovative approach fails to grapple with the realities of abuse. Under these laws, Californians must engage in extensive "privacy self-management" because the state forces them to exercise obscurity rights on a company-by-company basis.[36] Even the Safe at Home opt-out process – which was presumably designed with abuse victims in mind – operates from this fragmented premise by requiring victims to approach brokers individually and submit

[33] *See* Own Your Own Data Act, S. 806, 116th Cong., 1st Sess. (2019) (providing that "[e]ach individual owns and has an exclusive property right in the data that an individual generates on the internet"); Ignacio Cofone, *Beyond Data Ownership*, 43 CARDOZO L. REV. 501 (2021) (exposing flaws in the property approach to personal information); Health and Location Data Protection Act, S. 4408, 117th Cong., 2d Sess. (2022) (prohibiting brokers from sharing location and health data unless such data constitutes "newsworthy information of legitimate public concern").

[34] CAL. CIV. CODE § 1798.120.

[35] CAL. GOV. CODE § 6208.1; *Program Services*, CAL. SEC'Y STATE, https://perma.cc/DER2-3Q86.

[36] For background on privacy-self management, *see* Daniel J. Solove, *Introduction: Privacy Self-Management and the Consent Dilemma*, 126 HARV. L. REV. 1880, 1882–83 (2013), and Neil Richards & Woodrow Hartzog, *Taking Trust Seriously in Privacy Law*, 19 STAN. TECH. L. REV. 431, 444 (2016). Technological tools like the Global Privacy Control are seeking to streamline this process by enabling people to automatically assert their obscurity rights through settings on their browsers. Though this initiative still creates self-management burdens that will likely dampen its efficacy, it could be a step in the right direction. *See* GLOB. PRIV. CONTROL, https://perma.cc/QE8C-4972.

forms to each one regularly. Brokers, after all, continuously replenish their stocks, and concealing *some* data does not stop *other* data from soon taking its place. Given these features of the broker industry, laws like California's could actually entrench a disaggregated and detrimental obscurity process because brokers can seize on their legal compliance to justify not offering better services.

10.4 THE HARMS OF BROKERED ABUSE

With this legal survey in mind, let us return to the matter of harms: How do brokers enable and exacerbate abuse? How is the law inadequate and complicit? And how might legal procedures even contribute toward a person's suffering?

To answer these questions, I return to obscurity – a notion of privacy concerned with "the difficulty and probability of discovering or understanding information."[37] As Woodrow Hartzog and Evan Selinger have observed, obscurity can be a "protective state" that serves valuable privacy-dependent goals like "autonomy, self-fulfillment, socialization, and relative freedom from the abuse of power."[38] Understanding the full scope of brokered abuse requires parsing how data brokerage, including its surrounding legal constructs, undermines obscurity. As we'll see, brokered abuse encompasses an array of *intrinsic* and *extrinsic* harms, all of which implicate a person's obscurity.

10.4.1 *Intrinsic Harms*

Abuse. As an initial matter, brokers routinely create privacy losses by sharing people's information. Though this core of brokerage is not intrinsically harmful, such privacy *losses* can engender privacy *harms*.[39] Some of these privacy harms, to use Ignacio Cofone's terminology, are "consequential" because they are "external to privacy interests but occur as a consequence of privacy violations."[40] Brokers facilitate the surveillance of victims and their kin by systematically sharing personal information. An abuser armed with brokered data can perpetrate a slew of

[37] Woodrow Hartzog & Evan Selinger, *Surveillance as Loss of Obscurity*, 72 WASH. & LEE L. REV. 1343, 1355 (2015).

[38] Woodrow Hartzog & Evan Selinger, *Obscurity: A Better Way to Think About Your Data than "Privacy"*, ATLANTIC (Jan. 17, 2013), https://perma.cc/38TV-8KTL.

[39] *See* Ignacio N. Cofone & Adriana Z. Robertson, *Privacy Harms*, 69 HASTINGS L.J. 1039, 1042, 1049–55 (2018) (connecting but distinguishing the ideas of "privacy loss" and "privacy harm"); Ignacio Cofone, *Privacy Standing*, 2022 U. ILL. L. REV. 1367 (further developing these concepts in the context of standing to bring privacy claims); *see also* Ryan Calo, *The Boundaries of Privacy Harm*, 86 IND. L.J. 1131, 1131, 1143 (2011) (arguing that subjective and objective privacy harms represent "the anticipation and consequence of a loss of control over personal information"); Danielle Keats Citron & Daniel J. Solove, *Privacy Harms*, 102 B.U. L. REV. 793, 830–61 (2022) (offering a typology of privacy harms to show privacy's instrumental value in seven different contexts).

[40] *See* Cofone, *supra* note 39, at 1398, 1403–05.

"consequential" physical, emotional, economic, and reputational harms. This might not be a broker's goal, but it's certainly their role.

Risk. Beyond the direct harm of actually enabling abuse, brokers commit the kindred harm of increasing the risk of abuse by making it easier to surveil a person and their family, friends, or associates. This risk, in turn, can cause anxiety even if no abusive act ever occurs.[41] Without regulatory intervention, these threats will only grow as data proliferates and new technologies, like facial-recognition surveillance, further wreck obscurity.[42]

Isolation. Brokers also rob people of agency to "control their visibility within public space."[43] As Scott Skinner-Thompson has argued, digital and physical surveillance can cause forced publicity, which might then deter people from participating in public life.[44] This cycle, unsurprisingly, has unequal repercussions for those who are socially marginalized already – a special concern here because victims often hail from marginalized groups and because abuse can have ostracizing effects regardless of one's preexisting social status and personal characteristics.[45] Data brokerage can intensify a victim's isolation by foisting visibility on them, creating yet more reasons for them to retreat entirely from public spaces.

10.4.2 *Extrinsic Harms*

Some people respond to this trio of intrinsic harms – abuse, anxiety, and isolation – by trying to cull information from broker databases. Easier said than done. As we have seen, people must beg brokers to conceal their data with little guarantee of success, especially in jurisdictions where legal remedies are absent or incomplete. At best, people in places like California can contact every single broker separately to

[41] *Cf.* Daniel J. Solove & Danielle Keats Citron, *Risk and Anxiety: A Theory of Data Breach Harms*, 96 Tex. L. Rev. 737 (2018) (arguing that risk and anxiety can be legally cognizable harms caused by data breaches).

[42] *See* Amanda Levendowski, *Resisting Face Surveillance with Copyright Law*, 100 N.C. L. Rev. 1015, 1018, 1022–35 (2022) (identifying injustices of "face surveillance" – a term that "embraces multiple biometric systems that use algorithms to analyze faces, such as face detection, face classification, and ... face recognition"); Neil Richards & Woodrow Hartzog, *The Pathologies of Digital Consent*, 96 Wash. U. L. Rev. 1461, 1485 (2019) (discussing the threats posed by facial-recognition technology); Woodrow Hartzog & Evan Selinger, *Why You Can No Longer Get Lost in the Crowd*, N.Y. Times (Apr. 17, 2019), https://perma.cc/C2ST-9UUJ (exploring the importance of obscurity and observing that "[t]hreats to our obscurity are growing" due to advances in technology).

[43] Scott Skinner-Thompson, *Agonistic Privacy & Equitable Democracy*, 131 Yale L.J. F. 454, 456 (2021).

[44] *Id.* at 454–56, 459–61.

[45] *See* Mary Anne Franks & Ari Ezra Waldman, *Sex, Lies, and Videotape: Deep Fakes and Free Speech Delusions*, 78 Md. L. Rev. 892, 896 (2019); Ari Ezra Waldman, *Law, Privacy, and Online Dating: "Revenge Porn" in Gay Online Communities*, 44 Law & Soc. Inquiry 987, 1009 (2019); Thomas E. Kadri, *Drawing Trump Naked: Curbing the Right of Publicity to Protect Public Discourse*, 78 Md. L. Rev. 899, 950–51 (2019).

exercise their legal rights. The result? People facing physical and psychological peril must approach each broker individually over and over again. At a time of high vulnerability, this obscurity process creates a pair of extrinsic harms that are partly constructed by legal rules and procedures.

Annoyance. The first harm can be styled as annoyance, though it covers a range of unwanted emotions. Some people might reasonably feel indignant about having to demand their obscurity. (Imagine someone complaining: "It's *my* data, not *theirs*, so *they* should have to ask *me* before using it! Why should *I* have to contact *them*?") Others might resent spending time filling out forms or navigating brokers' laborious and complex bureaucracies. Some people might feel exasperated at how futile it all seems, especially given that "grey holes" in privacy law might give brokers enough room to resist obscurity requests or refill their databases.[46] Absent some compelling justification, the law should not be complicit in cultivating negative reactions to exercising legal rights. Feeling indignant, resentful, or exasperated is both unpleasant and likely to dissuade people from enforcing their rights.

Trauma. Taking annoyance seriously is important to understanding the law's failure to address brokered abuse. But to culminate this chapter, I want to stress something different and underappreciated. For abuse victims, an arduous and dispersed obscurity process can inflict a harm that goes beyond mere hassle or frustration. It's more than a matter of transaction costs. It's more even than a question of abuse and anxiety. Instead, it's about trauma – and how the law's failure to consider the role of trauma represents a failure of empathy toward victims of abuse.

The basic point is this: The process of preventing brokers from sharing information can trigger psychological harm by forcing victims to repeatedly revisit their abuse and recognize their vulnerability. A disaggregated and inefficient obscurity process might irritate some people, but the burden it can impose on victims is likely distinct and severe. In short, the obscurity process itself can be traumatic.

"Trauma is the experience and resulting aftermath of an extremely distressing event or series of events, such as disaster, violence, abuse, or other emotionally harmful experiences."[47] Though further research is required to explore how trauma manifests in the context of brokered abuse, existing studies point to likely connections between abuse, trauma, and technology. For example, a recent interdisciplinary study by researchers working directly with victims in the Clinic to End Tech Abuse at Cornell University examines how people's interactions with digital

[46] *Cf.* Alicia G. Solow-Niederman, *Algorithmic Grey Holes*, 5 J.L. & Innov. 116 (2023) (exploring the idea of how "grey holes" in law can include procedures that create the appearance but not the reality of constraints on government action).

[47] *See* Janet X. Chen, Allison McDonald, Yixin Zou, Emily Tseng, Kevin A Roundy, Acar Tamersoy, Florian Schaub, Thomas Ristenpart & Nicola Dell, *Trauma-Informed Computing: Towards Safer Technology Experiences for All*, CHI'22: Proceedings of the 2022 CHI Conference on Human Factors in Computing Systems 1 (2022).

technologies can cause trauma in the context of interpersonal abuse. As the authors observe based on a series of actual case studies, people's experiences with technology can "trigger existing trauma and even retraumatize a person," such as "when something in one's environment causes them to recall a traumatic experience, often with a recurrence of the emotional state during the original event."[48] Based on my own experiences – personally as an abuse victim and professionally when speaking with other victims – this accurately describes how prevailing obscurity processes involving data brokers can trigger trauma.

Even the most expansive obscurity rights fail to grapple with this extrinsic harm. Indeed, these laws risk aggravating matters by enshrining a decentralized process into law. While current procedures might be annoying for someone who's never faced abuse, for victims seeking obscurity it creates an extra injury that might further discourage them from enforcing their legal rights. Legislators have failed to account for the dynamics of interpersonal abuse from a victim's perspective. The law, it might be said, lacks empathy.

To compound matters, current processes to regain obscurity are often ineffective. Brokers can simply shun removal requests in the forty-odd states that lack data-privacy laws, and even a responsive broker can do no more than purge information from its own database. An abuser needs only one willing broker to facilitate surveillance, and the scattering of digital breadcrumbs among brokers can distress people even if an abuser never actually gets any data. A flawed obscurity process, then, solidifies all three intrinsic harms by enabling abuse, creating anxiety, and causing isolation, while also maintaining extrinsic harms like annoyance and trauma.[49]

I leave the matter of addressing brokered abuse for another day, but one thing seems clear: There's a dire need for an effective and empathetic obscurity process.[50] Though it's impossible to say how many people are harmed through brokered data, we know that many forms of technology-enabled abuse are rampant, rising, and ruinous. Recent empirical research has shown how abusers are exploiting technologies to intimidate, threaten, monitor, impersonate, and harass.[51] This essential work substantiates earlier scholarship revealing how technology can facilitate interpersonal harms and deepen social inequities.[52] We know, too, that abuse victims suffer

[48] *Id.* at 4–6.

[49] *See* Kadri, *supra* note 6, at 1095–96 (discussing how the mere existence of technologies that enable stalking can instill paranoia in abuse victims); Mara Hvistendahl, *I Tried to Get My Name Off People-Search Sites. It Was Nearly Impossible*, Consumer Reps. (Aug. 20, 2020), https://perma.cc/T52R-LG34.

[50] *See* Kadri, *supra* note 6, at 1078–80, 1118–19 (arguing that empathy should be a guiding regulatory principle in this area).

[51] Diana Freed, Jackeline Palmer, Diana Minchala, Karen Levy, Thomas Ristenpart & Nicola Dell, "A *Stalker's Paradise": How Intimate Partner Abusers Exploit Technology*, Ass'n Computing Mach. (2018).

[52] *See, e.g.*, Danielle Citron, Hate Crimes in Cyberspace (2014); Ari Ezra Waldman, *Safe Social Spaces*, 96 Wash. U. L. Rev. 1535 (2019); Mary Anne Franks, *Unwilling Avatars: Idealism and Discrimination in Cyberspace*, 20 Colum. J. Gender & L. 224 (2011).

significantly higher rates of depression, anxiety, insomnia, and social dysfunction than the general population.[53] Given these realities, we should not turn a blind eye to brokered abuse.

10.5 CONCLUSION

Data brokers are abuse enablers. By sharing people's information, brokers thwart obscurity, stimulate surveillance, and ultimately enable interpersonal abuse. This chapter has canvassed four regulatory responses to brokered abuse. Though these existing measures have some merit, none is adequate, and some laws can even make matters worse. Put simply, the current legal landscape is neither effective nor empathetic.

Of particular and yet underappreciated concern, the prevailing broker-by-broker approach to regaining obscurity likely causes victims' trauma by forcing them to engage repeatedly with their abuse and vulnerability. The flaws of this obscurity process also leave people vulnerable to serious physical, psychological, financial, and reputational harms. Regulating brokered abuse should be a priority for both lawmakers and technologists.

[53] Eric Blaauw, Frans W. Winkel, Ella Arensman, Lorraine Sheridan & Adriënne Freeve, *The Toll of Stalking: The Relationship between Features of Stalking and Psychopathology of Victims*, 17 J. INTERPERSONAL VIOLENCE 50, 57–58 (2002); *see also* Ari Ezra Waldman, *Amplifying Abuse: The Fusion of Cyberharassment and Discrimination*, 95 B.U. L. REV. ANNEX 83, 83 (2015) (discussing how cyberharassment victims commonly experience anxiety, panic attacks, fear, post-traumatic stress disorder, anorexia, bulimia, and clinical depression).

PART III

Platform Governance

11

Introduction

Platform Governance

Kyle Langvardt

The term "content moderation," a holdover from the days of small bulletin-board discussion groups, is quite a bland way to describe an immensely powerful and consequential aspect of social governance. Today's largest platforms make judgments on millions of pieces of content a day, with world-shaping consequences. And in the United States, they do so mostly unconstrained by legal requirements. One senses that "content moderation" – the preferred term in industry and in the policy community – is something of a euphemism for content *regulation*, a way to cope with the unease that attends the knowledge (1) that so much unchecked power has been vested in so few hands and (2) that the alternatives to this arrangement are so hard to glimpse.

Some kind of content moderation, after all, is necessary for a speech platform to function at all. Gus Hurwitz's "Noisy Speech Externalities" (Chapter 12) makes this high-level point from the mathematical perspective of information theory. For Professor Hurwitz, content moderation is not merely about cleaning up harmful content. Instead, content moderation becomes most important as communications channels approach saturation with so much content that users cannot pick out the signal from the noise. In making this particular case for content moderation, Professor Hurwitz offers a striking inversion of the traditional First Amendment wisdom that the cure for bad speech is more speech. When speech is cheap and bandwidth is scarce, any incremental speech may create negative externalities. As such, he writes, "the only solution to bad speech may be *less* speech – encouraging more speech may actually be detrimental to our speech values." Professor Hurwitz therefore suggests that policymakers might best advance the marketplace of ideas by encouraging platforms to "use best available content moderation technologies as suitable for their scale."

Laura Edelson's "Content Moderation in Practice" (Chapter 13) provides some detail on what these technologies might look like. Through a survey of the mechanics of content moderation at today's largest platforms – Facebook, YouTube, TikTok, Reddit, and Zoom – Dr. Edelson demonstrates that the range of existing techniques for moderating content is remarkably diverse and complex. "Profound differences in content moderation policy, rules for enforcement, and enforcement practices" produce similarly deep differences in the user experience from platform to platform. Yet all these platforms, through their own mechanisms, take a hardline approach toward content that is "simply illegal" or that otherwise contravenes some strong social expectation.

In Chapter 14, "The Reverse Spider-Man Principle: With Great Responsibility Comes Great Power," Eugene Volokh examines the hazards that arise when private go-betweens assume the responsibility of meeting public expectations for content regulation. As companies develop technical capabilities that insinuate them more deeply into human decision-making and interaction, there is a natural temptation to require them to use their powers for harm prevention. But as seen in the case of online platforms, these interventions can create discomfiting governance dynamics where entities micromanage private life without clear guardrails or a public mandate. Volokh argues that courts do grasp this Reverse Spider-Man Principle at some level, and that they have worked to avoid its dangers in diverse settings. Tort law, for example, does not generally hold landlords responsible for screening out allegedly criminal tenants, even if such screening might help protect other tenants from violent crime. If it were otherwise, then the law would appoint landlords as narcotics officers, with likely disastrous consequences for individual liberty.

Alan Z. Rozenshtein's "Moderating the Fediverse: Content Moderation on Distributed Social Media" (Chapter 15) points toward an alternative social media architecture that would address the Reverse Spider-Man problem by dialing down the reach, responsibility, and power of any one community of moderators. This "Fediverse" does not rotate around any single intermediary in the way that today's mainstream social media architecture does. Instead, the Fediverse is held together by a common *protocol*, ActivityPub, that allows any user to found and operate their own "instance." In the case of Mastodon, the Fediverse's most popular social media platform, each instance works a bit like a miniature X platform with its own content policies and membership criteria. Groups of instances, in turn, can enter into federative agreements with each other: Instance A may allow its users to see content posted in instance B, but not content posted in instance C.

This architecture ensures that no one group of moderators has the scale – or the responsibility, or the power – to set content rules that control the shape of public discourse. But achieving this result would require great *effort* in the form of a distributed, almost Jeffersonian moderation culture in which a much larger group of users participates intimately in content decisions. Moreover, it is unclear that the Fediverse lends itself to ad-based monetization in the same way that platformed social media does. The seemingly natural behavioral and economic inclination toward market concentration and walled gardens indicates that public policy will have to play some role in encouraging the Fediverse to flourish. Professor Rozenshtein's chapter offers some suggestions.

12

Noisy Speech Externalities

Gus Hurwitz

12.1 INTRODUCTION

A central tenet of contemporary First Amendment law is the metaphor of the marketplace of ideas – that the solution to bad speech is more, better, speech.[1] This basic idea is well established in both judicial and scholarly writing – but it is not without its critics. My contribution to this volume adds a new criticism of the marketplace-of-ideas metaphor. I argue that there are circumstances where ostensibly "good" speech may be indistinguishable by listeners from bad speech – indeed, that there are cases in which *any* incremental speech can actually make *other* good speech indistinguishable from bad speech. In such cases, seemingly "good" speech has the effect of "bad" speech. I call this process by which ostensibly good speech turns the effects of other speech bad "a noisy speech externality."

This thesis has important implications. First, it offers a poignant critique of the marketplace-of-ideas aphorism introduced by Justice Holmes in his *Abrams* dissent.[2] If the marketplace of ideas is subject to significant market failure, correctives *may* be justified. Market failures, after all, are a standard justification for regulatory intervention. But, second, my contribution goes a step farther, suggesting not only that there are circumstances in which good speech may fail as a corrective to bad speech but also that there are circumstances in which the addition of seemingly good speech may only yield more bad speech. In such cases, the only solution to bad speech may be *less* speech – encouraging more speech may actually be detrimental to our speech values. If that is the case, then correctives may be not only justified but

1 Whitney v. California, 274 U.S. 357, 377 (1927) (Brandeis, J., concurring) ("If there be time to expose through discussion the falsehood and fallacies, to avert the evil by the processes of education, the remedy to be applied is more speech, not enforced silence."), *overruled in part by* Brandenburg v. Ohio, 395 U.S. 444 (1969).

2 Abrams v. United States, 250 U.S. 616, 630 (1919) ("[T]he best test of truth is the power of the thought to get itself accepted in the competition of the market. … That at any rate is the theory of our Constitution.").

needed to satisfy an important societal interest. And, third, this chapter presents solutions for content-neutral ways in which to implement such correctives.

The insight underlying this thesis builds on my prior work applying the insights of Claude Shannon's information theory to social media.[3] That piece applied Shannon's work to social media to argue that, at least at a metaphorical level and potentially at a cognitive level, our capacity to communicate is governed by Shannon's channel-capacity theorem.[4] This theorem tells us that the capacity of a communications channel is limited by that channel's *signal-to-noise* ratio. Critically, once that capacity is exceeded, any additional signal is indistinguishable from noise – and this has the effect of worsening the signal-to-noise ratio, further reducing the communications capacity. In other words, after a certain threshold, additional speech is not merely ineffective: It creates a negative externality that interferes with other speech.

Other scholars have made similar arguments, which can casually be framed as exploring the effects of "too much information" or "information overload."[5] But the negative-externality element of this argument goes a step further. A "too much information" argument suggests that listeners are overwhelmed by the quantity of speech to which they may be subject. This argument suggests that speakers can – deliberately or otherwise – exercise a veto over other speakers by saturating listeners' information sources. For the listener, it is not merely a question of filtering out the good information from the bad (the signal from the noise): At the point of saturation, signal cannot be differentiated from noise and any filtering necessarily must occur upstream from the listener.

Filtering – reducing the overall amount of speech – has always been a key tool in fighting bad speech. All platforms must filter. Indeed, this is nothing new: Editorial processes have always been valuable to listeners. The question is how they do it, with a related question of the law surrounding that filtering. Under the current approach (facilitated through Section 230 of the Communications Decency Act and built upon First Amendment principles), platforms have substantial discretion over what speech they host. This chapter's normative contribution is to argue that liability shield should be contingent upon platforms using "reasonable best-available technology" to filter speech – a standard that most platforms, this chapter also argues, likely already meet.

The discussion in this chapter proceeds in four sections. It begins in Section 12.2 by introducing technical concepts from the field of information theory – most

[3] Justin "Gus" Hurwitz, *Madison and Shannon on Social Media*, 3 Bus. Entrepreneurship & Tax L. Rev. 249 (2019).

[4] Cognitive psychologists and neurobiologists have identified some of these limits. Some of this research, such as that showing that there is a roughly constant information density across spoken human languages despite their vastly different syntax, grammars, and word complexity, is considered in Hurwitz, *supra* note 3.

[5] *See infra* Section 12.3.2.

notably the ideas of channel capacity and the role of the signal-to-noise ratio in defining a channel's capacity. Section 12.3 then introduces the traditional "marketplace-of-ideas" understanding of the First Amendment and builds on lessons from information theory to argue that this "marketplace" may in some cases be subject to negative externalities – noisy speech externalities – and that such externalities may justify some forms of corrective regulation. It also considers other arguments that have a similar feeling ("too much information," "information overload," and "listeners' rights"), and explains how the negative-externalities consequence of exceeding a channel's carrying capacity presents an even greater concern than is advanced by those ideas. Sections 12.4 and 12.5 then explore the First Amendment and regulatory responses to these concerns, arguing that the negative-externalities concern might justify limited regulatory response. In particular, Section 12.6 argues that platforms can reasonably be expected to implement "reasonable best-available technologies" to address noisy speech externalities.

12.2 INFORMATION THEORY, CHANNEL CAPACITY, AND THE SIGNAL-TO-NOISE RATIO

Initially developed by Claude Shannon at AT&T Bell Labs in the 1940s to study how, and how much, information could be transmitted over the communications channels making up the telephone network, information theory studies how we encode and transmit usable information over communications channels.[6] While mathematical and abstract in its characterization of information and communication, it is quite literally at the foundation of all modern communications networks.[7]

To understand the questions that information theory answers, we can start with a counterfactual. Imagine a perfect, noiseless, communications medium being used by two people to share meaningful information between them – say a professor wants to transmit a 90,000-word "article" to a journal editor. Assuming no limits on the part of the two communicating individuals, how quickly can one transmit that information to the other? We can ask the same question in a slightly different way: Because we assume the speakers do not impose any constraints (i.e., we assume that each can speak or listen at any speed), we want to know how much information the communications medium can carry per unit of time – its "channel capacity."[8]

To answer this to a first approximation, one could imagine that a professor could read the article aloud in three hours. So, the channel capacity is at least 30,000 words per hour. But we have assumed that the communicating individuals aren't the constraint. So, in principle, the professor could read faster, and the editor could

[6] *See* Hurwitz, *supra* note 3, at 259.

[7] C. E. Shannon, *A Mathematical Theory of Communications*, 27 BELL SYS. TECH. J. 379 (1948).

[8] A communications medium is referred to as a "channel" – as in a communications channel. As defined by Shannon, a "channel is merely the medium used to transmit the signal from transmitter to receiver." *Id.* at 381.

transcribe faster – say, 90,000 words per hour, or even 180,000 words per hour, or even 180,000,000 words per hour. In the limit case, because we have assumed that the endpoints (the speaker and listener) do not impose any constraints *and* that the communications channel is a perfect, noiseless medium, the professor and the editor could communicate instantaneously.

This of course is not the case. But it illustrates two distinct limits we need to be aware of: the ability of the endpoints (speaker and listener) to encode and decode information at a given speed, and the ability of the communications channel to transmit, or carry, that information at a given speed.

Shannon studied both the encoding and carrying questions. We are focused on the carrying question, which for Shannon boiled down to two factors: the strength of the information-carrying signal and the amount of background noise. Taken together, these define the *signal-to-noise ratio* of the communications channel (mathematically, signal divided by noise, or signal/noise). Increasing this ratio increases the channel capacity. This means that you can increase the channel capacity either by increasing the signal strength *or* by decreasing the noisiness of the channel.

This should make intuitive sense to anyone who has ever had conversation in a noisy room. It is hard to have a conversation at a loud party – you generally need to speak more slowly and loudly to be heard clearly. You speak more slowly because the carrying capacity of the room (qua communications channel) is reduced by the noise; you speak more loudly to increase the strength of your communications signal.

The example of the noisy room also demonstrates three key takeaways from information theory. What is the source of the "noise" in the room? Mostly other people having their own conversations, or perhaps music is playing in the background. This is not meaningless "noise." Noise is not merely static or unintelligible sound (though static would be noise). Rather, noise is any signal that is not carrying meaningful information *for the recipient*. The recipient needs to expend mental energy trying to differentiate signal from noise (if there is enough signal available to reconstruct the intended communication), which slows down her ability to receive information.

Second, all noise is, therefore, reciprocal. Your conversation is noise to everyone else in the room! This means that when you speak more loudly so that your interlocutor can make out what you are saying, you are increasing the amount of noise that everyone else in the room must deal with – you are worsening their signal-to-noise ratio.

Something similar happens when you exceed the carrying capacity of a given communications channel, even if there is no one using that channel other than the speaker and listener. If you think about having a conversation on a phone line with a lot of noise in the background, there is a maximum speed at which you can talk and be understood. What happens when you speak faster than this? The sounds you make become unintelligible – they become noise. This is another lesson quantified by Shannon: When a channel's carrying capacity is exceeded, any additional information put onto that channel is interpreted not as signal but as noise.[9]

This last observation illustrates a third key takeaway: Signal and noise are interpreted by, and at, the receiver. There could be a thousand conversations going on in the room. Only those that reach the given individual's ears contribute to the signal and noise she must decipher. Similarly, in the online context, the signal-to-noise ratio is a function only of the message that an individual receives, not of the universe of messages that a platform carries. If a platform that carries a billion messages each day only delivers the relevant, meaningful ones to its users, it will have a very high signal-to-noise ratio; if another platform carries tens or hundreds of messages each day but delivers them all to a user regardless of their relevance, requiring her to sift through all of the messages in order to find those of relevance to her, that platform will have a relatively low signal-to-noise ratio.

12.3 EXTERNALITIES AND SPEECH REGULATION

The discussion above tells us something additional about shared communications channels: At a certain point, information added to a communications channel creates a negative externality, reducing the capacity of that channel for everyone using it. But additional foundation is needed before we can look at why this carries an important lesson for how we think about speech regulation. The discussion below revisits the metaphor of the marketplace of ideas, looks at other scholars who have considered the challenges of limited communications capacity, and then introduces the idea that the negative externality created when a channel's carrying capacity is exceeded can justify regulation. It concludes by discussing some examples to illustrate these concerns.

12.3.1 *Recapitulating the Marketplace of Ideas*

Justice Holmes's dissent in *Abrams v. United States* introduced one of the most enduring metaphors of American law: the marketplace of ideas.[10] The concept of the marketplace of ideas is more intuitive than it is appealing: Just as better products (in terms of either price or quality) brought to market will sell better than inferior ones, so too will better ideas curry more favor with the public than lesser ones. And,

9 Shannon, *supra* note 7, at 410 ("If an attempt is made to transmit at a higher rate than C, say $C + R_1$, then there will necessarily be an equivocation equal to or greater than the excess R_1. Nature takes payment by requiring just that much uncertainty, so that we are not actually getting any more than C through correctly.").

10 250 U.S. 616, 630 (1919) (Holmes, J., dissenting) ("[T]he best test of truth is the power of the thought to get itself accepted in the competition of the market. . . . That at any rate is the theory of our Constitution.").

in dynamic terms, just as overpriced or low-quality products will encourage new entrants into the market, lesser ideas will create an opportunity for better ideas to prevail.

This metaphor does important work toward vindicating the First Amendment's protection of individuals' speech against government interference – indeed, this is its true appeal, rather than the idea that speech will work as a marketplace. It promises that there is a mechanism to arbitrate between competing speech in the place of the government. Even where there may be some social need for speech to be moderated, state actors can take a step back and rely on this alternative mechanism to moderate in their stead – a need that might otherwise create demand for government intervention.

The marketplace-of-ideas metaphor has monopolized understandings of the First Amendment's protection of speech for the past century. While one can, and many do, debate its propriety and fidelity to the Amendment, I will posit that it was fit to task for most of this era. And the reason for this is that the listener-to-speaker ratio was relatively high. This was an era of rapidly changing technologies during which innovation ensured that new entrants and media were regularly entering the marketplace, but the high capital costs of those technologies inhibited entry, largely limiting it to those with the resources and ability to sincerely engage as a participant in this marketplace. A relative few broadcast platforms competed for market share based on the quality of their reporting, and a number of local media outlets pruned these broadcasters' speech even further as a means to reach local communities. And throughout much of the twentieth century, where media failed a community's needs, entry was both possible and often occurred.

12.3.2 *Other Characterizations of Speech Regulation*

As we entered the modern era of communications – with the widespread adoption of cable television and explosive growth of talk radio in the 1980s and the rapid digitalization of consumer-focused communications in the early 1990s[11] – increasing attention was paid to the idea of "too much information."[12] Indeed, television had famously been described as a "vast wasteland" as early as 1961.[13] By the early 1990s, the number of channels that cable systems could carry exceeded the number of channels of content being produced, satellite systems that could carry several times

[11] *Cf.* Note, *The Awareness Doctrine*, 135 Harv. L. Rev. 1907, 1911 (2022) (citing Steve Rendall, *The Fairness Doctrine: How We Lost It, and Why We Need It Back*, FAIR (Jan. 1, 2005), https://perma.cc/P557-C8FA), *with* Marvin Ammori, *The Fairness Doctrine: A Flawed Means to Attain a Noble Goal*, 60 Admin. L. Rev. 881 (2008) (discussing issues with the Fairness Doctrine in practice).

[12] *See, e.g.*, Cass Sunstein, Too Much Information: Understanding What You Do not Want to Know (2020).

[13] Newton N. Minow, *Television and the Public Interest*, 55 Fed. Commc'ns L.J. 395, 397 (2003).

that many channels were being developed, and the internet had come to the attention of sophisticated commentators.

Around the turn of the century, for instance, Cass Sunstein and Richard Posner both considered how the changing media landscape might affect our understanding of media regulation.[14] Sunstein, for instance, juxtaposed the marketplace-of-ideas approach to free speech with a Madisonian perspective, under which the purpose of the First Amendment is not merely to protect private speakers from government intrusion into their speech, but also affirmatively to promote and facilitate deliberative democracy.[15] Under the marketplace model, regulatory intervention had generally only been understood as appropriate in the face of scarcity – a lack of sufficient communications channels that prevented competition within the marketplace. As newer technologies increased the capacity of communications channels, and decreased the cost of deploying new ones, this rationale for regulating speech diminished. But, Sunstein argued, the Madisonian perspective suggested that regulation might nonetheless be appropriate if the new, emerging marketplace of ideas was not conducive to a functioning deliberative democracy.[16]

A decade later, Richard Posner considered many of the same issues that result from the decreasing costs of entering the market and sharing information in the information ecosystem.[17] He presented a different perspective than Sunstein, however, arguing that most consumers of information had always primarily wanted entertainment – not droll information – and that increased competition in the marketplace was catering to this interest.[18] In typical contrarian Posnerian fashion, he argued this was possibly not a bad thing: Just as increased competition in the marketplace catered to those citizens who were more interested in entertainment than in information, it would also better cater to those citizens who were more interested in information.[19]

[14] Cass R. Sunstein, *The First Amendment in Cyberspace*, 104 Yale L.J. 1757 (1995); Richard Posner, *Bad News*, N.Y. Times Book Rev. (July 31, 2005) (reviewing and discussing eight recent books on the changing media landscape).

[15] Sunstein, *supra* note 14, at 1759.

[16] *Id.* at 1804.

[17] Posner, *supra* note 14.

[18] *Id.* ("But increased competition has not produced a public more oriented toward public issues, more motivated and competent to engage in genuine self-government, because these are not the goods that most people are seeking from the news media. They are seeking entertainment, confirmation, reinforcement, emotional satisfaction; and what consumers want, a competitive market supplies, no more, no less.").

[19] *Id.* ("Yet what of the sliver of the public that does have a serious interest in policy issues? Are these people less well served than in the old days? Another recent survey by the Pew Research Center finds that serious magazines have held their own and that serious broadcast outlets, including that bane of the right, National Public Radio, are attracting ever larger audiences. And for that sliver of a sliver that invites challenges to its biases by reading The New York Times and The Wall Street Journal, that watches CNN and Fox, that reads Brent Bozell and Eric Alterman and everything in between, the increased polarization of the media provides a richer fare than ever before.").

More recently, there have been arguments about "too much information" and "information overload."[20] The general theme of these arguments is apparent on their face: Consumers of information face a glut of information that overwhelms their ability to process it all. A generation or two ago, there were relatively few sources of information. Consumers could reasonably assume that these sources had gone through some kind of vetting process and were therefore basically trustworthy. Indeed, should they so desire, an interested consumer could at least somewhat meaningfully undertake to investigate the quality of those competing information sources. The "too much information" argument says that neither of these is as possible today, if it is possible at all, as in it was prior generations – that the sheer quantity of information we encounter on a day-to-day basis undermines media sources' authority and interferes with listeners' purposes. And this resonates with the "marketplace-of-ideas" frame as well, for markets are driven, in part, by the consumer's ability to make informed choices – if that is not possible, the marketplace may not work.

There is another, more recent, argument that, again, challenges the marketplace orthodoxy: listeners' rights.[21] The listeners'-rights idea echoes the Madisonian (i.e., democracy-oriented) perspective on the First Amendment, though it may or may not be aligned with the marketplace concept. Under this view, the purpose of the First Amendment is not merely to ensure individuals' unfettered ability to speak without government interference, but also to ensure that individuals have access to (viz., the opportunity to listen to) information without undue government interference. Thus, if listeners want certain types of information but speakers interfere with their ability to obtain that information, the government may have some role in mediating that conflict and, when it does so, it should preference the listeners' choices about what information they want to receive over the speakers' efforts to influence the speakers.

12.3.3 *An Externalities Argument for Speech Regulation*

We can now return to the ideas introduced with information theory. The discussion in Section 12.2 concluded with the idea that any additional speech added to a saturated communications channel is interpreted as noise, not signal, by all parties to that communications channel. This has the effect of worsening the signal-to-noise ratio, which reduces the overall channel capacity for everyone using that communications channel. In effect, this combines both the "too much information" construct and the listeners'-rights understanding of the First Amendment.

More important, it introduces a fundamentally different justification for (and, as will be discussed in Sections 12.4 and 12.5, a different approach to) speech regulation: externalities. Both the "too much information" and listeners'-rights perspectives

20 SUNSTEIN, *supra* note 12.

21 James Grimmelmann, *Listeners' Choices*, 90 COLO. L. REV. 65 (2019).

present an information-asymmetry rationale for regulating the marketplace of ideas. Information asymmetries are a traditional justification for intervening to regulate a market: When one side of the market systematically has better information than the other, we might regulate to prevent harmful exploitation of that information.[22] For instance, we may require nutrition or energy-usage labels on products where consumers are not in a position to ascertain that information on their own. So too one could imagine requiring disclosures about the sources of information that speakers communicate to listeners, either as a way of helping consumers to meaningfully make use of the glut of information communicated to them or as a way of vindicating their rights to receive meaningful information as balanced against speakers' rights to share information.[23]

Externalities are another traditional justification for regulating markets.[24] Externalities occur where one party's private conduct has impacts on one or more third parties. Those impacts are "external" to the primary private conduct – as such, parties engaging in that conduct have little incentive to take them into account. Perhaps the most standard example of an externality is pollution: If I burn coal to generate electricity and no one has told me that I cannot put smoke into the air, I will not factor the environmental, health, or other costs of that pollution into my prices. The same can be said for many other types of activity (sometimes even individual conduct) and can be positive or negative. A neighborhood in which many people have dogs that they need to take on walks regularly (a private activity) may not be as welcoming to individuals who are scared of dogs (a negative externality) and also may have less crime (a positive externality).

Importantly, because the impacts of negative externalities are usually dispersed among many people and are difficult to measure except in aggregate, it may not be possible for injured parties to bring a lawsuit to recover for the injuries, either practically or as a matter of law. Lawmakers therefore might step in to address externalities, such as by prohibiting the underlying private conduct, requiring the parties to it to take care to prevent the externalities, or imposing taxes or fees on those parties that can be used to compensate any injured third parties to the case.

Additional speech – even ostensibly productive speech – added to a saturated communications channel has the characteristics of a negative externality. Because

[22] *See* THOMAS LAMBERT, HOW TO REGULATE: A GUIDE FOR POLICYMAKERS 185–218 (2017). *See also* George A. Akerlof, *The Market for "Lemons": Quality Uncertainty and the Market Mechanism*, 84 Q.J. ECON. 488 (1970); Howard Beales, Richard Craswell & Steven C. Salop, *The Efficient Regulation of Consumer Information*, 24 J.L. & ECON. 491 (1981).

[23] This is not meant to advocate for either of those outcomes. One could also imagine a Posnerian market-based approach in which information providers compete to be trustworthy by making the information they provide easy for consumers to verify. It is entirely possible that the market could address concerns about either listeners being overwhelmed by information or vindicating their rights against speakers better than regulatory approaches.

[24] *See* LAMBERT, *supra* note 22, at 22–59. *See also* Garrett Hardin, *The Tragedy of the Commons*, 162 SCI. 1243 (1968); Ronald Coase, *The Problem of Social Cost*, 3 J.L. & ECON. 1 (1960).

the carrying capacity of the channel is already saturated, the additional speech is interpreted by all who hear it as noise. This worsens the signal-to-noise ratio, further decreasing the carrying capacity of the channel. In a very real sense, noise is like air pollution: Just as pollution reduces the usability of air for all who breathe it, noise reduces the usability of a communications channel for all who communicate over it. Thinking back to the example of the loud room at a party, it is intuitive that if someone walks into a room in which several people are having conversations and turns up the volume on a stereo, this act will negatively impact the ability of all those in the room to continue their conversations.

12.3.4 *Some Examples of Noisy Speech Externalities*

Pointing to concrete examples of noisy speech externalities is challenging because the concept itself is somewhat abstract, and because the impacts may not be readily identifiable as discrete events.

The example of the noisy room presents a case study: At some point, a quiet room becomes too noisy to comfortably have a conversation; at a further point, it becomes impractical to have a conversation; at a further point, it becomes impossible to have a conversation. This transition charts the increasing harms that stem from noisy speech externalities. These harms most clearly need remedy when conversation becomes impossible. But in practice, the forum is likely to be abandoned by most participants before that point.

Useful forums have to solve the signal-to-noise problem somehow, then, and they differentiate themselves by addressing the problem in different ways. Newspapers are as much a filter of information as a source of information; so are television and radio stations. Bookstores sort their books into sections and by topics; publishers select books for publication, perhaps filtering by subject, genre, or audience, and ensuring a quality threshold. Noisy forums are not usually sought after as platforms for information sharing. One would not ordinarily negotiate a contract at a rock concert or debate politics with strangers in a busy subway station.

Social media presents the clearest setting for examples of noisy speech externalities – and mis- and disinformation are likely the clearest examples. The very promise of social-media platforms is that they allow users to communicate directly with one another – their defining feature is that they do *not* filter or select the information shared between users. And they also lack the traditional indicia of being too noisy to serve as a forum for information to be exchanged. A rock concert is a poor forum because all of the sound is heard at once – attendees attempting to have a conversation necessarily hear the loud music at the same time they are trying to hear their interlocutor – making it difficult to differentiate signal from noise. But in the social-media setting, content is presented in individual pieces, creating a perception for users that they have the ability to meaningfully engage with it.

We see the effects of noisy speech externalities, both intentionally and unintentionally created, with dis- and misinformation. For instance, there is some agreement that Russia weaponized disinformation around the 2016 U.S. election.[25] Commentators such as Bruce Schneier have argued that the purpose of Russian disinformation campaigns has been less to influence specific outcomes than to attack the American information ecosystem.[26] An adversary can win just as much by attacking our ability to separate fact from fiction as by convincing us to accept falsity as truth. But we do not need to turn to deliberate efforts to cause harm for examples. The inventor of X's "retweet" button, for instance, has described the retweet feature as "hand[ing] a 4-year-old a loaded weapon."[27] Speaking of an example, he said: "Ask any of the people who were targets at that time, retweeting helped them get a false picture of a person out there faster than they could respond. We did not build a defense for that. We only built an offensive conduit."[28]

It is important to note here – and to draw attention to a theme to which I will return in Part IV – that the point of these examples is not to say that they demonstrate that X (or any other particular platform) ought to be regulated. To the contrary, platforms like X have always tried to develop new features to address concerns like these. Even the retweet feature was initially envisaged as a way to improve the signal-to-noise ratio (the theory being that making it easier to quickly share good information would help users get more information that they wanted). Platforms like Reddit have comprehensive user-based moderation technologies and norms.[29] Facebook and X have invested substantially in addressing mis- and disinformation. The argument I make in Section 12.5 is that it may be reasonable and permissible for Congress to require firms to engage in such efforts, and that efforts such as these should satisfy any regulatory obligations.

12.4 PRELIMINARIES OF ADDRESSING NOISY SPEECH EXTERNALITIES

Whether there is need and legally justifiable reason to support regulating speech in the digital era has prompted substantial debate in recent years. Arguments against such regulations most often sound, on both fronts, in the metaphor of the marketplace of ideas: The ostensible problem we face today is that the cost of speech is too

[25] *See* Henry Farrell & Bruce Schneier, *Democracy's Dilemma*, BOS. REV. (May 15, 2019), https://perma.cc/MC27-J4K4; YOCHAI BENKLER, ROBERT FARIS & HAL ROBERTS, NETWORK PROPAGANDA: MANIPULATION, DISINFORMATION, AND RADICALIZATION IN AMERICAN POLITICS (2018).

[26] *Id.*

[27] Alex Kantrowitz, *The Man Who Built the Retweet: "We Handed A Loaded Weapon to 4-Year-Olds"*, BUZZFEED (July 23, 2019), https://perma.cc/5LQ8-QFWC.

[28] *Id.*

[29] *See Reddit Mod Education,* REDDIT, https://perma.cc/R8QX-V5WV.

low and the barriers to expression are too few, both of which would typically support the functioning of a robust marketplace.[30] The discussion below argues that concern about negative externalities derived from an information-theory-based understanding of channel capacity is sufficient to justify and overcome fundamental legal obstacles (i.e., First Amendment concerns) to regulation. It then considers what such regulation could look like, drawing from other settings where the law addresses externalities.

12.4.1 *Speech Regulation and the First Amendment*

The first question is simply, as a matter of law, whether noisy speech externalities provide a cognizable legal basis for speech regulation – that is, whether such regulation could survive First Amendment scrutiny. As above, debates about such speech regulation are often framed in terms of Madisonian vs Holmesian principles, whether the purpose of the First Amendment is to support robust democratic engagement or to foster a robust marketplace of ideas. But it may be useful to anchor the discussion in more doctrinal terms: Would regulation intended to address noisy speech externalities survive First Amendment scrutiny under existing doctrine?

There are two distinct lines of cases most relevant to this question: broadcast-regulation cases (e.g., *Red Lion*, *Pacifica*, *Turner*)[31] and the noise-regulation cases (such as *Ward v. Rock Against Racism*).[32] The broadcast cases are the foundation for media regulation in the United States – and, as foundations go, they are notably weak. They derive from midcentury understandings of spectrum and technological ability to use spectrum as a broadcast medium. The central concept of these cases is *scarcity*.[33] Because spectrum was a scarce resource that only supported relatively few television or radio broadcast stations in any geographic area, there was sufficient justification for the government to regulate who had access to that spectrum in order to ensure "the right of the public to receive suitable access to social, political, esthetic, moral and other ideas and experiences."[34] These cases expressly discuss this right in terms of the marketplace of ideas – importantly, scarcity is one of the most traditional justifications for regulation to intervene in the operation of markets – though it is arguably the case that this "right" is compatible with the Madisonian view of the First Amendment.

[30] *See* Posner, *supra* note 14; Eugene Volokh, *Cheap Speech and What It Will Do*, 104 YALE L.J. 1805 (1995).

[31] Red Lion Broad. Co. v. Fed. Commc'ns Comm'n, 395 U.S. 367 (1969); Fed. Commc'ns Comm'n v. Pacifica Found., 438 U.S. 726 (1978); Turner Broad. Sys., Inc. v. Fed. Commc'ns Comm'n, 520 U.S. 180 (1997).

[32] Ward v. Rock Against Racism, 491 U.S. 781 (1989).

[33] Nat'l Broad. Co. v. United States, 319 U.S. 190 (1943).

[34] *Red Lion*, 395 U.S. at 390.

Ward v. Rock Against Racism is best known for its treatment of content-neutral "time, place, and manner" restrictions on speech and its clarification that such regulations need only be narrowly tailored to address a legitimate government purpose, not the least restrictive means of doing so.[35] Curiously, *Ward v. Rock* itself dealt with noise regulations that limited the volume of music at a concert in New York's Central Park – though the Court's concern about "noise" in that case is understood in the colloquial sense of "disturbing or distracting sound" rather than in information theory's more technical sense. But even without resorting to information theory and the concern that noise reduces a channel's information-carrying capacity, this type of noise is a classic example of a negative externality.[36]

Where a communications channel is at its carrying capacity, we may see both scarcity and negative externalities coming into play. Scarcity does not necessarily implicate externalities, because the lack of options may not affect third parties. And externalities alone do not necessarily meaningfully implicate scarcity because they can adversely affect every option that a consumer may reasonably have. But if a communications channel reaches the point of saturation, that suggests that its users do not have a robust set of alternative channels available to them (as otherwise they would switch to a less congested channel) and so face scarcity, and that any additional information added to that channel worsens the signal-to-noise ratio for all users, creating a negative externality.

It is therefore likely, or at least plausible, that the government would have a substantial interest in narrowly tailored regulations intended to lessen these impacts on a content-neutral basis.

12.4.2 *Technical Responses to a Poor Signal-to-Noise Ratio*

Mathematically, the way to address a poor signal-to-noise ratio is to increase the strength of the signal or decrease the amount of noise in the signal. This guides technical approaches to addressing a poor signal-to-noise ratio. In settings where the communications channel's capacity is not exceeded, the signal strength can be directly increased (akin to speaking more loudly). Alternatively, filters can be added to reduce noise, either at the transmitter or receiver. Importantly, filters can both reject true "noise" (e.g., background static), or they can reject "unwanted signal." For instance, a radio receiver might use a filter to reject signal from adjacent radio stations (e.g., a radio tuned to FM station 101.3 might filter out signal from stations 101.1 and 101.5).

[35] *Ward*, 491 U.S. at 791.

[36] It bears emphasis that the negative externality of noise alone is less substantial than that which occurs when incremental speech is added to a saturated communications channel. In the latter case, the incremental speech is a negative impact on its own, but it has the more substantial effect of making otherwise-meaningful speech also on the communications channel indistinguishable from noise.

In more complex settings, such as cellular telephone networks, solutions are more sophisticated. In cellular networks, capacity can be increased by adding more "cells" (antennas spread across the network) and decreasing the power at which the antennas within them transmit. Adding more cells brings antennas closer to cell phones – the reduced distance decreases the minimum signal strength that is needed for communications. This, in turn, reduces the extent to which one's phone interferes with another's. And there is always the least-sophisticated solution to a poor signal-to-noise ratio: decreasing the speed of communications.[37]

12.4.3 *Legal Responses to Externalities*

On the legal side of the ledger, there are both public and private legal institutions that address externalities. On the public law side of the ledger, environmental regulation to reduce pollution presents the clearest analogy. Here, there are a few standard tools in the regulatory toolbox. Environmental regulations, for instance, might implement direct command-and-control-style regulations, prohibiting certain types of conduct (such as the emission of certain pollutants beyond a threshold, and an absolute prohibition on the use or emission of certain pollutants or chemicals).[38] In other cases, the EPA uses "best-available control technology" (BACT) or similar requirements, under which the agency will undertake a regulatory process to ascertain the state-of-the-art in pollution-control technologies and require sources of pollutants to use those technologies.[39]

There are also private law institutions that address externalities – though they are relatively rare to see implemented at scale. In common law, these are most often seen in the context of new or changing technologies that lead to new conflicts between individuals. For instance, when once-distant residential communities and industrial farming operations expand to the point that they are near-neighbors,[40]

37 While less sophisticated, this approach is nonetheless important. It is probably one of the two intuitive responses to overcoming a poor signal-to-noise ratio (the other being to increase signal strength – that is, to speak more loudly or clearly). It also finds analogy in discussions about online speech regulation, for instance with suggestions that platforms insert "friction" into speech.

38 *See, e.g.*, Bruce A. Ackerman & Richard B. Stewart, *Reforming Environmental Law*, 37 Stan. L. Rev. 1333 (1985); Rena Steinzor, *Reinventing Environmental Regulation: The Dangerous Journey from Command to Self-Control*, 22 Harv. Env't L. Rev. 103 (1998) ("Command and control rules impose detailed, legally enforceable limits, conditions, and affirmative requirements on industrial operations, generally controlling sources that generate pollution on an individual basis.").

39 Steinzor, *supra* note 38, at 114; Ackerman & Stewart, *supra* note 38, at 1335 (discussing best-available technology regulations); 42 U.S.C § 7475(a)(4) ("[T]he proposed facility is subject to the best available control technology for each pollutant subject to regulation under this chapter.").

40 Spur Industries v. Del E. Webb Development Co., 108 Ariz. 178 (1972).

noise-generating machinery is installed in areas where it was not previously used,[41] cement plants expand to serve the needs of growing communities,[42] new construction obstructs longstanding enjoyment of the sun,[43] or new technologies such as mills alter the character and landscape of a community,[44] judges may be called in to adjudicate the uncertain rights that exist between individuals engaging in these activities and the third parties affected by the externalities resulting from them. Most often, legal claims arising from these changing uses are styled as regarding public or private nuisance – although where they implicate rights that have been clearly established under the common law or statute, they may be treated as trespass or statutory violations.

12.5 HOW WE SHOULD REGULATE NOISY SPEECH EXTERNALITIES

This brings us to this chapter's ultimate question: How should we regulate online speech in response to noisy speech externalities? My answer is that we should adopt a model similar to that used by the EPA for pollution control – a best-available control technology – but rely on customary industry practices to determine whether such a standard is being met. Unlike the EPA model, the baseline requirement in this setting ought to be a "reasonable best-available technology" requirement, recognizing the vast variation between the capabilities of various platforms and needs of their users. One option for implementing this requirement is to make Section 230's liability shield contingent upon the use of such technologies.[45]

Section 12.4.3 introduced standard legal approaches to addressing externalities, including public law approaches such as environmental regulation and private law approaches such as nuisance and trespass claims. So far, neither of these approaches have been put into practice in the online environment. Rather, Section 230 of the Communications Decency Act creates a permissive self-regulatory environment.[46] Section 230 frees up platforms to moderate users' speech while making clear that they are under no obligation to do so.[47] Under this approach, platforms are shielded from liability for any harms caused by speech generated by their users, including to the speech interests of their other users.

[41] Sturges v. Bridgman, 11 Ch. D. 852 (1879).

[42] Boomer v. Atlantic Cement Co., 257 N.E.2d 870 (N.Y. 1970).

[43] Fontainebleau H. Corp. v. Forty-Five Twenty-Five, Inc., 114 So. 2d 357 (Fla. Ct. App. 1960); Prah v. Maretti, 108 Wis. 2d 223 (1982).

[44] Rylands v. Fletcher, L.R. 3 H.L. 330 (1868).

[45] The most trenchant response to proposals such as this is that weakening Section 230's liability shield creates a legitimately worrisome possibility of harming platforms – especially smaller platforms that cannot easily absorb the cost of litigation – by exposing them to potential claims sufficient to survive a motion to dismiss. This concern is addressed near the end of this section.

[46] 47 U.S.C. § 230.

[47] § 230(c)(2) provides that platforms shall not be held liable on account of their moderation activities and § 230(c)(1) provides that they shall not be held liable for information shared by their users.

Section 12.4.1, however, suggested that the government may have a sufficient interest in regulating this speech with narrowly tailored regulations intended to lessen the impacts of noisy speech externalities. We might look to aspects of both public and private law approaches to regulating externalities for a model of how the government could respond to noisy speech externalities. In the final analysis, this approach would combine the self-regulatory approach embraced by Section 230 with an affirmative requirement that platforms use best-available content-moderation technologies as suitable for their scale.[48]

Pollution and pollution control are the most traditional legal analogies for thinking about noisy speech externalities and their regulation – and the control-technologies analogy maps onto the concept of content-moderation technologies. A requirement that a platform uses "best-available content-moderation technology" to ensure as best as possible that its users have meaningful access to content on the platform is a content-neutral policy. More-prescriptive policies would run the risk of making content-based distinctions, especially if they were based in concerns that some types of speech on platforms were more or less in need of protection.[49] And while policies such as a common-carrier obligation would likely qualify as facially neutral, their effect on the signal-to-noise ratio of platforms would be to render the platforms useless for the vast majority of communications.[50]

Content-moderation techniques and technologies are akin to technological filters or amplifiers that reduce noise or increase the strength of desirable signal to improve the signal-to-noise ratio. These techniques or technologies may come in many forms (indeed, they need not be technological or algorithmic, but could result, for instance, from cultivating community norms or market mechanisms). Their defining characteristic is that they improve a platform's signal-to-noise ratio, making it easier for users to engage with desired information (signal) or less likely that they will encounter undesired information (noise). As with filters and amplifiers, these

[48] That last proviso, "as suitable for their scale," is likely redundant. A small platform likely has little need for significant content moderation practices because users are likely able to replicate the experience of that platform on any number of other platforms. As the scale of the platform grows, the value of content moderation grows, and the costs to the platform of poor practices potentially decreases as users face fewer competitive alternatives. In addition to potential competition considerations, it is potentially the case that as the signal-to-noise ratio decreases, so too will users' ability to evaluate the quality of the platform. This creates an endogenous challenge that might on its own justify some amount of regulatory intervention.

[49] *See, e.g.*, Turner Broad. Sys., Inc. v. Fed. Commc'ns Comm'n, 520 U.S. 180, 234 (O'Connor, J., dissenting) ("But appellees' characterization of must-carry as a means of protecting [local broadcast] stations, like the Court's explicit concern for promoting 'community self-expression' and the 'local origination of broadcast programming,' reveals a content-based preference for broadcast programming.").

[50] Indeed, one could argue that a common-carrier obligation would amplify certain types of speech over others in a social-media environment. If we need carriage guaranteed to ensure that some types of speech are viable on the platform, that suggests that the regulations are not, in fact, content-neutral. *Id.*

technologies can be misconfigured – content moderation can have the effect of amplifying harmful speech or filtering desirable speech. But this is a specific question of how a technology is implemented (including whether it is a "best-available" technology), not a question of the viability or desirability of the underlying technology.

The harder question is who decides what content-moderation technologies are reasonably considered "best available" and how regulation based upon those technologies may be implemented. In the environmental-regulation context, this is done through a regulatory process in which the regulator gathers information about industry practices and dictates what technologies to use. This is not a desirable approach in the speech-moderation setting. As an initial matter, different content-moderation technologies may have different effects on different speech or speakers. Unlike in the pollution context, this potentially creates substantial issues, including embedding content-based distinctions into regulations. That could bring us into the domain of strict scrutiny and concerns about government interference in private speech – a central concern against which the First Amendment is meant to protect.

An additional challenge is the range of speech and the range of platforms hosting that speech. This is a more dynamic environment than the environmental-pollution setting. The EPA regulates a small number of pollutants produced by a small number of chemical processes, which can only be addressed by a small number of control technologies. This makes assessing the best available among those control technologies a tractable task. Courts and regulators are unlikely to be able to keep up to speed with changing needs and capabilities of content moderation – indeed, they are likely to lack the sophistication needed to understand how the technologies even work. And different technologies may be better or worse suited to different types of speech or different types of communication platforms.

It is not unusual for courts to look to industry custom in the face of changing technologies or scientifically complex settings.[51] This is a setting where deference to customary industry practices, as opposed to prescriptive command-and-control regulation, makes good sense. And it is an important margin along which online speech platforms compete today. Indeed, platforms invest substantially in their content-moderation operations and are continually innovating new techniques to filter undesired speech, amplify desired speech, and generally to give users greater control of the information that they receive. To be sure, not all of these technologies succeed, and platforms often need to balance the effectiveness of these technologies with the business needs of the platform. To take one example of the former effect, the initial theory behind adding the ability to "like" and

[51] The classic case demonstrating the role of industry custom in judicial decision-making is *The T.J. Hooper*, 60 F.2d 737 (2d Cir. 1932). Medical-malpractice cases are an instance where courts rely on customary practices as a tool for understanding complex scientific settings. *See, e.g.*, Richard N. Pearson, *The Role of Custom in Medical Malpractice Cases*, 51 Ind. L.J. 528 (1976).

"retweet" content on X was to amplify desirable content – but its greater effect was to substantially worsen the platform's signal-to-noise ratio by increasing the velocity of lower-value content and superficial engagement with that content.[52] On the other hand, tools like verified accounts and the ability for high-reputation users to help moderate posts through systems like X's Birdwatch or Reddit's moderator system provide useful amplification and filters that help manage the platforms' signal-to-noise ratios.

Of course, any regulation of online platforms' speech practices needs to confront Section 230's liability shield. Today, Section 230 permits but does not require platforms to adopt content-moderation policies. As suggested above, if a platform is exceeding its channel-carrying capacity without losing users, this suggests there is a market failure keeping those users beholden to the platform. At that point, justification for Section 230's permissive no-moderation provisions are at their nadir and it becomes reasonable to expect the platform to adopt improved moderation practices.

This is no small recommendation, and I do not make it lightly. Weakening the protections of Section 230's liability shield significantly increases the cost of litigation, especially for smaller platforms. In its current form, it is difficult for a plaintiff in a Section 230 case to survive a motion to dismiss. Making that shield contingent upon a nebulous "reasonable best-available technology" requirement invites suits that would survive a motion to dismiss. Critically, this raises significant concerns that litigation could deprive platforms' users of their chosen venue for the exercise of their constitutionally protected speech rights. Any alteration to Section 230's liability shield should thus be accompanied by specific requirements to counterbalance these concerns, such as sanctions for sham or strategic litigation, fee-shifting requirements, specific pleading or discovery requirements, and safe harbors for smaller platforms. These should be accompanied by a presumption that any industry-standard content-moderation techniques satisfy a "reasonable best-available technology" benchmark. Policymakers might also consider a two-pronged requirement (a) that concerns about a platform's content-moderation practices must be reported to a state attorney general prior to the commencement of a suit and (b) that a private suit can only be brought after that attorney general non-prejudicially declines to conduct their own investigation.

12.6 CONCLUSION

A central tenet of contemporary First Amendment law is the metaphor of the marketplace of ideas – that the solution to bad speech is more, better speech. But this is built upon an assumption that more, better speech is possible. Information theory tells us that there are circumstances where any additional speech is necessarily bad speech. This is analytically equivalent to an externality, a common form of market failure and traditional regulatory intervention; and it is analogically

[52] Kantrowitz, *supra* note 27.

equivalent to a market failure in the marketplace of ideas. Indeed, examples of regulation in the face of such failures are common in cases such as pollution and nuisance law – as well as in the First Amendment setting.

This chapter has argued that regulation may be justified, and may survive First Amendment challenges, in cases where noisy speech externalities are likely to occur. It also argues that such regulation should draw from the examples of pollution control's use of best-available control technologies to mitigate these externalities – but that unlike the pollution setting, courts should look to customary industry practices to evaluate whether a particular platform is using such technologies. This chapter suggests that Section 230's liability shield, which currently allows but does not require platforms to implement any content-moderation technologies, should require platforms to adopt such technologies. However, this is likely a less radical suggestion than it may seem, as most platforms already actively use and develop content-moderation technologies in the standard course of business; such efforts should be sufficient to satisfy a "best-available content-moderation technology" requirement. Rather, only platforms that actively eschew content-moderation practices, or that otherwise neglect these technologies, would risk the loss of Section 230's liability shield.

13

Content Moderation in Practice

Laura Edelson

13.1 INTRODUCTION

Almost all platforms for user-generated content have written policies around what content they are and are not willing to host, even if these policies are not always public. Even platforms explicitly designed to host adult content, such as OnlyFans,[1] have community guidelines. Of course, different platforms' content policies can differ widely in multiple regards. Platforms differ on everything from what content they do and do not allow, to how vigorously they enforce their rules, to the mechanisms for enforcement itself. Nevertheless, nearly all platforms have two sets of content criteria: one set of rules setting a minimum floor for what content the platform is willing to host at all, and a more rigorous set of rules defining standards for advertising content. Many social-media platforms also have additional criteria for what content they will actively recommend to users that differ from their more general standards of what content they are willing to host at all.

These differences, which exist in both policy and enforcement, create vastly different user experiences of content moderation in practice. This chapter will review the content-moderation policies and enforcement practices of Meta's Facebook platform, YouTube (owned by Google), TikTok, Reddit, and Zoom, focusing on four key areas of platforms' content-moderation policies and practices: the content policies as they are written, the context in which platforms say those rules will be enforced, the mechanisms they use for enforcement, and how platforms communicate enforcement decisions to users in different scenarios.

Platforms usually outline their content-moderation policies in their community guidelines or standards. These guideline documents are broad and usually have rules about what kinds of actions users can take on their platform and what content can be posted. These guideline documents often also describe the context in which

[1] *Help*, ONLYFANS, https://perma.cc/WCW7-VDSY.

rules will be enforced. Many platforms also provide information about the enforcement actions they may take against content that violates the rules. However, details about the consequences for users who post such content are typically sparse.

More detail is typically available about different platforms' mechanisms for enforcement. Platforms can enforce policies manually by having human reviewers check content for compliance directly, or they can employ automated methods to identify violating content. In practice, many platforms employ a hybrid approach, employing automated means to identify content that may need additional human review. Whether they employ a primarily manual or primarily automated approach, platforms have an additional choice to make regarding what will trigger enforcement of their rules. Platforms can enforce their content-moderation policies either proactively by looking for content that violates policies or reactively by responding to user complaints about violating content.

Platforms also have a range of actions they can take regarding content found to be policy violating. The bluntest tool they can employ is simply to take the content down. A subtler option involves changing how the content is displayed by showing the content with a disclaimer or by requiring a user to make an additional click to see the content. Platforms can also restrict who can see the content, limiting it to users over an age minimum or in a particular geographic region. Lastly, platforms can make content ineligible for recommendation, an administrative decision that might be entirely hidden from users.

Once a moderation decision is made, either by an automated system or by a human reviewer, platforms have choices about how (and whether) to inform the content creator about the decision. Sometimes platforms withhold notice in order to avoid negative reactions from users, though certain enforcement actions are hard or impossible to hide. In other instances, platforms may wish to keep users informed about actions they take either to create a sense of transparency or to nudge the user not to post violating content in the future.

13.2 FACEBOOK

Facebook (owned by Meta) has made more information about its content-moderation policies and practices available compared to other social-media companies discussed here. However, it is also the only major platform at the time of this writing that gives an outside body, its external Oversight Board, discretion over the enforcement of its policies.

13.2.1 *Content Policies*

Facebook outlines its content policies in its Community Standards.[2] Broadly speaking, Facebook prohibits or otherwise restricts content that promotes violent or

[2] *Facebook Community Standards*, META, https://perma.cc/G36P-CAU8.

criminal behavior, poses a safety risk, or is "objectionable content," usually defined as hate speech, sexual content, or graphic violence.

Violent, sexual, hateful, and fraudulent content are all prohibited outright. However, there are limited exceptions for newsworthy content, such as police body-cam footage from shooting incidents, which must be shared behind a warning label if at all. Content that poses an immediate safety risk, such as non-consensual "outing" of LGBTQ+ individuals or doxing, is always prohibited. Many other forms of "borderline" content are restricted, rather than banned outright, if it is found to be satirical, expressed as an opinion, or newsworthy.

Meta's policy around misinformation is more ambiguous than these prohibited categories of content. The company's policy says, "misinformation is different from other types of speech addressed in our Community Standards because there is no way to articulate a comprehensive list of what is prohibited." The policy continues, "We remove misinformation where it is likely to directly contribute to the risk of imminent physical harm. We also remove content that is likely to directly contribute to interference with the functioning of political processes and certain highly deceptive manipulated media."[3] In practice, this policy has produced subcategories of misinformation with varying levels of protection. For example, over the past several years, the company has interpreted this policy as prohibiting vaccine misinformation but not climate change-related misinformation.

13.2.2 *Enforcement Practices*

Meta also provides some information about Facebook's policy-enforcement practices in its "Transparency Center."[4] Facebook says that it enforces its policies with a mix of automated methods and human reviewers who train the automated systems over time. In Meta's words, a new automated system "might have low confidence about whether a piece of content violates our policies. Review teams can then make the final call, and our technology can learn from each human decision. Over time – after learning from thousands of human decisions – the technology becomes more accurate."[5]

This quote describes a fairly standard process in machine learning where automated systems and humans collaborate to make decisions, with humans having a more significant role early in the process and automated systems "learning" from the decisions humans make over time. While Meta's documentation clearly states that human reviewers make the call when automated classifiers have low confidence, it is less clear about human reviewers' role in more established domains. Meta states that there are some circumstances where automated systems remove content

3 *Misinformation*, META, https://perma.cc/2DTC-R7CT.
4 *How Meta Enforces Its Policies*, META, https://perma.cc/82GV-37N6.
5 *Id.*

without human intervention: "Our technology will take action on a new piece of content if it matches or comes very close to another piece of violating content." According to Meta, their "technology [i.e., automated system] finds more than 90% of the content we remove before anyone reports it for most violation categories."[6] A careful reader will note that this does not say that 90 percent of content is *removed* before users report it, only that it is *found* before users report it. Still, it is likely a safe assumption that the vast majority of content moderation that happens on the Facebook platform is proactive, rather than reactive.

When Facebook removes content (as opposed to restricting who can see their content or reducing how often it recommends it in users' newsfeeds), it notifies the user who posted the content.[7] It then employs a "strike" system to restrict the accounts of users whom the company finds to have violated content policies repeatedly over time.[8] A first strike is only a warning, but after that, strikes result in increasingly longer bans from creating content. These range from a second strike resulting in a one-day ban to a fifth strike resulting in a thirty-day ban. Users can appeal decisions they think are incorrect, and Meta publishes statistics about how often they reinstate removed content in various categories of violations in its quarterly Community Standards Enforcement Report.[9] Finally, accounts that repeatedly post policy-violating content and thus receive five or more strikes can be disabled entirely.[10] As a final layer of oversight of their content-moderation practices, Meta, uniquely among major social-media companies, has established an Oversight Board.[11] The Board serves, among other things, as a final court of appeals for Facebook's moderation decisions. As of the time of this writing, Meta's Oversight Board has reviewed thirty-six appeals, and found in twenty-four cases that content should be reinstated.[12]

13.3 YOUTUBE

Rather than a standalone section of its website, YouTube outlines its content policies ("Community Guidelines") in a section of its Help pages.[13] YouTube prohibits nearly all the same categories of content as Facebook, although the companies' policies use different nomenclature in some cases and demonstrate different areas of focus. For example, both platforms prohibit sexual content, but Facebook groups this category under the umbrella of "offensive content" while

6 *How Technology Detects Violations*, META (Jan. 19, 2022), https://perma.cc/QC6Q-L9RM.
7 *Taking Down Violating Content*, META (Sept. 9, 2022), https://perma.cc/B3VX-388A.
8 *Restricting Accounts*, META (Oct. 4, 2022), https://perma.cc/A7BJ-AHPF.
9 *Community Standards Enforcement Report*, META, https://perma.cc/9BHW-SAPP.
10 *Disabling Accounts*, META (Jan. 19, 2022), https://perma.cc/RYR7-RZ6J.
11 OVERSIGHT BOARD, https://perma.cc/M32S-356A.
12 *Id.*
13 *YouTube's Community Guidelines*, YOUTUBE, https://perma.cc/85SE-MW4X.

YouTube groups it with "sensitive content." Similarly, both platforms broadly prohibit fraudulent content, but YouTube focuses more on preventing spam, while Facebook focuses on financial scams.

In contrast to its relatively well-developed documentation around its content policies, YouTube's documentation[14] of its policy-enforcement mechanisms is sparse. The company thoroughly describes how users can flag content that violates policy and how content is reactively reviewed when that happens (always by human reviewers). The policies state that YouTube does, however, "use technology to identify and remove spam automatically, as well as re-uploads of content we have already reviewed and determined violates our policies."[15] Google (YouTube's owner) also publishes data about content moderation on YouTube in quarterly Transparency Reports.[16] In these reports, Google breaks down the share of removals originating from automated systems versus users, with greater than 90 percent of removals originating from automated systems. Google also provides statistics on when in a post's lifecycle removals happen, breaking down the share that happens before a post receives any views at all, one to ten views, or greater than ten views.

Like Facebook, YouTube employs a "strike" system to nudge users into better behavior.[17] YouTube's strike system is significantly more aggressive, however. Users get a warning with no other penalty attached the first time YouTube finds that they have posted content that violates its policies. After that, users who receive three additional strikes in a ninety-day period will have their YouTube channel permanently removed. YouTube further says that "[i]f your channel or account is terminated, you may be unable to use, own, or create any other YouTube channels/accounts."[18] This implies that channel removal is indeed a complete ban of the user in some cases, but it's unclear how often this penalty is imposed in full.

13.4 TIKTOK

TikTok, similar to Facebook, maintains a separate "Community Guidelines" section of its website.[19] Content prohibitions are grouped slightly differently, but they generally resemble those of other platforms insofar as they focus on sexually explicit content, fraudulent content, and content deemed to pose a safety risk.

TikTok has released very little information about its mechanisms for enforcement, which violations will result in permanent bans, and how many "strikes" users might receive before getting a permanent ban. In 2021, TikTok published a blog

[14] *YouTube Community Guidelines Enforcement FAQs*, GOOGLE, https://perma.cc/X3FD-Q7RM.
[15] *See id.* (answering the question "Is flagged content automatically removed?").
[16] *YouTube Community Guidelines Enforcement*, GOOGLE, https://perma.cc/EAS7-X6NQ.
[17] *Community Guidelines Strike Basics on YouTube*, GOOGLE, https://perma.cc/6WPD-B2R3.
[18] *Channel or Account Terminations*, GOOGLE, https://perma.cc/Y6DC-FZHN.
[19] *Community Guidelines*, TIKTOK, https://perma.cc/XDM8-DQQ9.

post[20] announcing that the platform would begin automated proactive content removals for some categories of content. The platform also publishes quarterly Community Guidelines Enforcement reports[21] with details around content removal and restoration after appeal.

Unlike Meta and Google, TikTok does not give removal statistics by method of initial flagging. Rather, it breaks down final removals by "automated" versus "manual" means. The word "automated" is undefined, but one can reasonably infer it refers to removals without any human review. In TikTok's case, this appears to be about one-quarter of overall removals, but note that this metric is not equivalent to the ones given by other platforms around initial flagging type, so these numbers are not directly comparable. This is because this metric likely refers to human involvement at any point in the moderation process, instead of solely at the point of initial flagging.

At the same time as its automated proactive-content-removal announcement, TikTok also confirmed that it employs a strike system to ban users who repeatedly post violating content. TikTok does not currently disclose how many times (or at what frequency) users would have to violate policy to receive a ban. Its Community Guidelines make clear that they have a zero-tolerance policy for the most serious categories of violations, such as Child Sexual Abuse Material (CSAM) or violent content. In its transparency reports, the company provides data about the number of accounts removed on a monthly basis. Still, there is no way to connect the number of removed posts to the number of removed accounts without more intermediate data.

13.5 REDDIT

Like other platforms reviewed in this chapter, Reddit publishes Community Guidelines that apply across the entire platform.[22] However, these Community Guidelines are best thought of as a content-moderation "floor" that describes a substantially lower threshold than is actually enforced across the vast majority of the platform. This is because all Reddit content is posted to "subreddits" (also known as channels), each having its own set of policies and practices that users create and enforce themselves.[23] Reddit does require that channel moderators post their policies clearly and maintain an appeals process, but communities are otherwise free to self-moderate as they see fit.

This overarching policy of relatively few limitations on what content is permitted on the platform has naturally led to the existence of many groups with a great deal of

[20] Eric Han, *Advancing Our Approach to User Safety*, TikTok, https://perma.cc/V7Y2-ZG9Y.
[21] *Reports*, TikTok, https://perma.cc/L7YF-4KRF.
[22] *Reddit Content Policy*, Reddit, https://perma.cc/3A9D-3BJ7.
[23] *Moderator Code of Conduct*, Reddit (Sept. 8, 2022), https://perma.cc/GYS2-5UUP.

content that many users would find objectionable for one reason or another. To manage this issue, Reddit has a policy of "quarantining" subreddits that most users might find highly offensive or upsetting.[24] Reddit will not run ads on quarantined channels, which means they generate no revenue for Reddit. Content posted in these channels also does not appear in feeds of users not subscribed to the quarantined subreddits and will not be discoverable in user searches.

Similar to other platforms we have discussed, Reddit publishes a transparency report with details about its content-policy enforcement. However, it only publishes this report annually.[25] Reddit has some site-wide enforcement of its content-moderation policies, but subreddit moderators do the majority of content removal, according to its transparency report. To support the enforcement of both site- and community-specific content guidelines by moderators, Reddit makes an extensive set of moderator documentation[26] and tools[27] available to its army of volunteer channel moderators. One community moderation tool unique to Reddit among the platforms we have discussed is that of *flair*.[28] Flair are short text tags with single words, phrases, or emoticons. While flair can be used for a variety of purposes, when it is associated with user accounts, it typically conveys a user's reputation.

Due to the fragmented nature of both content policy and enforcement on Reddit, there is little that can be said about how enforcement decisions are communicated to users when they happen on the channel level. However, while subreddit moderators have broad autonomy to police their channels (and to ban users from them) as they see fit, only Reddit can ban user accounts from the site entirely. Reddit publishes data about both content and user-account removal in its transparency report, but the platform does not outline any explicit thresholds of policy violations (either what kind or how many) that would prompt a user's account to be suspended.

13.6 ZOOM

While Zoom is not generally considered a social-media company, it is still a platform for users to share content. Readers may be most familiar with Zoom as a tool for one-on-one video calling, but Zoom can also be used to host multi-party calls with up to 1,000 participants and webinars with up to 10,000, depending on the host's account type.[29] Zoom users can also record videos and save them to Zoom's cloud so that others can watch those videos at a later time. Therefore, the company

[24] *Quarantined Subreddits*, REDDIT, https://perma.cc/2FPP-66FQ.
[25] *Transparency Report 2021*, REDDIT, https://perma.cc/7HLX-BT2J.
[26] *Reddit Mods*, REDDIT, https://perma.cc/5HU2-DVRU.
[27] *Reddit Moderation Tools*, REDDIT, https://perma.cc/99P4-T8C3.
[28] *User Flair*, REDDIT, https://perma.cc/49JR-2M7W.
[29] Ajaay, *Zoom Limit: Maximum Participants, Call Duration, and More*, NERDS CHALK (Oct. 21, 2020), https://perma.cc/EWQ8-4YMM.

has published standards for what content it is and is not willing to host.[30] In their community standards, Zoom prohibits many of the same content categories as other platforms we have reviewed. These prohibited categories include hate speech, promotion of violence, and sexual or suggestive content, though some other commonly prohibited categories, such as misinformation, are allowed. However, unlike the other platforms we have discussed, Zoom only enforces its policies in reaction to user reports.[31]

Zoom appears to have no proactive enforcement of its content policies. Zoom also states that all moderation in response to user reports is done manually, rather than by automated means.[32] Notably, the company does not currently publish data about its content-policy enforcement. Instead, Zoom's annual transparency report only includes statistics about the company's responses to government requests of different types. The company has not made data available about how many pieces of content it has removed or how many users have been banned due to its content-policy enforcement.

Zoom does not have external oversight of its content-moderation decisions – only Meta does this – but interestingly, the platform does have several progressive tiers of internal content-moderation review to which users can appeal decisions. At the highest tier of review, an "appeals panel" makes decisions by majority vote. Panel members are chosen from a pool of Zoom employees and serve for no longer than two years. Panel decisions are documented so they can guide future internal decision-making. In many respects, Zoom's "appeals panel" is described quite similarly to Meta's Oversight Board.

13.7 DIFFERENCES IN CONTENT-MODERATION POLICY

Of the platforms we have reviewed, it is likely no coincidence that the three largest – Facebook, YouTube, and TikTok – have similar written policies on content moderation, as they are all attempting to serve very broad user bases and therefore face similar challenges. They all have platform-wide policies against many of the same types of content. They all take tiered approaches to enforcement, involving banning some kinds of content and limiting access or distribution of other kinds of content. They all describe (in greater or lesser detail) a policy of warning users who post violative content and banning those users who do so repeatedly.

Reddit's channel-specific approach is different in almost every respect from the approach taken at Facebook, YouTube, and TikTok. While there is a minimum standard for allowable content on Reddit, most policy rules are set by users themselves to facilitate the types of discussions they want to engage in within specific

[30] *Acceptable Use Guidelines*, Zoom, https://perma.cc/3SS4-86GN.
[31] *Acceptable Use Guidelines Enforcement*, Zoom, https://perma.cc/P8GZ-BKRF.
[32] *Our Tier Review System*, Zoom, https://perma.cc/25TT-JWKD.

groups. As they are written, Zoom's content policies fall somewhere between the permissiveness of Reddit and the broad prohibitions against offensive content that the largest platforms have. Zoom prohibits sexual and fraudulent content, as well as explicit calls for violence. However, the platform makes no explicit rules against many other categories of content, including misinformation, that are harder to define. In this respect, Zoom's content policies are significantly less aggressive than those of Facebook, TikTok, and YouTube.

13.8 DIFFERENCES IN CONTENT-MODERATION ENFORCEMENT RULES

The starkest differences between the platforms we have studied exist not in their policies as they are written, but in their rules for enforcing these policies. For example, Zoom's clear statement that it only enforces its policies in response to user reports creates manifestly different conditions for what content is allowed than exists on platforms that engage in proactive enforcement.

There are also meaningful differences between what consequences platforms impose on users who violate platform rules. Most platforms we have discussed employ "strike" systems of some kind, but not all are clear about what penalties will be enforced after which strike, or how long strikes will be counted. YouTube's clarity on these points is a notable exception. This ambiguity is likely strategic, giving platforms the freedom to adjust their policies in reaction to events without having to communicate every change publicly. It is interesting to note that one of Reddit's rules for its channel moderators is not to create "Secret Guidelines"[33] that aren't clearly communicated to users, even though Reddit itself is largely opaque about how it enforces its own guidelines.

Reddit and Zoom take a much more reactive approach to content moderation than Facebook, YouTube, and TikTok. Reddit, as discussed above, leaves most aspects of content moderation – including enforcement – to its user community. Zoom's content policies look much more like those of Facebook, YouTube, or TikTok on paper, but unlike those platforms, Zoom intervenes only in response to user complaints. In effect, then, any given group of users on a Zoom call can effectively agree on and enforce a local content-moderation policy – much as if they were on a subreddit. Unlike Reddit, however, there is no "floor" of allowable content for consenting users, because Zoom only enforces its content policies if it receives a complaint.

However, there do appear to be some areas where the effects of policy enforcement are relatively consistent across platforms, even if the mechanisms for achieving this effect differ. This is particularly true around content that is simply illegal, such as violent terrorist imagery or CSAM (Child Sexual Abuse Material). Every platform

[33] *Moderator Code of Conduct*, *supra* note 23.

we have discussed here makes clear that not only is this type of content prohibited, but that posting this type of content will result in users losing their accounts immediately, without strikes or warnings.

13.9 DIFFERENCES IN CONTENT-MODERATION ENFORCEMENT IMPLEMENTATION AND TRANSPARENCY

Differences around policy enforcement extend beyond rules for what policy enforcement looks like and what triggers it. There are also serious differences in platforms' implementation of enforcement systems. Zoom's all-manual, tiered enforcement system has very different accuracy characteristics than systems that use machine learning to evaluate content proactively. TikTok appears to rely more heavily on fully automated content moderation with an expectation that users will dispute some decisions and some content will be restored after those disputes. These details of implementation create very different user experiences than exist on other platforms.

Some of these differences are the result of platforms' differing structures. Reddit's uniquely manually intensive moderation system results from its channel-focused design. Reviewing the resources needed to build accurate machine-learning systems is beyond the scope of this chapter. However, the largest platforms that employ machine-learning techniques to identify violative content in an automated manner can do so, at least in part, because of the enormous training sets of data they can build because of the large volumes of user content they host.

All of the platforms we have reviewed publish transparency-report documents that provide some information about how their policies are implemented in practice. Each of these "transparency reports" have developed independently and, even when theoretically reporting data about the same category, often use different metrics to measure slightly different things. This means that while they can be individually informative, they are rarely directly comparable.

13.10 CONCLUSION

The platforms reviewed here have profound differences in content-moderation policy, rules for enforcement, and enforcement practices. How, then, can we compare them when they differ on so many dimensions? Ultimately, platforms (and their policies) exist to shape their user experience. This chapter, therefore, proposes that users' ultimate experience of platforms' content policies provides the most meaningful basis for comparison. This outcome-focused framework leads us to a series of questions that can be asked about different categories of content on each platform:

What content are users able to post?
What content will be taken down after users post it and how quickly will it be removed?

What content will be visible to users other than the poster?
What content will be recommended to other users?
What will the consequences be for users who post violating content?

An example of how to apply this framework to a category of content, in this case sexual content, is shown in the table below.

Sexually Explicit Content	Facebook	YouTube	TikTok	Reddit	Zoom
Can users post this content?	May be blocked at time of upload	May be blocked at time of upload	May be blocked at time of upload	Yes	Yes
Will this content be taken down?	Yes	Yes	Yes	Only if it goes against the rules of the channel in which it is posted	Only if a viewer objects
Will this content be visible to other users?	Generally no (because it will not be recommended)	Yes, until it is taken down	Generally no (because it will not be recommended)	Yes, unless it violates channel rules and is removed by a moderator	Yes, unless a viewer objects and the content is taken down
Will this content be recommended to other users?	No	No	No	Only if the user has subscribed to the channel	No. (Zoom does not recommend content)
What are the consequences for users who post this content?	One strike (out of an unknown number)	One strike (out of three to four)	One strike (out of an unknown number)	May be banned from channel (if in violation of channel rules)	Unclear

Platforms and policymakers often discuss aspects of content moderation in isolation. Our exploration of moderation policy and implantation demonstrates the degree to which these dynamic systems are the result of multiple interlocking parts, where aspects of one part of the system impact the efficacy of another. The reality of how policies are experienced by users is heavily impacted by how those policies are implemented. In closing, we encourage the reader, when attempting to make comparisons between platforms or even attempting to understand the impacts of changes to a single system, to consider the whole, rather than the parts.

14

The Reverse Spider-Man Principle

With Great Responsibility Comes Great Power

*Eugene Volokh**

14.1 INTRODUCTION

An entity – a landlord, a manufacturer, a phone company, a credit card company, an internet platform, a self-driving-car manufacturer – is making money off its customers' activities. Some of those customers are using the entity's services in ways that are criminal, tortious, or otherwise reprehensible. Should the entity be held responsible, legally or morally, for its role (however unintentional) in facilitating its customers' activities? This question has famously been at the center of the debates about platform content moderation,[1] but it can come up in other contexts as well.[2]

It is a broad question, and there might be no general answer. (Perhaps it is two broad questions – one about legal responsibility and one about moral responsibility – but I think the two are connected enough to be worth discussing together.) In this chapter, though, I'd like to focus on one downside of answering it "yes": what I call the Reverse Spider-Man Principle – with great responsibility comes great power.[3]

* Thanks to Nikita Aggarwal, Laura Edelson, Gus Hurwitz, Michael Karanicolas, Kyle Langvardt, Marc McKenna, Courtney Radsch, John Villaseñor, and Mark Verstraete for their help.

[1] *See, e.g.*, Dory Knight-Ingram, *Hate Speech in Social Media: How Platforms Can Do Better*, MICH. NEWS (Feb. 17, 2022), https://perma.cc/D6Z2-TR7E ("'the companies behind [social-media platforms] have civic responsibilities to combat abuse and prevent hateful users and groups from harming others'") (quoting Professor Libby Hemphill, author of an Anti-Defamation League report urging platforms to ban "white supremacist speech"); Karis Stephen, *The Social Responsibility of Social Media Platforms*, REG. REV. (Dec. 21, 2021), https://perma.cc/WT48-ZCRE.

[2] *See, e.g.*, Henry Fernandez, *Curbing Hate Online: What Companies Should Do Now*, CTR. FOR AM. PROGRESS (Oct. 25, 2018), https://perma.cc/Y83F-VMRE (arguing that payment processors have a responsibility to refuse to process payments to "hate groups").

[3] "With great power comes great responsibility" of course predates Spider-Man's Uncle Ben, though it is most associated with him. The phrase is often credited to, among others, Voltaire, *see, e.g.*, Montpelier US Ins. Co. v. Collins, No. CIV. 11-141-ART, 2012 WL 588799, *1 (E.D.

Whenever we are contemplating holding entities responsible for their customers' behavior, we should think about whether we want to empower such entities to surveil, investigate, and police their customers, both as to that particular behavior and as to other behavior.[4] And that is especially so when the behavior consists of speech, and the exercise of power can thus affect public debate.

Of course, some of the entities with whom we have relationships do have power over us. Employers are a classic example: In part precisely because they are responsible for our actions (through principles such as *respondeat superior* or negligent hiring/supervision liability), they have great power to control what we do, both on the job and in some measure off the job.[5] Doctors have the power to decide what prescription drugs we can buy, and psychiatrists have the responsibility (and the power) to report when their patients make credible threats against third parties.[6] And of course we are all subject to the power of police officers, who have the professional though not the legal responsibility to prevent and investigate crime.

On the other hand, we generally do not expect to be in such subordinate relationships to phone companies, or to manufacturers selling us products. We generally do not expect them to monitor how we use their products or services (except in rare situations where our use of a service interferes with the operation of the service itself), or to monitor our politics to see if we are the sorts of people who might use the products or services badly. At most, we expect some establishments to

Ky. Feb. 22, 2012). *But see With Great Power Comes Great Responsibility*, QUOTE INVESTIGATOR, https://perma.cc/5FAU-F655 (casting doubt on this attribution). *Luke* 12:48 (King James) – "For unto whomsoever much is given, of him shall be much required" – also seems to express a similar sentiment; in context, the "much is given" does appear to refer to power (*see Luke* 12:42 (King James), discussing someone "whom his lord shall make ruler over his household") rather than wealth.

The official name is apparently "Spider-Man" rather than "Spiderman," but not "Bat-Man" or "Super-Man." This was apparently deliberate product differentiation. *See* Patricia T. O'Conner & Stewart Kellerman, *Why the Hyphen in Spider-Man?*, GRAMMARLY (July 13, 2012), https://perma.cc/XXC4-QQEV (relying on, among other sources, a Tweet by Stan Lee).

[4] I assume in all such situations that the entities aren't acting with the specific purpose of promoting illegal behavior. If such a purpose is present, their actions may well be criminal aiding and abetting or even criminal conspiracy. *See, e.g.*, 18 PA. CONS. STAT. ANN. § 306 (aiding and abetting); TEX. PENAL CODE ANN. § 7.02 (2004) (likewise); United States v. Pino-Perez, 870 F.2d 1230, 125 (7th Cir. 1989) (likewise); Ocasio v. United States, 578 U.S. 282, 288 (2016) (conspiracy).

[5] Some statutes do limit employers' power to act on their employees' religious practices, speech, and certain off-the-job activities. *See, e.g.*, Title VII of the Civil Rights Act of 1964, 42 U.S.C. § 2000e; COLO. REV. STAT. ANN. § 24-34-402.5(1) (lawful off-the-job activities generally); N.D. CENT. CODE ANN. §§ 14-02.4-03, 14-02.4-08 (same); 820 ILL. COMP. STAT. ANN. 55/5 (off-the-job consumption of lawful products); MONT. CODE ANN. §§ 39-2-313(2), 39-2-313(3) (2011) (same); NEV. REV. STAT. ANN. § 613.333(1)(B) (same); N.C. GEN. STAT. ANN. § 95-28.2(B) (same); WIS. STAT. ANN. §§ 111.321, 111.35(2) (same); Eugene Volokh, *Private Employees' Speech and Political Activity: Statutory Protection against Employer Retaliation*, 16 TEX. REV. L. & POL. 295 (2012); Eugene Volokh, *Should the Law Limit Private-Employer-Imposed Speech Restrictions?*, 2 J. FREE SPEECH L. 269 (2023) (containing a map of such statutes throughout the country).

[6] *See, e.g.*, Tarasoff v. Regents of Univ. of Cal., 551 P.2d 334 (Cal. 1976).

perform some narrow checks at the time of a sale, often defined specifically and clearly by statute, for instance by laws that require bars not to serve people who are drunk or that require gun dealers to perform background checks on buyers.[7]

Many of us value the fact that, in service-oriented economies, companies try hard to do what it takes to keep customers (consider the mentality that "the customer is always right"), rather than expecting customers to comply with the companies' demands. But if we insist on more "responsibility" from such providers, we will effectively push them to exercise more power over us, and thus fundamentally change the nature of their relationships with us. If companies are required to police the use or users of their products and services (what some call "third-party policing"[8]) then people's relationship with them may become more and more like people's relationship with the police.

To be sure, none of this is a dispositive argument against demanding such responsibility. Perhaps sometimes such responsibility is called for. My point, though, is that this responsibility also carries costs. We should take those costs into account when we engage in "balancing," "proportionality tests," Learned Hand cost–benefit analysis, or something similar – whether as a matter of adjudication, policymaking, or even just moral judgment – in deciding whether to demand such responsibility.

14.2 THE VIRTUES OF IRRESPONSIBILITY

Let me begin by offering three examples of where some courts have balked at imposing legal liability, precisely because they did not want to require or encourage businesses to exercise power over their customers.

14.2.1 *Telephone and Telegraph Companies*

The first came in the early 1900s, when some government officials demanded that telephone and telegraph companies block access to their services by people suspected of running illegal gambling operations. Prosecutors could have gone after the bookies, of course, and they did. But they also argued that the companies should have done the same – and indeed sometimes prosecuted the companies for allowing their services to be used for such criminal purposes.

No, held some courts (though not all[9]); to quote one:

> A railroad company has a right to refuse to carry a passenger who is disorderly, or whose conduct imperils the lives of his fellow passengers or the officers or the

[7] *See, e.g.*, Cal. Bus. & Prof. Code § 25602(a); 18 U.S.C. § 922(t).

[8] *See, e.g.*, Lorraine Mazerolle & Janet Ransley, Third Party Policing (2005); Tracey L. Meares & Emily Owens, *Third-Party Policing: A Critical View*, *in* Police Innovation: Contrasting Perspectives 249, 273–87 (David Weisburd & Anthony A. Braga eds., 2019).

[9] For the contrary view, *see, e.g.*, Howard Sports Daily v. Weller, 18 A.2d 210 (Md. 1941).

> property of the company. It would have no right to refuse to carry a person who tendered or paid his fare simply because those in charge of the train believed that his purpose in going to a certain point was to commit an offense. A railroad company would have no right to refuse to carry persons because its officers were aware of the fact that they were going to visit the house of [the bookmaker], and thus make it possible for him and his associates to conduct a gambling house.
>
> Common carriers are not the censors of public or private morals. They cannot regulate the public and private conduct of those who ask service at their hands.[10]

If the telegraph or telephone company (or the railroad) were held responsible for the actions of its customers, the court reasoned, then it would acquire power – as "censor[] of public or private morals" – that it ought not possess.

And indeed, Cloudflare, a provider of internet services that prevents denial-of-service attacks, drew an analogy to a phone company in saying that it would generally not reject customers based on their views (though it might stop service to them if their services were actively being used to organize criminal attacks[11]):

> Our conclusion ... is that voluntarily terminating access to services that protect against cyberattack is not the correct approach.... Just as the telephone company does not terminate your line if you say awful, racist, bigoted things, we have concluded in consultation with politicians, policy makers, and experts that turning off security services because we think what you publish is despicable is the wrong policy. To be clear, just because we did it in a limited set of cases before does not mean we were right when we did. Or that we will ever do it again.[12]

14.2.2 *EMail Systems*

Telegraph and telephone companies were common carriers, denied such power (and therefore, those courts said, responsibility) by law. But consider a second example, *Lunney v. Prodigy Services Co.*, a 1999 case in which the New York high court held that email systems were immune from liability for allegedly defamatory material sent by their users.[13]

Email systems aren't common carriers, but the court nonetheless reasoned that they should not be held responsible for failing to block messages, even if they had

[10] Commonwealth v. W. Union Tel. Co., 67 S.W. 59, 60 (Ky. 1901) (paragraph break added); *see also* Pennsylvania Publications v. Pennsylvania Pub. Util. Comm'n, 36 A.2d 777, 781 (Pa. 1944) (cleaned up); People v. Brophy, 120 P.2d 946, 956 (Cal. App. 1942).

[11] Matthew Prince, *Blocking Kiwifarms*, CLOUDFLARE BLOG (Sept. 3, 2022), https://perma.cc/WG5N-6YPK.

[12] Matthew Prince & Alissa Starzak, *Cloudflare's Abuse Policies & Approach*, CLOUDFLARE BLOG (Aug. 31, 2022), https://perma.cc/J5KB-JRE9.

[13] The case turned on conduct that happened before the enactment of 47 U.S.C. § 230, which provided such immunity by statute. The court therefore addressed whether a libel claim was available in the first place, thus avoiding the need to determine whether § 230 was retroactive.

the legal authority to block them: An email system's "role in transmitting e-mail is akin to that of a telephone company," the court held, "which one neither wants nor expects to superintend the content of its subscribers' conversations."[14] Even though email systems aren't forbidden from being the censors of their users' communications, the court concluded that the law should not pressure them into becoming such censors.

14.2.3 *Landlords*

Courts have likewise balked at imposing obligations on residential landlords that would encourage the landlords to surveil and police their tenants. Consider *Castaneda v. Olsher*, where a mobile-home-park tenant injured in a gang-related shootout involving another tenant sued the landlord, claiming it "had breached a duty not to rent to known gang members."[15] No, said the California Supreme Court:

> [W]e are not persuaded that imposing a duty on landlords to withhold rental units from those they believe to be gang members is a fair or workable solution to [the] problem [of gang violence], or one consistent with our state's public policy as a whole....
>
> If landlords regularly face liability for injuries gang members cause on the premises, they will tend to deny rental to anyone who *might* be a gang member or, even more broadly, to any family one of whose members might be in a gang.[16]

This would in turn tend to lead to "arbitrary discrimination on the basis of race, ethnicity, family composition, dress and appearance, or reputation,"[17] which may itself be illegal (so the duty would put the landlord in a damned-if-you-do-damned-if-you-do-not position).

But even apart from such likely reactions by landlords possibly being illegal, making landlords liable would jeopardize people's housing options and undermine their freedom even if they aren't gang members, further subjecting them to the power of their landlords: "[F]amilies whose ethnicity, teenage children, or mode of dress or personal appearance could, to some, suggest a gang association would face an additional obstacle to finding housing."[18] Likewise, even if landlords respond only by legally and evenhandedly checking all tenants' criminal histories, "refusing to rent to anyone with arrests or convictions for any crime that could have involved a gang" would "unfairly deprive many Californians of housing."[19] This "likely social

[14] Lunney v. Prodigy Servs. Co., 723 N.E.2d 539, 542 (N.Y. 1999).
[15] Castaneda v. Olsher, 162 P.3d 610, 613 (Cal. 2007).
[16] *Id.* at 617. On this point, the Justices were unanimous.
[17] *Id.*
[18] *Id.* at 618.
[19] *Id.*

cost" helped turn the court against recognizing such a responsibility on the part of landlords.[20]

Other courts have taken similar views. In *Francis v. Kings Park Manor, Inc.*, for instance, the Second Circuit sitting en banc refused to hold a landlord liable for its tenants' racial harassment of fellow tenants, partly because of concern that such responsibility would pressure landlords to exercise undue power over tenants:

> [U]nder the alternative proposed by Francis, ... prospective and current renters would confront more restrictive leases rife with *in terrorem* clauses, intensified tenant screening procedures, and intrusions into their dealings with neighbors, all of which could result in greater hostility and danger, even culminating in (or beginning with) unwarranted evictions.
>
> Our holding should also be of special interest to those concerned with the evolution of surveillance by state actors or by those purporting to act at their direction. See Note 44, *ante* (warning against broad liability schemes that would encourage landlords to act as law enforcement).[21]

The New York intermediate appellate court took a similar view in *Gill v. New York City Housing Authority*, rejecting liability for tenant-on-tenant crime that the plaintiff claimed might have been avoided had the landlord dealt better with a tenant's mental illness:

> The practical consequences of an affirmance in this case would be devastating. The Housing Authority would be forced to conduct legally offensive and completely unwarranted "follow-up" of all those tenants within its projects known to have a psychiatric condition possibly ... injurious to another tenant.... [E]viction, which is described in the Housing Authority Management Manual as a "last resort," would become almost commonplace.[22]

A New Jersey intermediate appellate court took the same view in *Estate of Campagna v. Pleasant Point Properties, LLC*, rejecting a claim that landlords should be responsible for doing background checks on tenants.[23] Likewise, in the related context of university liability for students' consumption of alcohol, the Massachusetts high court concluded:

> As many courts have noted, requiring colleges and universities to police all on-campus use of alcohol would be inappropriate and unrealistic. Although "[t]here was a time when college administrators and faculties assumed a role in loco parentis" and "[s]tudents were committed to their charge because the students were considered minors," "[c]ollege administrators no longer control the broad arena of

[20] *Id.* at 619.
[21] 992 F.3d 67, 79 n.47 (2d Cir. 2021).
[22] 130 A.D.2d 256, 266 (N.Y. App. Div. 1987).
[23] 234 A.3d 348, 369 (N.J. App. Div. 2020); *see also* Anderson v. 124 Green St. LLC, No. CIV.A. 09-2626-H, 2011 WL 341709, at *5 (Mass. Super. Jan. 18, 2011), *aff'd*, 82 Mass. App. Ct. 1113 (2012).

> general morals." College-aged students, while sometimes underage for the purposes of the purchase and consumption of alcohol, otherwise are adults expected to manage their own social activities.... [T]he additional intrusion into the private lives of students that would be necessary to control alcohol use on campus would be both impractical for universities and intolerable to students.[24]

To be sure, the pattern here is not uniform. Sometimes landlords are held responsible (by statutes, ordinances, or tort law rules), for monitoring their tenants for potentially illegal behavior, such as the distribution of drugs; for failing to evict tenants who are violating the law,[25] or even tenants who are being victimized by criminals, and are thus calling 911 too often;[26] for failing to warn co-tenants of tenants' past criminal records;[27] or even for renting to tenants who have criminal records.[28] But the result of those decisions has indeed been what the courts quoted above warned about: greater surveillance of tenants by landlords, and greater landlord power being exercised over tenants.[29]

14.2.4 *The Limits of Complicity*

One way of understanding these cases is that they put limits on concepts of complicity. The law does sometimes hold people liable for enabling or otherwise facilitating others' wrongful conduct, even in the absence of a specific wrongful purpose to aid such conduct;[30] consider tort law principles such as negligent hiring and negligent entrustment. But there are often good public-policy reasons to limit this.

[24] Helfman v. Northeastern Univ., 149 N.E.3d 758, 768 (Mass. 2020) (citations omitted). The court recognized a university's duty to protect intoxicated students when it is aware of an "alcohol-related emergency," *id.* at 771, but concluded that universities are not responsible for monitoring alcohol use proactively, *id.* at 774–76.

[25] *See, e.g.*, Giggers v. Memphis Hous. Auth., 277 S.W.3d 359, 371 (Tenn. 2009).

[26] *See, e.g.*, Bd. of Trustees of Vill. of Groton v. Pirro, 152 A.D.3d 149, 157–58 (N.Y. App. Div. 2017); Erik Eckholm, *Victims' Dilemma: 911 Calls Can Bring Eviction*, N.Y. TIMES (Aug. 16, 2013); Matthew Desmond & Nicol Valdez, *Unpolicing the Urban Poor: Consequences of Third-Party Policing for Inner-City Women*, 78 AM. SOCIO. REV. 117 (2012).

[27] *See generally* Eugene Volokh, *Tort Law vs. Privacy*, 114 COLUM. L. REV. 879, 895–97 (2014).

[28] *See* David Thacher, *The Rise of Criminal Background Screening in Rental Housing*, 33 LAW & SOC. INQUIRY 5, 26 (2008) ("government efforts that encouraged landlords to adopt criminal history screening were partly motivated by a growing belief that private institutions should take more responsibility for their social impacts").

[29] *See generally, e.g.*, B.A. Glesner, *Landlords as Cops: Tort, Nuisance & Forfeiture Standards Imposing Liability on Landlords for Crime on the Premises*, 42 CASE W. RES. L. REV. 679, 780 (1992); Deborah J. La Fetra, *A Moving Target: Property Owners' Duty to Prevent Criminal Acts on the Premises*, 28 WHITTIER L. REV. 409, 439–59 (2006); Robert J. Aalberts, *Drug Testing Tenants: Does It Violate Rights of Privacy?*, 38 REAL PROP. PROB. & TR. J. 479, 481–82 (2003); Desmond & Valdez, *supra* note 26.

[30] *See supra* note 4.

Sometimes those reasons stem from our sense of professional roles. We do not fault a doctor for curing a career criminal, even if as a result the criminal goes on to commit more crimes. It's not a doctor's job to decide whether someone merits healing, or to bear responsibility for the consequences of successfully healing bad people.

Likewise, the legal system expects defense lawyers to do their best to get clients acquitted, and does not hold the lawyers responsible for the clients' future crimes. (Indeed, historically the legal system allowed courts to order unwilling lawyers to represent indigent defendants.[31]) When there is public pressure on lawyers to refuse to represent certain clients, the legal establishment often speaks out against such pressure.[32]

And sometimes those reasons stem from our sense of who should and who should not be "censors of public or private morals." The police may enforce gambling laws, or arrest gang members for gang-related crimes. The courts may enforce libel law. But various private entities, such as phone companies, email services, and landlords, should not be pressured into doing so.[33]

14.3 PRACTICAL LIMITS ON PRIVATE COMPANIES' POWER, IN THE ABSENCE OF RESPONSIBILITY

Of course, many such companies (setting aside the common carriers or similarly regulated monopolies) already have great power over whom to deal with and what to allow on their property, even when they aren't held responsible – by law or by public attitudes – for what happens on their property. In theory, for instance, Prodigy's owners could have decided that they wanted to kick off users who were using Prodigy email for purposes that they found objectionable: libel, racist speech, Communist advocacy, or whatever else. Likewise, some companies may decide not to deal with people who they view as belonging to hate groups or anti-American organizations, just because their shareholders or managers think that's the right thing to do, entirely apart from any social or legal norms of responsibility.

[31] *See, e.g.*, Sacandy v. Walther, 262 Ga. 11 (1992); David L. Shapiro, *The Enigma of the Lawyer's Duty to Serve*, 55 N.Y.U. L. Rev. 735 (1980).

[32] *See, e.g.*, *Guantanamo Remarks Cost Policy Chief His Job*, CNN (Feb. 2, 2007), https://perma.cc/236W-5DDP; Michel Paradis & Wells Dixon, *In Defense of Unpopular Clients – and Liberty*, Wall St. J. (Nov. 18, 2020); *cf.* Eugene Volokh, *Defending Guantanamo Detainees*, Volokh Conspiracy (Jan. 12, 2007), https://perma.cc/K3DD-CN4N.

[33] I set aside here still other reasons, for instance, stemming from the sense that excessive complicity liability may wrongly chill proper behavior as well as improper, or may unduly deter the exercise of constitutional rights. *See, e.g.*, New York Times Co. v. Sullivan, 376 U.S. 254 (1964) (limiting newspaper publisher's liability for publishing allegedly libelous ads); Protection for Lawful Commerce in Arms Act, 15 U.S.C. §§ 7901–7903 (limiting firearms manufacturers' and sellers' liability for criminal misuse of firearms by third parties).

But in practice, in the absence of responsibility (whether imposed by law or social norms), many companies will eschew such power, for several related reasons – even setting aside the presumably minor loss of business from the particular customers who are ejected:

1. Policing customers takes time, effort, and money.
2. Policing customers risks error and bad publicity associated with such error, which could alienate many more customers than the few who are actually denied service.
3. Policing customers risks allegations of discriminatory policing, which may itself be illegal and at least is especially likely to yield bad publicity.
4. Policing some customers will often lead to public demands for broader policing: "You kicked group X, which we sort of like, off your platform; why aren't you also kicking off group Y, which we loathe and which we view as similar to X?"[34]
5. Conversely, a policy of "we do not police our customers" – buttressed by social norms that do not require (or even affirmatively condemn) such policing – offers the company a simple response to all such demands.
6. Policing customers creates tension even with customers who aren't violating the company's rules – people often do not like even the prospect that some business is judging what they say, how they dress, or whom they associate with.
7. Policing customers gives an edge to competitors who publicly refuse to engage in such policing and who sell their services as "our only job is to serve you, not to judge you or eject you."

Imposing legal responsibility on such companies can thus pressure them to exercise power even when they otherwise would not have. And that is so in some measure even if responsibility is accepted just as a broad moral norm, created and enforced by public pressure (likely stemming from influential sectors of society, such as the media or activists or professional organizations), and not a legal norm.[35] That moral norm would increase the countervailing costs of non-policing. It would decrease the costs of policing: For instance, the norm and the corresponding pressure would likely act on all major competitors, so the normal competitive pressures encouraging a "the customer is always right" attitude would be sharply reduced. And

[34] Judge Alex Kozinski and I have labeled this "censorship envy," at least when it applies to speech-restrictive decisions. Alex Kozinski & Eugene Volokh, *A Penumbra Too Far*, 106 HARV. L. REV. 1639, 1655 n.88 (1993).

[35] Of course, some broad moral norms may be prompted or reinforced by government actors, such as elected representatives who are holding hearings. *See, e.g.*, Transcript, House of Representatives Energy & Commerce Comm., Subcomms. on Communications & Tech. and on Consumer Protection & Commerce, *Disinformation Nation: Social Media's Role in Promoting Extremism and Misinformation*, 117th Cong. (Mar. 25, 2021).

at some point, the norm might become the standard against which the reasonableness of behavior is measured as a legal matter.

Likewise, when people fault a company for errors or perceived discrimination, the company can use the norm as cover, for instance arguing that "regrettably, errors will happen, especially when one has to do policing at scale." "After all, you have told us you want us to police, have not you?"

Accepting such norms of responsibility could also change the culture and organization of the companies. It would habituate the companies to exercising such power. It would create internal bureaucracies staffed with people whose jobs rely on exercising the power – and who might be looking for more reasons to exercise that power.

And by making policing part of the companies' official mission, the acceptance of responsibility norms would subtly encourage employees to make sure that the policing is done effectively and comprehensively, and not just at the minimum that laws or existing social norms command. Modest initial policing missions, based on claims of responsibility for a narrow range of misuse, can thus creep into much more comprehensive use of such powers.[36]

Indeed, it appears that something like this happened with social-media platforms. Title 47 U.S.C. § 230 freed online companies of legal responsibility for the content of users' speech, and many such companies therefore did not exercise their legal power to restrict what users posted, or did so only lightly.[37] But the mid-2010s saw a combination of social and congressional pressure that held platforms responsible for supposed misinformation and other bad speech on their platforms, which caused the leading platforms to exercise such power more and more.[38] Platforms have now begun making decisions about which political candidates and officials to deplatform and which important political stories to block (including in the heat of an election campaign).[39] One might approve or disapprove of such power exercised by large business corporations over public discourse;[40] but my point here is simply that calls for great responsibility have indeed increased the exercise of such power.

36 *See* Eugene Volokh, *The Mechanisms of the Slippery Slope*, 116 HARV. L. REV. 1026, 1051–56 (2003) (discussing such "enforcement need" slippery slopes).

37 *See, e.g.*, Kate Klonick, The New Governors: The People, Rules, and Processes Governing Online Speech, 131 HARV. L. REV. 1598, 1618–21 (2018).

38 *Id.* at 1664, 1667; *cf.* Jack M. Balkin, *How to Regulate (and Not Regulate) Social Media*, 1 J. FREE SPEECH L. 71, 87–88 (2021) ("Public pressure and media coverage of social media companies can push them, at the margins, to behave as more responsible curators of public discourse."); Richard L. Hasen, *Deep Fakes, Bots, and Siloed Justices: American Election Law in a "Post-Truth" World*, 64 ST. LOUIS U. L.J. 535, 554 (2020).

39 *See* Eugene Volokh, *Treating Social Media Platforms Like Common Carriers?*, 1 J. FREE SPEECH L. 377, 395–96 (2021).

40 There is an element here of the debate about Citizens United v. FEC, 558 U.S. 310 (2010), though with the ideological polarity largely reversed. Volokh, *supra* note 39, at 388–95.

14.4 THE INTERNET OF THINGS, CONSTANT CUSTOMER/SELLER INTERACTION FOR TANGIBLE PRODUCTS, AND THE FUTURE OF RESPONSIBILITY

So far, there has been something of a constraint on calls for business "responsibility" for the actions of their customers: Such calls have generally involved ongoing business–customer relationships, for instance when Facebook can monitor what its users are posting (or at least respond to other users' complaints).

Occasionally, some have called on businesses to simply not deal with certain people at the outset – consider *Castaneda v. Olsher*, where the plaintiffs argued that the defendants just should not have rented the mobile homes to likely gang members. But such exclusionary calls have been rare.

I expect, for instance, that few people would think of arguing that car dealers should refuse to sell cars to suspected gang members who might use the cars for drive-by shootings or for crime getaways.[41] Presumably, most people would agree that even gang members are entitled to buy and use cars in the many lawful ways that cars can be used, and that car dealers should not see their job as judging the likely law-abidingness of their customers.[42] If the legislature wants to impose such responsibilities, for instance by banning the sale of guns to felons or of spray paint to minors, then presumably the legislature should create such narrow and clearly defined rules, which would rely on objective criteria that do not require seller judgment about which customers merely seem likely to be dangerous.

But now more and more products involve constant interaction between the customer and the seller.[43] Say, for instance, that I'm driving a partly self-driving

[41] *But see* Andrew Jay McClurg, *The Tortious Marketing of Handguns: Strict Liability Is Dead, Long Live Negligence*, 19 SETON HALL LEGIS. J. 777, 816 n.178 (1995) (quoting a proposal that gun sellers must, on pain of liability for negligence, "be especially alert to, and wary of, gun buyers who display certain behavioral characteristics such as … appear[ing] in unkempt clothing and hav[ing] a slovenly appearance").

[42] A few companies have said that they will refuse to do business with anyone "associated with known hate groups." *See An Update on Our Work to Uphold Our Community Standards*, AIRBNB (Mar. 18, 2021), https://perma.cc/SVJ7-RLT8; Michelle Malkin, *Why Airbnb Banned Me (And My Hubby, Too!)*, PRESCOTT ENEWS (Feb. 6, 2022), https://perma.cc/G8ER-GR3M; *Off Service Conduct*, TWITCH, https://perma.cc/37HD-66J7. Twitch also says it will ban users who are "[h]armful misinformation actors, or persistent misinformation superspreaders," even when none of the alleged misinformation was spread on Twitch.

[43] Rebecca Crootof, *The Internet of Torts: Expanding Civil Liability Standards to Address Corporate Remote Interference*, 69 DUKE L.J. 583 (2019), discusses this interaction in detail; but that article focuses on corporations monitoring and controlling the products they sell in order to promote their own financial interests (for instance, enforcing otherwise hard-to-enforce license terms, or electronically "repossessing" them in the event of failure to pay), rather than in order to fulfill some legally or socially mandated responsibilities to prevent supposed misuse by customers.

In addition to the question discussed in the text – whether the companies should have a responsibility for monitoring customer use of such connected products, and preventing misuse – there are of course other questions as well, such as (1) whether companies should

Tesla that is in constant contact with the company. Recall how Airbnb refused to rent to people who it suspected were going to a "Unite the Right" rally.[44] If that is seen as proper – and indeed is seen as mandated by corporate social responsibility principles – then one can imagine similar pressure on Tesla to stop Teslas from driving to the rally (or at least to stop such trips by Teslas owned by those people suspected of planning to participate in the rally).[45]

To be sure, this might arouse some hostility, because it's *my* car, not Tesla's. But Airbnb was likewise refusing to arrange bookings for other people's properties, not its own. Airbnb's rationale was that it had a responsibility to stop its service from being used to promote a racist, violent event.[46] Why would not Tesla then have a similar responsibility to stop its intellectual property and its central computers (assuming they are in constant communication with my car) from being used the same way?

True, the connection between the Tesla and its user's driving to the rally is somewhat indirect – but not more so than Airbnb's. Indeed, Tesla's connection is a bit more direct: Its product and the accompanying services would get the driver the last mile to the rally itself, rather than just providing a place to stay the night before. Indeed, there's just one eminently foreseeable step (a short walk from the parking space) between the use of the Tesla and the driver's attendance at the rally. And conversely, if we think Tesla should not be viewed as responsible for its cars being used to get to rallies that express certain views, what should that tell us about whether Facebook should be responsible for use of its service to convey those views?

Now, Tesla's sales contract might be seen as implicitly assuring that its software will always try to get me to my destination. But that is just a matter of the contract. If companies are seen as responsible for the misuse of their services, why wouldn't they have an obligation to draft contracts that let them fulfill that responsibility?

Of course, maybe some line might be drawn here: Perhaps, for instance, we might have a special rule for services that are ancillary to the sale of goods (Tesla, yes; Airbnb, no), under which the transfer of the goods carries with it the legal or moral obligation for the seller to keep providing the services even when one thinks the goods are likely to be used in illegal or immoral ways. (Though what if I lease my

have a responsibility to report possible misuse, *see* Volokh, *supra* note 27; (2) whether companies' records of user behavior should in some measure be shielded from law enforcement subpoenas and warrants, and from civil discovery; and (3) whether companies should be required to design their products in a way that facilitates law enforcement, *cf.* 47 U.S.C. §§ 1002, 1003, 1005 (requiring that telephone systems be designed to facilitate legally authorized surveillance).

44 Will Sommer, *Airbnb, Uber Plan to Ban 'Unite the Right' White-Supremacist Rally Participants*, Daily Beast (Aug. 10, 2018), https://perma.cc/TG4L-7L2V. Uber and Lyft apparently only stressed that their drivers could "refuse service to passengers connected to the ... rally," *id.*, rather than themselves forbidding their drivers from doing so.

45 Maybe Tesla's current owner, Elon Musk, would be reluctant to impose such rules, but then imagine some other car company that sells such cars.

46 *See, e.g.*, *Should Airbnb Ban Customers It Disagrees With?*, BBC (Aug. 8, 2017), https://perma.cc/C4MZ-9JBZ.

Tesla rather than buying it outright, or rent it for the day just as I might rent an Airbnb apartment for the night?) Or at least we might say there's nothing irresponsible about a product seller refusing to police customers' continuing use of the services that make those products work.

But that would just be a special case of the broader approach that I'm suggesting here: For at least some kinds of commercial relationships, a business should *not* be held responsible for what its customers do – because we do not want it exercising power over its customers' actions. We might then ask whether we should apply the same principle to other commercial relationships.

14.5 BIG DATA AND THE FUTURE OF RESPONSIBILITY

There has historically also been another constraint on such calls for business "responsibility": It's often very hard for a business to determine what a customer's plans are. Even if there is social pressure to get businesses to boycott people who associate with supposed "hate groups"[47] – or even if the owners of a business (say, Airbnb) just want to engage in such a boycott – how is a business to know what groups a person associates with, at least unless the person is famous, or unless someone expressly complains about the person to the business?[48]

But these days we can get a lot more data about people, just by searching the Internet and some other databases (some of which may cost money, but all of which are well within the means of most big businesses). To be sure, this might yield too much data about each prospective customer for a typical business to process at scale. But AI technology will likely reduce the cost of such processing by enabling computers to quickly and cheaply sift through all that data, and to produce some fairly reliable estimate: Joe Schmoe is 93 percent likely to be closely associated with one of the groups that a business is being pressured to boycott. At that point, the rhetoric of responsibility may suggest that what now can be done (identifying supposedly evil potential clients) should be done.

Consider one area in which technological change has sharply increased the scope of employer responsibility – and constrained the freedom of many prospective employees. American tort law has long held employers responsible for negligent hiring, negligent supervision, or negligent retention when they unreasonably hire employees who are incompetent at their jobs in a way that injures third parties,[49] or who have a tendency to commit crimes that are facilitated by the job.[50] But until at

[47] *See supra* note 42.

[48] *See, e.g.*, the Michelle Malkin incident cited in note 42; Malkin is a prominent commentator.

[49] *See, e.g.*, Carman v. City of New York, 14 Abb. Pr. 301 (N.Y. Sup. Ct. 1862) (noting liability for "want of sufficient care in employing suitable persons").

[50] *See, e.g.*, F. & L. Mfg. Co. v. Jomark, Inc., 134 Misc. 349 (N.Y. App. Term. 1929) (noting liability when a messenger hired by defendant stole property, when "[t]he most casual investigation would have disclosed that this messenger was not a proper person to whom defendant's

least the late 1960s, this had not required employers to do nationwide background checks, because such checks were seen as too expensive, and thus any such requirement "would place an unfair burden on the business community."[51] Even someone who had been convicted of a crime could thus often start over and get a job, at least in a different locale, without being dogged by his criminal record.

Now, though, as nationwide employee background checks have gotten cheaper, they have in effect become mandatory for many employers: "Lower costs and easier access provide [an] incentive to perform [background] checks, potentially leaving employers who choose not to conduct such checks in a difficult position when trying to prove they were not negligent in hiring."[52] As a result, people with criminal records now often find it especially hard to get jobs.

Perhaps that's good, given the need to protect customers from criminal attack. Or perhaps it's bad, given the social value of giving people a way to get back to productive, law-abiding life. Or perhaps it's a mix of both. But my key point here is that, while the employer's responsibility for screening his employees has formally remained the same – the test is reasonable care – technological change has required employers to exercise that responsibility in a way that limits the job opportunities of prospective employees much more than it did before.

Similarly, commercial property owners have long been held responsible for taking reasonable – which is to say, cost-effective – measures to protect their business visitors from criminal attack. Thus, as video surveillance cameras became cheap enough to be cost-effective, courts began to hold that defendants may be negligent for failing to install surveillance cameras,[53] even though such surveillance would not have been required when cameras were much more expensive.

We can expect to see something similar as technological change renders cost-effective other forms of investigation and surveillance – not just of employees or of outside intruders, but of customers. If it is a company's responsibility to make sure

goods might be intrusted," presumably because the investigation would have shown that the messenger was dishonest); Hall v. Smathers, 240 N.Y. 486, 490 (1925) (noting liability for an "assault upon a tenant of an apartment house by a superintendent kept in his position in spite of the complaints of the tenants, and with full knowledge of the defendants' agents of his habits and disposition").

51 *See* Stevens v. Lankard, 297 N.Y.S.2d 686, 688 (App. Div. 1968), *aff'd*, 254 N.E.2d 339 (N.Y. 1969).

52 Ryan D. Watstein, Note, *Out of Jail and Out of Luck: The Effect of Negligent Hiring Liability and the Criminal Record Revolution on an Ex-Offender's Employment Prospects*, 61 Fla. L. Rev. 581, 592–93 (2009); *cf., e.g.*, Malorney v. B & L Motor Freight, Inc., 496 N.E.2d 1086, 1089 (Ill. App. Ct. 1986) ("[T]here is no evidence . . . that the cost of checking on the criminal history of all truck driver applicants is too expensive and burdensome when measured against the potential utility [(preventing sexual assault of hitchhikers)] of doing so."); Carlsen v. Wackenhut Corp., 868 P.2d 882, 887–88 (Wash. Ct. App. 1994) (concluding employer may have duty to conduct background check for certain employees, including unarmed concert security guards).

53 *See* Volokh, *supra* note 27, at 918 n.176 (collecting cases).

that bad people do not use the company's products or services for bad purposes, then as technology allows companies to investigate their clients' affiliations and beliefs more cost-effectively, companies will feel pressure to engage in such investigation.

14.6 CONCLUSION

"Responsibility" is often viewed as an unalloyed good. Who, after all, wants to be known as "irresponsible"?[54] Sometimes we should indeed hold people and organizations legally or morally responsible for providing tools that others misuse. People and organizations are also of course entitled to choose to accept such responsibility, even if they are not pressured to do so.[55] And sometimes even if they do not feel responsible for doing something, they might still choose to do it, whether because they think it's good for their users and thus good for business, or because they think it's good for society. In particular, I'm not trying to take a position here on what sort of moderation social-media platforms should engage in.[56]

My point here is simply that such responsibility has an important cost, and refusal to take responsibility has a corresponding benefit. Those who are held responsible for what we do will need to assert their power over us, surveilling, second-guessing, and blocking our decisions. A phone company or an email provider or a landlord that's responsible for what we do with its property will need to control whether we are allowed to use its property, and control what we do with that property; likewise for a social-media platform or a driverless-car manufacturer. If we want freedom from such control, we should try to keep those companies from being held responsible for their users' behavior.

There is value in businesses being encouraged to "stay in their lane," with their lane being defined as providing a particular product or service. They should be free to say that they "are not the censors of public or private morals," and that they should not "regulate the public and private conduct of those who ask service at their hands."[57] Even if, unlike with telephone and telegraph cases, they have the legal

[54] Well, maybe it seems romantic at times – cf. BOBBY DARIN, *Call Me Irresponsible*, *on* FROM HELLO DOLLY TO GOODBYE CHARLIE (Capitol Records 1962), https://perma.cc/5C62-W2P4 – but we can set that aside here.

[55] Occasionally people's felt moral or religious obligation to avoid what they see as complicity with evil behavior will clash with public accommodations laws, and will raise interesting questions under various religious freedom statutes and constitutional regimes; but this is a separate matter. *See, e.g.*, Eugene Volokh, *A Common-Law Model for Religious Exemptions*, 46 UCLA L. REV. 1465, 1525–26 (1999); Eugene Volokh, *Religious Exemption Regimes and Complicity in Sin*, VOLOKH CONSPIRACY (Dec. 6, 2021), https://perma.cc/FZ3U-8N94; Eugene Volokh, *Bans on Political Discrimination in Places of Public Accommodation and Housing*, 15 NYU J. L. & LIB. 709 (2021).

[56] *Cf.* Laura Edelson, *Content Moderation in Practice*, 3 J. FREE SPEECH L. 183 (2023) (describing some actual moderation practices of various social-media platforms); Volokh, *supra* note 39 (discussing some arguments in favor and against limiting social-media platform moderation).

[57] *See supra* note 10 and accompanying text.

right to reject some customers, they should be free to refrain from exercising that right. Sometimes the responsibility for stopping misuse of the product should be placed solely on the users and on law enforcement – not on businesses that are enlisted as largely legally unsupervised private police forces, doing what the police are unable to do or (as with speech restrictions) are constitutionally forbidden from doing.

15

Moderating the Fediverse

Content Moderation on Distributed Social Media

*Alan Z. Rozenshtein**

15.1 INTRODUCTION

Current approaches to content moderation generally assume the continued dominance of "walled gardens": social-media platforms that control who can use their services and how. Whether the discussion is about self-regulation, quasi-public regulation (e.g., Facebook's Oversight Board), government regulation, tort law (including changes to Section 230), or antitrust enforcement, the assumption is that the future of social media will remain a matter of incrementally reforming a small group of giant, closed platforms. But, viewed from the perspective of the broader history of the internet, the dominance of closed platforms is an aberration. The internet initially grew around a set of open, decentralized applications, many of which remain central to its functioning today.

Email is an instructive example. Although email is hardly without its content-moderation issues – spam, in particular, has been an ongoing problem – there is far less discussion about email's content-moderation issues than about social media's. Part of this is because email lacks some of the social features that can make social media particularly toxic. But it is also because email's architecture simply does not permit the degree of centralized, top-down moderation that social-media platforms can perform. If "ought" implies "can," then "cannot" implies "need not." There is a limit to how heated the debates around email-content moderation can be, because there's an architectural limit to how much email moderation is possible. This raises

* For helpful comments I thank Laura Edelson, Kyle Langvardt, Erin Miller, Chinmayi Sharma, and participants at the Big Tech and Antitrust Conference at Seton Hall Law School, the Information Society Project and the Freedom of Expression Scholars Conference at Yale Law School, the Association for Computing Machinery (ACM) Symposium on Computer Science and Law, and the Max Weber Programme Multidisciplinary Research Workshop at the European University Institute. For excellent research assistance I thank Caleb Johnson and Isabel Park.

the intriguing possibility of what social media, and its accompanying content-moderation issues, would look like if it too operated as a decentralized protocol.

Fortunately, we do not have to speculate, because decentralized social media already exists in the form of the "Fediverse" – a portmanteau of "federation" and "universe." Much like the decentralized infrastructure of the internet, in which the HTTP communication protocol facilitates the retrieval and interaction of webpages that are stored on servers around the world, Fediverse protocols power "instances," which are comparable to social-media applications and services. The most important Fediverse protocol is ActivityPub, which powers the most popular Fediverse apps, notably the X-like microblogging service Mastodon, which has over a million active users and continues to grow, especially in the wake of Elon Musk's purchase of X.[1]

The importance of decentralization and open protocols is increasingly recognized within Silicon Valley. X co-founder Jack Dorsey has launched Bluesky, an X competitor built on the decentralized ATProtocol. Meta's Mark Zuckerberg has described his plans for an "open, interoperable metaverse" (though how far this commitment to openness will go remains to be seen).[2] And established social media platforms are building in interoperability with ActivityPub applications.[3]

Building on an emerging literature around decentralized social media,[4] this brief essay seeks to give an overview of the Fediverse, its benefits and drawbacks, and how government action can influence and encourage its development. Section 15.2 describes the Fediverse and how it works, first distinguishing open from closed protocols and then describing the current Fediverse ecosystem. Section 15.3 looks at the specific issue of content moderation on the Fediverse, using Mastodon as a case study to draw out the advantages and disadvantages of the federated content-moderation approach as compared to the currently dominant closed-platform model. Section 15.4 considers how policymakers can encourage the Fediverse through participation, regulation, antitrust enforcement, and liability shields.

1 *See* Barbara Ortutay, *Twitter Drama Too Much? Mastodon, Others Emerge as Options*, AP NEWS (Nov. 12, 2012), https://perma.cc/PY4F-8GD9.

2 Andrew Hayward, *An 'Open, Interoperable' Metaverse Is 'Better for Everyone': Meta's Mark Zuckerberg*, YAHOO! NEWS (Oct. 11, 2022), https://perma.cc/E32U-FQ7C.

3 David Pierce, *Can ActivityPub Save the Internet?*, VERGE (Apr. 20, 2023).

4 *See, e.g.*, Mike Masnick, *Protocols, Not Platforms: A Technological Approach to Free Speech*, KNIGHT FIRST AMEND. INST. (Aug. 21, 2019), https://perma.cc/J2QD-YVF7; FRANCIS FUKUYAMA ET AL., STANFORD CYBER POL'Y CTR., MIDDLEWARE FOR DOMINANT DIGITAL PLATFORMS: A TECHNOLOGICAL SOLUTION TO A THREAT TO DEMOCRACY (2021), https://perma.cc/S54K-JVEX; Daphne Keller, *The Future of Platform Power: Making Middleware Work*, 32 J. DEMOCRACY 168 (2021); Chand Rajendra-Nicolucci & Ethan Zuckerman, *What If Social Media Worked More Like Email?*, *in* AN ILLUSTRATED FIELD GUIDE TO SOCIAL MEDIA 24 (Chand Rajendra-Nicolucci & Ethan Zuckerman eds., 2021), https://perma.cc/F3LC-LGR4; Robert W. Gehl & Diana Zulli, *The Digital Covenant: Non-centralized Platform Governance on the Mastodon Social Network*, INFO., COMMC'N & SOC'Y (forthcoming), https://perma.cc/H4XN-9F9K.

15.2 CLOSED PLATFORMS AND DECENTRALIZED ALTERNATIVES

15.2.1 *A Brief History of the Internet*

A core architectural building block of the internet is the *open protocol*. A *protocol* is a rule that governs the transmission of data. The internet consists of many such protocols, ranging from those that direct how data is physically transmitted to those that govern the most common internet applications, like email or web browsing. Crucially, all these protocols are *open*, in that anyone can set up and operate a router, website, or email server without needing to register with or get permission from a central authority.[5] Open protocols were key to the first phase of the internet's growth because they enabled unfettered access, removing barriers and bridging gaps between different communities. This enabled and encouraged interactions between groups with various interests and knowledge, resulting in immense creativity and idea-sharing.

But starting in the mid-2000s, a new generation of closed platforms – first Facebook, YouTube, and X, and later Instagram, WhatsApp, and TikTok – came to dominate the internet habits of most users.[6] Today's internet users spend an average of seven hours online a day, and approximately 35 percent of that time is spent on closed social-media platforms.[7] Although social-media platforms use the standard internet protocols to communicate with their users – from the perspective of the broader internet, they just operate as massive web servers – their internal protocols are closed. There's no Facebook protocol that you could use to run your own Facebook server and communicate with other Facebook users without Facebook's permission. Thus, major social-media platforms are the most important example of the internet's steady, two-decades-long takeover by "walled gardens."[8]

There are many benefits to walled gardens; otherwise, they would not have taken over. Closed systems are attractive for the companies that run them because the companies can exert greater control over their platforms through content and user

[5] The distinction between open and closed protocols is not clear-cut. Some of the core technology behind the internet – for example, the Domain Name System, which maps IP addresses to human-readable domain names – has a centralized registration system. But this system imposes relatively minimal control, and the entity that runs it, the Internet Corporation for Assigned Names and Numbers (ICANN), is a multistakeholder nonprofit that prioritizes openness and interoperability.

[6] An early challenge to the open internet came from the first generation of giant online services providers like America Online, Compuserve, and Prodigy, which combined dial-up internet access with an all-encompassing web portal that provided both internet content and messaging. But as internet speeds increased and web browsing improved, users discovered that the limits of these closed systems outweighed their benefits, and they faded into irrelevance by the 2000s.

[7] Simon Kemp, *Digital 2022: Global Overview Report*, DataReportal (Jan. 26, 2022), https://perma.cc/XM4G-DLND.

[8] The other major example of a move to a closed system is the dominance of smartphones, which (especially iOS devices) are far more closed than are personal computers.

moderation. But the draw for platform owners is insufficient; only by providing users with a better experience (or at least convincing them that their experience is better) could closed platforms have come to dominate social media.

Closed platforms have indeed often provided more value to users. The logic of enclosure applies as much to virtual spaces as it does to real ones: Because companies can more thoroughly monetize closed platforms, they have a greater incentive to invest more in those platforms and provide better user experiences. One can create an X account and begin posting tweets and interacting with others within minutes; good luck setting up your own microblogging service from the ground up. And because companies have full control over the platform, they can make changes more easily – thus, at least in the short term, closed platforms can improve at a faster rate than can open platforms, which often struggle with cumbersome, decentralized consensus governance.

Most important, at least from the perspective of this chapter, are closed platforms' advantages when it comes to moderation. Closed platforms can be moderated centrally, which enables greater control over what appears on the network. And the business models of closed platforms allow them to deploy economic and technological resources at a scale that open, decentralized systems simply cannot match. For example, Meta, Facebook's parent company, has spent over $13 billion on "safety and security" efforts since the 2016 election, employing, both internally and through contractors, 40,000 employees on just this issue. And Meta's investments in AI-based content-moderation tools have led it to block billions of fake accounts.[9] Content moderation, as Tarleton Gillespie notes, "is central to what platforms do, not peripheral" and "is, in many ways, the commodity that platforms offer."[10] Indeed, this concern with security – whether about malicious code, online abuse, or offensive speech – is one of the most important drivers of the popularity of closed systems.[11]

But closed platforms have become a victim of their own success. They have exacerbated the costs of malicious action by creating systems that are designed to be as frictionless as possible within the network (even if access to the network is controlled by the platform). At the same time, they have massively increased user expectations regarding the moderation of harmful content, since centralization allows (in theory, though not in practice) the complete elimination of harmful content in a way that the architecture of an open system does not. Closed platforms impose uniform, top-down standards, which inevitably leave many users unsatisfied.

9 *Our Progress Addressing Challenges and Innovating Responsibly*, Facebook (Sept. 21, 2021), https://perma.cc/3FHT-3TB8.

10 Tarleton Gillespie, Custodians of the Internet: Platforms, Content Moderation, and the Hidden Decisions That Shape Social Media 13 (2018).

11 Jonathan Zittrain, The Future of the Internet and How to Stop It 59 (paperback ed. 2008).

And they raise concerns about the handful of giant companies and Silicon Valley CEOs exercising outsized control over the public sphere.[12]

In other words, large, closed platforms are faced with what might be called the *moderator's trilemma*. The first prong is that platform user bases are large and diverse. The second prong is that the platforms use centralized, top-down moderation policies and practices. The third prong is that the platforms would like to avoid angering large swaths of their users (not to mention the politicians that represent them). But the content-moderation controversies of the past decade suggest that these three goals cannot all be met. The large closed platforms are unwilling to shrink their user bases or give up control over content moderation, so they have tacitly accepted high levels of dissatisfaction with their moderation decisions. The Fediverse, by contrast, responds to the moderator's trilemma by giving up on centralized moderation.

15.2.2 *The Fediverse and Its Applications*

The term "Fediverse" refers collectively to the protocols, servers, applications, and communities that enable decentralized social media. The most popular of these protocols is ActivityPub, which is developed by the World Wide Web Consortium, the main international standards organization for the World Wide Web, and which has also developed the HTML, XML, and other foundational internet standards.[13]

To understand how ActivityPub operates, it's important to appreciate that all social-media platforms are built around the same core components: users creating and interacting with pieces of content, whether posts (Facebook), tweets (X), messages (WhatsApp), images (Instagram), or videos (YouTube and TikTok). When a user tweets, for example, they first send the tweet to an X server. That X server then distributes that tweet through the X network to other users. Like all platforms, X has its own internal protocol that processes the data representing the tweet: the tweet's content plus metadata like the user handle, the time the tweet was

[12] When Elon Musk first made his bid to purchase X, X co-founder Jack Dorsey tweeted:

> In principle, I do not believe anyone should own or run Twitter. It wants to be a public good at a protocol level, not a company. Solving for the problem of it being a company however, Elon is the singular solution I trust. I trust his mission to extend the light of consciousness.
>
> @jack, Twitter (Apr. 25, 2022, 9:03 PM), https://perma.cc/VD56-QNRQ.

The chaos that has roiled X since Musk's takeover suggests that Dorsey's faith in Musk's "mission to extend the light of consciousness" was misplaced while underscoring the observation that X would be better as "a public good at a protocol level, not a company." To his credit, Dorsey has since recognized Musk's faults as X's owner. *See* Faiz Siddiqui & Will Oremus, *Twitter Founder Jack Dorsey Says Musk Wasn't an Ideal Leader after All*, Wash. Post (Apr. 29, 2023).

[13] *ActivityPub*, W3C, https://perma.cc/L84U-C5D6.

made, responses to the tweet ("likes" and "retweets"), and any restrictions on who can see or reply to the tweet.

ActivityPub generalizes this system. The ActivityPub protocol is flexible enough to accommodate different kinds of social-media content. This means that developers can build different applications on top of the single ActivityPub protocol; thus, Friendica replicates the main features of Facebook, Mastodon replicates those of X, and PeerTube of YouTube. But unlike legacy social-media platforms, which do not naturally interoperate – one can embed a YouTube link in a tweet, but X sees the YouTube content as just another URL, rather than a type of content that X can directly interact with – all applications built on top of ActivityPub have, in principle, access to the same ActivityPub data, allowing for a greater integration of content.[14]

The most important feature of ActivityPub is that it is decentralized. The servers that users communicate with and that send content around the network are independently owned and operated. Anyone can set up and run an ActivityPub server – generally called an "instance" – as long as they follow the ActivityPub protocol. This is the key feature distinguishing closed platforms like X or Facebook from open platforms like ActivityPub – or email or the World Wide Web, for that matter: Anyone can run an email or web server if they follow the relevant protocols.

ActivityPub's decentralized nature means that each instance can choose what content flows across its network and use different content-moderation standards. An instance can even choose to block certain users, types of media (e.g., videos or images), or entire other instances. At the same time, each instance's content-moderation decisions are locally scoped: No instance can control the behavior of any other instance, and there is no central authority that can decide which instances are valid or that can ban a user or a piece of content from the ActivityPub network entirely. As long as someone is willing to host an instance and allow certain content on that instance, it exists on the ActivityPub network.

This leads to a model of what I call *content-moderation subsidiarity*. Just as the general principle of political subsidiarity holds that decisions should be made at the lowest organizational level capable of making such decisions,[15] content-moderation subsidiarity devolves decisions to the individual instances that make up the overall network.

A key guarantor of content-moderation subsidiarity is the ability of users to switch instances if, for example, they are dissatisfied with how their current instance moderates content. If a user decides to move instances, their followers will

[14] For example, as PeerTube, a video-sharing platform, notes, "you can follow a PeerTube user from Mastodon (the latest videos from the PeerTube account you follow will appear in your feed), and even comment on a PeerTube-hosted video directly from your Mastodon's account." PEERTUBE, https://perma.cc/RT9C-9TVH.

[15] *See generally* Andreas Føllesdal, *Subsidiarity*, 6 J. POL. PHIL. 190 (1998).

automatically refollow them at their new account.[16] Thus, migrating from one Mastodon instance to another does not require starting from scratch. The result is that, although Fediverse instances show some of the clustering that is characteristic of the internet as a whole,[17] no single instance monopolizes the network.[18]

Using Albert Hirschman's theory of how individuals respond to dissatisfaction with their organizations,[19] we can say that the Fediverse empowers users to exercise powers of *voice* and *exit* more readily and meaningfully than they could on a centralized social-media platform. Rather than simply put up with dissatisfactions, the Fediverse permits users to choose the instance that best suits them (exit) and to use that leverage to participate in instance governance (voice). Of course, users on closed platforms can (and frequently do) express their grievances with how the platform is moderated – perhaps most notably on X, where a common (and ironic) subject for tweets is how terrible X is – but such an "affective voice" is far less likely to lead to meaningful change than the "effective voice" that the Fediverse enables.[20]

Some existing companies, though they remain centralized in most respects, have enhanced users' voice and exit privileges by decentralizing their platform's moderation practices. For example, Reddit, the popular message-board platform, grants substantial autonomy to its various subreddits, each of which has its own moderators. Indeed, Reddit is frequently held up as the most prominent example of bottom-up, community-based content moderation.[21] One might thus ask: does the Fediverse offer anything beyond what already exists on Reddit and other sites, like Wikipedia, that enables user-led moderation?

Indeed it does, because the Fediverse's decentralization is a matter of *architecture*, not just policy. A subreddit moderator has control only insofar as Reddit, a soon-to-be public company,[22] permits that control. Because Reddit can moderate any piece of content – and can even ban a subreddit outright – no matter whether the subreddit moderator agrees, the company is subject to public pressure to do so.

[16] Mastodon does not currently allow moving posts from one instance to another, but it does allow users to download a record of their posts. *How to Migrate from One Server to Another*, MASTODON, https://perma.cc/Y4XY-KM6W.

[17] *See* Lada A. Adamic & Bernardo A. Huberman, *Zipf's Law and the Internet*, 3 GLOTTOMETRICS 143, 147–48 (2002), https://perma.cc/H8LL-G9LY ("[T]here are many small elements contained within the Web, but few large ones. A few sites consist of millions of pages, but millions of sites only contain a handful of pages. Few sites contain millions of links, but many sites have one or two. Millions of users flock to a few select sites, giving little attention to millions of others.").

[18] A list of Mastodon instances, sorted by number of users, is available at https://perma.cc/S8JU-GGTW.

[19] *See* ALBERT O. HIRSCHMAN, EXIT, VOICE, AND LOYALTY: RESPONSES TO DECLINE IN FIRMS, ORGANIZATIONS, AND STATES (1970).

[20] *See* Seth Frey & Nathan Schneider, *Effective Voice: Beyond Exit and Affect in Online Communities*, NEW MEDIA & SOC'Y (Sept. 2021), https://perma.cc/VQ6K-6CBY.

[21] *See, e.g.*, James Grimmelmann, *The Virtues of Moderation*, 17 YALE J.L. & TECH. 42, 94–101 (2015).

[22] Cory Weinberg, *Reddit Aims for IPO in Second Half as Market's Gears Quietly Turn*, INFORMATION (Feb. 14, 2023), https://perma.cc/XT6C-CS35.

Perhaps the most famous example is Reddit's banning of the controversial pro-Trump r/The_Donald subreddit several months before the 2020 election.[23]

Taken as a whole, the architecture of the Fediverse represents a challenge not only to the daily operations of incumbent platforms, but also to their very theoretical bases. Media scholars Aymeric Mansoux and Roel Roscam Abbing have developed what is so far the most theoretically sophisticated treatment of the Fediverse's content-moderation subsidiarity, which they characterize as a kind of "agonism": the increasingly influential[24] model of politics that seeks a middle ground between, on the one hand, unrealistic hopes for political consensus and, on the other hand, the zero-sum destructiveness of antagonism:

> The bet made by agonism is that by creating a system in which a pluralism of hegemonies is permitted, it is possible to move from an understanding of the other as an enemy, to the other as a political adversary. For this to happen, different ideologies must be allowed to materialize via different channels and platforms. An important prerequisite is that the goal of political consensus must be abandoned and replaced with conflictual consensus. ... Translated to the Fediverse, it is clear that it already contains a relatively diverse political landscape and that transitions from political consensus to conflictual consensus can be witnessed in the way communities relate to one another. At the base of these conflictual exchanges are various points of view on the collective design and use of the software stack and the underlying protocols that would be needed to further enable a sort of online agonistic pluralism.[25]

The Fediverse is a truly novel evolution in online speech. The question is: It works in theory, but does it work in practice?

15.3 CONTENT MODERATION ON THE FEDIVERSE

15.3.1 *The Mastodon Case Study*

Although the organization that runs the Mastodon project recommends certain content-moderation policies,[26] each Mastodon instance is able to choose whether

[23] Mike Isaac, *Reddit, Acting against Hate Speech, Bans "The_Donald" Subreddit*, N.Y. Times (June 29, 2020).

[24] For a recent attempt to bring agonism into the mainstream of legal scholarship, *see* Daniel E. Walters, *The Administrative Agon: Democratic Theory for a Conflictual Regulatory State*, 132 Yale L.J. 1 (2022).

[25] Aymeric Mansoux & Roel Roscam Abbing, *Seven Theses on the Fediverse and the Becoming of FLOSS*, *in* The Eternal Network: The Ends and Becomings of Network Culture 124, 131 (Kristoffer Gansing & Inga Luchs eds., 2020). For an influential general account of agonism, *see* Chantal Mouffe, Agonistics: Thinking the World Politically (2013).

[26] Specifically, the Mastodon project has promulgated a "Mastodon Server Covenant," whereby instances that commit to "[a]ctive moderation against racism, sexism, homophobia and transphobia" such that users will have "confidence that they are joining a safe space, free from white

and how much to moderate content. The large, general-interest instances tend to have fairly generic policies. For example, Mastodon.social bans "racism, sexism, homophobia, transphobia, xenophobia, or casteism" as well as "harassment, dogpiling or doxxing of other users."[27] By contrast, other instances do not specify prohibited categories of content;[28] this, of course, does not prevent the instance administrators from moderating content on an ad hoc basis, but it does signal a lighter touch. Content moderation can also be based on geography and subject matter; for example, Mastodon.social, which is hosted in Germany, explicitly bans content that is illegal in Germany,[29] and Switter, a "sex work friendly social space" that ran from 2018 to 2022, permitted sex-work advertisements that mainstream instances generally prohibited.[30] Mastodon instances can also impose various levels of moderation on other instances, which can be: (1) fully accessible (the default); (2) filtered but still accessible; (3) restricted such that users can only view content posted on the restricted instances if they follow users on those instances; and (4) fully blocked.

Mastodon instances thus operate according to the principle of content-moderation subsidiarity: Content-moderation standards are set by, and differ across, individual instances. Any given Mastodon instance may have rules that are far more restrictive than those of the major social-media platforms. But the network as a whole is substantially more protective of speech than are any of the major social-media platforms, since no user or content can be permanently banned from the network and anyone is free to start an instance that communicates both with the major Mastodon instances and with the peripheral, shunned instances.

The biggest content-moderation challenge for Mastodon has been Gab, an X-like social network that is popular on the far-right. Gab launched in 2016, and, in 2019, switched its software infrastructure to run on a version of Mastodon, in large part to get around Apple and Google banning Gab's smartphone app from their app stores. By switching its infrastructure to Mastodon and operating as merely one of Mastodon's many instances, Gab hoped to hitch a ride back to users' smartphones.[31]

supremacy, anti-semitism and transphobia of other platforms" are eligible to be listed on the project's homepage as recommended instances. *See* Eugen Rochko, *Introducing the Mastodon Server Covenant*, MASTODON (May 16, 2019), https://perma.cc/GP8H-MXXK. But the covenant is not binding on any Mastodon instance, and noncomplying instances remain full-fledged members of the overall Mastodon network, subject only to the moderation decision of other instances.

27 *Welcome*, MASTODON, https://perma.cc/326M-JW5A; *see also mas.to!*, MASTODON, https://perma.cc/TBH6-BKWA.

28 *See, e.g.*, *Mastodon.cloud*, MASTODON, https://perma.cc/7YQQ-ZX87.

29 *Welcome*, MASTODON, *supra* note 27.

30 SWITTER, https://perma.cc/B8FA-X7JY.

31 Adi Robertson, *How the Biggest Decentralized Social Network Is Dealing with Its Nazi Problem*, VERGE (July 12, 2019), https://perma.cc/QA6F-J54U. Gab is not the only right-wing social-media network to use Mastodon as its base. Truth Social, Donald Trump's social-media site, is

Gab is a useful case study in how decentralized social media can self-police. On the one hand, there was no way for Mastodon to expel Gab from the Fediverse. As Mastodon's founder Eugen Rochko explained, "You have to understand it's not actually possible to do anything platform-wide because it's decentralized.... I do not have the control."[32] On the other hand, individual Mastodon instances could – and the most popular ones did – refuse to interact with the Gab instance, effectively cutting it off from most of the network in a spontaneous, bottom-up process of instance-by-instance decision-making. Ultimately, Gab was left almost entirely isolated, with more than 99 percent of its users interacting only with other Gab users. Gab responded by "defederating": voluntarily cutting itself off from the remaining instances that were still willing to communicate with it.[33]

15.3.2 *Benefits and Drawbacks of Federated Moderation*

As the Gab story demonstrates, the biggest benefit of a decentralized moderation model is its embrace of content-moderation subsidiarity: Each community can choose its own content-moderation standards according to its own needs and values, while at the same time recognizing and respecting other communities' content-moderation choices. This is in stark contrast to the problem faced by large, centralized platforms, which by their nature must choose a single moderation standard that different groups of users will inevitably find either under- or overinclusive.

The difference in business models also lowers the need for content moderation generally. The business models of the major platforms – selling advertisements – require them to maximize "user engagement," and the discovery algorithms designed to promote this goal tend to emphasize conflict across users. By contrast, Fediverse applications can, and often are, engineered with "antivirality" in mind.[34] For example, Mastodon's lack of X's "quote tweet" feature was an intentional design choice on Eugene Rochko's part, who judged that such a feature "inevitably adds toxicity to people's behaviours" and encourages "performative" behavior and "ridiculing."[35] The same considerations underpin Mastodon's lack of full-text search and eschewal of algorithmic amplification in favor of reverse-chronological feeds.[36] In addition, Fediverse instances, which are generally run by volunteers and without a profit imperative, can afford to focus on smaller communities in which

also built off of Mastodon. Michael Kan, *Trump's Social Media Site Quietly Admits It's Based on Mastodon*, PCMAG (Dec. 1, 2021), https://perma.cc/3CJE-S2AA.

[32] Robertson, *supra* note 31.

[33] Rob Colbert (@shadowknight412), GAB (May 27, 2020), https://perma.cc/G82J-73WX.

[34] Clive Thompson, *Twitter Alternative: How Mastodon Is Designed to Be "Antiviral"*, MEDIUM (Nov. 9, 2022), https://perma.cc/49N4-YWGZ.

[35] Eugen Rochko (@Gargron), MASTODON (Mar. 10, 2018), https://perma.cc/VXE7-XVLC.

[36] Thompson, *supra* note 34.

like-minded users do not suffer the problem of "context collapse" that frequently leads to conflicts on the major social-media platforms.[37]

Of course, if the Fediverse proves popular, for-profit entities may enter the space, thus introducing the problematic incentives of the major platforms. But even if this were to occur, the ability of users to switch Fediverse applications and instances will limit the extent to which the Fediverse's architecture will reflect the values of the extractive attention economy.

The main objection to the Fediverse is that what some see as its key feature – its decentralized model – is for others its main bug. Because there is no centralized Fediverse authority, there is no way to fully exclude even the most harmful content from the network. And, as noted above, Fediverse administrators will generally have fewer resources as compared to giant social-media platforms.[38] By contrast, if Facebook or X want to fully ban a user or some piece of content, they can in principle do so (although in practice it can be a challenge given the size of their networks and users' ability to evade content moderation).

In considering the limits of decentralized content moderation, it is helpful to distinguish between two categories of objectionable conduct. The first category consists of content that is broadly recognized as having no legitimate expressive value. Examples of such content are child-exploitation material, communication that facilitates criminal conduct, and spam. The challenges of moderating these types of content are technological and organizational, and the main question is whether decentralized social media can handle the moderation challenges at scale. Ultimately, it's an empirical question and we'll have to wait until the Fediverse grows to find out the answer. But there are reasons for optimism.

First, the Fediverse itself may be up to the task. Automated scanning, while hardly foolproof, could lower moderation costs. For example, many of the major platforms use Microsoft's PhotoDNA system to scan for child pornography,[39] and the same software could be used by Fediverse instances for content that they host. And if effective moderation turns out to require more infrastructure, that could lead to a greater consolidation of instances. This is what happened with email, which – in part due to the investments necessary to counter spam – has become increasingly dominated by Google and Microsoft.[40]

If similar scale is necessary to fight spam and bot accounts on the Fediverse, this could serve as a centripetal force to counter the Fediverse's decentralized architecture and lead to a Fediverse that is more centralized than it is today (albeit still far more decentralized than architecturally closed platforms). Partial centralization

37 *See, e.g.*, Jenny L. Davis & Nathan Jurgenson, *Context Collapse: Theorizing Context Collusions and Collisions*, 17 Info., Commc'n & Soc'y 476 (2014).

38 *See supra* notes 9–11 and accompanying text.

39 *See* Hany Farid, *Reining in Online Abuses*, 19 Tech. & Innovation 596 (2018).

40 *See* Enze Liu et al., *Who's Got Your Mail?: Characterizing Mail Service Provider Usage*, *in* Proceedings of the 2021 ACM Internet Measurement Conference 113 (2021).

would reintroduce some of the content-moderation dilemmas that decentralization is meant to avoid,[41] and there is a trade-off between a vibrant and diverse communication system and the degree of centralized control that would be necessary to ensure 100 percent filtering of content. The question, to which the answer is as yet unknown, is how stark that trade-off is.

A second reason to think that federalized systems can have sufficient content moderation is that governments could step in to deal with instances that cannot, or choose not to, deal with the worst content. Although the Fediverse may live in the cloud, its servers, moderators, and users are physically located in nations whose governments are more than capable of enforcing local law.[42] A Mastodon instance that hosted child pornography would not only be blocked by all mainstream Mastodon instances, but would also be quickly taken offline – and have its members prosecuted – by the relevant jurisdictions. Even the threat of state action can have large effects. For example, Switter, which by the end of its life was the third-largest Mastodon instance, shut down because its organizers concluded that Switter's continued existence was increasingly untenable as major jurisdictions like the United States, Australia, and the United Kingdom advanced online-safety and antitrafficking legislation.[43]

When it comes to the second category of content moderation – content that is objectionable to one group but that others view as legitimate, even core, speech – the Fediverse will host content that current platforms prohibit. But whether this is a weakness or a strength depends on one's substantive views about the content at issue. What looks to one group like responsible moderation can appear to others as unjustified censorship. And when platforms inevitably make high-profile moderation mistakes – moderation, after all, is not an exact science – they undermine their credibility even further, especially where determinations of "misinformation" or "disinformation" are perceived as tendentious attempts to suppress conflict over politics, health, or other important social and culture issues.[44]

41 For example, the outsize importance of a few email providers has led to complaints of censorship. *See, e.g.*, *Republican National Committee Sues Google over Email Spam Filters*, Reuters (Oct. 24, 2022), https://perma.cc/49EU-JFEQ.

42 *See generally* Jack Goldsmith & Tim Wu, Who Controls the Internet?: Illusions of a Borderless World (2006).

43 *See* Switter, *supra* note 30.

44 A high-profile example is X and Facebook's decision on the cusp of the 2020 election to block news reports of Hunter Biden's stolen laptop. While X and Facebook, both of whom played an important role in amplifying Russian election interference in 2016, were understandably concerned that the laptop story was foreign disinformation, later revelations suggesting that the laptop was in fact authentic have further undermined many conservatives' faith in the platforms, and even the platforms themselves have conceded the mistake. *See* Cristiano Lima, *Hunter Biden Laptop Findings Renew Scrutiny of Twitter, Facebook Crackdowns*, Wash. Post (Mar. 31, 2022); Jessica Bursztynsky, *Twitter CEO Jack Dorsey Says Blocking New York Post Story Was "Wrong"*, CNBC (Oct. 16, 2020), https://perma.cc/7CMJ-5VGA; David Molloy,

The benefit of decentralized moderation is that it can satisfy both those that want to speak and those that do not want to listen. By empowering users, through their choice of instance, to avoid content they find objectionable, the Fediverse operationalizes the principle that freedom of speech is not the same as freedom of reach. In a world where there simply is not consensus on what content is and is not legitimate, letting people say what they want while giving others the means to protect themselves from that speech may be the best we can do.

A different concern with decentralized moderation is that it will lead to "filter bubbles" and "echo chambers" in which members will choose to only interact with like-minded users.[45] For Mansoux and Abbing, this state of affairs would produce a watered-down, second-best agonism:

> Rather than reaching a state of agonistic pluralism, it could be that the Fediverse will create at best a form of bastard agonism through pillarization. That is to say, we could witness a situation in which instances would form large agonistic-without-agonism aggregations only among both ideologically and technically compatible communities and software, with only a minority of them able and willing to bridge with radically opposed systems.[46]

This concern, though understandable, can be addressed several ways. First, filter bubbles are not a Fediverse-only phenomena; closed platforms can design their systems so as to keep dissimilar users from interacting with each other.

Second, it is important to not overstate the effect of filter bubbles; even the most partisan users frequently consume and even seek out information that challenges their beliefs.[47] While Fediverse applications like Mastodon may make it easier for users to communicate only with like-minded peers, users can still go outside their instances to access whatever information they want.

And third, even if filter bubbles exist, it is unclear whether they are a net negative, at least from the perspective of polarization and misinformation. The "backfire effect" (also known as belief perseverance) is a well-established psychological phenomenon whereby individuals who are exposed to evidence that challenges their views end up believing in those views more rather than less.[48] In this view, a more narrowly drawn epistemic environment, while hardly a model of ideal democratic public reason, may actually be better than a social-media free-for-all.

Zuckerberg Tells Rogan FBI Warning Prompted Biden Laptop Story Censorship, BBC (Aug. 26, 2022), https://perma.cc/XG9Q-5PWQ.

45 *See generally* Cass R. Sunstein, #Republic: Divided Democracy in the Age of Social Media (2018).

46 Mansoux & Abbing, *supra* note 25, at 132.

47 *See* Peter M. Dahlgren, *A Critical Review of Filter Bubbles and a Comparison with Selective Exposure*, 42 Nordicom Rev. 15 (2021).

48 *See* Brendan Nyhan & Jason Reifler, *When Corrections Fail: The Persistence of Political Misperceptions*, 32 Pol. Behav. 303 (2010).

Put another way, the smaller communities of the Fediverse may be a useful corrective to the "megascale" of contemporary social media, which pushes us to "say so much, and to so many, so often."[49]

15.4 ENCOURAGING THE FEDIVERSE

The Fediverse is still a very small part of the broader social-media ecosystem. Mastodon's several million users pale in comparison with Facebook's billion or X's hundreds of millions of users. Whether the Fediverse ever grows large enough to challenge the current dominance of closed platforms is very much an open question, one that will ultimately depend on whether it provides a product that ordinary users find superior to what is currently available on the dominant platforms.

Such an outcome is hardly preordained. It would require millions of people to overcome the steeper learning curves of Fediverse applications, commit to platforms that are often intentionally less viral than the engagement-at-all-costs alternatives, and navigate the culture shock of integrating into an existing community.[50] After experiencing a mass influx of X users that defected after Elon Musk purchased the platform, Mastodon has seen its active users drop from its late-2022 high of 2.5 million, suggesting that, for many users, Mastodon does not work as an X replacement.[51]

But Mastodon has demonstrated that, for millions of people, decentralized social media is a viable option. And even if Mastodon's market share remains modest, other decentralized applications, whether operating on ActivityPub or other protocols (as with the ATProtcol-powered Bluesky) will continue to grow, especially if they combine Mastodon's emphasis on decentralization with Silicon Valley's engagement-at-all-costs priorities. In the end, the current dominance of the incumbent platforms may prove illusory. They are, after all, themselves subject to shake-ups, as is demonstrated by the meteoric rise of apps like TikTok.

Although decentralized social media will have to stand on its own merits, public-policy interventions could nevertheless encourage its growth. Here I briefly consider four such interventions, ranging from most- to least-direct government involvement.

First, governments could support the Fediverse by participating in it as users or, better yet, as instances. This would both directly contribute to the Fediverse's growth but, more importantly, would help legitimate it as the preferred social-media architecture for democratic societies. For example, shortly after Musk announced plans to purchase X, the European Commission, the executive branch of the

[49] Ian Bogost, *People Are Not Meant to Talk This Much*, ATLANTIC (Oct. 22, 2021), https://perma.cc/U3NT-7MGF.

[50] *See* Alan Rozenshtein, *Mastodon's Content-Moderation Growing Pains*, VOLOKH CONSPIRACY (Nov. 21, 2022), https://perma.cc/5MPT-3WYK.

[51] Amanda Hoover, *The Mastodon Bump Is Now a Slump*, WIRED (Feb. 7, 2023), https://perma.cc/TJ5W-YRLZ.

European Union, launched EU Voice, a Mastodon instance that "provides EU institutions, bodies and agencies with privacy-friendly microblogging accounts that they typically use for the purposes of press and public relations activities."[52] Other governments and international organizations could follow suit.

Second, governments could mandate that large social-media platforms interoperate with the Fediverse. For example, under such a regime, Facebook would be allowed to choose what users or content appear on its servers, but it would have to allow other Fediverse instances to communicate with it. This would allow users to access content that Facebook removes and also still be able to interact with the broader Facebook community.[53] Such regulation would have to specify to what extent Facebook could block other instances entirely, since otherwise Facebook could effectively defederate. But even a limited interoperability mandate would enable a balance between what are the currently envisioned options: totally unfettered control by closed platforms or common-carrier-type regulations that make any sort of moderation impossible.[54]

Such regulation is already being pursued in Europe, where the Digital Services Act would require large platforms to interoperate, a requirement that could easily be modified to include the Fediverse.[55] In the United States, interoperability legislation, which has already been introduced in Congress,[56] would be a welcome alternative to recent overbroad state laws from Texas, Florida, and other Republican-governed states that purport to limit the ability of major social-media platforms to moderate content. These laws, in addition to being poorly thought out and overtly political, may also violate the First Amendment, at least in their more extreme versions.[57]

Third, antitrust regulators like the Department of Justice and the Federal Trade Commission could use an incumbent platform's willingness to interoperate as a

[52] EU Voice, https://perma.cc/2NTM-9N6E.

[53] Interestingly, Meta is reportedly working on a decentralized text-based social media platform that would interoperate with Mastodon. Deepsekhar Choudhury & Vikas Sn, *Exclusive: Meta Mulls a Twitter Competitor Codenamed "P92" That Will Be Interoperable with Mastodon*, MoneyControl (Mar. 10, 2023), https://perma.cc/6E8L-BFC6.

[54] To be sure, interoperability mandates are not without their own risks, especially to user privacy. *See, e.g.*, Thomas E. Kadri, *Digital Gatekeepers*, 99 Tex. L. Rev. 951, 999 (2021); Jane Bambauer, *Reinventing Cambridge Analytica One Good Intention at a Time*, Lawfare (June 8, 2022), https://perma.cc/7V7W-GML6.

[55] At the same time, other requirements of the Digital Services Act, especially around mandatory content moderation, might hinder the Fediverse's development. *See* Konstantinos Komaitis & Louis-Victor de Franssu, *Can Mastodon Survive Europe's Digital Services Act?*, Tech Pol'y Press (Nov. 16, 2022), https://perma.cc/W8RC-2XVL.

[56] *See, e.g.*, Press Release, Sen. Mark R. Warner, *Lawmakers Reintroduce Bipartisan Legislation to Encourage Competition in Social Media* (May 25, 2022), https://perma.cc/SC2Z-3XQL.

[57] *See, e.g.*, Alan Z. Rozenshtein, *First Amendment Absolutism and the Florida Social Media Law*, Lawfare (June 1, 2022), https://perma.cc/WXT9-4HAL; *see generally* Alan Z. Rozenshtein, *Silicon Valley's Speech: Technology Giants and the Deregulatory First Amendment*, 1 J. Free Speech L. 337 (2021).

consideration in antitrust cases.[58] Interoperability could then be an alternative to calls to "break up" social-media giants, a tactic that is both controversial and legally risky.[59]

Finally, policymakers should consider how the background legal regime can be tweaked to improve the incentives for the Fediverse. In the United States, the most important factor is Section 230 of the Communications Decency Act of 1996, which shields platforms from liability as publishers of content created by users.[60] Although Section 230 has come under increasing controversy, especially as it applies to giant platforms, it's hard to imagine how the Fediverse could function without it. The open nature of the Fediverse – with users being able to travel between and communicate across instances – limits the scope of monetization, since users can choose instances that limit advertisements and algorithmic ranking. But this also means that Fediverse instances will lack the resources necessary to perform the sort of aggressive content moderation that would be necessary were they to be held liable for their users' content. The rationale for Section 230 immunity when it was enacted in the mid-1990s – to help support a nascent internet – no longer applies to the technology giants. But it does apply to the current generation of internet innovators: the federated social-media platforms.

[58] *See generally* Chinmayi Sharma, *Concentrated Digital Markets, Restrictive APIs, and the Fight for Internet Interoperability*, 50 U. Mem. L. Rev. 441 (2019).

[59] *See* Herbert Hovenkamp, *Antitrust and Platform Monopoly*, 130 Yale L.J. 1952 (2021).

[60] 47 U.S.C. § 230(c)(1).

PART IV

Sustaining Journalistic Institutions

16

Introduction

Sustaining Journalistic Institutions

Gus Hurwitz

Media have traditionally relied on a mix of advertising and subscription revenue to keep the lights on – and to produce a mix of high-quality, thoughtful, well researched, compelling news, information, educational, and other content that is necessary in a modern democracy. The internet has disrupted those revenue streams. And while some media outlets have shored themselves up on other sources of support – grants, government transfers and licensing fees, wealthy patrons, or the like – such funding is both the exception and de minimis in the overall operation of our media ecosystem.

The chapters that follow consider these institutions' struggle to survive technological disruption. Can traditional media enterprises survive internet-era market forces? And if not, can they survive the governmental interventions (and governmental controls) that may be necessary to ride the market out?

In the first contribution to this section, Professor Laurie Lee looks to the relative success of local television news compared to newspapers over the recent past, to explore whether there are lessons that can be learned from the local television business model that can help print news to continue as a going concern. Her chapter surveys a significant amount of material, both historical and regulatory, to understand the enduring success of local television news – as well as to ponder how likely it is to continue to survive, if at all. And in an observation that bears on the other contributions to this cluster, Professor Lee notes that broadcast's most significant advantage may lie in the "regulatory protectionist policies" it enjoys under federal telecommunications law. It is doubtful under the First Amendment that these same policies could be carried over to newspapers.

Paul Matzko carries the discussion forward from here in a chapter that considers a recent mechanism advanced to support traditional media institutions in Australia. This mechanism, commonly referred to as a "link tax," requires social media platforms to pay some amount to Australian media outlets for links on the social media platform to content hosted by the Australian firms. As innovative as it may seem, Matzko argues that the link tax has an early twentieth-century forbear in the "hot news" doctrine. "Hot news" meant that news organizations could claim fresh scoops as their own exclusive quasi-property for short periods of time – and sue competitors who picked up the story too soon. This judicially created doctrine secured some established news organizations' revenue against the technological disruption of the day (competitive entry in the telegraph market). But critics including Matzko have argued that hot news created entrenchment effects that negated whatever benefit to journalism courts claimed it would provide. The "link tax," Matzko argues, will do the same: "If redistribution of online revenue is a priority for policymakers, then almost any other mechanism for accomplishing that goal would be preferable."

Lee's and Matzko's chapters both focus on what could be considered business models that distribute revenues from one set of (profitable) stakeholders to another set of (unprofitable, or at least less-profitable) stakeholders though a regulatory mechanism. The final two papers go a step further, considering permutations of direct public support for uneconomic media platforms. It bears note that all four authors contributing to this discussion consider at least a minimal level of regulatory intervention in markets – even if Lee ponders whether it is necessary and Matzko urges caution against the dangers of the Australian link tax that he examines.

In his contribution, Professor Kyle Langvardt minces no words, starting with the clear statement that "The commercial market for local news in the United States has collapsed." Two-thirds of the United States, he tells us, have no local newspaper; those papers that still serve their communities are struggling. What is the remedy? Considering the unviability of private markets to provide a solution, at least outside of edge cases such as Substack and other idiosyncratic markets, Langvardt looks to the clear alternative: public subsidies for traditional media institutions. Public funding of the press is traditionally disfavored in the United States – but, Langvardt notes, "A[a]lmost all wealthy democracies [other than the United States] give substantial financial support to the news media." Why should not we? Indeed, he notes that even in the United States there are various subsidies for media – such as discounted postage.

Professor Langvardt argues that American concerns about First Amendment rights and state control (or capture) of critical media institutions explain much of America's public stinginess toward the news. He considers a range of options that a public option for media may take, focusing on designs that may pass First Amendment muster. His discussion touches on several points, from the unresolved standing of government speech under the First Amendment (it may not be constitutionally problematic for the government itself to establish a media platform) to voucher-based programs directed through plebiscite.

Rounding out this section, and this volume, Professor Ramsi Woodcock also considers a model for traditional media businesses that involves more intervention in the market. Unlike Langvardt's argument for direct public subsidies to support traditional media, Woodcock proposes two indirect interventions, one aimed at newspapers' market for readers and the other at newspapers' market for advertisers.

On the reader side, Woodcock would use the postal service's letter-box monopoly to tax high-visibility social media posts. This would force lower-quality content out of the market, creating space for newspapers to shift resources back from the opinion-reporting that has proliferated in recent years to the more fact-oriented reporting that characterized mid- and late-twentieth century journalism. He believes this would restore the moderating influence that newspapers once exerted over American politics.

On the advertiser side, Woodcock would raise advertising revenues for newspapers by restricting advertising on social-media platforms, with the goal of pushing advertisers to spend more on advertising in traditional media. Unlike the link tax considered by Matzko, advertising restrictions would be more likely to restore newspapers' revenues because they would not depend on social-media companies' demand for news, which Woodcock believes to be small. Both of Woodcock's proposals are grounded in a frank, unsparing recognition that social media is simply built for attention and advertising in a way that traditional journalism is not and never can be – and that public policymakers will have to rebuild the playing field if they want journalism to survive competition in the digital economy.

17

How Local TV News Is Surviving Disruption as Newspapers Fail

Lessons Learned

Laurie Thomas Lee

17.1 INTRODUCTION

Despite the sharp decline in the number of local newspapers, it's important to understand that other legacy news-delivery platforms – particularly local TV news – have not been suffering the same degree of loss. Pew Research Center found that local TV news actually saw its audience *increase* across the evening and late-night timeslots in 2020, and that local TV companies earned more revenue than the previous year.[1] In fact, local TV was deemed to be on par with or outpacing cable and network TV. Pew survey data show more Americans still prefer to get their local news from television than from any other medium, including online. Even with an increasing preference for digital delivery, "local television stations have retained a strong hold in the local news ecosystem."[2]

Why and how has local TV news managed to stay afloat while local newspapers close their doors? Even as we mourn the loss of local news from print media, we should not overlook its surviving sibling that continues to churn out news to small and medium markets. Why do some media survive in the face of competition from new, disruptive media technologies? What lessons might be learned? Is there a role that government might play? Yet with the loss of local newspapers, are broadcast stations and online platforms adequate substitutes for providing local news? Or is local broadcast news actually just on a slower decline compared to newspapers?

17.2 SURVIVING DISRUPTION

Much of the blame for the fall of the newspaper industry rests with the rise of the internet and online competition. For example, digital offerings have cannibalized

[1] *Local TV News Fact Sheet*, Pew Rsch. Ctr. (July 13, 2021), https://perma.cc/37JZ-XNHC.

[2] *For Local News, Americans Embrace Digital but Still Want Strong Community Connection*, Pew Rsch. Ctr. (Mar. 26, 2019), https://perma.cc/C86L-ZD43.

the editorial side of the business as online aggregators. Social-media sites have become the alternate entry point for daily news as readers rapidly migrate to social media.

Newspapers have also been hit with a loss of advertising revenue to online companies like Facebook and Google.[3] The most devasting blow is from the online siphoning of roughly $5 billion in classified ad revenues – a critically important revenue source for newspapers.[4] Dedicated online businesses, such as Craigslist, and social-media companies, like Facebook, are able to easily provide less-expensive access to their online “Marketplace” for individuals and merchants to buy and sell goods and services.

As a result, cost-cutting ownership practices[5] – particularly by hedge-fund owners[6] – have led to a death spiral for newspapers. Granted, trends have shown that revenue growth from advertising expenditures had been weakening and not keeping up with inflation enough to be sustainable.[7] But newspapers’ shrinking page counts, staff layoffs, and general financial crises are largely due to the advent of the internet and the online business competitors it spawned.

17.3 UNDERSTANDING LOCAL TELEVISION NEWS SUCCESS

To understand how local television news has fared compared to local newspapers, we should examine distinguishing factors such as regulation and technology, as well as other market forces, including consumer behavior.

17.3.1 *Regulation*

Both industries have faced similar disruptive effects over the years, but the one element that most notably separates broadcasting from the newspaper industry is federal regulation and oversight. Governmental authority has shaped the broadcast industry in terms of invention, competition, and content, including how it serves local communities with news and information. It has controlled but also protected local broadcast stations in ways that may explain their continued success in the digital age.

3 Jon Wertheim, *Local Newsrooms Strained by Budget-Slashing Financial Firms*, CBS NEWS: 60 MINUTES (Feb. 27, 2022), https://perma.cc/27GS-7EL7.

4 Alexis Madrigal, *Local News Is Dying, and Americans Have No Idea*, ATLANTIC (Mar. 26, 2019), https://perma.cc/N44P-SVZ8.

5 *Town by Town, Local Journalism Is Dying in Plain Sight*, CNBC (Mar. 10, 2019), https://perma.cc/4RND-LP25.

6 Wertheim, *supra* note 3.

7 Robert Picard, *Shifts in Newspaper Advertising Expenditures and Their Implications for the Future of Newspapers*, 9 JOURNALISM STUD. 704 (2008).

17.3.1.1 Local and Educational Coverage Requirements

Unlike newspapers, TV and radio stations have always been and continue to be subject to federal licensing requirements. Since broadcasting signals naturally cross state lines,[8] the U.S. government's authority over broadcasting comes from the Commerce Clause,[9] which provides for oversight of interstate commerce. A period of chaotic interference by early radio entrepreneurs during the 1920s prompted calls for some sort of licensing and coordination of the airwaves akin to a traffic cop. The rationale for supporting licensing was then based on the legal premises of the scarcity doctrine and public ownership of the airwaves. Simply put, the range of frequencies in the electromagnetic spectrum that broadcasting stations use to transmit their signals is a limited resource, and that resource belongs to the public.[10]

As a result, one regulatory distinction is the assurance that all communities are served by at least one TV station. The federal government intentionally created a system of channel allocations that would ensure small markets are served.[11] Congress was concerned that licenses would become concentrated around major cities and would thus leave remote and less populated areas of the country without service.[12] The Federal Communication Commission (FCC) believed that the public interest would best be served by ensuring that every community had its own television station that was locally oriented and controlled.[13] So, a "Table of Allotments" was created that established a formula for the geographical distribution of local television and commercial FM radio frequencies across the country.[14] These channel assignments are set. Unlike newspapers, stations cannot abandon their local communities and move to larger markets or regionalize the scope of their coverage. They must serve their local communities of license.

The FCC further ensured that local communities would be served by increasing the number of stations available. Given the limited number of allocated broadcast TV channels and the high costs of entry into the market, the Low Power Television Service (LPTV) system was established, which provided flexible and less-expensive entry into television broadcasting while also permitting fuller use of the broadcast

8 Even if a signal does not migrate across a state's borders, federal regulation pertains.

9 U.S. CONST. art. I, § 8.

10 Red Lion Broad. Co. v. Fed. Commc'ns Comm'n, 395 U.S. 367 (1969).

11 Section 307(b) requires the FCC to "make such distribution of licenses, frequencies, hours of operation, and or power among the several States and communities as to provide a fair, efficient, and equitable distribution of radio service to each of the same." 47 U.S.C. § 307(b).

12 *See, e.g.*, David M. Silverman & David N. Tobenkin, *The FCC's Main Studio Rule: Achieving Little for Localism at a Great Cost to Broadcasters*, 53 FED. COMMC'NS L.J. 469 (2001).

13 *Id.*

14 Sixth Report and Order on Television Allocations, 41 FED. CMMC'NS COMM'N 148 (1952). *See* 47 C.F.R. § 73.606. This included standards for operation, such as allowable power and antenna height.

spectrum.[15] This was "primarily intended to provide opportunities for locally-oriented television service in small communities, ... delivering programming tailored to the interests of viewers in small localized areas, providing a means of local self-expression."[16] As a result, many communities are served by LPTV stations that are "operated by diverse groups and organizations, including high schools and colleges, churches and religious groups, local governments, large and small businesses, and individual citizens."[17] Today, these stations provide local news, community affairs, weather, and emergency information to millions of viewers across the country, particularly in small markets and rural areas.[18]

Along similar lines, the federal government in its frequency-allocation system required certain channels be set aside for noncommercial, educational broadcasting.[19] This meant that markets would be served by TV stations that are unconstrained by the quest for advertising dollars.[20] This also lead to a system of federal financial support for noncommercial stations when Congress recognized the need for federal funding in 1962 to help facilitate the development of such stations by passing the Educational Television Facilities Act.[21] In 1967, Congress also passed the Public Broadcasting Act, which considerably broadened the federal role in noncommercial broadcasting through the creation of the Corporation for Public Broadcasting (CPB), a nongovernmental and nonprofit corporation, to provide public broadcasting and network interconnection needs.[22] Notably, the CPB receives a federal appropriation for public broadcasting that it distributes to member stations. The CPB's role is to shield stations from political influence while delivering federal support in a way that allows stations to operate independently.[23] Their taxpayer-funded support in the form of direct station grants amounted to about 18.3 percent of the average public television station's total revenue in 2020.[24] Other federal funds may come from the National Telecommunications and Information Administration (NTIA) at the Department of Commerce as well as

15 *Low Power Television (LPTV)*, FED. COMMC'NS COMM'N (last updated June 15, 2021), https://perma.cc/V2CD-QU7T.

16 *Id.*

17 *Low Power Television Service*, FED. COMMC'NS COMM'N (last updated Dec. 9, 2019), https://perma.cc/6PJG-7CKH.

18 *Proposed Bill Would Allow LPTVs To Seek Class A Status*, RADIO & TELEVISION BUS. REP. (Dec. 20, 2021), https://perma.cc/JKC4-T7AK.

19 The FCC revised its table of frequency allocations in 1952 to spur the development of educational television broadcasting. It set aside 242 channels for exclusive use of noncommercial educational television (ETV), increasing that number to 329 by 1966. *Federal Support Educational Broadcasting*, STATEUNIVERSITY.COM EDUC. ENCYCLOPEDIA, https://perma.cc/4Y7Z-XBE6. *See* 47 C.F.R. § 73.621.

20 *Id.* at § 73.621(e), which prohibits promotional announcements on behalf of for-profit entities in exchange for consideration. However, acknowledgments of contributions can be made.

21 *Federal Support*, *supra* note 19.

22 *Id.*

23 *About Public Media*, CPB, https://perma.cc/86NB-DMKC.

24 *Federal Appropriation*, CPB, https://perma.cc/RJ5J-MFJT.

through programming grants from various federal agencies such as the National Science Foundation.[25] The remaining station revenue comes from public donations and underwriting. While these stations have national sources for programming such as PBS and its *PBS Newshour*, they also produce their own programming. A few public television stations – albeit in the largest markets – each provide a daily local-news program that is thirty minutes or longer.[26]

Newspapers, on the other hand, are typically for-profit enterprises, highly dependent on diminishing advertising revenue and without government support. There is, however, a movement by nonprofit outfits to take over or start news outlets. In fact, several notable publications are now run as nonprofits, such as the *Chicago Sun-Times*, which in 2018 was acquired by Chicago Public Media – a noncommercial/public radio broadcaster.[27] The deal moved a money-losing investment into the nonprofit tax space where revenue – including advertising, donations, and membership fees – are tax-exempt, and the need to please stockholders is eliminated.[28] Congress has even introduced legislation to help make it easier for newspapers to become nonprofits.[29] But while the CPB provides funding for TV stations, there is no comparable source of federal funding for newspapers. Still, Congress has introduced legislation that could help ease some financial concerns for local newspapers. Instead of direct grants, a series of tax credits has been proposed that would: (1) provide a tax credit of up to $250 for consumers to subscribe or donate to local newspapers; (2) provide a payroll tax credit to local news organizations for each local news journalist employed; and (3) provide a tax credit to small businesses that advertise with local newspapers – as well as local radio and television stations.[30] Although there appears to be some bipartisan support,[31] such measures would need to be passed, and it's not clear whether tax credits may be "too little, too late" for local newspapers on life support. There is also concern that this content-neutral approach may have unintended consequences of benefiting and spurring the

[25] *Federal Support*, *supra* note 19.

[26] Adam Ragusea, *Topple the Towers: Why Public Radio and Television Stations Should Radically Reorient toward Digital-First Local News, and How They Could Do It*, Knight Found. (2017), https://perma.cc/MWE4-JDJQ.

[27] Jack Shafer, *Your Newspaper's Not Making Money? Make It Permanent as a Nonprofit!*, Politico (Jan. 25, 2022), https://perma.cc/DV3T-ZU76. Other newspapers that have turned nonprofit include the *Texas Tribune*, *Baltimore Banner*, and *Salt Lake Tribune*.

[28] *Id.*

[29] Saving Local News Act, H.R. 6068, 117th Cong. (2021). The bill makes possible the publication of written news articles as a tax-exempt purpose for organizations. It amends Section 501(c)(3) of the Internal Revenue Code of 1986 by including "publication (including electronic publication) of written news articles." A local news resolution (H. Res. 821) was also introduced to recognize the importance of local media outlets to society and urge Congress to help stop the further decline of local media.

[30] Local Journalism Sustainability Act, H.R. 3940, 117th Cong. (2021).

[31] Margaret Sullivan, *Congress May Be About to Help Local News. It Cannot Happen Soon Enough*, Wash. Post (Aug. 31, 2021).

creation of hyper-partisan aggregation sites that only mimic local newspapers while promoting political agendas, contrary to the spirit of the legislation.[32]

17.3.1.2 Ownership Limits

For broadcasting, structural regulation has ensured a diversity of local voices through broadcast ownership limits. Initially adopted in 1964, the Local Television Ownership Rule restricted the number of local television stations that any one entity can own in a single market. This ensured that TV stations in a market cannot be bought out by one another, effectively reducing the number of stations and the diversity of viewpoints serving a community.

Contrast this with the treatment of the newspaper industry, which at the time was seeing a sharp decline in the number of cities and towns with two or more competing newspapers. In 1970, Congress passed the Newspaper Preservation Act to enable the Justice Department to make antitrust exceptions so that two newspapers in a community could combine their noneditorial functions to reduce costs.[33] Yet despite this regulatory effort to keep a second newspaper voice alive by allowing newspaper joint agreements, few survived.[34] For broadcasting, the local TV ownership limit continues, albeit modified slightly.

17.3.1.3 Localism and Public Interest Requirements

Another regulatory distinction from newspapers is the requirement that, as licensees of the public's airwaves, broadcast stations must serve the public interest. When Congress enacted the Communications Act of 1934,[35] it created the FCC to license broadcast stations that would serve in the "public interest, convenience, or necessity."[36] Broadcasters are essentially granted a limited-term "lease" to serve as public trustees of the airwaves.

A cornerstone of this public-interest requirement is a commitment to "localism."[37] Licensees must air programming that is responsive to the needs and interests of their communities of license. For years, broadcasters were required to conduct detailed ascertainments of their local communities and to indicate how their stations were addressing community problems through programming and outreach.[38] They

[32] *Id.*

[33] Douglas Gomery, The FCC's Newspaper-Broadcast Cross-Ownership Rule: An Analysis (2002).

[34] *Id.*

[35] 47 U.S.C. § 151 *et seq.*

[36] 47 U.S.C. § 307(a).

[37] Sixth Report and Order, 17 Fed. Reg. 3905 (1952).

[38] Report & Statement of Policy Re: Commission En Banc Programming Inquiry, 44 F.C.C. 2303, 2314 (1960); *see, e.g.*, Primer on Ascertainment of Community Problems by Broadcast Applicants, 27 F.C.C. 2d 650 (1971).

even had to dedicate a percentage of their programming to local programs, news, and public affairs.[39] At one point, TV stations had to observe the Prime Time Access Rule, which effectively required them to carry at least one hour of non-network programming each night in an FCC effort to promote independent and locally originated programming.[40] Although the FCC deregulated many of their behavioral rules in the 1980s and 1990s in favor of marketplace forces, the Commission has continued its commitment to ensuring licensees achieve the goal of localism. For example, stations must provide public inspection files of their operations and service to their community, which include quarterly lists of the most significant programs they have aired concerning issues of importance to their community.[41]

Of course, this is not to say that newspapers are not dedicated to or are uninterested in serving the public interest and their local communities. Quite the contrary, as this is a core part of their journalistic principles.[42] But newspapers are unregulated and enjoy greater First Amendment protections to make editorial decisions about their content than TV stations.[43] This can open the door to brazen abuse by a wave of hedge-fund owners and others who can ignore the public interest without government penalty. Indeed, evidence shows that community service by newspapers has been giving way to corporate profit centers over the years.[44] This situation produces a newspaper aimed not at the whole community it serves but at an audience valued by advertisers who provide roughly three-quarters of their revenues.[45]

For broadcasters, however, the consequences of ignoring the public interest can be dire. Licenses must be renewed, and the FCC will review applications to see if "the station has served the public interest, convenience, and necessity" and not violated any rules and regulations.[46] If an applicant for renewal has not met the

39 Delegations of Authority to the Chief, Broadcast Bureau, 59 F.C.C. 2d 491, 493 (1976). The guidelines required TV stations to air at least 5 percent total local programming, 5 percent informational (news and public affairs) programming, and 10 percent total non-entertainment programming.

40 Prime Time Access Rule, Section 73.638(k) (repealed in 1995).

41 47 C.F.R. §§ 73.3526(e)(11)(i), 73.3527(e)(8).

42 The Society of Professional Journalists Code of Ethics states, for example, that journalists should "[r]ecognize a special obligation to serve as watchdogs over public affairs" and "[s]-upport the open and civil exchange of views." *SPJ Code of Ethics*, Soc'y Pro. Journalists (Sept. 6, 2014), https://perma.cc/K48S-5YWR.

43 *See* Miami Herald Publ'g Co. v. Tornillo, 418 U.S. 241 (1974) (unanimously striking down a Florida law granting a right to reply to political candidates whose personal character or official record had been attacked by newspapers). This decision giving the print media constitutionally protected editorial autonomy is sharply contrasted to the treatment of broadcast media in Red Lion Broad. Co. v. Fed. Commc'ns Comm'n, 395 U.S. 367 (1969), where the Court upheld a regulation (the Fairness Doctrine) that required broadcasters to (among other things) give free reply time to persons attacked on the air.

44 *See, e.g.*, Gomery, *supra* note 33.

45 *Id.*

46 47 C.F.R. § 309(k)(1).

standards, the Commission can deny or condition the application, including reducing the license term.[47] This has implications for any potential hedge-fund buyers since licenses may not be granted to or renewed for broadcast stations that engage in layoffs and cost-cutting measures to maximize profits, failing to serve the public interest.

17.3.1.4 Regulatory Protections

Compared to newspapers, the greatest regulatory distinction for broadcasting may be less about constraints and more about the regulatory *protections* that broadcasting has uniquely enjoyed. The sustainability and growth of television broadcasting has been supported by government regulation, primarily in the name of localism. Such regulatory protections have not been afforded to newspapers.

For example, laws were created to ensure that TV stations would be receivable by all Americans. In 1962, Congress passed the "All Channel Receiver Act," requiring television manufacturers to produce TV receivers capable of receiving both VHF and UHF signals.[48] This meant that Americans would have free and ready access to stations in the UHF band (channels 14 and above).[49] Later, when the industry transitioned from analog to digital in 2009, the federal government spent over $2 billion to ensure that Americans with analog TV sets could receive the new digital signals with $40 digital converters.[50]

In the same vein, Congress and the FCC required – and continue to require – cable-television systems to carry all local TV stations in their cable-TV channel lineup. These "must-carry" rules were upheld by the Supreme Court as being

[47] *Id.* at § 309(k)(4). Losing a license for failure to serve the public is extremely rare, however. In fact, the only time a television station owner permanently lost their license was in the well-known case of WLBT in Jackson, Mississippi, when during the 1950s and 1960s the station's pro-segregationist owner made racist programming decisions such as preempting, ostensibly on the grounds of "technical difficulties," any network programs that covered the Civil Rights Movement, addressed racial injustice, or otherwise depicted African-Americans in a positive light. Civil rights protesters had filed formal complaints and lawsuits. The U.S. Court of Appeals for the D.C. Circuit ruled that the public had the right to take part in FCC license renewal hearings in order to protect the public interest. Office of Commc'n of the United Church of Christ v. Fed. Commc'ns Comm'n, 359 F.2d 994 (D.C. Cir. 1966).

[48] 47 U.S.C. § 303(s); All Channel Receiver Act of 1962, Pub. L. No. 87-529, 76 Stat. 150. "All television broadcast receivers manufactured after April 30, 1964, and shipped in interstate commerce or imported from any country into the United States, for sale or resale to the public, shall be capable of adequately receiving all channels allocated by the Commission to the television broadcast service." *All-Channel Television Broadcast Receivers*, 27 Fed. Reg. 11,698, 11,700 (Nov. 28, 1962); 47 C.F.R. § 15.70(a) (1962) (current version at 47 C.F.R. § 15.117(b)).

[49] The UHF band originally consisted of seventy channels (14–83), although that number was reduced when the less desirable channels 70–83 were reallocated in 1983 and when the recent digital transition completed in 2020 "repacked" the channels and reduced the usable UHF channels to 14–36 in the U.S.

[50] Ernie Smith, *The Long, Weird Transition from Analog to Digital Television*, ATLAS OBSCURA (Oct. 25, 2016), https://perma.cc/S7HM-R25Z.

consistent with the First Amendment.[51] TV stations have a right to be carried for free or to negotiate carriage for a price.[52] Such "retransmission consent fees" are now a significant and rapidly growing revenue source for TV stations,[53] accounting for roughly a quarter of the average station's revenue.[54]

This is in sharp contrast to what the newspaper industry faces. Newspapers do not benefit from such guaranteed content-redistribution revenues unless, for example, they are successful in collecting copyright-licensing fees from news aggregators which otherwise claim fair use.[55] The rise of online news aggregators – which have captured an increasing share of the news-consumer market[56] – is considered one of the significant reasons for the crisis facing the newspaper industry.[57]

Protectionist rules were also created to ensure that TV broadcasting would remain successful in the face of competition. Early subscription television services and cable television were seen as disruptive threats to the preservation of local broadcast services, which prompted the FCC to impose onerous rules that hindered their development. Competing content was restricted. Early rules prevented cable systems from carrying most movies and local sporting events in order to give local TV stations the opportunity to carry such programming.[58] Cable systems were also prevented from carrying distant television stations that were in competition with local stations.[59] Duplicate network signals still cannot be imported by cable systems

51 The Court ruled that the FCC's interest "in preserving a multiplicity of broadcasters" was not a violation of cable's freedom of speech. Turner Broad. Sys., Inc. v. Federal Commc'ns Comm'n, 520 U.S. 180 (1997).

52 Cable Television Consumer Protection and Competition Act of 1992, H.R. 4850, 102nd Cong. (1992).

53 Brad Adgate, *Why Are TV Stations Up for Sale?*, Forbes (Mar. 5, 2019), https://perma.cc/TVQ2-2JAT.

54 Knight Found., *The Future of Local TV News: Part 4, in* Local TV News and the New Media Landscape 116 (2020), https://perma.cc/7V5S-6MSX.

55 *Ten Reasons Why It Makes No Sense to Try to Charge News Aggregators*, Enrique Dans (Apr. 19, 2014), https://perma.cc/S8YF-W84L. *But see, e.g.*, Associated Press v. Meltwater U.S. Holdings, Inc., 931 F. Supp. 2d 537 (S.D.N.Y. 2013) (holding that a company's conduct in scraping and aggregating copyrighted news articles was not protected by fair use).

56 Already as to online news traffic alone, a study from 2009 found news-media users were more likely to turn to an aggregator (31 percent) than to a newspaper site (8 percent). Another study from 2015 found aggregators such as Google News, Buzzfeed, and Huffington Post attracted 80 percent of the online news traffic. Doh-Shin Jeon, *Economics of News Aggregators* (Toulouse School of Economics, Working Paper No. 18-912, 2018), https://perma.cc/6H23-399D.

57 Reporters Comm. for Freedom of the Press, *Content Aggregation: Spreading or Stealing the News?* (2012), https://perma.cc/QTT7-39M4.

58 Home Box Office, Inc. v. Fed. Commc'ns Comm'n, 567 F.2d 9 (D.C. Cir. 1977), *citing* 47 C.F.R. §§ 73.643, 76.225 (1975). The stated purpose of these rules was to prevent competitive bidding ("siphoning") away of popular program material from the free broadcast television service. *Id.* In 1977, the U.S. Court of Appeals held that the FCC had exceeded its jurisdiction and that the cable television rules were inconsistent with the First Amendment. *Id.*

59 First Report and Order, 38 F.C.C. 683 (1965).

or satellite carriers in competition to local network affiliates.[60] And, in order to protect local TV broadcasters from viewers migrating to cable channels, cable systems and satellite carriers are also prevented from carrying syndicated programming that is licensed exclusively to local TV stations.[61]

17.3.2 *Technical Advantages*

The continued success of broadcast-television news stations may also be explained by certain technological advantages inherent to the medium. Their method of delivery has enjoyed certain efficiencies and steady costs. Local TV stations have also more easily adapted to digital delivery, allowing them to meet and embrace internet disruption head on.

In the first place, advances in technology have led to noticeably lower operating costs for TV stations. While newspapers have struggled with rising print costs, TV stations have benefited from steadily dropping prices for cameras, computers, and transmission equipment.[62] On average, the annual operating expenses for U.S. television stations have remained fairly steady since 2013.[63] In contrast, newspapers have been stricken with newsprint costs that have soared by over 50 percent in just a matter of months.[64] This comes after having reduced the size of their papers and losing their supportive partnerships with paper mills.[65]

Local TV news stations are also highly – if not more – suited to adapt to the digital revolution, given their technological roots. They have already transitioned from electronic to digital media production with cameras, editing, switching, and other equipment. TV stations also successfully weathered the very-expensive transition from analog to digital delivery when the government required all terrestrial TV signals in the U.S. to be transmitted in digital format by 2009.[66] TV stations have the

60 *Network Nonduplication Rule*, 47 C.F.R. § 76.92, which gives a local station the exclusive right to distribute a network program, meaning that a cable system cannot carry a duplicate network program from a distant station. This also applies to satellite carriers. 47 U.S.C. § 339; 47 C.F.R. § 76.122 (Satellite Network Non-Duplication).

61 47 C.F.R. § 76.101 (Cable Syndicated Program Exclusivity), § 76.123 (Satellite Syndicated Program Exclusivity).

62 *Id.*

63 Macrotrends reports that U.S. broadcast television's annual operating expenses in 2013 were $462 million, reached a high of $522 million in 2018, and then dropped to $400 million by 2020. They were $466 million in 2021. *Television Broadcasts Operating Expenses 2010–2021*, MACROTRENDS, https://perma.cc/Q4XW-95J9.

64 *Soaring Newsprint Costs Make Life Even Harder for Newspapers*, ECONOMIST (Nov. 6, 2021), https://perma.cc/CZ9T-6ZN3.

65 *Id.*

66 *See Digital Television*, FED. COMMC'NS COMM'N (last updated Dec. 9, 2016), https://perma.cc/AT9D-SG66. It would cost TV stations between $5 million and $10 million to make the conversion, "with little to no return on a station owners' investment." Rich Kirchen, *Digital TV: It's Too Expensive and You Cannot Get It*, MILWAUKEE BUS. J. (Oct. 24, 1999), https://perma.cc/99SE-G3YG.

workforce and the workflow to embrace new distribution opportunities, from news video for social media, to over-the-top (OTT) news clips, to streaming news coverage.[67]

These moves into the digital realm have especially positioned television stations to be able to innovate and adopt new strategies. For example, digital antennas are now being promoted as the next frontier of TV viewing that will meet the needs of consumers who are shifting to streaming services but want to supplement their maxed-out monthly subscription services with free, local TV station content that includes local news and sports.[68] Already 40 percent of Americans own a digital antenna, up from 29 percent at the end of 2019 and pre-pandemic quarantines. Digital technology has also allowed TV stations to generate additional revenue from "multicasting" – transmitting additional digital TV signals that typically carry low-cost programming and provide more opportunities to sell advertising.[69] As much as 5 percent of some TV stations' *total* revenue now comes from multicasting.[70] Some local TV-station groups have also introduced their own national OTT service that uses a data platform to provide local and national advertisers with advanced audience targeting and automated buying, thus giving stations an additional, growing source of revenue.[71]

Most importantly, digital television can seamlessly integrate with the internet and directly challenge online competition. Consumers can use virtually any screen – and even the same screen at the same time – to watch TV, browse the internet, or engage with social media. In fact, multiscreen use is one of the most significant changes in modern media consumption.[72] It has long been expected that television and the internet would effectively merge, and television entrepreneurs have been successful in developing technologies to capitalize on this integration.[73] Most notable is NextGen TV, or ATSC 3.0, which is the next generation of local TV services approved for implementation by the FCC in 2017.[74] NextGen TV is essentially 4K TV that merges over-the-air antenna TV with the internet.[75] It allows local stations to personalize their news, sports, live events, and shows with

67 Knight Found., *The Future of Local News Video: Part 3*, *in* Local TV News and the New Media Landscape, *supra* note 54, at 93.

68 Alex Sherman, *How Local TV Stations Plan to Remain Relevant as Viewers Shift to Streaming*, CNBC (Apr. 24, 2021), https://perma.cc/ZUS3-QHF8.

69 Knight Found., *The State of the Industry: Part 1*, *in* Local TV News and the New Media Landscape, *supra* note 54, at 1.

70 *Id.*

71 Adgate, *supra* note 53.

72 Peter Hirshberg, *First the Media, Then Us: How the Internet Changed the Fundamental Nature of the Communication and Its Relationship with the Audience*, *in* Ch@nge: 19 Key Essays on How the Internet Is Changing Our Lives (2013), https://perma.cc/4JXQ-PPVV.

73 Gomery, *supra* note 33.

74 Adgate, *supra* note 53.

75 Sherman, *supra* note 68.

interactive features that give viewers the content that is most relevant to them.[76] And it gives advertisers the ability to geo-target viewers with addressable advertising.[77] Aside from picture and audio improvements, NextGen TV gives viewers the ability to watch broadcast content on phones, tablets, and in cars.[78] It can be repurposed for streaming at a time when the creation of streaming options, especially for mobile devices,[79] is particularly important as more people turn to the internet for their television content.[80]

Of course, many print newspapers have also successfully responded to digital disruption by going digital themselves – creating e-editions, news websites, and digital news services for mobile access, often with video and audio. Traffic on newspaper websites has steadily increased – at least for the top fifty daily newspapers in the U.S.[81] Thus, making the technical shift to digital production has not been a barrier to success for most newspapers. Instead, economic failure is primarily attributed to waiting too long to make the transition, trying to hold on to a traditional print model.[82]

Nonetheless, most local television stations have similarly developed station websites and embraced social media, and some are outperforming their local digital newspaper competitors.[83] TV-station websites have become an important and increasingly profitable distribution platform for local news video.[84] Local TV has an advantage over newspapers and other competitors on digital platforms in that it is already equipped to better deal with breaking news and video. Local TV newsrooms know best how to engage in video storytelling, and most will post these videos to the web as part of their daily workflows.[85] Given an increasing consumer demand for video news, some stations now boast about having the top news website in their city, with 50 percent more daily visitors than the local newspaper site.[86] Although both

76 *Id.* (citing NextGen's website).

77 Adgate, *supra* note 53.

78 Sherman, *supra* note 68.

79 *Id.*

80 Knight Found., *The Future of Local TV News*, *supra* note 54.

81 *Newspapers Fact Sheet*, Pew Rsch. Ctr. (June 29, 2021), https://perma.cc/7T4T-3BH3. In the fourth quarter of 2020, there was an average of 13.9 million monthly unique visitors (across all devices) for the top 50 newspapers. This was up 14 percent from 2019, which itself was 5 percent higher than in 2018. *Id.* Measuring the digital audience for the rest of the newspaper industry is difficult, since many daily newspapers do not have enough website traffic to be measured by data company Comscore. *Id.*

82 Ray Glenn, *Reports of Newspapers' Demise Have Been Greatly Exaggerated*, Nw. Fl. Daily News (Feb. 13, 2022), https://perma.cc/39KY-USSY.

83 A study by the Knight Foundation found that of 37 small markets analyzed, television websites came out on top in 23 while newspapers came out on top in 13. Knight Found., *The State of the Industry*, *supra* note 69.

84 Knight Found., *The Future of Local News Video*, *supra* note 67.

85 Knight Found., *The Future of Local TV News*, *supra* note 54.

86 *Id.* WBAY-TV in Green Bay, Wisconsin, is an example of a station that in five years became the top website in Green Bay.

newspapers and television websites earn about the same amount of advertising dollars per online visitor,[87] some advertisers are willing to pay more to be featured with online video than text.[88]

TV stations are also using social media more fully. While newspapers tend to focus more on X, some are arguably ceding Facebook and other social media.[89] TV broadcasters enjoy a social-media presence advantage, being responsible for a significant portion of the news video published on social media, especially Facebook.[90] One study has shown that the median social-media share for TV was 85.5 percent, while the median share for newspapers was only 11.7 percent.[91] While newspapers certainly have extensive content to offer, social media is said to particularly play well to TV's strengths, namely, "timely, emotional, video" content.[92]

17.3.3 *Consumer and Advertiser Demand*

Consumer and advertising demand further distinguish broadcast television from newspapers when it comes to the ability to thrive in the local news media market. Factors such as the growing demand for video, promotional opportunities, a sense of community, and economic value tend to favor broadcast television. These factors also help give broadcast television a more competitive footing against rival internet services.

Overall, a majority of Americans choose local TV news as their go-to news source. Roughly 50 percent of U.S. adults say they often get their news from local television, compared to only 18 percent from print newspapers and 25 percent from radio.[93] The margin for online news sources has tightened, but trails at 43 percent.[94] Also reinforcing the popularity of local TV news is the fact that adults are watching more minutes of news in a typical week and spending more of their TV-viewing time (18.2 percent) watching news.[95]

A key advantage that sets TV apart from newspapers in general is its visual storytelling appeal and the increasing demand for video. Videos have become the most popular choice for content consumption.[96] Nearly a quarter billion people in the U.S. watched digital videos in 2020 – a number that far exceeded expert

87 *Id.*
88 Knight Found., *The Future of Local News Video*, *supra* note 67.
89 Knight Found., *The Future of Local TV News*, *supra* note 54.
90 Knight Found., *The Future of Local News Video*, *supra* note 67.
91 Knight Found., *The State of the Industry*, *supra* note 69.
92 *Id.* at 20 (citing Sean McLaughlin, Vice President of Content at E.W. Scripps).
93 *Id.* This is according to Nielsen television data.
94 *Id.*
95 *Id.* Up from 14.7 percent in 2015.
96 Maryam Mohsin, *10 Video Marketing Statistics*, Oberlo (Apr. 13, 2022), https://perma.cc/ZG68-BSSH.

predictions.[97] This has certainly been driven by online use. But while the internet and smartphones are increasingly popular platforms for video-viewing, television has dominated with the most content and the most time spent viewing.[98] Americans watch TV an average of five hours per day, largely consuming live content,[99] while watching videos online for about two hours per day.[100] This is also the case for video-news consumption, where Americans "show a clear preference for getting news on a screen, and the TV screen still leads the way."[101] The average adult spends nearly six hours each week watching TV news.[102] It's therefore not surprising that 90 percent more local news is being broadcast today than twenty years ago, and that viewers can find local news on 39 percent more TV stations.[103]

Of course, disruptive internet services – such as various streaming services, YouTube, and social-media sites like Instagram, Snapchat, and TikTok – are quickly gaining market share in competition to both TV broadcasters and newspapers. One-third of all online activity is spent watching videos, and the vast majority of global internet traffic is from streaming videos and downloads.[104] In fact, it is suggested that more video content is being uploaded in just thirty days than what the major television networks in the U.S. have created in the past thirty years.[105] Online video consumption is up for all age groups, but especially teens and young adults.[106] Yet, as previously mentioned, local TV websites are also increasingly popular and are ideally suited to deliver online news videos, giving them a strong, competitive grip in the online market.

The video advantage also helps broadcasters when it comes to advertising, particularly on their local TV websites. The preference for video content is not just limited to entertainment and news; it extends to brands. More than two-thirds of consumers say they prefer video over text when learning about a product or service.[107] And studies show that more than half of consumers want to see more video content from the brands or businesses they support.[108] Advertisers recognize

97 *Id.* The number of people watching digital videos in the U.S. reached 244.4 million in 2020.

98 Knight Found., *The State of the Industry*, *supra* note 69.

99 *Id.*

100 Mohsin, *supra* note 96. In 2019, users spent a weekly average of 6 hours and 48 minutes watching online videos. This is an increase of 59 percent from 2016. A more recent study by Wyzowl says that people watch an average of 16 hours of online videos per week. Jacinda Santora, *Video Marketing Statistics: What You Must Know for 2022*, OptinMonster (Jan. 7, 2022), https://perma.cc/8VFM-HUC4.

101 Knight Found., *The State of the Industry*, *supra* note 69, at 6 (quoting a 2016 Pew Research Center study, *The Modern News Consumer*).

102 *Id.* The amount of time spent consuming TV news is 5:47 per week.

103 *Id.*

104 Sarika, *135 Video Marketing Statistics You Cannot Ignore in 2022*, InVideo (June 20, 2022), https://perma.cc/4LZQ-AVLG.

105 *Id.*

106 Knight Found., *The State of the Industry*, *supra* note 69, at 6.

107 Santora, *supra* note 100.

108 Mohsin, *supra* note 96.

the power of video when it comes to convincing consumers to purchase a product or service.[109] They prefer video ads because people are more likely to pay attention to them than to audio and written content, which they may otherwise skip or skim.[110] Advertisers often try to tell visual stories within their ads to create an emotional impact on viewers.[111] This means giving TV websites the preferred nod to carry their ads. Indeed, digital advertising revenue for local TV stations has been growing, increasing 6 percent in 2020 alone.[112]

Television also draws in large numbers of viewers, which means greater promotional and cross-promotional opportunities for its local news product. Since roughly 2000, television has been in a second "Golden Age," enjoying an era of "Peak TV"[113] with the creation of a wider array of critically acclaimed content leading to more viewers watching – and even binging – on more television than ever before.[114] This resurgence in television entertainment programming has attracted more viewers, many of whom will also end up watching a station's local newscasts. Not only does popular entertainment content provide an effective lead-in and lead-out programming strategy for local newscasts, it also serves as an excellent vehicle for station newscast promotions that can be strategically placed throughout the programming schedule. Cross promotions may also run on other Multichannel Video Programming Distributors (MVPDs). This benefit also applies to a station's website, which draws users for its entertainment program listings and social engagement and then captures interest in its local news content and on-air newscasts. Newspapers, on the other hand, do not enjoy a similar cross-promotional advantage. Aside from some entertaining columnists, comic strips, puzzles, and entertainment-related supplements, newspapers generally do not have a comparable cache of non-news options to attract readers to their news product, and this also applies to their news websites.

For the same matter, television programming is effective at cultivating fan-based communities and is a driver for social-media interaction, which offers even more cross-promotional opportunities for local news. Among the most widely discussed topics on social media is television.[115] TV viewers like to interact with one another about their favorite shows over Facebook, X, and TV-network websites. In fact, over

[109] Sarika, *supra* note 104 (reporting that 72 percent of customers say they would rather learn about a product or service by way of video, and 84 percent say they have been convinced to buy a product or service after watching a brand's video).

[110] Mohsin, *supra* note 96.

[111] Neil Kokemuller, *What Is the Advantage of Using TV & Radio Media for Advertising?*, CHRON. (Feb. 4, 2019), https://perma.cc/RBT7-ERCL.

[112] PEW RSCH. CTR., *Local TV News Fact Sheet*, *supra* note 1.

[113] Alex Mell-Taylor, *From The Sopranos to BoJack Horseman: The End of the Second Golden Age of Television*, CULTURE CORNER (Mar. 10, 2020), https://perma.cc/SK5X-UFD8.

[114] Hirshberg, *supra* note 72.

[115] *Id.*

40 percent of viewers watch TV while also using a social network,[116] and nearly 24 percent will post, vote, share, or otherwise comment on a TV show on social media.[117] These communities of fans share a common experience, which is important to the success of television. These communities will then connect favored programs with the networks, streamers, and stations that distribute them. And once again, local television news can indirectly benefit from the promotion of shows carried on their station, potentially converting those users into local broadcast-news consumers.

Generating a sense of trust and local community is another advantage for local television stations, although this is also true for newspapers, distinguishing both legacy media from their online competitors. Nearly eight in ten Americans say they have more trust in their local news to give them information they need to get involved in their community.[118] In addition, they are almost twice as likely to express trust in local news as compared to national news.[119] Still, broadcast news may have an edge when it comes to trust. Aside from reaching the largest share of local news consumers, there is some sense that TV provides viewers with more accurate news that is from professional journalists.[120] Television-oriented local-news consumers also appear to have a stronger attachment to their preferred source of news than those with digital preferences do. U.S. adults who prefer getting local news online are less likely to follow local news very closely, compared to those who prefer television news.[121]

Perhaps the greatest distinguishing factor for local television news, however, is its cost and perceived value by consumers. Simply put, local over-the-air TV stations have always been and continue to be available for free. There are no subscriptions, messy contracts, or onerous online agreements with terms and conditions.

Local print newspapers, on the other hand, customarily charge subscription and per-issue fees, and even their digital newspapers employ some type of paywall model. While some well-known national newspaper outlets have had success charging subscribers, local publishers have been much less successful in converting their

[116] L. Ceci, *Frequency of U.S. Smartphone Social Usage While Watching TV 2019*, Statista (2019), https://perma.cc/ZUV8-KVNG.

[117] Troy Dreier, *24% of U.S. Adults Use Social Media to Comment on TV Shows*, Streaming Media (Apr. 14, 2017), https://perma.cc/QPN3-R5ST.

[118] Sarah Fioroni, *Local News Most Trusted in Keeping Americans Informed About Their Communities*, Knight Found. (May 19, 2022), https://perma.cc/FLN9-NRM5.

[119] *Id.*

[120] Nakedi Phala, *Three Reasons Why TV Is Still the Best for News Consumption*, Media Update (Mar. 6, 2020), https://perma.cc/54XW-LWSG. There is still a demand for credible and authentic information.

[121] *For Local News, Americans Embrace Digital but Still Want Strong Community Connection*, Pew Rsch. Ctr. (Mar. 26, 2019), https://perma.cc/VL7J-SKX6. This is 21 percent compared to 40 percent for those who prefer TV. *Id.*

online readers into paying subscribers.[122] Yet it's important for digital newspapers to attract a large base of subscribers in order to have a sustainable business model. One analysis found that small towns of less than 10,000 residents will not have enough subscribers to support the operation of a digital publication.[123] If the price point is set at only $5, for example, 20 percent of the town's population would need to subscribe to cover the publication's overheads, salaries, and other expenses. Unfortunately, most local outlets are already only converting less than 1 percent of their population.[124]

Value is also a top consideration for advertisers. Both TV stations and newspapers rely heavily on advertising revenues, and both have seen a decline in advertising over the years. But for local TV, the loss of ad revenue is far less concerning than it is for newspapers. Television stations reap the benefits of political-advertising revenue in election years, for example. Although this revenue is cyclical, in election year 2020, local TV over-the-air advertising revenue actually increased by 8 percent over 2019.[125] In the meantime, additional income is generated by the increasing fees related to retransmission consent from MVPDs, as mentioned earlier. TV does not depend on subscription or circulation revenues, and there is less reliance on digital ad revenue, which accounted for only 7 percent of total TV ad revenue in 2020.

For newspapers, however, total advertising revenues have been dropping significantly. In fact, 2020 saw a 25 percent decline from 2019.[126] Even the top six publicly owned newspaper chains, which own and operate more than 300 daily newspapers, reported a 42 percent advertising revenue loss.[127] For the first time, advertising revenue was less than newspaper-circulation revenue,[128] which has also been in decline.[129] Digital advertising now comprises 39 percent of newspapers' remaining ad revenue. This is particularly troublesome when the Big Tech companies of Facebook and Google have reportedly siphoned away 77 percent of the digital ad revenue in local markets.[130] Moreover, while traffic has increased, consumers are spending less time on newspaper websites, with the average number of minutes per visit for the top fifty daily newspapers dropping to less than two minutes in 2020.[131]

122 Simon Owens, *Why Local News Outlets Struggle with Digital Subscriptions*, WHAT'S NEW IN PUBL'G (Feb. 28, 2020), https://perma.cc/3P33-JJH6.

123 *Id.*

124 *Id.* Even big city digital news publications with their larger editorial staff to support are only able to convert 1 or 2 percent of the populations they serve. The *Seattle Times*, for example, has only converted 1.2 percent of the population it serves to digital subscribers. *Id.*

125 PEW RSCH. CTR., *Local TV News Fact Sheet*, *supra* note 1.

126 PEW RSCH. CTR., *Newspapers Fact Sheet*, *supra* note 81.

127 Mike Vorhaus, *Traditional TV Advertising Is Growing – Unlike Newspapers*, FORBES (Nov. 29, 2020), https://perma.cc/5Q39-JP7Z.

128 PEW RSCH. CTR., *Newspapers Fact Sheet*, *supra* note 81.

129 Vorhaus, *supra* note 127.

130 Owens, *supra* note 122. This is compared to a digital ad revenue loss of 58 percent nationwide. *Id.*

131 PEW RSCH. CTR., *Newspapers Fact Sheet*, *supra* note 81.

This, along with the use of online paywalls, impacts the attractiveness of local news websites for advertisers, resulting in the dreaded revenue death spiral for newspapers.[132]

17.4 DISCUSSION

It's clear that, while newspapers are struggling economically, local television news enjoys a number of comparative advantages that have kept it afloat. Of course, it is unclear how long these advantages will continue and whether they will be enough to counter the disruptive forces of the internet. And if local TV news does continue to thrive, it is additionally unclear whether it and competing online news platforms would be sufficient substitutes for the loss of a strong newspaper presence in their respective communities. There have been various approaches suggested to help the newspaper industry readjust, recover, and possibly regain market share and its important role of watchdog journalism. Looking to local TV news as a model is one approach to consider.

17.4.1 *Sustainable Success?*

It is important to first recognize, however, that the success of local TV news may not be sustainable. Disruption is a process, after all, and for television, this may simply be a slower process than it has been for newspapers. In fact, some have suggested that local television as an industry has been "very, very mildly contracting."[133] It's quite possible that TV stations could face declining audiences and revenues, and fail to adapt. Or the disruption may not only be slow, but incomplete.

17.4.2 *Following a TV-News-Station Model*

Nonetheless, local TV news appears to have the only media-revenue model likely to sustain itself for at least the next decade.[134] Covering local news continues to earn a profit for at least two-thirds of local stations that run local news.[135] In fact, TV news directors report that 55 percent of station revenues come from their news operations, even though news constitutes less than a quarter of a station's daily broadcast schedule.[136]

Although there are inherent differences between TV- and newspaper-delivery platforms, there are some lessons that can be gleaned from the TV-news business

[132] Vorhaus, *supra* note 127.
[133] Madrigal, *supra* note 4.
[134] Knight Found., *The Future of Local TV News*, *supra* note 54. This will be largely aided by retransmission revenue, increasing political revenue, and industry consolidation.
[135] *Id.*
[136] *Id.*

model that may help newspapers going forward. While newspapers have responded to TV competition in the digital realm by adding audio and video, for example, they should evaluate what is working well for local television news and consider adopting those winning strategies where possible. Newspapers could model themselves more on what has helped sustain local TV news in the face of internet competition. Taking a page from their TV competitor's playbook, so to speak, could open the door to new opportunities and ultimately success for the industry.

For example, newspapers might lower their technology costs by eliminating their expensive print-newspaper operations and going all digital. Small-town newspapers, in particular, should make the digital leap and even let go of their legacy print model entirely. As with broadcasters, this would take advantage of lower-cost video equipment and other production technologies.

Newspapers need to take full advantage of digital technology and its opportunities for instantaneous, breaking-news posts and live streams, including audio and video. To be competitive with broadcasters and digital platforms, newspapers will need to meet them where they are at by excelling at visual storytelling by incorporating more video in their online stories. This will also give advertisers more video options for their ads, which they prefer.

Daily newspapers would then need to continue increasing their digital readership and significantly bolstering their website traffic, attracting users to their sites as well as keeping those users engaged for a longer time in order to yield more views on revenue-supporting advertising. This might mean engaging in "clickbait" strategies, pushing more enticing headlines and incorporating more entertainment/non-news elements alongside higher social-media engagement. In order to compete with more-popular local television websites, newspapers will need to find additional exclusive or niche content that they can promote. Journalists are excellent storytellers and they can capitalize on that strength. The additional content could also help with effective promotions, which newspapers need in order to draw users to their digital news sites, especially younger users whom advertisers covet. More cross-promotional arrangements with other media outlets could also be explored.

Newspapers should also borrow from broadcasting's revenue model and rethink their reliance on subscription revenue. Even digital newspapers struggle with getting a large-enough base of subscribers to be sustainable. Paywalls have not been as successful an approach for smaller daily papers as they have been for national newspapers, such as *The New York Times* and *Washington Post*.[137] Charging a fee for base access simply makes it hard to compete with freely available television news and other online news offerings.

Of course, removing or reducing subscription revenue would require a greater reliance on advertising revenue, which the newspaper industry has already fought hard to grow with limited success. The industry has earned more than twice as much

[137] *Id.*

money in digital advertising than local TV has, but after factoring in daily visitor use, both newspapers and TV are earning the same amount of advertising money per online visitor.[138] Content improvements, including producing more video, could help turn the tables and pull digital-advertising revenue away from Facebook, Google, and the like. Newspapers might further bolster advertising revenue by embracing more sponsored content or "native advertising" on their digital sites,[139] which – similar to broadcasting's "infomercials" – can be offered while adhering to the journalistic ethical principles that require news and advertising be distinguished from one another.[140] They might also take a cue from broadcasting and find a way to capture the cyclical but highly lucrative political-advertising revenue. Ever since the U.S. Supreme Court in 2010 opened the political-advertising floodgates with the *Citizens United* case, the broadcasting industry has seen their political-ad revenue shoot to over $3 billion in 2020.[141] By creating a space for effective audio and video political ads, newspapers could capture a piece of this revenue pie.

Newspapers might also follow the trend of becoming nonprofit enterprises, much like noncommercial public-broadcasting stations. As mentioned earlier, this would allow newspapers to generate revenue that would be tax-exempt. Legislation such as the Saving Local News Act would make this possible by amending the Internal Revenue Code to include "publication (including electronic publication) of written news articles."[142] In addition, nonprofit newspapers could receive additional federal support with something comparable to a federally funded Corporation for Public Broadcasting that distributes funds to them. This could be in the form of grants, just as the CPB provides to public-broadcasting stations, which constitutes about 18.3 percent of their annual revenue.[143] There would have to be provisions and oversight to ensure that such nonprofits were not just hyper-partisan aggregation sites mimicking local newspapers. There could be conditions that require that they, like broadcasters, serve the public interest to ensure that funding recipients are responsive to their local communities. These conditions might go as far as requiring that a certain percentage of the news-editorial content be locally originated as opposed to syndicated or aggregated. Like broadcast stations, any nonprofit newspapers that receive government funding might be expected to provide regular reports indicating the issues and needs of the community and how these were addressed by the newspapers. Of course, care would need to be taken to ensure that this funding approach

[138] *Id.*

[139] Freddy Mayhew, *Shifting to a Digital-First Strategy and the Steps to Making It Pay for Publishers*, PRESS GAZETTE (Jan. 19, 2022), https://pressgazette.co.uk/digital-first-strategy-and-steps-making-it-pay-for-publishers/.

[140] *SPJ Code of Ethics*, *supra* note 42. Publishers need to "Act Independently" by being sure to "distinguish news from advertising and shun hybrids that blur the lines between the two. Prominently label sponsored content." *Id.*

[141] KNIGHT FOUND., *The Future of Local TV News*, *supra* note 54.

[142] Saving Local News Act, H.R. 6068, 117th Cong. (2021).

[143] CPB, *Federal Appropriation*, *supra* note 24.

was content-neutral and did not violate First Amendment rights. Another condition for funding might require that owners and staff, including journalists, live in the community they serve. This would help ensure the involvement of local editorial voices and commitment. Having nonprofit status and local ownership would also ward off hedge-fund owners and other corporate profit centers that are currently crippling the newspaper industry.

Some of the regulatory protectionist policies of the FCC for broadcasting, however, cannot be extended to newspapers. For example, it would not be possible to mandate a system whereby all Americans receive at least one local newspaper as they do with the allocation of regulated television signals. Moreover, aggregators and other media outlets cannot be required to carry local newspapers on their services like MVPDs are required to carry local TV broadcast stations, nor can they be required to negotiate retransmission fees. Such fees, as noted, constitute a significant part of broadcast-station revenues. Yet, it's possible that some creative regulatory approach could be taken to at least assist newspapers in collecting fees from online news aggregators, similarly to broadcasting's retransmission fees from MVPDs.

Likewise, there is no regulatory authority to protect newspapers and promote a diversity of local voices with structural ownership rules for newspapers. The Newspaper/Broadcast Cross-Ownership rule that existed up until recently was an FCC regulation that applied to broadcasting. That said, elimination of that broadcast rule creates new possibilities for the survivability of local newspapers. Taking advantage of the opportunity to now merge with local TV news stations in the same market may prove to be the ultimate solution for saving newspapers. And despite concerns that consolidation will result in a diminution of local voices, some believe that cross-ownership could actually lead to *more* coverage of local issues. The synergies produced by such a merge could also balance the playing field, stimulate investment, and potentially save local news media.

17.5 CONCLUSION

Even if local TV news remains resilient to internet disruption and is the last local news medium standing, there is concern that it is not a perfect substitute for the kind of journalism that daily print newspapers have traditionally provided. Since TV-station coverage areas largely encompass towns and cities, smaller communities and even neighborhoods will likely not receive the same level of journalistic attention as would their weekly print newspaper. TV stations may employ fewer and less experienced reporters. Many fear that deeper forms of reporting and investigative explorations that make civic journalism valuable to communities will be lost.[144]

Still, if local TV news proves to be the model of success for legacy media, local journalism will remain available for most communities nationwide. TV news

[144] Madrigal, *supra* note 4.

stations can ensure that large "news deserts" do not develop, where citizens become even more politically polarized, less engaged civically, and lose their ability to hold government officials accountable.[145] But this situation is made much better if local newspapers – even co-owned with broadcasters – are enabled to prosper.

[145] Sullivan, *supra* note 31.

18

From Hot News to Link Tax

The Dangers of a Quasi-Property Right in Information

Paul Matzko

18.1 INTRODUCTION

In February 2021, the Australian federal government enacted the "News Media and Digital Platforms Mandatory Bargaining Code," which requires Facebook and Google to pay domestic news outlets for linking to their websites. It was a first-of-its-kind mechanism for redistributing revenue from Big Tech platforms to legacy journalism, and it has attracted global attention from policymakers looking to halt the internet-fueled decline of the traditional news industry. Thus, the success or failure of what critics call Australia's "link tax" has significant implications for the future of both the World Wide Web and the news industry writ large.

But while the full consequences of Australia's regulatory innovation will not be apparent for several years, there is a precedent from the United States that could shine light on the possible outcomes. In the early twentieth century, U.S. courts created a "hot news" doctrine to bolster the Associated Press newswire service when it faced new competitors and navigated the technological disruption caused by the spread of the telegraph. The intended and unintended consequences of the American hot news doctrine offer a cautionary tale to contemporary policymakers interested in an Australian-style link tax. Both hot news and the link tax are forms of enclosure that turn a category of information into a novel form of property. Doing so has radical implications: rewarding politically connected incumbent firms, punishing insurgent competitors, and producing ideological consensus.

It is not breaking news that newspapers in the twenty-first century have experienced a general decline that has dramatically affected circulation, advertising, and revenue. The rise of the consumer internet eroded classified advertising, once the single most significant source of newspaper revenue. In Australia, classified revenue fell from $1.5 billion in 2002 to just $0.2 billion by 2018. At the same time, overall Australian newspaper revenue fell by nearly the same margin – from $4.4 billion to $3 billion – suggesting that the migration of classified ads to online clearinghouses like Craigslist was a principal factor in the collapse of the old newspaper financial model.[1]

18.2 WHO SHOULD PAY AND HOW?

Australian newspapers had a revenue problem and looked to their national government for redress. A straightforward solution would have been to tax the online classified-ad platforms and redistribute the money to bereft newspapers, whose market share had fallen from 96 percent to 12 percent. However, such an approach would have been straightforwardly anti-competitive, would have generated costs that fell directly on consumers, and would have targeted domestic classified-ad platforms. Instead, Australian newspapers sought to take a slice from a much-larger financial pie: online search-and-display advertising, which enjoys quadruple the revenue of online classifieds.[2] Since two companies that are headquartered abroad – Facebook and Google – dominate search-and-display in Australia, the costs of a link tax would not fall as directly on Australian consumers (so long as neither company pulled out of the market entirely).

Online classified platforms derive nothing from newspapers, so taxing them to subsidize newspapers would not have seemed equitable (nor would it have been particularly lucrative). By contrast, Facebook and Google operate as news aggregators, linking to newspaper articles in order to sell ads and garner user data. Since aggregators have a proximate relationship to the news, it is easy to claim that they are free-riding off of journalists' hard work and should pay a fair share.[3] As Australia's Federal Treasurer Josh Frydenberg put it, "This is really a question of fairness. If you prepare the content and the digital platforms are using it to bring traffic to their websites, then they should pay for it."[4]

Note that the justification offered is moral, rooted in a particular concept of what is fair. It is not a proposition that translates well in the offline world. For instance, it would be strange to suggest that brick-and-mortar retailers have a moral obligation to pay manufacturers not only for their product but also for the mere right to resell and

[1] AlphaBeta, Australian Media Landscape Trends (Sept. 2020), https://perma.cc/845D-GKBT.

[2] *Id.* at 15. The four largest Australian classified advertising companies by revenue are REA Group, Seek, Carsales, and Domain, each headquartered in Australia. It is worth noting that many newspapers have since migrated their classified sections online, meaning that they are now direct competitors with non-newspaper platforms.

[3] "'How do you value fact-based news absent advertising? News has always been valued on the back of how much ads that the outlet can sell. Because Google and Facebook have dominated the advertising market and taken that out of the equation, we are now trying to work out the value of public interest journalism.'" Associated Press, *Australian Media Law Raises Questions about "Pay for Clicks,"* USA Today (Feb. 19, 2021), https://perma.cc/8T9U-LVWJ (quoting Peter Lewis, Director of the Australia Institute's Center for Responsible Technology).

[4] Richard Holden, *Australia's News Media and Digital Platforms Bargaining Code Is Great Politics but Questionable Economics*, ProMarket (Sept. 21, 2020), https://perma.cc/2596-96S8.

display the product on their shelves. (Typically, the relationship is reversed, with manufacturers paying major retailers for prime shelf space. Efficient distribution is a value-added proposition.)[5] Fundamentally, the problem that the link tax is meant to address is not moral but structural, as policymakers attempt to buttress traditional media organizations that are coping with technological disruption, albeit with varying degrees of success.

Yet news aggregators had little to do with the financial decline of the newspaper industry. They were not major players in the rise of online classified advertising. Additionally, online advertising has shifted display-ad revenue away from its traditional proximity to the news. Advertisers have more non-news digital options for placing their ads – social media, streaming, etc. – than they did back when print newspapers were one of the few mediums for reaching large audiences. For example, a clothing store would have once placed an ad in the local newspaper by necessity (and not because it was a newspaper per se); how else could they affordably reach a large group of potential customers? Today, however, that clothing company would be more likely to place an ad with a TikTok influencer or to buy a display ad on Pinterest, neither of which has anything to do with news reporting. Only a miniscule fraction of the revenue lost from display ads in print newspapers was transferred over into advertising on online news aggregators.[6] In other words, even if one were to somehow abolish online news aggregation, it would not return significant display-advertising revenue to newspapers.

Nevertheless, after several years of studying a variety of financial redistribution mechanisms – including a per-click hyperlink tax, the source of the now somewhat-misleading "link tax" moniker – the Australian Competition and Consumer Commission opted for a mandatory-bargaining scheme. News aggregators are expected to negotiate revenue sharing deals with news producers in exchange for linking to their articles and videos. If they fail to do so within three months, the treasurer is given sole authority to appoint an arbitrator, require the parties to submit competing offers, and then choose whichever offer they find fairest.[7] Thus far, the mandatory-bargaining component has remained notional, given that the treasurer has yet to exercise his authority. But the mere possibility of enforcement was enough to convince Google and Facebook – after some brief initial resistance – to quickly strike a number of deals with Australia's largest news producers.[8]

[5] Fed. Trade Comm'n, Slotting Allowances in the Retail Grocery Industry: Selected Case Studies in Five Product Categories (Nov. 2003), https://perma.cc/AQW3-DTRT.

[6] Ads on news searches account for as little as 1 percent of Google's total revenue. Kamil Franek, *How Google News Makes Money: Business Model Explained* (Dec. 17, 2019), https://perma.cc/H9S7-K9Q4.

[7] *Treasury Laws Amendment (News Media and Digital Platforms Mandatory Bargaining Code) Bill 2021* (Cth) 28 (Austl.), https://perma.cc/Q6WH-44Q5.

[8] Facebook imposed a one-week ban on news-article-sharing on its platform, sparking a public backlash among Australian users. Rod McGuirk, *Unfriended No More: Facebook to Lift Australia News Ban*, AP News (Feb. 23, 2021), https://perma.cc/N3A7-C6DX.

The early returns from the law have heartened proponents. Australia's largest newspaper and magazine conglomerate, News Corp Australia, negotiated a $50 million deal with Google, while broadcasters Seven and Nine got $30 million apiece. The total reported transfer to all news outlets from both Google and Facebook as of March 2022 was $200 million, with 90 percent going to News Corp, Seven, and Nine. Flush with cash – for instance, Nine Entertainment reported a 39 percent increase in earnings because of the payments – the outlets have embarked on a journalist-hiring spree.[9]

However, the newly fattened bottom lines of Australia's largest media enterprises are unlikely to assuage critics of the link tax. Indeed, given that News Corp is owned by Rupert Murdoch, opponents have dubbed it the "Fox News tax," raising concerns that the link tax will merely entrench the global news magnate's disproportionate share of the Australian news industry and bolster his ability to influence politics in a particular ideological direction.[10] Others have argued that the link tax is an example of ham-fisted government intervention, an "extraction of money at the point of the proverbial gun" rather than an "honest attempt at collective bargaining."[11] The boldest claim, however, comes from Sir Tim Berners-Lee, the inventor of the World Wide Web, who was "concerned that the Code risks breaching a fundamental principle of the web by requiring payment for linking between certain content online" and "could make the web unworkable around the world."[12]

18.3 MADE IN AMERICA

This is not the first time a national news industry has successfully pushed for government intervention to subsidize operations via a novel legal mechanism in response to technological disruption and financial competition. In the early twentieth century in the United States, the Associated Press (AP) newswire service found itself facing a similar crisis. Half a century earlier, a group of New York City newspapers had banded together to share the costs of producing original journalism. For example, a journalist on assignment in Charleston, South Carolina, or London, England, could send back dispatches about the latest events, from which each AP

[9] Mathew Ingram, *Facebook and the News after Australia: What Happens Now?*, COLUM. J. REV. (2021); Christopher Warren, *Diversity Hit between the Eyes as Old Media Pockets about 90% of Big Tech Cash*, CRIKEY (Feb. 24, 2021), https://perma.cc/PA3D-GKPQ; Nic Fildes, *Australia's Media Thrives after Forcing Big Tech to Pay for Content*, FIN. TIMES (Mar. 11, 2022), https://perma.cc/59CJ-8CPB.

[10] James Allworth, *Australia's Proposed "Fox News Tax"*, MEDIUM (Jan. 25, 2021), https://perma.cc/3DA4-GQAW; *Saving the Free and Diverse Press: Hearing Before the Subcomm. on Antitrust, Com., and Admin. L.*, 116th Cong. (2021) (statement of Jeff Jarvis, Leonard Tow Professor of Journalism Innovation, City Univ. of New York).

[11] Ben Allworth, *Australia's News Media Bargaining Code, Breaking Down the Code, Australia's Fake News*, STRATECHERY (Aug. 20, 2020), https://perma.cc/D56N-K9GP.

[12] Timothy Berners-Lee, *Testimony to the Senate Standing Committee on Economics* (Jan. 18, 2021), https://perma.cc/E58F-KPLZ.

member could then construct a news story with their own stylistic spin. This system allowed newspapers to focus their efforts on the local news beat while defraying the high cost of national and international coverage. In addition, as historian Richard Schwarzlose puts it, the AP "was partner in a common-law marriage with Western Union," which enjoyed a functional trans-continental telegraph monopoly.[13] As a result, the AP could not only share costs across a national pool of member newspapers, but it could transmit dispatches more quickly than could its various regional competitors.

The AP's competitive advantages made membership a desirable privilege. By the turn of the twentieth century and by design, only about 30 percent of American newspapers had been allowed to join the AP fold. First-class AP members were given the right to exclude from membership all other newspapers in a 120-mile radius. It was a trade-off. On the one hand, more members meant that shared costs could be spread more widely; however, adding too many members would dilute the value of existing memberships by introducing local competition between member newspapers. And since AP membership rights were transferable, when a member newspaper folded, its membership could sell for the modern equivalent of hundreds of thousands or millions of dollars at auction. As one newspaper owner put it, "The exclusive character of the news [was] an essential element of its value, and incentive to its collection."[14]

But that value proposition was under serious pressure by the turn of the century. Antitrust action against Western Union and the rise of competing telegraph lines had eroded AP's technological advantage. Newspaper owners clamoring for AP membership lobbied state governments and appealed to the courts, asking for a mandate that the AP sell its wire service to all comers as a "quasi-public utility affected with a public interest."[15] But when the Illinois Supreme Court ruled against the AP in *Inter-Ocean Publishing Co. v. Associated Press* in 1900, the AP dodged this requirement by moving to New York and re-organizing under a designation intended for fish and game clubs.[16]

Hunting club or not, by the 1900s, dissatisfied newspaper owners like magnate William Randolph Hearst – better known today as the inspiration for the movie *Citizen Kane* – took aim at the AP cartel and founded competing newswires, including United Press and the International News Service. Hearst was a sensationalist and innovator, the first newspaperman to print letters to the editor and color cartoons (including the popular *Yellow Kid* strip, which originated the phrase

[13] Richard Schwarzlose, The Nation's Newsbrokers Volume 2: The Rush to Institution: From 1865 to 1920, at 14 (1990).

[14] *Id.* at 184; Jonathan Silberstein-Loeb, The International Distribution of News: The Associated Press, Press Association, and Reuters, 1848–1947, at 49–50 (2014).

[15] Schwarzlose, *supra* note 13, at 193.

[16] Richard M. Harnett & Billy G. Ferguson, Unipress: United Press International, Covering the 20th Century 16 (2003).

"yellow journalism" as a description of Hearst's often-lurid article topics).[17] Instead of the AP's dry, boring dispatches full of legislative votes and business mergers, the new wire services provided colorful accounts that had human-interest angles. Furthermore, they were early adopters of the faster, cheaper teletype technology.

The Associated Press, then under the leadership of Melville Stone, needed to find a mechanism that would stymie external competitors, quiet restive AP affiliates, and preserve the value of possessing an AP membership. Stone believed that the AP would find its salvation in "hot news" (a name derived from the saying that news was "hot off the press," pages still warm from the printing process). Stone believed that newswires deserved an exclusive, time-limited, legal right to disseminate information collected by one of its correspondents or affiliated newspapers. This was a significant departure from the standard newsgathering practices of the time; it had been routine to extract facts from competing newspaper stories and rewrite them into stories for one's own paper. An entire ecosystem of evening-edition and West Coast newspapers had sprung up around the practice, repurposing information gathered from morning editions and East Coast papers.

This system had been tolerated because it helped morning newspapers by making it "notorious" – as early AP member Horace Greeley put it – that "certain journals have the earliest news" while evening papers were forced to regurgitate from the leavings of the morning papers. And the practice was so beneficial to the morning papers that Greeley said he "would rather that those [evening newspapers] who do not take it should copy than not."[18] Indeed, the Associated Press itself engaged in so-called "news piracy." As Stone reported to the AP Board of Directors after the U.S. Supreme Court ruling in *INS v. AP*, the "proprietary news case had not only great advantage for us, but it had some disadvantage" by "necessarily put[ting] an end to our pirating news from the London papers."[19] But the loss of that benefit was outweighed by the way in which the hot news doctrine would reinforce the competitive advantages of the Associated Press. Since the AP had the largest newsgathering network, decreasing the amount of free-riding performed by non-member newspapers and insurgent newswires would simultaneously raise costs for competitors, increase the value of an AP franchise, and convince current AP members to remain in-network and continue paying the substantial membership fees required.

Stone found a test case involving an employee of an AP affiliate in Cleveland, Ohio, who had been bribed by the International News Service to relay information gathered from the newsroom's bulletin board. The AP sued, the federal district court ruled in its favor, INS appealed, and the case then went to the U.S. Supreme Court, which upheld the district court's decision in *International News Service v. Associated Press* (1918). Melville Stone got his wish for a hot news standard when the Supreme

[17] Ben Proctor, William Randolph Hearst: The Later Years, 1911–1951, at 5–6 (2007).

[18] Frederic Proctor, Journalism in the United States, from 1690 to 1872, at 541–42 (1873).

[19] Silberstein-Loeb, *supra* note 14, at 207.

Court granted newswires and newspapers a "*quasi*-property" right over freshly collected news as rightful recompense for "one who gathers news, at pains and expense, for the purpose of lucrative publication" and to prevent unfair competition.[20] The Supreme Court did not set a cooling-off period for hot news, though the district court had suggested a minimum of "three or four hours," as long as "sufficient time has elapsed to afford opportunity for general publication."[21] Regardless, the Supreme Court had created something wholly new, a category of property separate from copyright, trademarks, trade secrets, stock tips, and other established categories of proprietary information.

18.4 ENCLOSURE OF AN INFORMATIONAL COMMONS

Both the hot news doctrine and the link tax have created a novel, quasi-property right in information. The proper term for describing that process is "enclosure," an echo of how rentiers in early modern Europe turned previously common pasture, open to the use of all village residents, into private property by erecting fences and legal boundaries. Similarly, as legal scholar Yochai Benkler wrote in 1999, "We are in the midst of an enclosure movement in our information environment," as "our society is making a series of decisions that will subject more of the ways in which each of us uses information to someone else's exclusive control."[22] The invention of the internet undermined the value that could be extracted by a class of quasi-monopolistic newsgatherers who had been able to charge consumers inflated prices for access to news information and the classifieds marketplace.

With those geographically defined news-distribution monopolies under threat from digital disruption, it is understandable why the formerly landed newspapers would seek a legal mechanism to enclose their corner of the World Wide Web – to erect a high regulatory fence that could keep out all those who would graze on their news without permission. The metaphor breaks down, however, given that in the case of internet news aggregation, the grazing does not crop the grass, thus starving the animals and leaving the owner bereft; rather, the aggregator funnels users to the news originator, expanding their audience at no marginal cost to them. It is hardly the fault of the aggregator that the news producer lost an entirely different form of income (from classified ads) and has suffered as a result.

Proponents of hot news and a link tax often justify a quasi-property right on the basis that reporting the news takes hard work and great expense. As the Associated Press had argued in its brief, "News is a business commodity, because it costs money and labor to produce and because it has value for which those who have it not are

20 Int'l News Service v. Associated Press, 248 U.S. 215, 216 (1918).

21 *Id.* at 426, 428.

22 Yochai Benkler, *Free as the Air to Common Use: First Amendment Constraints on Enclosure of the Public Domain*, 74 N.Y.U. L. Rev. 354, 354–55 (1999).

ready to pay."[23] In other words, it is property because we have it, it was hard to produce, and you want it so much that you will pay for it. The U.S. Supreme Court in *INS v. AP* had agreed, adopting what would later become known as the "sweat of the brow" standard for property in information.[24] Factual news itself, not merely copyrightable stories about that news, was considered a form of time-limited property under the hot news doctrine.

By contrast, the traditional standard for those "noblest of human productions – knowledge, truths ascertained, conceptions, and ideas" – was that they should be, in the words of Justice Louis Brandeis (from his dissent to *INS v. AP*), "free as the air to common use." Exceptions could be made to this rule, especially "productions which, in some degree, involve creation, invention, or discovery" – a standard which certainly applies to newsgathering – but it was an exception that proved the rule.[25] For instance, copyright was a form of property invented to be, as Lord Thomas Macaulay put it, "a tax on readers for the purpose of giving a bounty to writers."[26] According to dissenters like Justice Brandeis, the question of whether or not an abstraction should be proprietized was a function of the social utility derived and not the labor that went into making it. The goal was not payment for authors per se but rather the creation of a necessary incentive that would lead to greater literary production and thus net social benefit.

This is an old debate, which legal scholar Richard Epstein has summarized as the difference between "those who see the source of property rights in the positive law" and "as a command of the sovereign" versus those who ground "property rights on the traditions and common practices within a given community" and see property arising "from the bottom up, and not from the top down." In the latter conception, the state ought to play merely a discovery role, figuring out "what the community has customarily regarded as binding social rules" and then enforcing those organically generated rules. Indeed, this debate underlines the current contest over the link tax. Should the government of Australia use positive law – given "its administrative ease of application," to quote Epstein again – to subsidize news outlets via the

[23] *Id.* at 221–22.

[24] Feist Publ'ns, Inc. v. Rural Tel. Serv. Co., 499 U.S. 340 (1991). The U.S. Supreme Court overturned the standard despite the admitted expenditure of effort and expense that went into compiling telephone numbers for a white-pages publisher.

[25] *Int'l News*, 248 U.S. at 250.

[26] Thomas Babington Macaulay, *First Speech to the House of Commons on Copyright, in* Macaulay's Speeches on Copyright and Lincoln's Address at Cooper Institute 201, 201 (James Fleming Hosic ed., 1915). Indeed, Macaulay expressly opposed the extension of copyright terms postmortem because, as he put it, doing so tipped copyright into mere "encouragement to expenditure." Thomas Babington Macaulay, Copyright 1394 (Thomas Curson Hansard 1842). Notably, Melville Stone's moment of inspiration for his hot news crusade came while reading Isaac Disraeli's *Calamities and Quarrels of Authors*, in which he wrote, "Is it wonderful ... that even successful authors are indigent? ... [F]or, on the publication of their works, these cease to be their own property." *See* Melville Stone, Fifty Years a Journalist 355 (1921).

creation of a novel, quasi-property right over links to news articles? Or should it instead constrain itself to conforming the law to the spontaneously evolving technical and community standards of the World Wide Web?[27]

18.5 WRECK-IT RUPERT BREAKS THE INTERNET

It is important to recognize just how radical a departure such a link tax enclosure is from the norms of the World Wide Web. This was the source of Sir Timothy Berners-Lee's concerns about the link tax's effect on the future of the internet. Berners-Lee invented the concept of hypertext in 1980 – which links text on one site to text in another location – and then connected it to emerging protocols for transmission and identification, thus creating the first modern website in December 1990. As he later described, his intention was always that "normal links should simply be references," meaning that a hyperlink did not imply endorsement or claim ownership of the linked site. The link was no more the property of the reference site than the bare footnote to this paragraph is the property of the cited author.[28] The resulting spiderweb of interconnections spread quickly and globally, thus earning the name "World Wide Web."

The Australian link tax, however, turns the hyperlink itself into a form of quasi-property by granting an exclusive right of control and compensation to the reference site.[29] As internet-theorist Konstantinos Komaitis notes, this "changes fundamentally the meaning and scope of hyperlinks" and "ascribes to them a meaning they are not meant to have."[30] Links to news sites are no longer "normal links" under Berners-Lee's taxonomy. Google and Facebook can no longer legally share a mere link to one of Rupert Murdoch's papers without paying for his permission to do so (or, at least, without risking the wrath of the treasurer of Australia for their failure to bargain). Yet, according to Berners-Lee, it is "the ability to link freely ... without limitations regarding the content of the linked site and without monetary fees" that "is fundamental to how the web operates, how it has flourished till present, and how it will continue to grow in decades to come."[31] The link tax, by proprietizing the hyperlink and legally enclosing online news, threatens to snip a set of threads tying

[27] Richard Epstein, *International News Service v. Associated Press: Custom and Law as Sources of Property Rights in News*, 78 VA L. REV. 85, 85–88 (1992).

[28] Tim Berners-Lee, *Axioms of Web Architecture, Links and Law: Myths*, W3 (Apr. 1997), https://perma.cc/6456-NGJZ.

[29] I prefer the term "quasi-property" for the link tax both because it echoes its use by the U.S. Supreme Court to describe hot news and because it's a nonformalized form of property. The Australian government could have instead formalized a full property right over hyperlinks via copyright law.

[30] *In the Case of Australia vs. Facebook, the Internet Is the Casualty*, KONSTANTINOS KOMAITIS (Feb. 19, 2021), https://perma.cc/68RH-NYY5.

[31] Berners-Lee, *supra* note 12.

together the World Wide Web.[32] Australia has been a relatively minor player in global internet development, so the Web can likely survive even so fundamental a challenge. But the success of the link tax Down Under could propel the rise of an imitative, rentier class across the globe, each nation snipping away at the threads that bind together the Web. The days of a truly "world-wide" web may be numbered.

To understand just how radical the legal enclosure of hyperlinks could be, consider other similar forms of information and how social benefit is derived from their remaining publicly accessible. Compare a news website to the house you occupy; both required significant expense and effort to construct and furnish. However, owning a house at a particular location does not give the title holder ownership of the street address. That is because there is immense social and civil benefit derived from that address remaining public information – remaining "free as the air." Its nonownership is a traditional, well-established communal norm. It is useful for taxing authorities, commercial entities, and social connectedness; in the internet age, it is a vital part of services such as Google Maps that greatly benefit travelers.

Turning street addresses into private property could have potential upsides, like helping shield celebrities from stalkers or domestic-abuse survivors from former partners. Perhaps it could even generate rents for those holding these novel rights in street addresses by forcing phone-book companies and registries to pay for listing rights. But more likely, enclosure would simply destroy these networks that provide socially beneficial uses without returning any monetary benefit to the owner.

Indeed, this is the reason why, when looking at the global map of Google Street View locations, you will find large blank spots in Germany. Based on an understandable, historical fear of government surveillance and an emphasis on personal privacy rights, German courts have upheld "informational self-determination" and prohibited corporations from using images of people's homes or even listing their street addresses without obtaining express permission. Enclosing this category of information – which is freely available in other parts of the world – destroyed much of the social utility derived from Google Street View and did so without returning any kind of monetary benefit to German residents. Given the value Germans place on privacy, it appears to be a price they were willing to pay.[33] But it serves as a reminder that the decision to enclose a commons can generate distributed social costs and informational deadweight losses.[34]

32 Although the mechanism of enclosure is different, the current debate over enclosing hyperlinks is reminiscent of concerns about the rise of internet "walled gardens" in the late 1990s and early 2000s. Facebook is a descendant of those older walled gardens – including AOL and Yahoo – though Google helped blow them apart. *AOL's 'Walled Garden'*, Wall St. J. (Sept. 4, 2000).

33 Frank Jacobs, *Why Germany Is a Blank Spot on Google's Street View*, Big Think (Feb. 11, 2022), https://perma.cc/S8BF-G73G.

34 It is worth noting that the proximate problem for Google Street View in Germany was not the creation of a privacy property right per se but the way that doing so functionally increased

Or imagine a world in which authors – jealous of the revenue extracted from their hard work by used bookstores or the loss of revenue from library borrowing – convinced the government to proprietize factual information about books.[35] In this imaginary world, in order to display a book cover on its shelves or list a book title or description in its catalog, a bookstore or library would need to obtain and pay for the express permission of the newly endowed rights holder. This might create some financial benefit for authors, but it would certainly devastate the used-bookstore and library industries. Given the costs of regulatory compliance and decreased competition, that would leave consumers literarily impoverished with fewer titles carried in fewer locations and at higher prices.[36] Likewise, the future of a World Wide Web in which an increasing number of hyperlinks are considered property is an internet composed of fewer links, offering fewer services, and providing less information, even as it returns only a fraction of that lost consumer value to a handful of websites.

18.6 PASS GO AND COLLECT $200

The desirability of a new property right should be determined by weighing its social benefits and detriments. To do so, it is first necessary to study the contexts from which hot news and the link tax originated. Both were rooted in efforts – by the Associated Press in the U.S. in the 1910s and Australian news outlets in the 2010s – to protect natural advantages that were crumbling under technological disruption. In the mid-nineteenth century, a natural monopoly in telegraphy developed in response to its high capital costs and the need for government-granted easements, a situation from which the Associated Press, via its relationship with Western Union, derived a massive competitive advantage. As discussed previously, the late-nineteenth-century erosion of the AP's derived telegraph

transaction costs. *See* Michael Heller, *The Tragedy of the Anticommons: A Concise Introduction and Lexicon*, 76 MOD. L. REV. 6 (2013), https://perma.cc/6U9Z-F8ST.

[35] The fair-use right to share print books in libraries is traditional and well established. However, digital books are newer and the loss of profits from library use of e-books has been hotly contested. Alison Flood, *Writers Sue US University Libraries for Copyright Infringement*, GUARDIAN (Sept. 13, 2011), https://perma.cc/B2QV-MP42.

[36] Compare this imaginary scenario to the very real devolution of publisher liability for U.S. bookstores over the course of the twentieth century. It was once routine for booksellers to be considered equivalent to publishers and thus held criminally responsible for the content of the books they sold. But the courts eventually recognized the downsides of that approach, exempting bookstore middlemen that stand between producers and consumers from liability. That principle was then enshrined for the internet in Section 230 of the Communications Decency Act. Or to put that another way, the mere carrying of a book title did not imply approval or ownership of book by the store, which is the same principle behind Timothy Berners-Lee's conception of hyperlinking. Brent Skorup & Jennifer Huddleston, *The Erosion of Publisher Liability in American Law, Section 230, and the Future of Online Curation*, 72 OKLA. L. REV. 3 (2020).

monopoly launched both a wave of new competition and Melville Stone's reactionary hot news crusade.

Australian newspapers at the turn of the twenty-first century did not have a comparable technological advantage, but newspapers in the pre-internet era typically enjoyed a different kind of natural advantage: a geography-based regional monopoly in news provision. As Berkshire Hathaway CEO Warren Buffett once put it, "If you have a monopoly newspaper . . . your idiot nephew could run it."[37] Buffett backed his words with his wallet, going on a U.S.-newspaper buying spree in the 1970s. By that point, Australian newspaper magnate Rupert Murdoch had already inherited the family newspaper in Adelaide and embarked on his own buying spree of distressed newspapers as the industry consolidated. Classified-ad revenue – which Murdoch once described as "rivers of gold" – was the financial bedrock on which Murdoch ultimately built a network of domestic broadcast stations, international newspapers, and, in 1996, a new American cable news network, the Fox News Channel.[38]

But by the 2000s, it was apparent that technological disruption of the newspaper industry was on the horizon. Online classified-ad platforms provided a better, faster, and cheaper service to consumers than print newspapers could, and newspaper owners were generally slow to pivot and create their own online platforms lest they cannibalize their existing business model. In addition, some of the earliest online news aggregators did not merely share links to articles hosted on the newspaper's own websites – driving display-ad revenue – but simply copied the content wholesale and posted it on their own sites. By the end of the decade, the newspaper industry's income had fallen precipitously; at *The New York Times*, for example, revenue had halved from $3.27 billion in 2006 to $1.59 billion in 2012.[39] But the paper's executive editor Bill Keller blamed not the direct copiers – which could be, and often were, sued for copyright violations – but aggregators like *The Huffington Post*, which merely linked to *The Times*' articles, and which Keller dramatically compared to Somali pirates.[40]

The frustrations of newspaper owners percolated up to the Associated Press, which announced its intent to spend more on its legal efforts to win "appropriate compensation" for its newsgathering. Like in Australia, the primary cause of newspaper revenue decline was the loss of classified ads, but there was nothing the *NYT*

37 Interview with Warren Buffett, Chairman & CEO, Berkshire Hathaway (May 26, 2010), https://perma.cc/D4UW-GM9J.

38 *Classified Calamity*, Economist (Nov. 17, 2005), https://perma.cc/3K9C-7WJB; George Munster, Rupert Murdoch: A Paper Prince (1985); William Shawcross, Murdoch: The Making of a Media Empire (1997).

39 Amy Watson, *New York Times Company's Revenue from 2006 to 2021*, Statista (Mar. 21, 2022), https://perma.cc/68AQ-DYH8.

40 Seth Mnookin, *The Kingdom and the Paywall*, N.Y. Mag. (July 24, 2011), https://perma.cc/4LDA-A724.

or AP could do about the likes of Craigslist and other classified ad platforms. They could, however, target early news aggregators like *The Huffington Post* and *Drudge Report*, which were dependent on linking to newspapers. The Associated Press had waged a war against news piracy in the early twentieth century; and in the early twenty-first century, the Associated Press and member newspapers charged once more into the breach, albeit one opened by the advent of the internet instead of the decline of a telegraphic monopoly.

Little about the rhetoric involved had changed in a century. Back in 1917, district court judges had accused the International News Service of being a "parasite," which by "taking the news" would kill off the Associated Press and then "meet the same fate that every parasite meets," dying "with the stock upon which it feeds."[41] Likewise, a 2009 article in the *Los Angeles Times* was titled "Internet Parasites" and opened with an elaborate analogy in which newspapers were compared to the hardworking, bread-baking Little Red Hen of the eponymous folk tale, while online aggregators played the role of the lazy dog, cow, and pig who "undercut her price and each other's" until all were driven out of the bread business.[42]

The moment also demonstrated the continuing relevance of Melville Stone's crusade for hot news. From 2008 to 2012, a wave of scholarship and activism called for a revival of a federal hot news doctrine (which had lapsed in the 1930s) with *INS v. AP* as a precedent.[43] If news itself – and not just copyrightable stories about the news – were considered a form of quasi-property, then free-riding online papers and bloggers would have to either wait to publish their own derivative articles or pay the newspapers for the right to do so promptly. Yet while a closely watched Federal Trade Commission panel in 2009 discussed "potential revenue sources from changes in law" to bail out the newspaper industry – including federal hot news legislation – the proposals went nowhere in either Congress or the courts.[44] In part, that was because early aggregators were small fry; the oft-maligned *Huffington Post*, for example, had only $30 million in revenue in 2010, at which point the *NYT* was seeking to recoup nearly fifty times that amount.[45]

[41] Int'l News Serv. v. Associated Press, 248 U.S. 215, 585 (1918).

[42] David Marburger & Dan Marburger, *Internet Parasites*, L.A. Times (Aug. 2, 2009).

[43] *See, e.g.*, Ryan Holte, *Restricting Fair Use to Save the News: A Proposed Change in Copyright Law to Bring More Profit to News Reporting*, 13 J. Tech. L. & Pol'y 1 (2008); Lindsay Rabicoff, *The Hot News Misappropriation Doctrine: Confusion in the Internet Age and the Call for Legislative Action*, 53 Jurimetrics 1 (2012); Eric Schmidt, *Hot News Misappropriation in the Internet Age*, 9 J. on Telecomm. & High Tech L. 313 (2011); Elaine Stoll, *Hot News Misappropriation: More than Nine Decades after INS v. AP, Still an Important Remedy for News Piracy*, 79 U. Cin. L. Rev. 3 (2011).

[44] Fed. Trade Comm'n, *Federal Trade Commission Staff Discussion Draft: Potential Policy Recommendations to Support the Reinvention of Journalism* (2010), https://perma.cc/LPJ8-QTEU.

[45] Jim Romenesko, *Huffington Post Says It'll Post First Annual Profit This Year*, Poynter (Dec. 14, 2010), https://perma.cc/M735-E333.

18.7 "ADVERTISING ONLY IS DEAD"

In any case, by the middle of the decade, the larger American news outlets had discovered a new, even more successful financial model. The newspapers might have lost classified ads and their regional monopolies, but they now enjoyed a potentially global audience in which the marginal cost of every additional subscriber was zero. They slapped up subscription paywalls, dribbled out a handful of free news articles each month to inveigle new subscribers, and watched their subscription bases swell. For example, *The New York Times* had flipped its $88 million operating loss in 2012 into a $109 million profit by 2021, in large part by multiplying its online subscriber count from less than one million readers to more than ten million.[46] With growth and profits this torrid, demand for a revived hot news doctrine went cold.

However, the idea of a quasi-property right in news persisted Down Under. While the *NYT* and Associated Press complained and dithered, Rupert Murdoch acted. In an insightful speech at a Federal Trade Commission Workshop in 2009, Murdoch acknowledged that "the old [newspaper] business model based on advertising-only is dead" and any replacement "that relies primarily on online advertising cannot sustain newspapers over the long term.[47] The reason is simple arithmetic.... The old model was founded on quasi-monopolies such as classified advertising – which has been decimated by new and cheaper competitors." Instead, "good journalism will depend on the ability of a news organization to attract customers by providing news and information they are willing to pay for." By 2009, Murdoch had already begun to pivot to a subscription model, well before his peers.[48]

Murdoch's acute business analysis did not, however, alleviate his sense that news aggregators were unfairly appropriating his content. He decried those who "take our news content and use it for their own purposes without contributing a penny to its production," and some who "rewrite, at times without attribution, the news stories of expensive and distinguished journalists . . . all under the tattered veil of 'fair use'" but which is truly "theft." Bear in mind that his speech was titled, "From Town Crier to Bloggers: How Will Journalism Survive the Internet Age," suggesting a capacious definition of unfair online competition. Murdoch might have made the smart move and pivoted his newspapers to a subscription model, but he was still determined to

[46] Amy Chozick, *New York Times Co. Posts $88 Million Loss, Citing About.com Write-Down*, N.Y. Times (July 26, 2012); Alexandra Bruell, *New York Times Tops 10 Million Subscriptions as Profit Soars*, Wall St. J. (Feb. 2, 2022).

[47] Rupert Murdoch, *From Town Crier to Bloggers: How Will Journalism Survive the Internet Age?*, Fed. Trade Comm'n (Dec. 1, 2009), https://perma.cc/RV9M-Q96C.

[48] R. Johnson & A. Gutiérrez, Reinventing the Business Model of the Newspaper Industry: Electronic Business Models and the Newspaper Industry, The Wall Street Journal as Case Study (2010) (M.A. thesis, Blekinge Institute of Technology), https://perma.cc/QE8K-5UH7.

crack down on bloggers, aggregators, and copiers by restricting their right to profit from his news articles without his express permission. "There's no such thing as a free news story," Murdoch enjoined, "and we are going to ensure that we get a fair but modest price for the value we provide."[49] Of course, what Murdoch saw as collecting a "fair but modest price," critics saw as him extracting a pound of flesh – vengefully taking that which was not his by right.

While the push for an enhanced property right in news in the United States stalled, Murdoch was able to take advantage of his even greater influence over Australian media and politics. As Rod Sims – the head of the Australian Competition and Consumer Commission, which drafted the mandatory-bargaining rules – acknowledged, it was Rupert Murdoch who first proposed a link tax.[50] Sims recently stepped down, but Murdoch's personal influence within the link tax regime is likely to continue given that the new head of the competition committee, Gina Cass-Gottlieb, is a former director of the Murdoch family trust.[51]

18.8 CONCENTRATE, CONSOLIDATE

Rupert Murdoch is both the driving force behind the Australian link tax and its greatest beneficiary. That is because the Australian newspaper industry is one of the most highly concentrated in the world. One study of media concentration ranked it third out of thirty countries, behind only China and Egypt, which have nationalized news outlets and authoritarian governments. It is so concentrated that more than half – 51.9 percent – of all newspaper readership in Australia goes to newspapers affiliated with Murdoch's News Corp. Throw in the next three networks by size, and only 7.4 percent of the market is left for independently owned papers.[52] It should not be a surprise that Murdoch's News Corp and the Nine Network together received over 90 percent of the total money brokered between Google, Facebook, and Australian newspapers. The largest conglomerates in a highly concentrated industry are naturally best able to extract the greatest financial returns from the new regulations they helped design.[53]

49 Murdoch, *supra* note 47.

50 Mike Masnick, *Australian Official Admits that of Course Murdoch Came Up with Link Tax, but Insists the Bill Is Not a Favor to News Corp.*, TECHDIRT (June 17, 2021), https://perma.cc/N9PX-FSYV.

51 Hannah Wootton, *'Go for Your Life': ACCC's New Chief Hailed as a Win for All Sides*, AUSTL. FIN. REV. (Dec. 14, 2021), https://perma.cc/D8QW-3X5U; Hannah Wootton & John Kehoe, *New ACCC Chairwoman Is Murdoch Family Insider*, AUSTL. FIN. REV. (Dec. 15, 2021), https://perma.cc/WHM6-QBTH; Bill Grueskin, *Millions of Dollars for News, Shrouded in Mysterious Deals*, ED. & PUBLISHER (Mar. 10, 2022), https://perma.cc/52MS-2VKF.

52 ELI NOAM, WHO OWNS THE WORLD'S MEDIA?: MEDIA CONCENTRATION AND OWNERSHIP AROUND THE WORLD (2016); Nick Evershed, *Australia's Newspaper Ownership Is Among the Most Concentrated in the World*, GUARDIAN (Nov. 13, 2020), https://perma.cc/U9CY-HYBP.

53 Warren, *supra* note 9.

This is an expected outcome from informational enclosure. As legal scholar Yochai Benkler notes, enclosure increases input costs for everyone "because some information previously available at no charge from the public domain is now available only for a price."[54] Previously, another website or aggregator could freely link to a news article; doing so now, however, comes at a cost. News producers and distributors can compensate for those higher costs by either sharing fewer links or by adjusting their organizational strategy to reduce costs – merging, in this case.[55]

Benkler's taxonomy of organizational structures can be adapted to the Australian media landscape. News Corp is a blend of two organizational forms. It is, like most traditional newspapers, a "quasi-rent seeker," an entity that sells exclusive access to a time-sensitive product.[56] But News Corp is also something that Benkler calls a "Mickey" (after Disney's famous Mouse), meaning a highly integrated firm with a large catalog of valuable content. News Corp is horizontally integrated across a national network of newspapers and radio and television stations. A quasi-rent-seeking "Mickey" has the most to gain from enclosure because the value of its large informational holdings increases; and it has the least to lose since horizontal integration mitigates increased transaction costs by allowing resource-sharing from across the firm. In short, member newspapers do not have to pay to link to each other, while non members do.

This incentivizes smaller newspapers to merge or to join with larger existing firms. Enclosure thus propels consolidation "of a greater portion of the information production function in the hands of large commercial organizations." In 1999, Benkler presciently predicted that "a world dominated by Disney, News Corp., and Time Warner appears to be the expected and rational response to excessive enclosure of the public domain."[57] Given that Australia already has one of the most concentrated news industries in the world, the anti-competitive effects of enclosure should be a particular concern.[58]

There has already been a severe imbalance that is evident when looking at which companies have benefited from Australia's mandatory-bargaining regime. Big newspaper conglomerates like News Corp, Seven, and Nine have each won tens of millions of dollars from Google and Facebook. But smaller, nonprofit, and public outlets have struggled to receive the same consideration. Ostensibly, the mandatory-bargaining rules allow these outlets to appeal to the Australian federal treasurer, who can impose arbitration (although the treasurer has yet to do so in any instance). However, even if the rules functioned as designed, smaller outlets would still simply

[54] Benkler, *supra* note 22, at 406.

[55] *Id.* at 401–06.

[56] Benkler's use of "rent-seeker" differs from the narrower sense of the term as used in the public choice literature. *See* David Henderson, *Rent Seeking*, Econlib, https://perma.cc/Q5QP-BY8F.

[57] Benkler, *supra* note 22, at 359.

[58] *Id.* at 401–06, 410.

have "less clout than a bigger player, than a News Corp," in the words of media critic Jeff Jarvis.[59] That includes Croakey Health Media, which reaches indigenous communities with health information. Croakey's editor-in-chief, Melissa Sweet, has asked the federal treasurer to compel Google and Facebook to begin mandatory bargaining, but she worries that they "do not have that political power." A system that requires companies to "bend the ear of the Treasurer" if they are unable to strike a deal with Google or Facebook on their own is a system that will be more responsive to the likes of Rupert Murdoch than to those like Melissa Sweet.[60]

Furthermore, an anti-small bias is designed into the mandatory-bargaining code. It expressly limits mandatory-bargaining rights to news organizations with a minimum of $150,000 in revenue. That excludes most bloggers, newsletters, nonprofits, and even small startup newspapers. The $150,000 limit would be an unusual criterion if the goal of the link tax, as originally stated, was truly to enforce "fairness" in the distribution of the news by ensuring that aggregators pay all newsgatherers. But if the goal is merely financial redistribution from Big Tech to Big Ink – from Google and Facebook to News Corp and other news conglomerates – then it makes perfect sense.[61]

The problem is that enclosure, in general, creates incentives for consolidation, just as Yochai Benkler predicted a quarter of a century ago; creating this kind of size threshold only heightens the consolidation pressure for companies that would benefit by meeting it. For example, Broadsheet Media – a small Australian city guide specializing in restaurant reviews – falls below the mandatory-bargaining threshold and thus cannot compel Google to offer them compensation for linking users to their restaurant recommendations. But if a larger conglomerate newspaper were to start a competing culture guide in Broadsheet's market, it would be qualified for mandatory bargaining, thus driving Broadsheet out of business or into a merger.[62]

18.9 "PROPERTY RIGHTS TALK"

The early returns from Australia's link tax suggest that there will be anti-competitive outcomes. The history of the hot news doctrine is instructive in this regard. After the victory in *INS v. AP*, the Associated Press grew enormously, with membership swelling from 35 percent of all daily newspapers in 1912 to 67.8 percent by 1948, while total revenues nearly tripled. The ratio was even more skewed for morning newspapers, of which a remarkable 96 percent were affiliated with the AP by the

[59] Rod McGuirk, *Facebook to Lift Australia News Ban after Dispute over Paying for Journalism*, PBS (Feb. 23, 2021), https://perma.cc/EKU8-MSJB.

[60] Grueskin, *supra* note 51; Hal Crawford, *Comment: Why Australia's Dishonest News Media Code Is a Bad Way to Tax Google and Facebook*, PressGazette (Oct. 14, 2021).

[61] My thanks to Kyle Langvardt for coming up with the phrase "Big Tech to Big Ink."

[62] Mariam Cheik-Hussein, *Explainer: The Arguments against the News Media Bargaining Code and What Happens Next*, AdNews (Feb. 1, 2021), https://perma.cc/E5LF-VLYH.

1940s.[63] Indeed, AP head Melville Stone had worried that the U.S. Supreme Court's decision was so useful to the AP's enterprise that it might "destroy our competition or hamper it in such measure that it will make us seem a monopoly," thus attracting "very dangerous" antitrust attention. The longstanding goal of Associated Press leadership in the early twentieth century was not monopoly power but "moderated competition."[64]

From Stone's perspective, the hot news doctrine would cement the AP's control over existing members, who were restive over high telegraphy fees, worried about the promise and peril of radio news, and tempted to leave because of the AP's reluctant decision in 1915 – under antitrust pressure from the U.S. attorney general – to allow members to receive news from competing wire services.[65] By reducing free-riding by non-members, the hot news standard would theoretically raise the costs of leaving the AP fold. However, Stone stepped down from his active duties shortly after the legal victory, and his successor, Kent Cooper, did not share Stone's interest in pursuing a hot news-based, anti-competitive strategy. Instead, Cooper reduced fees while increasing the number of member newspapers.

Cooper's approach worked to the benefit of William Randolph Hearst, who was not only the head of the INS but also the single largest owner of newspapers with AP memberships. Hearst had lost *INS v. AP* in his capacity as INS head, but his AP holdings hedged that loss significantly. Indeed, the post-case boom in the size of the AP meant that even more of Hearst's papers were quickly added to the AP fold. For Hearst, creating the INS was at least in part a way to increase his bargaining power *within* the AP – a way to pressure it to loosen its cap on the number of newspapers allowed into membership.

It is also a reminder that the point of asserting an informational property right can be something other than the direct financial benefit that it entails. Even if a property right is never formalized nor defended in court, its mere existence – and the implied threat of assertion – can boost negotiating power or constrain unwanted behavior. Publisher and AP member Horace Greeley once described the inveterate complaints about news piracy as something "talked of for effect's sake."[66] Complaining has its own utility, a function that the AP's Stone sought to boost by inventing a novel property right in hot news.

This "property-rights talk," to use legal scholar Douglas Baird's phrase, may bear on the Australian link tax situation.[67] If the goal of inventing a novel quasi-property right over hyperlinks was the creation of an equitable and transparent redistribution process, then the chosen mechanism has already proven itself to be a failure. But if

63 Schwarzlose, *supra* note 13, at 231; Silberstein-Loeb, *supra* note 14, at 67, 80.
64 Silberstein-Loeb, *supra* note 14, at 77.
65 Douglas Baird, *Property, Natural Monopoly, and the Uneasy Legacy of INS vs. AP* 2, Chi. Unbound (2005), https://perma.cc/KW6B-FCRS; Schwarzlose, *supra* note 13, at 84.
66 Hudson, *supra* note 19, at 541.
67 Baird, *supra* note 63, at 36.

the link tax's goal was instead to bolster the bargaining power of well-connected, incumbent newspaper conglomerates, then the link tax has been a major success. That distinction also makes sense of the fact that the mandatory-bargaining system has yet to be formally invoked by Australia's federal treasurer. The system's nominal purpose and actual function are quite different. By persuading Google and Facebook to sit down with large outlets like News Corp, the link tax may have already fulfilled its true purpose.

18.10 CENSORSHIP AND CONSENSUS

There are other negative consequences that stem from informational enclosure beyond industry consolidation and diminished competition. When the consolidated power of an industry is dependent on governmental support, it exacerbates the risk of either overt censorship or the creation of an artificial consensus. It is too early to predict any particular outcomes from Australia's link tax in this regard, but there are warning signs. The tax vests a great deal of discretionary power in a single, appointed position: the federal treasurer. And the mandatory-bargaining process is a black box. Initial negotiations between news outlets and aggregators are private. If those negotiations fail and an appeal is filed, the federal treasurer is under no obligation to explain why they mandated arbitration or chose not to. When concerns about the opacity of the bargaining process were raised, the head of the Australian Competition and Consumer Commission retorted that "the objective was never transparency. … The simple thing was evening out the bargaining power. If deals are done that the media companies are happy with, then it's a success."[68] It is hard to imagine a design more likely to result in regulatory capture and untoward political influence on behalf of favored media groups.

There is a subtler danger than overt censorship. News media consolidation tends to favor centrist politics and the creation of ideological consensus. Smaller, more radical newspapers will naturally have greater difficulty than larger firms in building the political capital needed to "bend the ear" of a partisan treasurer or their appointed arbitrators. Without intending to, the link tax could set the stage for decreased ideological diversity in the output of the Australian newspaper industry.

Something similar happened in the aftermath of the hot news doctrine. Although the test case in *INS v. AP* involved news piracy in Cleveland, Ohio, the subject of the pirated wires was the world war being waged in Europe. Hearst had developed a pro-German reputation prior to U.S. entry into the conflict, becoming the "most hated man in the country" (though he averred that his anti-war views made him "the only powerful sane man on the mad planet"). Hearst changed his tune after the U.S. declaration of war in 1917, but by that point, each of the major Allied governments had already barred INS reporters from using their cables or postal services, angry

[68] Grueskin, *supra* note 51.

about INS newspapers running unapproved (but mostly true) stories about various military setbacks and political machinations. Hearst sounded a defiant note – "I will not supplicate England for news"! – but his newspapers still needed coverage from the front.[69] Hearst was forced to rely heavily on information obtained from the AP's wire reports and did so until he was caught in Cleveland. By contrast, Stone and the AP had deferred to French and British censors and had earned special, expedited privileges for AP reports.[70] Back in the United States, the AP encouraged President Wilson to create a censorship board and pledged its "hearty support" for the war effort.[71]

In this context, granting a property right over hot news reinforced wartime censorship by guaranteeing that the most enthusiastically pro-government wire service carried the freshest news. In his dissent from *INS v. AP*, Justice Brandeis recognized this problem, noting the "danger involved in recognizing such a property right in news" when it aligned with "prohibitions imposed by foreign governments."[72] There were even concerns within the AP about the situation. Stone's successor, Kent Cooper, later said that he "disliked the idea of the Associated Press having exclusive access to and being an outlet for the propaganda tainted announcements of foreign governments, which in effect set The Associated Press up as the exclusive mouthpiece in America for these governments."[73] That kind of knock-on government censorship is relatively easy to spot. There is, as of yet, no evidence of a similar problem in Australia today involving the link tax.

However, what is less visible but no less pernicious are the ways in which enclosure and consolidation can stifle peripheral voices, creating an artificial ideological consensus even without formal censorship. By the early twentieth century, the Associated Press had earned a reputation for conservatism, opposition to organized labor, and disinterest in racial issues. Garrison Villard, owner of *The Nation*, accused the AP of siding "in ninety-nine cases out of a hundred" with "the views of the employing class."[74] INS, on the other hand, reflected Hearst's more progressive politics, his desire to "see the press fulfill its noble calling, and as the mouthpiece of the people, rule, regulate, and reform the world."[75] Other, smaller newswires

69 Proctor, *supra* note 17.

70 Stone, *supra* note 26, at 245–46.

71 *Id.* at 325–26; Harnett & Ferguson, *supra* note 16, at 54; for more on the censorship board, *see* Steven Vaughn, Holding Fast the Inner Lines: Democracy, Nationalism, and the Committee on Public Information (1980).

72 Int'l News Serv. v. Associated Press, 248 U.S. 215, 263 (1918).

73 Schwarzlose, *supra* note 13, at 82.

74 Harnett & Ferguson, *supra* note 16, at 40; Christopher Wadlow argues that Justice Mahlon Pitney, who authored the majority opinion in INS v. AP, was primarily motivated by his longstanding malice towards labor union agitation. INS v. AP was thus an attempt to create a precedent for enhanced protection of commercial property from union organization. Christopher Wadlow, *A Riddle Whose Answer Is 'Tort': A Reassessment of International News Service v Associated Press*, 76 Mod. L. Rev. 4 (2013).

75 Proctor, *supra* note 17, at 6.

cropped up in the 1900s and 1910s to address the oversights of the AP, including the Federated Press, which served a group of socialist newspapers, and the Associated Negro Press, which reached a growing national network of black-owned newspapers. The hot news standard was never strictly enforced, but a rigorous hot news regime would have been damaging for these second-tier newswires, which often relied upon basic information gleaned from the AP. Through its cozy relationship with the federal government and a relative disinterest in serving radical or marginalized communities, the AP's rise to predominance by the 1940s may have played an important role in the formation of the post–World War II liberal consensus.[76]

18.11 FRIEND OR FOE?

Censorship concerns aside, it is possible that the link tax's bark will be worse than its bite, as was the case with the hot news doctrine. The mandatory-bargaining rule has yet to be formally invoked or challenged in court. And the major news conglomerates do have a substantial interest in keeping news aggregators in the Australian market. Perhaps the strangest aspect of the rhetoric revolving around the link tax is that it often assumes an unnecessarily adversarial relationship between news producers and news aggregators. Remember, aggregators did not cause the decline of local newspapers. Aggregators actually provide crucial assistance to papers that have been able to transition away from peddling classified ads and instead pivoted towards a subscription-based financial model. Aggregators function as global discovery and distribution networks for newspapers, which is why newspapers almost invariably keep their websites open to search-engine indexing. If news-aggregator "piracy" were truly a problem, stopping Google would be as easy as inserting a simple text file (robots.txt) into a website's code. It is so easy that U.S. courts have recognized that the failure to implement such code grants an "implied license" to aggregators to index and link to a website.[77]

That discovery-and-distribution function has significant monetary value. Google claims to direct consumer referrals worth $218 million to Australian media companies yearly. Facebook claims $407 million.[78] Both companies have an incentive to exaggerate their contribution, but their willingness to pay hundreds of millions to stay in the Australian news market suggests that it is not too far from the truth. And

[76] For instance, the AP's coverage of the Dies Committee was highly deferential. Peter Barker, Un-Americanism in the Papers: Anti-Communists and Their Use of the Press (2009) (MA thesis, Miami University), https://perma.cc/83N8-CH9X. The concept of a postwar "liberal consensus" comes from Godfrey Hodgson. *See* ROBERT MASON & IWAN MORGAN, THE LIBERAL CONSENSUS RECONSIDERED: AMERICAN POLITICS AND SOCIETY IN THE POSTWAR ERA (2017).

[77] Monika Jasiewicz, *Copyright Protection in an Opt-Out World: Implied License Doctrine and News Aggregators*, 122 YALE L.J. 3 (2012).

[78] Holden, *supra* note 4; Bianca O'Neill, *Is the News Media Bargaining Code the Start of a New Internet Era?*, ROLLING STONE AUS. (Feb. 18, 2021), https://perma.cc/NMJ3-QL3K.

the value of news aggregation is backed by research from overseas. When Spain passed a tax on snippets (the brief description of a website that appears below the hyperlink), Google News pulled out of the country entirely, giving researchers a natural experiment about the effects of (dis)aggregation of online news. All eighty-four major Spanish online newspapers lost a huge amount of traffic and revenue, with the losses concentrated among the smallest newspapers.[79] By severing the mutually beneficial relationship between news producers and news aggregators, Spain's snippet tax left everyone poorer and consumers less informed.

Australian newspapers will naturally wish to maximize their share of the revenue from mutually beneficial deals struck with aggregators. But they also have an incentive not to completely drive aggregators away, as happened in Spain. The best-case scenario would be that the link tax is an extreme example of "property-rights talk" or jawboning, not an effort to create a quasi-property right over hyperlinks. If it is jawboning, the link tax is a signal that Australian newspapers want to be taken seriously, not literally. It would then merely reset the bargaining equilibrium at a different value proposition than if the link tax did not exist. Such a scenario may be true, but it is a dangerous game to play, given the high stakes involved.

Policymakers in Canada, the United Kingdom, and the European Union are looking to Australia's experience for guidance while considering implementing their own versions of a link tax.[80] But a link tax can undermine mutually beneficial exchange, that is, news producers receiving free distribution and distributors accessing free content, and generate significant downside risks, for example, inequitable enclosure, corporate consolidation, ideological consensus, and a snipped World Wide Web. Thus, a link tax is a questionable option for addressing the decline of the legacy news industry. If redistribution of online revenue is a priority for policymakers, then almost any other mechanism for accomplishing that goal would be preferable.

79 Mike Masnick, *Study of Spain's 'Google Tax' on News Shows How Much Damage It Has Done*, Techdirt (July 29, 2015), https://perma.cc/DZF6-UMH2.

80 David Ljunggren, *Canada Plans Digital Tax in 2022 on Global Tech Giants*, Reuters (Nov. 30, 2020), https://perma.cc/82AQ-TFY5; Sam Dumitriu, *The EU's Link Tax Is Bad Enough, but the UK's Version Would Be Even Worse*, CapX (Feb. 2, 2022), https://perma.cc/EA6L-HLRC.

19

Structuring a Subsidy for Local Journalism

*Kyle Langvardt**

19.1 INTRODUCTION

The commercial market for local news in the United States has collapsed. Many communities lack a local paper. These "news deserts," comprising about two-thirds of the country, have lost a range of benefits that local newspapers once provided. Foremost among these benefits was investigative reporting – local newspapers at one time played a primary role in investigating local government and commerce and then reporting the facts to the public. It is rare for someone else to pick up the slack when the newspaper disappears.

The local newspapers that do remain in operation are badly diminished. Most have cut their print circulation either by narrowing geographical reach,[1] distributing the paper only a few days a week,[2] or moving to an online-only model. Almost all surviving newspapers have made severe cuts to reporting staff. These cuts have diminished the quantity and depth of local coverage. Investigations that dig beneath the surface of police reports and press releases are costly and beyond most surviving newspapers' means. It is much more convenient, and much more common, to run low-cost pro forma stories that merely repeat the official line.

Local newspapers of the twentieth century had their own problems, but overall these problems were much less dire. When newspapers made cuts and their quality

* The author thanks Eric Berger, Gus Hurwitz, Arlen Langvardt, Laurie Thomas Lee, Paul Matzko, Ramsi Woodcock, and Elana Zeide for helpful comments at various points in the process. Thanks also to Robert Drust and Paige Ross for excellent research assistance. This work was supported by a McCollum Grant.

[1] *E.g.*, Nikki Usher, News for the Rich, White, and Blue: How Place and Power Distort American Journalism 73–74 (2021).

[2] *Id.*

suffered, it was usually because management wanted to report high profit margins to investors.[3] But revenues themselves remained quite high.[4]

Revenues were high because twentieth-century papers inhabited a technological "Goldilocks zone."[5] The high cost of printing created economies of scale – big papers with big printers incurred less cost per page, so markets naturally encouraged papers to grow their operations. Distribution costs went up over long distances, though, so it was not generally in a publication's interest to grow the audience by acquiring long-distance subscribers. Instead, the most successful operations achieved scale by saturating the local market.

Under these conditions, most local markets could only support one or two such printer/distributors – and this monopoly or duopoly on printing and distribution served as an anchor for a newspaper's entire operation. The lack of competing publisher-distributors, in turn, created opportunities to package and sell a "bundle" of sports, lifestyle, home and garden, and local and national news. The inclusion of classified ads and advertiser-friendly "soft" content in the bundle allowed newspapers to cross-subsidize the costly work of investigative reporting.

The internet has destroyed the Goldilocks zone that made this business model possible. Today the marginal cost of distribution is zero, and geographical distance is irrelevant. Economies of scale remain, but local journalism institutions are in no position to capture them. Many readers access content on an à la carte basis, typically mediated by some type of online recommendations platform, and the old bundle of "hard" and "soft" content, "local" and "national" content, is no longer marketable.

These market changes have not wiped local news out completely. Some high-quality paywalled products have enjoyed significant success. Mega-papers such as *The New York Times* or *The Guardian* can still thrive by marketing a multimedia super-bundle to far-flung subscribers. But this model only seems possible in very large urban markets, and even when it works, the need to reach out-of-town readers

3 Victor Picard, *Can Charity Save Journalism from Market Failure?*, CONVERSATION (Apr. 27, 2017), https://perma.cc/JXJ6-HEEM.

4 U.S. Census Bureau data shows that newspaper publishers earned over twice the revenue in 2002 ($46,179,000) that they did in 2020 ($22,149,000) – and that is before adjusting for inflation. Adam Gundy, *Service Annual Survey Shows Continuing Decline in Print Publishing Revenue*, U.S. CENSUS BUREAU (June 7, 2022), https://perma.cc/XF9H-3CV .Adjusted for inflation, total revenue from newspapers and periodicals in 1998 would be approximately $131,889,507 in 2022. Newspapers alone would be around $83,225,792 and periodicals about $64,990,383. Calculated using the U.S. Inflation Calculator based on the latest U.S. government CPI data. *Inflation Calculator*, US INFLATION CALCULATOR, www .usinflationcalculator.com/. Based on original numbers compiled by Douglas Galbi at Douglas Galbi, *Historic Patterns of Paying for Content*, PURPLE MOTES (June 14, 2009), https://perma.cc/PR9J-3M2P.

5 My usage varies from that of Nikki Usher, who uses the term "Goldilocks newspaper" to refer to legacy papers like the *Miami Herald* or *Des Moines Register* that were not quite local, not quite national. *See* USHER, *supra* note 1.

can create pressures for a newspaper like *The New York Times* to divert reporting resources away from New York City concerns.[6]

Other publications have found success by publishing some kind of a smaller product, such as a newsletter, behind a paywall. *The Charlotte Ledger*, for example, offers a daily Substack letter to about 2,000 subscribers for $99 per year. *Downtown Albuquerque News* offers a weekday online-only paper to 450 subscribers for $100 per year. This appears to be a sustainable business model, but one that is probably incapable of producing a volume of content that is comparable to that of a traditional paper.[7]

Some philanthropy-funded, donor-funded, and/or VC-funded outlets have emerged as well, and these often produce high-quality content. But even in large markets, these outlets are unlikely to have the bandwidth to produce the volume and variety of content found in a traditional newspaper, or to achieve the market saturation necessary to play the central role in community life that local newspapers did during most of the twentieth century.[8]

At one time, many hoped that the internet would create new opportunities for volunteers to produce free community journalism – and at some level it has. Quite a bit of social-media activity involves communications that some might consider reporting – even on the low-profile app NextDoor, users "report" (and misreport)

[6] Other publications, meanwhile, produce high-quality niche reporting for a small readership at very high subscription prices. Nic Newman, *Journalism, Media, and Technology Trends and Predictions 2022*, Reuters Inst. (Jan. 10, 2022), https://perma.cc/4VAM-U7RP. "Almost half of news leaders (47%) worry that subscription models may be pushing journalism towards super-serving richer and more educated audiences and leaving others behind. Many leaders of PSBs and others committed to open journalism are amongst those who disagree with this statement, but our own research shows that even these organisations are struggling to build connections with younger and less educated groups online." Sara Fischer, *Media Experts Sound Alarm on Rise of Paywalled Content*, Axios (Jan. 11, 2022), https://perma.cc/S7ST-2RYB.

[7] *Why DAN's Business Model Is the Future of Local News*, Downtown Albuquerque News, https://perma.cc/Z9UM-XDNH; *see also* Mark Jacob, *Subscriber-Only Newsletters Aim to Build Local News Loyalty*, Local News Initiative (Oct. 23, 2019), https://perma.cc/6RQ2-H2EQ. *Chicago Tribune*'s newsroom began offering two subscriber-only newsletters: *The Spin*, a political newsletter, and *10 Thoughts*, a Bears newsletter. According to Christine Taylor, the Managing Editor for Audience, subscriber-only newsletters create a benefit in "convenience and reader experience, putting content where readers are already spending time – their inbox." *Id.* *10 Thoughts* acquired over 1,000 new subscribers in the first week, and has attained an open rate of over 100 percent, meaning that people are opening the newsletter and coming back to it multiple times to actually finish it.

[8] *The Daily Memphian* may be an exception to this trend, as it offers a high-quality full-service newspaper for around $10 per month. But "The Memphian's unorthodox and opaque fundraising strategy has been controversial among many, both in the bubbling new news landscape and in Memphis. Transparency in funding has become a mantra in the nonprofit news movement, and there the Memphian is lacking. 'Give or take, the original $6.7 million was all raised anonymously, which caused some consternation with journalists and INN [Institute for Nonprofit News],' says [Memphian CEO Eric] Barnes." Ken Doctor, *Newsonomics: In Memphis' Unexpected News War, The Daily Memphian's Model Demands Attention*, NiemanLab (Feb. 20, 2020), https://perma.cc/DFR2-ZESV.

suspicious activity on their block. But volunteer reporting, typically uncoordinated, has obvious limits as a substitute for an industry that employs full-time professional reporters.[9] Indeed, the low-quality information that amateurs and saboteurs circulate on social media and in similar settings only intensifies the public need for professional journalists to play a corrective role.

This is all to say that there is little reason to expect the private sector to produce any reliable, widely reproduceable model to recover what has been lost – or that it is unlikely, at least, that any such model will emerge on an acceptable timescale.[10] If commerce, philanthropy, and volunteerism will not sustain high-quality, wide-circulation local journalism, then the only viable models for journalism will have to depend for financial support on the government.

19.2 PUBLIC MEDIA AND SUBSIDIZED PRIVATE MEDIA

Almost all wealthy democracies give substantial financial support to news media. But in the United States, there is a widespread and deep-seated fear among American policymakers and journalists themselves that government actors will inevitably capture and exploit media organizations that depend on public support. This fear explains – or at least provides a rationalization for – America's uniquely stingy approach to its news media. According to research conducted by Timothy Neff and Victor Pickard, the United States spends just $3.16 per person on its public media, while Germany spends $142.42 on public media per person, Norway $110.73, and the UK $81.30.[11]

America's concern about state capture is probably somewhat excessive – the sky has not fallen in Iceland, where per-capita state expenditures on media outstrip those in the United States by a factor of about 13 to 1. Yet state capture is not an

9 *See, e.g.*, *The Future of Journalism: Hearing before the S. Comm. on Com., Sci., and Transp.*, 111th Cong., 1st sess. 28, 32–33 (2009) (statement of David Simon, former reporter, *The Baltimore Sun* and Blown Deadline Productions) (quoted in VICTOR PICKARD, DEMOCRACY WITHOUT JOURNALISM?: CONFRONTING THE MISINFORMATION SOCIETY 41 (2019)) ("[T]o read the claims that some new media voices are already making, you would think they need only bulldoze the carcasses of moribund newspapers aside and begin typing. They do not know what they do not know – which is a dangerous state for any class of folk – and to those of us who do understand how subtle and complex good reporting can be, their ignorance is as embarrassing as it is seemingly sincere. Indeed, the very phrase citizen journalist strikes my ear as nearly Orwellian. A neighbor who is a good listener and cares about people is a good neighbor; he is not in any sense a citizen social worker. Just as a neighbor with a garden hose and good intentions is not a citizen firefighter. To say so is a heedless insult to trained social workers and firefighters.").

10 *See* PICKARD, *supra* note 9, at 61 ("'[A]s news media institutions continue to search desperately for new commercial models, one central fact usually remains unsaid: There is precious little evidence to suggest that market-based initiatives and new media technologies can effectively replace everything being lost with the downfall of traditional news outlets.'"). *See more generally id.* at 70–89 for a discussion of the "New US Media Landscape."

11 *Id.* at 9.

entirely unrealistic concern either – state institutions in flawed democracies around the world have used subsidies to influence news coverage, and America's increasingly troubled political system is nothing if not "flawed." The question, then, is how to structure a subsidy for local journalism that mitigates the state-capture concern as well as is reasonably achievable.

There are, broadly, two ways for the public sector to support journalism financially. The United States practices both methods in modest ways, but at nowhere near the levels that most wealthy democracies do.

19.2.1 *Public Options*

The first approach would provide a journalistic "public option" that operated alongside any number of private media companies. The UK's British Broadcasting Company offers a famous and highly successful example of this approach. The United States has its own public options – the Corporation for Public Broadcasting, Radio Free Europe/Asia, Stars and Stripes, and so on – but at a much smaller scale. In principle, the United States could dramatically expand these offerings at all levels, including local levels, until they compensated for the collapse of the commercial market for journalism.

There is no reason to worry, under existing First Amendment doctrine, that an expanded public media system would run into serious constitutional trouble.[12] But the politics look almost prohibitive. Since its inception, Republican leaders have called to defund the CPB, and at various points they have come close. At one time, PBS and NPR relied on direct federal funding as a primary revenue source; today, federal funding accounts for only about 15 percent of PBS's budget and 2 percent at NPR.[13] Republicans have historically lambasted NPR and PBS for alleged "liberal bias," and the "bias" against the GOP has only grown stronger during the Trump years and beyond as party leaders have embraced flagrant lies about the 2020 election

[12] Arkansas Educ. Television Comm'n v. Forbes, 523 U.S. 666, 675 (1998) ("Although public broadcasting as a general matter does not lend itself to scrutiny under the forum doctrine, candidate debates present the narrow exception to the rule."). Under *Forbes*, candidate debates conducted on public television must remain open on a viewpoint-neutral basis. Otherwise, the Court indicated that the First Amendment does not – in the absence of some legislative design to "regiment" broadcasters another way – impose any free-standing requirement of content- or viewpoint-neutrality on public broadcasters.

[13] Amy Bingham, *Mitt Romney Cannot Roast Big Bird with PBS Cuts*, ABC News (Oct. 4. 2012), https://perma.cc/EX8P-AZDF (stating that "[a]bout 15 percent of PBS's budget comes from federal funds."). *See also* Suevon Lee, *Big Bird Debate: How Much Does Federal Funding Matter to Public Broadcasting?*, ProPublica (Oct. 11, 2012), https://perma.cc/E4MS-GPH7 (explaining that the Corporation for Public Broadcasting (CPB) created by Congress in 1967 to disperse funds to nonprofit broadcast outlets like PBS and NPR was set to receive $445 million from 2012–2014. "PBS draws roughly 15 percent of its revenue from the CPB. NPR's revenue mostly comes from member station dues and fees, with 2 percent coming from CPB-issued grants.").

and other crucial matters. Short of a realignment in American politics, it is hard to see how a serious expansion of domestic public media could make its way into law.

19.2.2 *Broad-Based Subsidies*

An alternative to a public media option would involve direct subsidies for private media institutions. Almost since its founding, the U.S. Postal Service has subsidized newspapers and magazines, albeit indirectly, with free or reduced-rate ("second-class") postage. Today, several media organizations have registered with the IRS as tax-exempt charitable organizations. And as discussed in Laurie Thomas Lee's chapter in this volume, private local broadcasters receive an effective subsidy from cable carriers in the form of carriage fees that are required under law.[14]

These kinds of policies have never attracted the same kind of political attacks as public broadcasting. One can speculate why. Perhaps public broadcasting makes an easier target simply because PBS, NPR, and the Corporation for Public Broadcasting are high-visibility brands, while second-class postage and Section 501 (c) of the tax code are not. Maybe public broadcasting's Great Society roots trigger a vindictive reflex in Republicans, and none of the media-subsidy programs have a similarly partisan pedigree.

Or perhaps the reason that media subsidies do not draw significant fire is that so many of their would-be critics – small-government think-tanks, conservative print media, local broadcasters – are themselves beneficiaries of the subsidy. Such institutions may argue from time to time that some other organization should be either included or excluded in the subsidy.[15] But few organizations are likely to argue that "their" subsidy should be cancelled across the board.

[14] Laurie Thomas Lee, *How Local TV News Is Surviving Disruption as Newspapers Fail: Lessons Learned*, 3 J. FREE SPEECH L. 241, 251 (2023).

[15] *See* Alan Rappeport, *In Targeting Political Groups, I.R.S. Crossed Party Lines*, N.Y. TIMES (Oct. 5, 2017) (explaining the results of the I.R.S. targeting controversy investigation: "The exhaustive report, which examined nine years' worth of applications for tax-exempt status, comes after a similar audit in 2013 found that groups with conservative names like 'Tea Party,' 'patriot,' or '9/12' were unfairly targeted for further review.... The new report found that the I.R.S. was also inappropriately targeting progressive-leaning groups. While the investigation does not specify the political affiliations of the groups, the names that were flagged included the words 'progressive,' 'occupy,' 'green energy,' and Acorn.... Organizations that were flagged by the I.R.S. as potentially political had to undergo intensive requests for information about any legislative activities."). *See also* Emily Cochrane, *Justice Department Settles with Tea Party Groups after I.R.S. Scrutiny*, N.Y. TIMES (Oct. 26, 2017) ("While the I.R.S. acknowledged wrongly targeting groups based on political leanings, a report this month found that behavior crossed party lines."). *See also* Bob Jones Univ. v. United States, 461 U.S. 574 (1983) (holding that the Religion Clauses of the First Amendment did not prohibit the Internal Revenue Service from revoking the tax-exempt status of a religious university whose practices are contrary to a compelling government public policy, such as eradicating racial discrimination).

Despite disputes there is no apparent desire anywhere on the political spectrum to eliminate nonprofit status altogether, and one naturally suspects that this has something to do with the

These observations suggest that a broad-based, boring, and ideally bipartisan subsidy for local news could hold up well politically. A broad-based subsidy would mollify its own would-be critics; a boring subsidy would be hard to campaign against; and a bipartisan subsidy, if possible, would be harder to attack as the other party's dastardly deed.

19.3 CONCERNS ABOUT CONSTITUTIONALITY AND STATE CAPTURE

Even assuming that a broad-based subsidy is politically achievable, however, it is also likely to draw a constitutional challenge. Such a challenge would almost certainly center on the program's eligibility criteria and the compatibility of these criteria with the First Amendment.

A completely neutral subsidy available to any media organization that wants it is not desirable. However broadly the subsidy might be drawn, it will have to exclude at least some media institutions to achieve its goals. A subsidy for local news, for example, would probably exclude media institutions that do not report news at all, or that consist entirely or primarily of commentary on national developments. Beyond this basic criterion, one can also expect that the subsidy would require beneficiaries to meet some minimum threshold of quality and human decency.

All these requirements would favor some kinds of speech over others. This favoritism could pose a serious problem if courts apply the "public-forum" doctrine – an uneven but often severe set of First Amendment rules for public programs that underwrite private speech. But it is also conceivable that courts would view a local-news subsidy as *the government's own speech* rather than as a form of regulation and, on that basis, exempt the program from any kind of First Amendment scrutiny at all. The stark difference between these two doctrinal worlds – government speech versus public forum – makes it very important to determine which one of them we are in. And if it is impossible to answer this question conclusively up front, then we should determine how likely it is that a court would apply public-forum principles to the kind of broad-based subsidy we have in mind. If it seems likely that courts would apply the public-forum doctrine to the subsidy, then the subsidy's designers would have to tread lightly to avoid invalidation.

19.3.1 *Subsidies as a Public Forum*

The discussion in *Rosenberger v. Rector and Visitors of the University of Virginia*,[16] a seminal public-forum holding, illustrates why a subsidy would likely be construed as a public forum. In that case, the University of Pennsylvania maintained a fund to

fact that American politicians depend on 501Ic(3) organizations and 501(c)(3) organizations depend on 501(c)(3) status.

16 Rosenberger v. Rector & Visitors of the Univ. of Va., 515 U.S. 819 (1995).

cover printing costs for publications by student groups. Under the policy, these publications could cover "student news, information, opinion, entertainment, or academic communications media groups."[17] The policy nevertheless excluded "religious activities," which in relation to the printing fund meant any publication that "primarily promotes or manifests a particular belie[f] in or about a deity or an ultimate reality."[18]

The Supreme Court held that the exclusion for "religious activities" violated the First Amendment. "[V]iewpoint-based restrictions are [not] proper," it explained, "when the University does not itself speak or subsidize transmittal of a message it favors but instead expends funds to encourage a diversity of views from private speakers."[19] For the Court, it was untenable to frame the University's printing fund as a government speech when the University itself had "declared that the student groups eligible for SAF support are not the University's agents, are not subject to its control, and are not its responsibility. Having offered to pay the third-party contractors on behalf of private speakers who convey their own messages, the University may not silence the expression of selected viewpoints."[20]

Now consider a hypothetical subsidy program to shore up local media around the country. The parallels to *Rosenberger* seem unavoidable. Like the university fund, our subsidy for local news organizations would subsidize private speech with government funds. And to preserve the credibility of news organizations that took the subsidy, the subsidy's enabling law would almost certainly include some express public assurance – much like the University's in *Rosenberger – that* the subsidy's recipients were "not [government] agents, not subject to its control, and not its responsibility."[21] Such assurances are routine when the government underwrites media, and it is hard to see why a subsidy for local news would not work the same way.[22] Indeed, the norm is so accepted that a court might read some protection for

[17] *Id.* at 824.

[18] *Id.* at 825.

[19] *Id.* at 834.

[20] *Id.*

[21] Turner v. U.S. Agency for Glob. Media, 502 F. Supp. 3d 333, 342 (D.D.C. 2020), *appeal dismissed*, No. 20-5374, 2021 WL 2201669 (D.C. Cir. May 17, 2021). Central to the success of this critical foreign policy work, however, is the premise that, in contrast to the state-run propaganda that dominates media in the countries where VOA and its sister networks broadcast, U.S.-funded international broadcasting outlets combat disinformation and deception with facts, told through an American lens of democratic values. Thus, "to transform" these outlets "into house organs for the United States Government" would be "inimical to [their] fundamental mission." Ralis v. RFE/RL, Inc., 770 F.2d 1121, 1125 (D.C. Cir. 1985). Instead, to provide a model of democratic debate and deliberation informed by the contributions of a free press, VOA and its sister networks must "present the policies of the United States clearly and effectively," alongside "responsible discussions and opinion on these policies." 22 U.S.C. § 6202(c)(3); *see also id.* § 6202(b)(3).

[22] Past practice shows that Congress recognizes the relationship between editorial independence and journalistic credibility. The U.S. Agency for Global Media, for example, is a fully public organization housed within the State Department; it runs Voice of America, Radio Free

editorial independence into a statute that did not provide for it expressly.[23] In any event, a broad subsidy with protections for editorial protection would be hard to characterize as government speech, and easy to characterize as a public forum.

19.3.2 *Avoiding "Viewpoint Discrimination"*

If our subsidy is indeed a public forum, then it must be held out on broadly equal terms. The details are complex, but suffice it to say that viewpoint discrimination in such a "forum" is broadly prohibited. Discrimination on the basis of *subject matter*, meanwhile, is often upheld "where a government 'reserv[es a forum] for certain groups or for the discussion of certain topics,'"[24] so long as the subject-matter rules are reasonable and viewpoint-neutral.[25]

In practice, however, the allowance for viewpoint-neutral subject-matter restrictions does not go as far as one might expect. This is because courts throw the phrase "viewpoint" around rather liberally, and in a way that sometimes covers classifications that read more intuitively as having to do with topic or subject matter. In *Rosenberger*, for instance, the category of "religious publications" included publications that either represented or opposed any religion; this, for the Court, was a viewpoint-based category in spite of its seeming even-handedness.[26] In other

Europe, Radio Free Asia, the Office of Cuba Broadcasting, and the Middle East Broadcasting Networks. Congress has every right under the Constitution to make these platforms into state mouthpieces. Instead, these organizations operate under a longstanding "statutory firewall" that requires the agency director to maintain "respect [for] the professional independence and integrity of the [Broadcasting Board of Governors], its broadcasting services, and the grantees of the Board," § 6204(b). An early court decision involving the firewall policy noted that in Congress, "to transform [Radio Free Europe] from independent broadcasters into house organs for the United States Government was seen as inimical to [their] fundamental mission." *Ralis*, 770 F.2d at 1125.

23 In Legal Servs. Corp. v. Velazquez, 531 U.S. 533 (2001), the Supreme Court struck down a statutory limitation on funds for litigation challenging public welfare restrictions. In doing so, the Court distinguished Rust v. Sullivan, 500 U.S. 173 (1991), in which it had upheld, as government speech, the Hyde Amendment's restriction on the use of federal funds to underwrite abortion counseling by physicians. The Court's rationale here was that litigation against the government was so inherently adversarial to the government that it could not plausibly be characterized as speech by the public: to do so would "distort[] the legal system by altering the traditional role of the attorneys." Legal Servs. Corp., 531 U.S. at 544. The press, with its own tradition of adversariness, might suffer a similar "distortion" if by taking funds it became a "government speaker."

24 Walker v. Texas Div., Sons of Confederate Veterans, Inc., 576 U.S. 200, 201 (2015) (quoting Rosenberger, *supra* note 16 at 829 (1995)).

25 *See* Barrett v. Walker Cnty. Sch. Dist., 872 F.3d 1209, 1225 (11th Cir. 2017) ("content-based discrimination … is permitted in a limited public forum if it is viewpoint neutral and reasonable in light of the forum's purpose").

26 515 U.S. 819, 831–32 (1995) ("It is as objectionable to exclude both a theistic and an atheistic perspective on the debate as it is to exclude one, the other, or yet another political, economic, or social viewpoint. The [notion] that debate is not skewed so long as multiple voices are silenced is simply wrong; the debate is skewed in multiple ways.").

cases, the Court has treated pharmaceutical-marketing regulations as viewpoint-discriminatory if they treated generic drugs more favorably than the name brand.[27] And in a number of cases, the Court has treated general bans on racial or ethnic disparagement, no matter whose group is disparaged, as bans on a viewpoint rather than as bans on a general topic or theme.[28] Offensiveness itself is considered a viewpoint.[29]

Some of the Court's more activist Justices have blurred the nature of the viewpoint-discrimination rule even further by invoking it to strike down "controversial" speech regulations that offend the "viewpoint" of one of the regulated parties. Unions are "controversial," for example, so for Justice Alito, it is viewpoint discrimination to pay for collective bargaining from mandatory union fees.[30] Abortion is "controversial," so for Justice Thomas, it is viewpoint discrimination to require crisis pregnancy centers to disclose true information about the availability of family-planning services in the area.[31] Note that neither the paycheck deduction nor the disclosure requirement actually regulated advocacy or opinion on unions, abortion, or any other "controversial" subject.

I do not mean to suggest that the Court should give the government a pass on genuine viewpoint discrimination when it subsidizes speech. The Court is right – obviously right – that viewpoint discrimination qualifies as a "particularly egregious" form of content discrimination. In the context of media subsidies, viewpoint discrimination marks the line between public media and state propaganda.

What I *do* mean to point out, though, is that the First Amendment bar against viewpoint discrimination is susceptible to overextension and abuse by courts. This oversensitivity to "viewpoint" concerns could make it very difficult for subsidy designers and administrators to run a competent program.

To illustrate this problem, suppose that the local news subsidy is available only to organizations that spend some given amount of time or space *covering local news.* This seemingly modest requirement could create a lot of trouble.

19.3.2.1 Localism

Suppose that to receive the subsidy, a local newspaper must show that at least one-third of the stories it runs deal with people who reside or events that occur within a 100-mile radius. Such a rule – the "local" half of a "local news" requirement – would undoubtedly have to do in some sense with the "content" of subsidized papers. But on its own, this localism requirement would be hard to strike down as any kind of "viewpoint" restriction.

27 Sorrell v. IMS Health Inc., 564 U.S. 552 (2011).
28 R.A.V. v. St. Paul, 505 U.S. 377 (1992); Matal v. Tam, 137 S. Ct. 1744 (2017).
29 Iancu v. Brunetti, 139 S. Ct. 2294 (2019).
30 Janus v. Am. Fed'n of State, Cnty. & Mun. Emps., 138 S. Ct. 2448 (2018).
31 Nat'l Inst. of Fam. & Life Advocs. v. Becerra, 138 S. Ct. 2361 (2018).

A recent case involving an Austin, Texas, signage ordinance deals with a similar issue. The law there put a restriction on the use of digital signs: Owners could use them to display messages about "on-premises" concerns (e.g., "eat here" at a restaurant on the premises) but not "off-premises" concerns (e.g., "Biden/Harris 2020"). The Supreme Court upheld it as a content-neutral time-place-manner regulation because it did not "single out any topic or subject matter for differential treatment."[32]

I grant that the analogy between the Austin signage law and a national media subsidy is somewhat unsatisfying. The expressive stakes in the Austin case were low, after all, and removed from the media context. But the Austin case is not the first time that the Court has upheld a locality preference as content-neutral. It has also upheld a requirement that cable-service providers, notwithstanding their "editorial discretion" under the First Amendment, can be required to carry local television stations as part of a basic cable package.[33] This, for the Court, was also a content-neutral requirement.

Again, there are significant contextual differences between the "editorial discretion" exercised by a newspaper as opposed to a cable-service provider. But very broadly, both cases suggest a somewhat relaxed attitude on the Court toward localism requirements. If the Court was unwilling in these cases to scrutinize locality restrictions as even being *content*-based, then there is some reason to hope that a locality criterion in the context of a news subsidy would not be considered *viewpoint*-based.

19.3.2.2 Quality and Professionalism

So far, so good. But realistically, the "local news" concept would incorporate a number of cross-cutting content lines beyond localism. The subsidy might reasonably be limited to reporting on matters of public importance rather than trivial personal matters or neighborhood gossip. There may be some threshold for journalistic quality, or a mechanism to ensure that "hard news" and investigative reporting get the bulk of the subsidy. Chronic defamers or conspiracy spreaders might be disqualified somehow. And so on.

At least some of these lines could become proxies for viewpoint discrimination or state capture. A "journalistic quality" criterion will raise some particularly delicate issues; even if it is defined in a relatively objective way and administered with safeguards against corruption, journalistic quality will correlate at some level with viewpoint. In some situations, such a "journalistic quality" criterion will correlate even *more* strongly with partisan viewpoint if it is administered well.

32 City of Austin v. Reagan Nat'l Advert. of Austin, LLC, 142 S. Ct. 1464, 1472 (2022).

33 Turner Broad. Sys., Inc. v. FCC (*Turner I*), 512 U.S. 622 (1994); Turner Broad. Sys., Inc. v. FCC (*Turner II*), 520 U.S. 180 (1997).

Correlation, of course, is not causation or motivation, and under basic doctrinal principles, the First Amendment does not bar policies that have a disparate ideological impact so long as they are neutral by design.[34] But the distinction between a neutral requirement and a discriminatory one can be more slippery than one might think.

Journalistic ethics codes, for example, routinely require objectivity in reporting, a wall between reporting and commentary, and fair and respectful treatment of subjects and sources. But even standards designed to promote objectivity and neutrality embody something that could reasonably be called a viewpoint: namely, the "viewpoint from above" that is the hallmark of professionalized mainstream journalism.

At a policy level, one might question how serious a concern this particular kind of viewpoint discrimination really is, and what measures if any might be taken to mitigate or offset it. But under First Amendment law, any subsidy that is conditioned on journalistic professionalism will be vulnerable to challenges based on the formalistic and somewhat obtuse position that the AP reports the news from one viewpoint and Breitbart reports the news from another.

The upshot here is that if the government (1) offers subsidies on a broad basis to journalistic institutions and (2) includes protections for editorial independence, then courts are likely to treat that program as a public forum.[35] If the subsidy is a public forum, then it must be defined and administered in a viewpoint-neutral manner. Institutions excluded from the subsidy will therefore bring constitutional challenges that attack various boundary-setting features of the subsidy as being viewpoint-based. And given how broadly and sometimes capriciously the concept of "viewpoint" has been interpreted in the past, it may be very difficult to draft content requirements that are entirely safe from invalidation.

19.3.3 *Government Speech?*

Recall, however, that there are *two* conceivable ways to frame a media-subsidy program under the First Amendment: as a public forum or as government speech. So far, I have focused on the public-forum framing because, for reasons I have already discussed, it fits a lot better. But the government-speech framing is also worth discussing – not because it fits the policy particularly well, but because it presents such a tempting shortcut around the meddlesome public-forum doctrine.

34 "A regulation that serves purposes unrelated to the content of expression is deemed neutral, even if it has an incidental effect on some speakers or messages but not others." Ward v. Rock Against Racism, 491 U.S. 781, 791 (1989).

35 More specifically, courts would probably regard this kind of program as a "limited public forum." In a "limited public forum," the government is free to set rules that discriminate on the basis of *content*, so long as those rules are viewpoint-neutral, they relate reasonably to the purpose of the forum, and they are defined up front and enforced consistently.

The government-speech doctrine rests on the principle that government must be free to project *its own* viewpoint, and to exclude others', when it communicates with the public. That implies that when the government enlists private speakers as mouthpieces for the government, the government is not opening any kind of public forum. The government may impose whatever kind of messaging restrictions it pleases on these speakers without triggering any kind of First Amendment scrutiny.

To expand on this theme, one might say that if the government wishes to use its "voice" via media subsidies to strengthen democracy and public knowledge through a strong, independent, and pluralistic press, then it should not also have to underwrite propaganda outlets that lie to the public and undermine democracy.[36] The government-speech concept, at first impression, captures this idea in an appealing way. As Justice Alito has memorably observed, the United States did not, by accepting the Statue of Liberty from France, assume a duty to accept "other statues of a similar size and nature (e.g., a Statue of Autocracy, if one had been offered by, say, the German Empire or Imperial Russia)."[37]

The catch, of course, is that the government-speech doctrine cuts both ways. The government can always accept the Statue of Autocracy and reject the Statue of Liberty. And applied to a media subsidy, the government-speech framing would empower the government to structure the subsidy in abusive and anti-democratic ways without any meaningful judicial oversight.

Between the highly restrictive public-forum doctrine and the completely ambivalent government-speech doctrine, the Court has thus put forward an all-or-nothing model for analyzing governmental speech supports under the First Amendment. And as noted above, I think the Court would be far more likely to put a broad-based, even-handed local media subsidy into the "public forum" box than the "government speech" box.[38] But note that in holding out these two alternatives, the Court signals perverse incentives to Congress. If Congress designs up a subsidy that encourages a "diversity of views"[39] and includes protections for editorial autonomy, then its program will become a litigation magnet under the public-forum doctrine; if Congress strips out the editorial protections and encourages newspapers to toe the government's line, then the program might be upheld as government speech. Or at least that is how the existing case law makes it look.

National Endowment for the Arts v. Finley[40] illustrates, in a lower-stakes context, the kinds of political and legal difficulties that legislators, administrators, and courts may someday face when considering a national subsidy for local news. The National Endowment for the Arts awards grants to artists and arts organizations based on a

36 *See* Adam Shinar, *Democratic Backsliding, Subsidized Speech, and the New Majoritarian Entrenchment*, 69 Am. J. Comp. L. 335 (2021).

37 Pleasant Grove City, Utah v. Summum, 555 U.S. 460, 479 (2009).

38 *See supra* notes 16–23 and accompanying text.

39 Rosenberger, *supra* note 16.

40 Nat'l Endowment for the Arts v. Finley, 524 U.S. 569 (1998).

standard of "artistic excellence and artistic merit." In the early 1990s, the NEA sustained heavy criticism for funding works that were in one way or another created to shock mainstream sensibilities. The most controversial among these works involved religious desecration, nudity, or explicit depictions of sex.[41] Congress responded to the controversy by amending the NEA's statutory guidelines to require the NEA to "take into consideration ... general standards of decency and respect for the diverse beliefs and values of the American public."[42]

The NEA was set up to be administered apolitically. But by requiring the NEA to consider "decency and respect," Congress obviously wanted the NEA to consider whether an artist's work offended mainstream sensibilities. And "giving offense," as the Court has noted more recently, "is a viewpoint."[43] This viewpoint discrimination is not a problem if the NEA's subsidy is seen as government speech; but it is a big problem if NEA funding is considered a public forum.

Finley presented Congress with a problem similar in some respects to the one the government might face if it was trying to exclude fringe publications – neo-Nazis, jihadists, QAnoners – from a media-subsidy program. Any viable, politically sustainable program has an interest in not getting caught funding flamboyantly offensive projects. Yet preventing offense is exactly what the First Amendment forbids the government to do when it sets up a public forum. Read simply, the public-forum doctrine would seem to force the government to choose between an unconstitutional policy and a politically vulnerable one.[44]

Justice O'Connor, writing for a six-Justice majority in *Finley*, found a way to finesse the issue: She and the majority upheld the program based primarily on the fact that the "decency" criterion was merely one factor to be considered as part of a competitive grantmaking process rather than a binding requirement for funding. Even assuming the NEA was a public forum, the new statutory guidelines were

41 *Id.* at 574–75.

42 20 U.S.C. § 954(d)(1). *See also* 20 U.S.C. §954(d)(2) (NEA "regulations and procedures shall clearly indicate that obscenity is without artistic merit, is not protected speech, and shall not be funded").

43 Matal v. Tam, 582 U.S. 218, 243 (2017).

44 *See* Ark. Educ. Television Comm'n v. Forbes, 523 U.S. 666, 681–82 (1998):

> Were it faced with the prospect of cacophony, on the one hand, and First Amendment liability, on the other, a public television broadcaster might choose not to air candidates' views at all. A broadcaster might decide "'the safe course is to avoid controversy,' ... and by so doing diminish the free flow of information and ideas." Turner Broadcasting System, Inc., 512 U.S., at 656 (quoting Miami Herald Publishing Co. v. Tornillo, 418 U.S. 241, 257 (1974)). In this circumstance, a "[g]overnment-enforced right of access inescapably 'dampens the vigor and limits the variety of public debate.'" *Id.* (quoting New York Times Co. v. Sullivan, 376 U.S. 254, 279 (1964)).
>
> These concerns are more than speculative. As a direct result of the Court of Appeals' decision in this case, the Nebraska Educational Television Network canceled a scheduled debate between candidates in Nebraska's 1996 United States Senate race. LINCOLN JOURNAL STAR, Aug. 24, 1996, p. 1A, col. 6. A First Amendment jurisprudence yielding these results does not promote speech but represses it.

simply too ineffectual for the Court to "perceive a realistic danger that [they would] compromise First Amendment values."[45]

Yet this "merely a factor for consideration" reasoning ultimately dodges the issue, as Justice Souter argued in a lone dissent: "What if the statute required a panel to apply criteria 'taking into consideration the centrality of Christianity to the American cultural experience,' or 'taking into consideration whether the artist is a communist,' or 'taking into consideration the political message conveyed by the art,' or even 'taking into consideration the superiority of the white race'?" he asked.[46] In any of these situations, it would be impossible to disregard the censorial implications.

Justice Souter's point here is surely correct. Yet Justice O'Connor's small concession to political reality may well have done more to preserve the arts as a going concern in American life. Even so, it is hard to read Justice O'Connor's opinion as anything but a punt – a way to give Congress a pass in *this* case while still preserving the option, under public-forum doctrine, to invalidate some other more troubling restriction on arts funding in a later case.

Justice Scalia, concurring in the judgment, would have cut the Gordian knot by calling the whole NEA a form of government speech and unshackling the government to set the message however it wants.[47] But in a country where arts organizations typically rely on NEA funds to cover about a third of their budget, the "government-speech" approach would allow the government to play a disturbingly authoritarian role in the arts world. It would leave the government free, for example, to withdraw sustaining support from community theaters whose programming is critical of the president's party. In recent years, the leaders of countries experiencing "democratic backsliding" have exploited subsidies for arts, science, and journalism in just this way.[48]

19.4 LIMITED OPTIONS

In sum, the First Amendment as currently interpreted seems to allow three broad strategies to support local media:

1. Congress may create its own media institutions and then provide them the financial resources to run local affiliates around the country. These institutions may be in the mold of the Agency for Global Media, which is housed within the State Department, or it may be a publicly funded nonprofit corporation like the Corporation for Public Broadcasting. The Supreme Court has held that government may do this without inadvertently opening a public forum. That means that Congress should have

[45] *Finley*, 524 U.S. at 583.
[46] *Id.* at 610 (Souter, J., dissenting).
[47] *Id.* at 590 (Scalia, J., concurring).
[48] Shinar, *supra* note 36, at 341 (discussing the phenomenon in Israel, Poland, and Hungary).

the ability to require the new media institution to observe norms of professionalism, objectivity, and balance, and to create institutional firewalls to protect for editorial independence.

2. Congress may give subsidies to existing private media institutions and guarantee these institutions' editorial independence in much the same way that it guarantees editorial independence at the Corporation for Public Broadcasting and the Agency for Global Media. But in guaranteeing that it will not withdraw the subsidy based on editorial decisions, Congress is very likely to become committed to a full "viewpoint-neutrality" requirement under the public-forum doctrine. This viewpoint-neutrality requirement will make it very difficult for Congress to set minimum standards for journalistic quality.
3. Congress might give subsidies to existing private media institutions as in strategy 2 while also clarifying somehow that these media institutions now speak on behalf of the government and that the government has control over the message. This strategy would allow the government to avail itself of the "government speech" doctrine, which means that the government could safely deny the subsidy to low-quality outlets. The problem, obviously, is that this kind of incursion onto the independence of the press would largely defeat the purpose of having a press at all.

Among these options, the first one – a massive expansion of public media – is in most respects the best. There is American precedent for this model in a dramatically smaller form. PBS and NPR enjoy broad public support despite their perennial funding battles, and their journalistic operations are widely respected.

This model is relatively uncomplicated from a legal perspective as well. Insofar as the courts have applied the First Amendment to public broadcasting, they have generally done so in a way that supports editorial independence at these institutions. Courts have not, so far, given any reason to fear that First Amendment litigation will undermine or interfere with these programs' operations. For all these reasons, a public media expansion would be an attractive and straightforward way to provide economic support for local journalism.

The one real shortcoming of this approach – other than the longstanding political opposition to public media – is that on its own, it would not support private news institutions that may already be established in a community. If struggling private news institutions are forced to compete with better-funded public options, then a public media expansion seems certain to accelerate their decline. Even with strong public media, the loss of these private institutions would badly diminish the plurality and resiliency of the overall media landscape in ways that may be hard to foresee.[49]

[49] *See* Brian Asher Rosenwald, Mount Rushmore: The Rise of Talk Radio and Its Impact on Politics and Public Policy (2015) (PhD dissertation) (on file with the University of Virginia Library), https://perma.cc/C9KT-28VH (arguing that subsidized NPR affiliates' hold over

Therefore, some kind of subsidy for nonpublic media institutions is probably desirable in any event, either as a standalone program or as a supplement to a public media expansion.

19.5 DESIGNING A SUBSIDY

The question, then, is how to design this kind of program in a manner that is least likely to fall under constitutional challenge. As I have discussed, it is likely that courts would construe a broad media-subsidy program as a public forum for First Amendment purposes. In principle, this would allow the government to set some viewpoint-neutral rules for the kind of content the program will support, and at what level. But in practice, it can be hard to predict where the line lies between content classifications and viewpoint classifications. This uncertainty introduces a degree of litigation risk into any element of a subsidy that turns on content. Program designers will be well-advised to avoid content classifications to the greatest extent practicable.

Some degree of content classification is probably unavoidable and relatively safe. A program designed to promote local journalism can probably get away with requiring local coverage.[50] But it is less certain whether content classifications designed to ensure that funds go to legitimate institutions would survive review.

Bob McChesney has proposed to hold referenda in which voters would name a short list of news outlets in their community to receive federal funds. The few top-ranking outlets then would become eligible to take "journalism vouchers" that individual community residents allocate to the participating institution of their choice.

Vouchers are promising. The Supreme Court has upheld school tuition-voucher programs over objections that these vouchers gave an unconstitutional benefit to religious schools. Direct, preferential grants by government to parochial schools might have violated the First Amendment's Establishment Clause. But if the government left the final choice with individuals who overwhelmingly awarded their vouchers to parochial institutions, then the government's hands were clean.[51] A similar line of reasoning could inoculate a journalism voucher from First Amendment-based challenges: It is not viewpoint discrimination or even content discrimination for the government to give funds to individuals who then spend them according to personal preference.

The primary difficulty with a voucher-oriented program, however, is that one still must set some conditions to determine which organizations may collect vouchers and seek public reimbursement. Otherwise, program funds could be diverted to uses

center-to-left listeners played a role in preventing left-wing talk radio from flourishing) (thanks to Paul Matzko for this tip).

[50] *See supra* notes 32–33 and accompanying text.

[51] Zelman v. Simmons-Harris, 536 U.S. 639 (2002).

that are not related to the purpose of the fund. Churches, for example, might encourage members to use their voucher to buy the church bulletin; or retailers might give incentives for customers to "subscribe" to "news" about products on sale. And for the program to have the most impact, it will probably make sense to concentrate vouchers on a small menu of publications within a community.

McChesney's proposal of a ranked referendum is likely to address these concerns without requiring government *officials* to set content criteria. But the Supreme Court has indicated fairly clearly that it would view even a popular referendum as yet another form of viewpoint discrimination. In *Board of Regents v. Southworth*, the Court warned that a campus referendum to decide funding for student groups would violate the First Amendment. "To the extent the referendum substitutes majority determinations for viewpoint neutrality it would undermine the constitutional protection the program requires.... Access to a public forum ... does not depend upon majoritarian consent."[52]

An irony here is that in the glory days of local news, the business model of a robust community newspaper really *did* depend on something like popular consent in the form of large market share, which enabled high economies of scale. It is only when majorities express themselves through a *political* process – here a direct referendum, but legislative action would count as well – that the First Amendment kicks in and concerns about majoritarian tyranny flare up.

Whether or not this dichotomy between political majoritarianism and market majoritarianism makes any sense, it is bedrock in American constitutional culture. And it may provide an opening for a public subsidy program to concentrate its funds on widely read and widely trusted community papers. Rather than asking community members to *choose* which local news outlets are worthy to receive public subsidies, the government might implement a system of content-neutral subsidies to simulate the monopolistic incentive structure that made the old local newspapers viable. The government might, for example, provide matching funds for each subscription a local publication picks up – and then sharply escalate the degree of match as the publication achieves a higher degree of saturation within a defined geographical radius.

Such a system would involve some degree of technical challenge, as well as several difficult design choices. But it would also seem to avoid the concerns about state influence and content neutrality that have traditionally underlain the American suspicion toward public news subsidies. In many ways, the incentive structure I propose would offer a spiritual successor to the postal subsidies that Congress has at various points extended to the press.

Those subsidies, too, came with content-neutral conditions that Congress adjusted over the years to achieve different structural goals. In some years, the subsidies were drawn to reward long-distance readership. In other years,

[52] Bd. of Regents of Univ. of Wisconsin Sys. v. Southworth, 529 U.S. 217, 235 (2000).

the subsidies were drawn to reward local readership. A twenty-first-century subsidy for local newspapers might be drawn to reward *popular* outlets that are capable of reaching a large segment of the community and offering a common reference point on local events.

Hopefully, many recipients of a program like this one would use their new revenues to pick up the hard, investigative reporting work that so many legacy papers have been forced to forego. But even "soft" news on culture, sports, and community events could provide real value by helping to consolidate a sense of place and local community. If nothing else, a consistent source of local news might help to displace the excess of ideologically polarizing national news that dominates most contemporary news consumers' media diets.

20

Saving the News

Ramsi A. Woodcock[*]

20.1 INTRODUCTION

It is usually a mistake to suppose that a company is the best judge of how its business works.[1] Or that an industry is the best judge of how the industry works. AT&T is a good example. When the Justice Department sat down with management in 1981 to negotiate a breakup of what was then a monopoly provider of telephone service, government lawyers asked which part of the company management wanted to keep after the breakup – the long-distance operations or the regional networks.[2] The long-distance operations had long been the company's most profitable, so management asked for those.[3]

It was a mistake. The long-distance operations had been profitable only because AT&T had owned the regional networks and could use them to deny access to competing long-distance companies seeking to complete calls.[4] Once AT&T had spun off the regional networks, the company could no longer do that.[5] Competitors

* Since submitting this chapter for publication, I have abandoned my view that charging postage for online posts would be a desirable method of promoting fact-reporting. I have come to believe, based on my observation of newspaper reporting during Israel's 2023 invasion of Gaza, that competition in the news industry can be insufficient to support such an approach, and that democracy can be preserved only through free and otherwise unfettered access to social media. I stand by the other points made in the chapter.

1 This chapter draws heavily on two working papers of mine. *See* Ramsi Woodcock, *Ruinous Competition in News, the Postal Internet, and the Three Laws of Techno-Legal Change* (2022), https://perma.cc/J643-RP4J; Ramsi Woodcock, *The Fourth's Estate* (2022), https://perma.cc/AXC6-F823.

2 *See* Richard H. K Vietor, Contrived Competition: Regulation and Deregulation in America 210–11, 223–25 (1994); Alan Stone, Wrong Number: The Breakup of AT&T 318–19, 326 (1989).

3 *See* Stone, *supra* note 2, at 318–19.

4 *See id.* at 168.

5 *See id.* at 328 (noting that as part of the breakup the regional networks were required to provide equal access to their networks to all long-distance providers).

flooded the long-distance market, driving down AT&T's profits. But the regional networks remained protected from competition thanks to the prohibitive cost of running new wires to individual homes. They flourished. Management had failed to grasp that the real source of AT&T's power was its regional-network monopolies, not its long-distance operations. Two decades later, AT&T was forced to sell itself – to one of the regional networks.[6]

If management sometimes has trouble understanding the value proposition of the single company that it runs, we can forgive newspapers for not understanding the value proposition of the entire industry that they constitute.

Over the past decade, the newspaper industry has been trying to stave off collapse brought on by the very low cost of internet communication.[7] That low cost has all but eliminated barriers to entry into both the news industry and the broader market for reader attention. That has forced newspapers to engage in ruinous competition for a shrinking share of overall public engagement.[8] In local news markets, the result has been bankruptcy as newspapers' declining share of reader attention has reduced the value of newspapers' main product – advertising distribution – to advertisers.[9] In national newspaper markets, which still attract enough attention to sustain the market, the result has been fragmentation and quality destruction. Newspapers have replaced fact-reporting with opinion-reporting to differentiate themselves in a more viewpoint saturated national conversation and cut costs.[10]

The newspaper industry's response has betrayed a lack of comprehension regarding the source of its misfortune. The industry has responded to the overall decline in its share of reader attention by calling for antitrust action against the Tech Giants – particularly Google and Facebook – which are principally responsible for the decline.[11] But Google and Facebook have prospered because social media is more engaging than newspapers, not because the Tech Giants are monopolies. Whether there is one social media company or hundreds, readers are not going to start substituting more newspaper time for the time they spend on social media. In a fit of blind egomania, the industry has also responded by trying to negotiate payments from the Tech Giants as compensation for their use of links to newspaper

6 *See* Nilay Patel, *Look at This Goddamn Chart*, VERGE (Oct. 24, 2016), https://perma.cc/F45B-BM7F; Matthew Stuart, *How AT&T Conquered All Forms of Communication after the Government Forced It to Break Up*, BUS. INSIDER (Mar. 5, 2018), https://perma.cc/U892-PLJ4.

7 *See* Fred Dews & Eric Bull, *The Decline of Newspapers, in Four Charts*, BROOKINGS (Oct. 23, 2014), https://perma.cc/76MN-BZ8L.

8 *See* Woodcock, *Ruinous Competition in News*, *supra* note 1, at 17–20; Woodcock, *The Fourth's Estate*, *supra* note 1, at 9–10.

9 *See* Dews & Bull, *supra* note 7.

10 *See* Woodcock, *Ruinous Competition in News*, *supra* note 1, at 17–20.

11 *See* Staff, *Alliance Releases New White Paper Outlining Google's Dominant Market Behavior, Harming of Journalism*, NEWS MEDIA ALLIANCE (Jun. 18, 2020), https://perma.cc/EH73-LXH2; David Chavern, *Statement: News Media Alliance Applauds House Report on Dominant Online Platforms and Market Power*, NEWS MEDIA ALLIANCE (Oct. 6, 2020), https://perma.cc/9PUC-VKC9.

articles – part of a broader project of obtaining intellectual-property protection for news articles.[12] But social media has captured the public's attention for reasons other than the opportunity it provides to share news. Accordingly, the Tech Giants are not willing to pay much for the privilege of linking, whether newspaper articles are protected by intellectual-property rights or not. They would do just fine without linking to news. Finally, the industry has experimented with a microjournalism model of subscriptions for independent journalists and niche reporting. But while microjournalism may prevent the total demise of journalism at the local level and stem losses at the national level, high-quality fact production requires scale in newsgathering that is fundamentally incompatible with such decentralization.[13]

To save newspapers, other approaches are needed. Ruinous competition may be addressed by attacking the root of the problem: the low cost of communication. Policymakers could raise the cost of communication by taxing internet post views at levels just high enough to discourage excessive entry into national news markets and thereby to enable national newspapers to maintain the scale and profitability they need to invest in the production of high-quality investigative journalism.[14] Organizations that cannot pay the tax required to reach a broad audience will be driven from the market. The resulting reduction in competition will alleviate the pressure on newspapers to differentiate themselves through opinion-reporting. It will also drive up revenues, creating both the means and the incentive for newspapers to invest more in fact-reporting. The federal government, in the form of the U.S. Postal Service, already has the tools to impose such a tax by reinterpreting its "letter-box monopoly" to include electronic letter boxes, allowing the postal service to charge postage for the receipt of electronic communications of any kind.[15]

Internet postage would solve the problem of excessive competition within the newspaper industry but not the problem of competition for reader attention from the Tech Giants that has hit local newspapers particularly hard. Internet postage should not be set so high as to discourage social media use as a general matter, but only high enough to limit the number of users having large numbers of post views.[16]

[12] Paul Matzko, *From Hot News to a Link Tax: The Dangers of a Quasi-Property Right in Information*, 3 J. Free Speech L. 269 (2023). *See also* Joshua Benton, *Facebook Got Everything It Wanted out of Australia by Being Willing to Do What the Other Guy Wouldn't*, Nieman Lab, https://perma.cc/5TZP-6A37.

[13] *See* James Hamilton, Democracy's Detectives: The Economics of Investigative Journalism 131 (2018) (noting that the cost of a single investigation can run into the hundreds of thousands of dollars).

[14] *See* Woodcock, *Ruinous Competition in News*, *supra* note 1, at 35–39. The tax might be implemented as follows. For those unwilling to pay the tax, distribution of the post would be broken off after the tax-exempt number of views is reached. Those who do view the post would be free to repost it but would themselves be subject to the tax were views of the reposted material to exceed the quota. Automated reposting to evade payment of postage could be prohibited.

[15] *See id.* at 40–46.

[16] *See id.* at 37–38.

Social media is, overall, a good thing. Taxing it out of existence would therefore destroy value.[17]

To solve the problem of Tech Giant competition, government could adopt a second policy, complementary to the policy of charging internet postage, that would channel advertising revenues back to the newspaper industry. That policy would be to cap the number of ad impressions that social media companies are permitted to sell per year.[18] Because advertising is ultimately a race to the bottom – firms are compelled to do it to counteract the advertising of competitors – advertisers would respond by shifting their advertising dollars back to newspapers, despite the inferiority of newspaper advertising, in order to keep up with each other. For the same reason, modern militaries would purchase bows and arrows if prevented from purchasing more sophisticated equipment.[19] This race-to-the-bottom characteristic of advertising would, incidentally, allow the government to place a cap on all advertising without reducing the amount of revenue generated by advertising distributors.[20] Because advertising distorts preferences and therefore leads to misallocation of resources, such a cap would improve economic efficiency – and could be piggybacked on policies targeting Tech Giant advertising.

Neither internet postage nor advertising caps would violate the First Amendment.[21] The Supreme Court long ago ruled that the U.S. Postal Service's letter-box monopoly does not violate the First Amendment because people are free to use alternative means of communication such as placing phone calls, slipping paper under front doors, or making in-person appointments.[22] And advertising caps must pass constitutional muster because, in the information age, advertising's information function is obsolete.[23] Consumers can get all the product information they want from a quick Google search, which they can also use to educate themselves about products that they do not yet know to seek out.[24] Advertising's only remaining function is to manipulate consumers into buying products that they do not prefer. But the Supreme Court has extended First Amendment protection only to advertising that enhances consumers' ability to make independent choices about which products they wish to buy.[25]

17 *See id.*

18 *See* Woodcock, *The Fourth's Estate*, *supra* note 1, at 19–29.

19 *See id.* at 26–27.

20 *See id.* at 29–33.

21 *See* Woodcock, *Ruinous Competition in News*, *supra* note 1, at 44–46; Woodcock, *The Fourth's Estate*, *supra* note 1, at 43–52.

22 *See* Postal Service v. Council of Greenburgh Civic Ass'ns, 453 U.S. 114, 129 (1981).

23 *Cf.* Citizens United v. Fed. Election Comm'n, 558 U.S. 310, 917 (2009) (rejecting caps on corporate expenditures on political, as opposed to commercial, speech); Ramsi A. Woodcock, *The Obsolescence of Advertising in the Information Age*, 127 Yale L.J. 2270, 2334–36 (2018) (explaining why the rationale for a commercial advertising ban would not extend to political advertising).

24 *See* Woodcock, *supra* note 23, at 2299–2308, 2328–36.

25 *See* Va. State Bd. of Pharmacy v. Va. Consumer Council, 425 U.S. 748, 765 (1976) (noting that "the allocation of our resources in large measure will be made through numerous private

20.2 NEWSPAPERS' CHALLENGES

Newspapers were perhaps the most successful monopolies of the twentieth century, the sort of asset with a "moat" around it that the likes of savvy investor Warren Buffet coveted.[26] Newspapers enjoyed protection from competition both because distribution costs were high – paper is costly, and heavy – and because advertisers prefer newspapers that have more readers.[27] As a result, a single newspaper serving all advertisers was able to charge lower prices than a smaller newspaper serving a fraction of the market; the larger newspaper could spread distribution costs over more customers. This newspaper could also offer broader distribution to advertisers than a newspaper serving a fraction of the market, making it more appealing to advertisers, as well.[28] Nearly, every city therefore came to have a single major newspaper and a handful of papers served the national news market.[29]

The monopoly position of newspapers created a number of positive externalities. One was independence for the press from interference by either government or corporate advertisers. Monopoly profits meant that newspapers did not require government subsidies and a monopoly position meant that advertisers strove to please newspapers, not the other way around. Another positive externality of monopoly was that newspapers enjoyed both the means and incentive to invest in expensive fact-reporting.[30] In a competitive news market, each newspaper caters to a relatively small, ideologically homogenous readership.[31] Any attempt to attract ideologically distant readers fails because those readers have access to alternative options that are better aligned with their political views.[32] In a monopoly news market, the monopolist caters to a large, ideologically diverse group of readers because readers who are ideologically distant from the monopolist have no

economic decisions. It is a matter of public interest that those decisions, in the aggregate, be intelligent and well informed. To this end, the free flow of commercial information is indispensable.").

26 *See* Buffalo Courier-Exp. v. Buffalo Evening News, 601 F. 2d 48, 50–52 (2d Cir. 1979); Michael Hiltzik, *Column: How Warren Buffett, Who Says the News Business is "Toast," Tried to Kill My First Paper*, L.A. TIMES (Jun. 4, 2019); Tae Kim, *Warren Buffett Believes This Is "the Most Important Thing" to Find in a Business*, CNBC (May 7, 2018), https://perma.cc/DZB5-ZQWS.

27 *See* DAVID S. EVANS & RICHARD SCHMALENSEE, MATCHMAKERS: THE NEW ECONOMICS OF MULTISIDED PLATFORMS 22–27, 99 (2016).

28 *See id.* at 22–27.

29 *See, e.g.*, Robert G. Picard, *The Economics of the Daily Newspaper Industry*, *in* MEDIA ECONOMICS: THEORY AND PRACTICE 109, 110 (Alison Alexander et al. eds., 2003) ("The newspaper industry in the United States is characterized by monopoly and its attendant market power, with 98% of newspapers existing as the only daily paper published within their markets. In the few cities where local competition exists, it nearly always occurs between differentiated newspapers such as a broadsheet and a tabloid intended for different audiences or between papers that target substantially different geographic markets than their competitors[.]").

30 *See* Woodcock, *Ruinous Competition in News*, *supra* note 1, at 22–24.

31 *See id.* at 15–17.

32 *See id.*

alternative newspaper to which they can turn.[33] To induce such readers to subscribe rather than forgo news entirely, a newspaper monopolist must deemphasize ideology to the greatest extent possible and invest in fact-reporting. Facts have broad appeal across ideological lines, even if each reader prefers a different spin on the facts.[34] The scoop rather than the hot take was therefore king. And, as monopolies, newspapers could afford to invest in scoops. It is no accident that the ethic of objectivity in reporting came to dominate journalism over the course of the twentieth century as newspaper monopolies arose and became more entrenched.[35] The result was a willingness to invest in high-cost investigative journalism that incidentally served democracy.[36] Finally, the monopoly position of newspapers paid a dividend in terms of social stability. There is, of course, no such thing as a neutral or objective report of the facts. Each newspaper must choose a location along the ideological spectrum. As median-voter theory has taught in the context of elections, however, the point that has the broadest appeal is the center. Newspapers therefore tended to promote viewpoints that interpolated between political extremes, exerting a moderating influence on national debates.[37] All this was true even in markets, such as national news markets, that had a small number of newspapers as opposed to a single monopolist. In those markets, the small number of competitors meant that most readers still lacked ideologically aligned news sources, creating an incentive for papers to use fact-reporting and centrism to reach them. And the small number of competitors meant that papers still earned handsome profits.

The low cost of communication created by the internet dealt a death blow to newspaper monopoly on the reader-facing side of the business and created new competitors on the advertiser-facing side, eliminating the positive externalities that had come with newspapers' privileged market position. Printing and distribution of paper editions on a daily basis requires large, up-front investments in printing presses, trucks, paper, and of course labor, making entry into paper news markets

[33] *See id.*

[34] *See id.*

[35] *See* MICHAEL SCHUDSON, DISCOVERING THE NEWS: A SOCIAL HISTORY OF AMERICAN NEWSPAPERS 121–59 (2011); Woodcock, *Ruinous Competition in News*, *supra* note 1, at 35.

[36] *See* JENNIFER KAVANAGH ET AL., RAND CORP., NEWS IN A DIGITAL AGE: COMPARING THE PRESENTATION OF NEWS INFORMATION OVER TIME AND ACROSS MEDIA PLATFORMS 119 (2019) (stating that since 2020 "news coverage has shifted away from a more traditional style characterized by complex, detailed reporting that emphasizes events, context, public figures, time, and numbers toward a more personal, subjective form of reporting that emphasizes anecdotes, argumentation, advocacy, and emotion"); HAMILTON, *supra* note 13, at 131.

[37] *See* Markus Prior, *Media and Political Polarization*, 16 ANN. REV. POL. SCI. 101, 119 (2013) ("In the 1970s, about a quarter of Americans identified strongly with a political party. Media in the broadcast era were probably too centrist for these people's tastes. Technological change has made it economically viable to cater to smaller audience segments."); Roger D. Congleton, *The Median Voter Model*, *in* THE ENCYCLOPEDIA OF PUBLIC CHOICE 382, 382 (Charles K. Rowley & Friedrich Schneider eds., 2004).

difficult.[38] With the maturation of the internet, anyone who could post news online – and that was almost everyone – could compete with *The New York Times*.[39] Low-cost communication also introduced new competition into advertising markets. It created an entire new category of media – social media – that gave advertisers a desirable alternative to advertising in newspapers, putting pressure on news industry revenues.[40]

Low-cost communication tore down barriers to entry into news markets, increasing competition for the attention that consumers devote to news. Social media made new categories of consumer attention available to advertisers by causing interactions that might once have been carried out around the dinner table or by email to be conducted on internet platforms through which they could be subjected to advertising.[41] People spend more time engaging in these interactions than they spend reading news, and the interactions themselves are more revealing than news-reading. That enabled social media companies to offer advertisers a larger audience than newspapers and to profile consumers and target advertising in ways that newspapers – even in digital form – cannot.[42] This shifted the flow of advertising dollars from newspapers to social-media giants like Google and Facebook.[43]

[38] *See* Picard, *supra* note 29, at 116.

[39] *See* Mahmud Hasan et al., *A Survey on Real-Time Event Detection from the Twitter Data Stream*, 44 J. Info. Sci. 443, 443 (2018) ("With around 310 million monthly-active Twitter users producing content from all over the world, Twitter has essentially become a host of sensors for events as they happen.").

[40] *See* Penelope Muse Abernathy, *The Loss of Local News: What It Means for Communities*, Expanding News Desert, https://perma.cc/3XQQ-7NJX.

[41] *Cf.* Jennifer Allen et al., *Evaluating the Fake News Problem at the Scale of the Information Ecosystem*, 6 Sci. Advances 1, 2–3 (Apr. 3, 2020) ("For online consumption, which includes mobile and desktop, news is dominated by several other categories such as entertainment, social media, and search.").

[42] *See* Woodcock, *The Fourth's Estate*, *supra* note 1, at 10–11.

[43] *See Google May Employ More People than the Entire U.S. Newspaper Industry*, Bloomberg (Feb. 12, 2019), https://perma.cc/S4GN-V3NV. Craigslist, which distributes classified advertising for free online, did some of the initial damage to local newspapers' advertising revenues, but it would be a mistake to suppose that Craigslist alone is responsible for newspapers' advertising woes. *See* Robert Seamans & Feng Zhu, *Responses to Entry in Multi-Sided Markets: The Impact of Craigslist on Local Newspapers*, 60 Mgmt. Sci. 476, 490 (2014). News industry advertising revenues have fallen 80 percent, from a peak of $49 billion in 2005 to $9.6 billion in 2020, far more than the third of advertising revenues accounted for by classified advertising in 2005. *Newspapers Fact Sheet*, Pew Rsch. Ctr. (Jun. 29, 2021), https://perma.cc/86S4-TV43; Robert G. Picard, *Shifts in Newspaper Advertising Expenditures and Their Implications for the Future of Newspapers*, 9 Journalism Stud. 704, 713 (2008). Clearly, national and retail advertising, in which the Tech Giants specialize, have also sustained catastrophic declines. Meanwhile, advertising on Google, Facebook, and Amazon were up from nearly zero to $10 billion over the same period. Reid Wilson, *New Data Shows Newspaper Revenues Down Sharply*, Hill (Jun. 9, 2022), https://perma.cc/Y377-K3B3. A recent study commissioned by Google itself shows that almost half of advertising revenue declines between 2003 and 2019 were due to declines in nonclassified advertising. *See* Eero Korhonen, *Research: What Really Happened to Newspaper Revenue*, Google: Keyword (Jun. 3, 2021), https://perma.cc/2NQ2-7TTA. That study focused on Western European news markets but may

The result was the fragmentation of national news markets and the demise of many local news markets. In national news markets, competitors fanned out across the ideological spectrum, picking off legacy papers' ideologically nonaligned readers, who had been weakly held to the legacy papers by an interest in facts.[44] Expensive fact-reporting could no longer pay dividends in the form of a broader readership and newspapers now had to defend their own ideological turf against assault from new internet entrants, including both news websites and social media users with large followings. A turn to inexpensive opinion-reporting was the only option.[45] This was ruinous competition in the economic sense.[46] Firms were forced to degrade their own products' quality in order to survive in the market. High-quality fact-oriented reporting was replaced with low-quality opinion-based reporting. This effect was magnified by competition for advertising from social media companies, which reduced the revenues flowing into news, creating a further incentive to substitute opinion-reporting for expensive fact-reporting. In many local news markets, which were too small to support newspapers on reduced advertising revenues, competition from social media had an even more catastrophic effect; newspapers simply disappeared.[47]

By the 2020s, the positive externalities created by the monopoly position of twentieth-century newspapers were gone. Newspapers no longer had the incentive or the revenues to invest in high-quality fact production. Ideological centrism had been replaced by ideological fragmentation, and so newspapers no longer exerted a moderating influence on politics. And the influx of competition into news markets, combined with the competition for advertising from social media companies, had

be probative of the situation in news markets in the United States as well. It also bears noting that, in recent years, Facebook Marketplace has made inroads into online classifieds; if the Tech Giants were not the original diverters of newspapers' classified advertising revenues, they are increasingly so today.

44 *See* Woodcock, *Ruinous Competition in News*, *supra* note 1, at 17–20; David M. J. Lazer et al., *The Science of Fake News*, 359 Sci. 1094 (2018) ("The internet has lowered the cost of entry to new competitors – many of which have rejected [objectivity] norms – and undermined the business models of traditional news sources that had enjoyed high levels of public trust and credibility.").

45 *See* Hamilton, *supra* note 13, at 315 ("Costly delivery and distribution methods once meant consumer, producer, entertainment, and voter information came bundled in a dominant local newspaper or widely viewed national broadcast. Cable, Internet, and social media broke the bundle, making a wider variety of entertainment and expression possible. This also reduced bundling's support for information with relatively higher costs, … namely accountability journalism.").

46 Ruinous competition is usually defined as competition that prevents firms in an industry from covering fixed costs. *See* Alfred E. Kahn, The Economics of Regulation: Principles and Institutions 173 / II (1971). But when a firm is systematically unable to cover fixed costs, the firm may reduce those costs by reducing product quality. Thus ruinous competition is ultimately competition that degrades quality. *See id.* at 176 / II ("The decline in price to average variable costs can lead to a skimping on safety, reliability, and frequency of service that consumers may have difficulty in detecting promptly.").

47 *See* Abernathy, *supra* note 40.

starved national newspapers of revenue and driven many local newspapers out of business entirely. Far from being in a position to speak truth to power, newspapers' continued existence was in doubt, leading to calls for government subsidization.[48]

20.3 NEWSPAPERS' INADEQUATE RESPONSE

20.3.1 *To Social Media*

Newspapers' responses to these challenges betray a lack of understanding regarding their causes. The basic premise of newspapers' response to competition from social media companies in their advertising markets has been to argue that social-media companies are stealing newspaper content. Specifically, newspapers argue that social-media companies are using links to news content to attract social-media users without providing newspapers with adequate compensation in return.[49] This premise underlies a campaign by newspapers over the past decade to drum up support for antitrust action against Google and Facebook.[50] Not only has the News Media Alliance – newspapers' lobbying organization – explicitly called for antitrust action, but newspapers from across the political spectrum have appeared to use favorable reporting, editorials, and the publication of op-eds by antitrust activists to promote it as well.[51] Whether the apparent pro-antitrust slant to reporting is a product of deliberate policy or anti-tech sentiment among journalists, who believe that their livelihoods are threatened by social media, is unclear.[52] But the premise that Google and Facebook are appropriating something of value from newspapers is not. Newspapers hope that the introduction of more competitors into social-media markets via antitrust action will make it easier for newspapers to negotiate compensation from the social-media industry.

The premise that social media is stealing from newspapers also underlies newspapers' attempt to lobby Congress for an antitrust exemption that would permit the industry to form a cartel to negotiate compensation from social-media companies.[53] If newspapers can negotiate as a block, they reason, they will be able to extract larger payments from social-media companies than they might otherwise. The theft

[48] *See* Robert G. Picard, *Subsidised News Sounds Good, but Is No Panacea to News Industry Challenges*, 13 J. MEDIA BUS. STUD. 136, 136 (2016).

[49] *See* Kate Ackley, *News Media Alliance Pushes for New Senate Antitrust Bill*, ROLL CALL (Jun. 4, 2019), https://perma.cc/JNA6-X4Q5. This is the subject of Paul Matzko's contribution to this volume. *See* Matzko, *supra* note 12.

[50] *See* Woodcock, *The Fourth's Estate*, *supra* note 1, at 5–7; Ramsi A. Woodcock, *Big Ink vs. Bigger Tech*, TRUTH ON THE MARKET (DEC. 30, 2019), https://perma.cc/Q92L-MFWA.

[51] *See* Chavern, *supra* note 11; Woodcock, *Big Ink vs. Bigger Tech*, *supra* note 50; Woodcock, *The Fourth's Estate*, *supra* note 1, at 5–7.

[52] *See* Woodcock, *The Fourth's Estate*, *supra* note 1, at 5–7.

[53] *See* Ackley, *supra* note 49; Staff, *Newspapers Nationwide Run Coordinated Ad Campaign, Urge Congress to Pass JCPA*, NEWS MEDIA ALL. (Jul. 19, 2022), https://perma.cc/7299-TYFX.

premise also underlies the News Media Alliance's interest in achieving intellectual-property protection for news-article links or news content more generally.[54] At present, newspapers have no legal right to demand payment from social-media companies for links to news content.[55] All newspapers can do to encourage payment is threaten to program their websites to reject incoming web traffic from social-media platforms.[56] The hope is that intellectual-property protection for linking would strengthen newspapers' bargaining position.

It is hard to view newspapers' conviction that the Tech Giants' success is built on appropriation of newspaper content as anything other than narcissistic pathology. The news industry seems unable to conceive that its readers might wish to do something on social media other than find news. But, in fact, they do.[57] While some small fraction of the attention that social-media companies generate may represent attention that once would have been devoted to newspapers – and may even be attention poached from newspapers in the sense that news article links are used to attract this attention – the lion's share is not.[58] The success of social media comes not from poaching news readers' attention but from expanding the overall pool of commercializable attention in the economy. Social-media companies will, therefore, be unwilling to pay newspapers anything but a small fraction of the advertising revenues that newspapers have lost to social media. This is true whether the social-media industry is concentrated into a few Tech Giants or deconcentrated into large numbers of small providers. Either way, an industry that relies little on news links is not going to pay much for access to them.

The importance of news to social media was demonstrated in early 2021 when the government of Australia sought to compel social-media companies to pay newspapers for links.[59] Facebook responded by disabling news-linking on its platform and pointing out that only 4 percent of the material shared on its platform involves

[54] *See* Marshall Kosloff & David Chavern, *Day Three, Session VI: Can News Be Profitable on the Internet?*, Reboot 2020 Conference (Nov. 10, 2020), https://perma.cc/XS7W-HCJ9.

[55] *See* News Media All., How Google Abuses Its Position as a Market Dominant Platform to Strong-Arm News Publishers and Hurt Journalism 2–4 (2020), https://perma.cc/5MWH-QCW9 (arguing that legal rulings that suggest that newspapers have no copyright over links to their content should be overturned).

[56] *See* Benton, *supra* note 12.

[57] *See id.* (noting that, according to Facebook, only one in every twenty-five Facebook posts shares news); Allen et al., *supra* note 41, at 3 ("Even including passive exposure to news content on social media sites [Facebook, X, Reddit, and YouTube], search engines [Google, Bing, and Yahoo!], and portals [Yahoo!, MSN, and AOL], news accounts for only 4.2% of total online consumption.").

[58] *See* Joshua Benton, *Do not Expect McConnell's Paradox to Help News Publishers Get Real Money out of Google and Facebook*, Nieman Lab (Jan. 8, 2020), https://perma.cc/T3TC-X862.

[59] *See* Bill Grueskin, *Australia Pressured Google and Facebook to Pay for Journalism. Is America Next?*, Colum. Journalism Rev. (Mar. 9, 2022), https://perma.cc/KS4T-99GX. It may not be a coincidence that Australia is the birthplace of news magnate Rupert Murdoch, a leading proponent of the strategy of making social media pay for news

news.[60] Facebook simply did not need the news. While Facebook and Google eventually agreed to make some payments for news, the amounts – which are estimated to be in the low tens of millions of dollars per year – were an infinitesimal of the Tech Giants' own advertising revenues and an order of magnitude below annual declines in newspaper advertising revenues. Newspapers declared victory, if only to save face.[61]

20.3.2 *To News Competition*

There has been no analogous industry-wide initiative to counter the threat of ruinous competition in national news markets. By its nature, intra-industry competition pits news providers against each other, complicating collective action. Instead, the ruinous-competition problem has been left to individual newspapers and journalists to solve in decentralized fashion. Left to their own devices, newspapers and independent journalists have sought shelter from the competitive gale in news through two strategies: product differentiation and abandonment of the ad-based funding model in favor of subscription models.[62] Newspapers have differentiated their product based on ideological orientation, making the problem of ruinous competition worse, further fragmenting news markets, and forcing opinion-reporting on their competitors. Newspapers have also differentiated their product based on subject matter, reporting on a particular industry, profession, neighborhood, or other area of interest. At an extreme, it involves independent journalists taking refuge in subscription-based blogging services like Substack. Differentiation of this and also the ideological variety can help newspapers or independent journalists avoid bankruptcy. But it also results in insufficient revenues to sustain high-quality fact production except in the few ideological or subject matter markets having well-heeled audiences, such as markets for opinion that support moneyed interests or for news about Silicon Valley, Wall Street, or Capitol Hill.[63] Thus while there might still be years-long investigations of Silicon Valley, there will be no years-long investigations of corruption at City Hall. There have been some notable attempts to overcome the revenue squeeze through pooling of resources across organizations to carry out specific investigations.[64] But these are limited by inter-

[60] *See* Benton, *supra* note 58; Benton, *supra* note 12.

[61] *See* Grueskin, *supra* note 59; Benton, *supra* note 58; Emma Shepherd, *Print Advertising Expected to Decline 10.2% Annually until 2025, PwC Finds*, MUMBRELLA (JUL. 19, 2021); Carmen Ang, *How Do Big Tech Giants Make Their Billions?*, VISUAL CAPITALIST (Apr. 25, 2022), https://perma.cc/ZX4C-WMWY.

[62] *See* Ben Smith, *Bail Out Journalists. Let Newspaper Chains Die.*, N.Y. TIMES (Mar. 29, 2020); Will Oremus, *What Substack Is Really Doing to the Media*, SLATE (Apr. 23, 2021), https://perma.cc/4YNX-R5BT.

[63] *See* HAMILTON, *supra* note 13, at 131 (discussing the cost of investigative reporting).

[64] *See The Panama Papers: Exposing the Rogue Offshore Finance Industry*, INT'L CONSORTIUM INVESTIGATIVE JOURNALISTS (Apr. 3, 2016), https://perma.cc/BLC5-T2FX.

organization coordination costs that the old newspaper monopolies did not face. The move to subscription-based funding models is also unlikely fully to replace lost advertising revenues. If it could do that, then newspapers would have relied more on subscriptions than advertising in the first place.[65]

20.4 POSTAGE AND AD CAPS AS ALTERNATIVES

20.4.1 *Charging Online Postage*

One way to restore newspapers' dwindling revenues would be through direct government subsidization along the lines of what Britain does for the BBC in the broadcast arena.[66] To maintain the political independence of the press, government could impose a special tax on communications – in Britain, all television hookups are taxed at a flat rate – and dedicate the proceeds to newspapers, ensuring that any attempt to punish newspapers by directing the funding elsewhere would be viewed by voters as a misappropriation of public funds.[67] Britain does this by taxing all television hookups at a flat rate. On a similar theory, Franklin D. Roosevelt insisted that Social Security tax be charged as a separate line item to taxpayers in the United States in order to protect Social Security from rollback.[68] A few state and local governments are already dabbling in direct subsidization as a way of rescuing local news. But the direct subsidization model is unlikely to spread thanks to America's deeply engrained anti-statism, which resists both taxation and government influence over public debate, however tenuous.[69] Even if it were to spread, it could be no more than a partial solution to fragmentation and political polarization at the national level. Entry into that market would remain free and readers would continue to be drawn to the private news sources that best fit their ideological preferences. But so long as subsidies were to reward fact-reporting, more of that would be supplied to the market.

Another approach would target fragmentation and political polarization in national news markets in particular, and avoid the pitfalls of direct subsidization. That approach would be to leverage a mode of indirect support for the news with which Americans are comfortable and which is so firmly embedded in the nation's

[65] *See* EVANS & SCHMALENSEE, *supra* note 27, at 50, 99 (observing that newspapers have "rebalanc[ed] their pricing" to generate more revenue from readers as opposed to advertisers and that "[w]ith less advertising revenue, newspapers could not spend as much on content").

[66] *See* Jim Waterson, *How Is the BBC Funded and Could the Licence Fee Be Abolished?*, GUARDIAN (Dec. 16, 2019), https://perma.cc/ANS7-FBKD.

[67] *See id.*

[68] *See* Matthew H. Hawes, *So No Damn Politician Can Ever Scrap It: The Constitutional Protection of Social Security Benefits*, 65 U. PITT. L. REV. 865, 904 (2004).

[69] *See* Jack Shafer, *The State of New Jersey Wants to Subsidize News. Uh-Oh.*, POLITICO MAG. (Jul. 6, 2018), https://perma.cc/WL8T-9X5M; Sarah Bartlett & Julie Sandorf, *How New York City Is Saving Its Local News Outlets*, N.Y. TIMES (May 20, 2021).

history that it was one of the means by which the country obtained independence from Britain in the eighteenth century: the postal service.[70] Although Americans today think of the postal service as a rapidly obsolescing mode of private communication through the exchange of paper letters, it started life as a method of distributing newspapers.[71] The British Crown had a monopoly over the provision of postal services in the colonies and its postmasters leveraged this monopoly to favor carriage of newspapers that they themselves published, excluding competing viewpoints.[72] In response, the American revolutionaries created a national postal service that lavishly subsidized the distribution of American newspapers, enabling any newspaper to transmit the news to customers at virtually no cost.[73] Alexis de Tocqueville, viewing the results some decades later, remarked with awe that, thanks to America's subsidized news distribution, a backwoodsman in Michigan knew more about the rest of the world than a suburban Parisian.[74]

By the start of the twentieth century, the postal service had largely ceased to be an important disseminator of news. The advent of the telegraph and a general decline in transportation costs allowed newspapers to build private distribution networks that disseminated the news far more quickly.[75] The challenges faced by newspapers today give the postal service an opportunity once again to carry out its original mission to sustain the press.[76] Whereas the challenge faced by the press at the nation's founding was how to overcome an excessively high cost of communication, today the challenge faced by the press in national news markets is how to overcome an excessively low cost of communication that has led to ruinous competition and political polarization. It follows that, whereas the job of the postal service at the founding was to lower the cost of distributing the news by charging low, subsidized postage rates to newspapers, the job of the postal service today should be to raise the cost of distributing the news by charging postage for online posts.[77]

70 *See* Anuj C. Desai, *The Transformation of Statutes into Constitutional Law: How Early Post Office Policy Shaped Modern First Amendment Doctrine*, 58 Hastings L.J. 671, 681–83 (2007) (describing the abandonment of the "parliamentary Post" by American colonials in favor of a private network established by a pro-independence newspaper publisher seeking a means of distributing his newspapers free of British control as "the first institutional change of the American Revolution").

71 *See id.* at 683 (describing the "initial establishment" of the forerunner to the U.S. Postal Service as "due to a printer's attempt to ensure delivery of his newspapers to the populace at large").

72 *See id.* at 678–81.

73 *See id.* at 694 (noting that whereas the cost to the post office of delivering a four-sheet newspaper more than 450 miles was a dollar, postage in 1792 was "a cent and a half").

74 *See* Richard R. John, Spreading the News: The American Postal System from Franklin to Morse 1–2 (1995).

75 *See* Paul Starr, The Creation of the Media: Political Origins of Modern Communications 174–75, 179, 252 (2006); Woodcock, *Ruinous Competition in News*, *supra* note 1, at 34.

76 *See* Woodcock, *Ruinous Competition in News*, *supra* note 1, at 32–46.

77 *See id.* at 35.

The goal would not be to drive distribution costs back to pre-internet days. The low cost of communication has created immense value for society by allowing a greater diversity of voices and information to enter public debate. Rather, the goal would be to drive costs up enough to strike a balance between the benefits and harms of easy entry into news markets.[78] Just as the Federal Reserve uses data on capital markets to set interest rates, the postal service could use data on news markets to adjust online postage rates to achieve a level of ease of entry that properly balances benefits and harms.[79] By imposing a zero price of postage for posts to social-media sites, blogs, or newspaper websites that garner small numbers of views but a substantial fixed price for posts to such platforms that have a moderate number of views, the postal service could impose a fixed cost on writing for the general public as opposed to private friend groups. That cost would drive down the number of news organizations in the market. With competition reduced, the news organizations that would remain in the market would have the opportunity and incentive to maximize their readership through fact-reporting.[80] Scale would be rewarded, and fragmentation and product differentiation discouraged.[81]

The postal service already has the statutory authority to act.[82] Federal law gives the postal service a "letter-box monopoly" – the sole right to deliver mail to mailboxes – and the authority to define, by regulation, what a mailbox is.[83] By redefining mailboxes to include electronic mailboxes, including email and social-media accounts, the postal service could acquire the exclusive right to deliver internet communications.[84] It could then grant a license to make those deliveries to the firms, such as Google and Facebook, that actually deliver them today. But the postal service could retain the right to charge postage for such delivery. To minimize the resemblance of such postage to a tax, the postal service could distribute the proceeds to the public. This would demonstrate that, even if internet postage would have the

78 *See id.*

79 *See* David Zaring, *Law and Custom on the Federal Open Market Committee*, 78 Law & Contemp. Probs. 157, 162–63, 171–72 (2015); Woodcock, *Ruinous Competition in News*, *supra* note 1, at 37.

80 *Cf.* Evans & Schmalensee, *supra* note 27, at 50.

81 Kyle Langvardt, *Structuring a Subsidy for Local Journalism*, 3 J. Free Speech L. 297 (2023). *See also* Woodcock, *Ruinous Competition in News*, *supra* note 1, at 37–38. For example, if the postal service were to charge $1 million in postage for a post that receives more than 10,000 views, most posters would need to be able to derive revenue from such an audience in order to be able to afford to post to it. And the bigger the audience, the better, because, operating costs aside, every dollar of revenue generated above the $1 million fee would be profit. Moreover, unable to cover postage, many ideological posters would no longer be able to reach large audiences. Ideological posters would be too few to give every viewer a fellow traveler to prefer over an ideologically different poster of facts. Fact-reporting would, therefore, once again be rewarded and ideological differentiation would become less important to success.

82 *See id.* at 40–46.

83 18 U.S.C. § 1725 (2018); J. Gregory Sidak, *Abolishing the Letter-Box Monopoly*, 1 Criterion J. Innovation 401, 408 (2016).

84 *See* Woodcock, *Ruinous Competition in News*, *supra* note 1, at 40–46.

effect of a tax on participants in news markets, its purpose would not be to raise revenue for the postal service or the government more generally, or to subsidize the news industry à la the BBC's tax on television hookups, but only to alter the structure of news markets in ways that improve the quality of the news and reduce political polarization.

20.4.2 *Capping Advertising*

Internet postage would insulate national newspapers from ruinous competition from other news sources, but it would not restore the revenues that national newspapers have lost to social media. Internet postage also would not help local newspapers, which lack the advertising revenues they need to stay in business, much less engage in ruinous competition. Some additional policy is required to address newspapers' loss of advertising revenue to social media. One approach would be for the postal service to use high postage rates for social-media views to destroy social media. That would eliminate the competition that is diverting newspapers' advertising revenue flows. But that is not a desirable solution. Social media represents a genuine improvement upon communication, which is why it is so popular.[85] Destroying it would be wasteful.

A better solution would be for government to place a cap on the number of advertising impressions that social-media companies distribute each year.[86] Normally, a restriction on the sale of a superior product will not necessarily help a competitor offering an inferior product because buyers might exit the product category entirely rather than purchase the inferior product. If you cannot obtain a high-quality ice cream, you might purchase a pastry instead, rather than poor-quality ice cream. So, in principle, capping social-media advertising, which advertisers view as superior because of its reach and the opportunities it affords for targeting, would not necessarily induce advertisers to advertise in newspapers. They might choose to stop advertising entirely and invest in improving the technology of their products instead.

But advertising is different. Firms rarely have a choice about whether to advertise because their competitors already advertise. If they do not use counter-advertising to cancel out their competitors' advertising, they will lose business.[87] It follows that firms that are locked out of high-quality advertising distribution will substitute low-quality advertising distribution because they fear that their competitors will substitute low-quality advertising distribution.[88] A cap on the amount of advertising that social media can distribute would, therefore, channel advertisers' dollars back to

85 *See* Woodcock, *The Fourth's Estate*, *supra* note 1, at 42.
86 *See id.* at 19–29.
87 *See* Kyle Bagwell, *The Economic Analysis of Advertising*, *in* 3 Handbook of Industrial Organization 1701, 1729 (2007); Woodcock, *The Fourth's Estate*, *supra* note 1, at 26 n. 129.
88 *See* Woodcock, *The Fourth's Estate*, *supra* note 1, at 27–28.

newspapers rather than away from advertising entirely.[89] By adjusting the cap, a regulator could adjust the precise amount of advertising revenue that would be returned to the newspaper industry. The regulator could even set the cap so low as to redirect all social-media profits to newspapers, allowing the social-media industry only enough revenue to cover costs.[90] Thus a cap would not have the redistributive limitations inherent in the news industry's current approach of seeking to extract payment from social-media companies that place a low value on access to news content. While the Federal Communications Commission (FCC) currently enjoys some authority to regulate advertising, new legislation would be required to enable the FCC or another regulator to implement this approach.[91]

An advertising cap has the virtue of continuing the newspaper industry's tradition of funding itself through advertising.[92] That approach is the principal way in which an anti-statist society such as the United States funds information-related public goods, including not just newsgathering but also the arts, entertainment, and sports.[93] All of these activities provide benefits to society as a whole – newsgathering is critical to a successful democracy, for example – for which consumers are sometimes not willing to pay in full if charged directly.[94] Rather than fund these activities through taxation – the textbook means of funding public goods – the United States for the most part leaves it to those engaged in these activities to acquire their own funding through the distribution of advertising. Consumers still end up paying for these activities, but they do so indirectly by purchasing advertised products. Advertising manipulates consumers into paying higher prices for goods and services. Advertisers pay a portion of the additional revenues they generate from those higher prices to the providers of informational public goods who distribute their advertising. In this way, advertisers end up manipulating consumers into paying for public goods for which consumers would not be willing to pay if asked to do so directly.[95] The result is a decentralized model of public goods financing that

89 *See id.*

90 *See id.* at 29. For an estimate of those costs, *see* Woodcock, *supra* note 23, at 2340 n. 345.

91 *See* Woodcock, *The Fourth's Estate*, *supra* note 1, at 21 n. 96.

92 *See* Starr, *supra* note 75, at 86.

93 *See* David A. Moss, When All Else Fails: Government as the Ultimate Risk Manager 317 (2002) (discussing American anti-statism).

94 *See* Hal R. Varian, Intermediate Microeconomics: A Modern Approach 670–71 (7th ed. 2006).

95 *See id.* Advertising's manipulative properties are consistent with advertising's cancelling effect. When a firm that is alone in an industry advertises, the advertising draws customers away from competitors and makes these customers willing to pay higher prices, because the advertiser must charge higher prices to cover the cost of advertising. To counteract this effect, the other firms in the industry must also advertise, drawing customers to their products to make up for those they have lost. These may be customers who were drawn away by the first firm's advertising or legacy customers of the first firm. Regardless, these customers must now pay a higher price for the other firms' products in order to cover the other firms' advertising costs. From the perspective of firms, nothing has been achieved by advertising other than to defend against each other's advertising. But, from the perspective of consumers, much has changed.

minimizes the influence of government over the news and culture more generally. Such minimization of government influence is not necessarily good for either the news or culture.[96] Moreover, there is something odd about using a practice that manipulates consumers into buying products they would not otherwise buy to fund a newspaper industry devoted to empowering citizens to think for themselves.[97] But this funding model may be the only approach to subsidizing the news that Americans will accept, at least in the short term.

An added benefit of placing a cap on social-media advertising is that it would afford government the opportunity to reduce the overall amount of advertising in the economy.[98] Reducing advertising is desirable because advertising short-circuits free markets. Free markets enable consumers to impose their preferences on firms, showering profits on those that please them and starving those that do not.[99] Consumers who have been manipulated by advertising into buying things that they would not otherwise buy are unable to impose their will on firms, however. Firms use advertising to ensure that consumers buy products that *firms* prefer rather than products that consumers prefer.[100] While counter-advertising by other firms tends to prevent advertising from raising demand for individual firms – that's the canceling effect of advertising – it does not prevent consumers from being manipulated by advertising. The net effect of advertising may well be that those who prefer Coke drink Pepsi and those who prefer Pepsi drink Coke, even if advertising does not increase overall demand for either product.[101] The result is inefficiency: Advertising prevents markets from allocating resources in ways that consumers would value the most.[102] It was once possible to argue that advertising had an offsetting benefit in the form of the product information that it provided to consumers. In the world before the internet, a consumer might not have been able to find a product that they really did prefer without the aid of advertising.[103] But in the information age, advertising's information function has become redundant. Consumers can find all the product

Some have been manipulated into buying products that they would not have purchased otherwise. All have been manipulated into paying higher prices.

96 *See* Jean-Jacques Rousseau, Letter to d'Alembert and Writings for the Theater 113 (Alan Bloom et al. eds., 2004) (arguing against the establishment of a theater in Geneva on the ground that the theater would "attack" the morals and constitution of the city).

97 *See* Ramsi A. Woodcock, *Advertising Is Obsolete – Here's Why It's Time to End It*, Conversation (Aug. 20, 2018), https://perma.cc/A9GQ-CYYA.

98 *See* Woodcock, *supra* note 23, at 2278–90.

99 *See id.*

100 *See id.*

101 *Cf.* Samuel M. McClure et al., *Neural Correlates of Behavioral Preference for Culturally Familiar Drinks*, 44 Neuron 379, 384 (2004) (finding that study participants were unable to distinguish Coke from Pepsi in blind taste testing but that they exhibited strong brand preferences that were reflected in imaging of their brains).

102 *See* Woodcock, *supra* note 23, at 2278–90.

103 *See id.*

information they desire – much of it in the form of unvarnished consumer reviews that are more informative than any advertisement – through a Google search.[104]

A regulator empowered to place a cap on social media advertising could go one step further and place a cap on all advertising.[105] For the same reason that the canceling aspect of advertising ensures that capping social-media advertising would not reduce the total amount of money spent by firms on advertising but would merely shift it to newspaper advertising, capping all advertising would not reduce the total amount of money spent by all firms on advertising either. But because now there would be no alternative form of advertising to which the money could flow, capping social-media advertising would instead cause advertisers to bid up the price of the advertising that would remain available under the cap. Indeed, because firms advertise in order to cancel the advertising of others, a cap on all advertising would lead firms to bid up the price of advertising impressions – so as not to lose the opportunity to counteract a competitor's employment of this scarce resource – until they find themselves spending the same amount on advertising as they did before the cap.[106] Funding for public goods financed through the distribution of advertising – whether the good is news, the arts, or sports – would, therefore, not be reduced by a cap on all advertising.[107] So long as the regulator were to cause the cap to fall disproportionately on social-media advertising relative to newspaper advertising, dollars would still be diverted from social media to newspapers, but the overall number of advertising impressions served up by the advertising-distribution industry would fall.

20.4.3 *First Amendment Concerns*

Both internet postage and advertising caps regulate speech. Postage burdens internet communication and advertising caps prevent advertisers from speaking about their products. Neither of these policies would violate the First Amendment, however. In *Postal Service v. Council of Greenburgh Civic Ass'ns*, the Supreme Court rejected a challenge to the postal service's letter-box monopoly on the ground that regulation of the speech that passes through mailboxes does not prevent speakers from communicating by other means.[108] According to the Court, the postal service's control over mailbox speech is rather like the military's control over speech on military bases – necessary for government to act.[109]

To be sure, were the postal service to redefine the definition of "letter-box" to include all virtual receptacles of online communications, the definition would be

[104] *See id.* at 2299–2308.
[105] *See* Woodcock, *The Fourth's Estate*, *supra* note 1, at 29.
[106] *See id.* at 29–33.
[107] *See id.*
[108] *See* Postal Service v. Council of Greenburgh Civic Ass'ns, 453 U.S. 114, 129 (1981).
[109] *See id.* at 129–30.

far more expansive than the physical mailbox on a stick on the front lawn contemplated by the Supreme Court in *Greenburgh*.[110] But all of that expansion would be to areas that did not exist when the Supreme Court decided *Greenburgh* in 1981.[111] If, at a time when virtual mailboxes were not an extant alternative to mailing letters, the Court thought that depriving Americans of the right to speak through physical mailboxes without paying a toll left Americans enough alternative modes of communication for free speech to remain uninfringed, then it is hard to see why depriving Americans of the freedom to speak un-tolled through new virtual mailboxes that did not exist at the time *Greenburgh* was decided could deprive Americans of sufficient alternative modes of communication to pose a threat to free speech.[112] Moreover, in both the case of the physical letter-box and the virtual letter-box, regulation is essential to the government activity of promoting a healthy news industry that is the original purpose of the postal service.

Advertising caps do not violate the First Amendment because advertising's manipulativeness – which is its exclusive function now that its information function has been rendered obsolete by the information age – places all advertising in the same unprotected First Amendment category as false advertising.[113] The Supreme Court has said that false advertising receives no protection because it tends to impair the ability of consumers to make "intelligent and well informed" purchase decisions.[114] That is, false advertising impairs consumers' ability to impose their preferences on markets. All other forms of advertising today do the same, but they do it by manipulating consumer preferences rather than hiding the true characteristics of products from consumers, as false advertising does.[115] While advertising's information function, which does help consumers make well-informed purchase decisions, once enabled advertising to enjoy First Amendment protection, the obsolescence of that function has eliminated this rationale for protecting advertising.[116] The notion that the First Amendment no longer protects *any* advertising would seem to clash with the apparent alacrity with which the Court has extended the First Amendment to ever-larger amounts of commercial speech in recent decades.[117] But a careful reading of the cases shows that the Court has never extended protection to advertising that it has understood to be exclusively manipulative in function, as all advertising is today.[118]

[110] *See id.* at 129.
[111] *See id.* at 114.
[112] *See* Woodcock, *Ruinous Competition in News, the Postal Internet*, *supra* note 1, at 44–45.
[113] *See* Woodcock, *supra* note 23, at 2328–36.
[114] *See* Va. State Bd. of Pharmacy v. Va. Consumer Council, 425 U.S. 748, 765 (1976).
[115] *See* Woodcock, *supra* note 23, at 2308–19.
[116] *See id.* at 2299–2308.
[117] *See id.* at 2330–36.
[118] *See id.* at 2334.

20.5 CONCLUSION

By lowering the cost of communication almost to zero, the internet created two challenges for newspapers. The first was that, by making possible the creation of the social-media industry, the internet greatly expanded the amount of commercializable attention in the economy, relegating the quality of the advertising distribution product offered by newspapers to second-class status, and driving revenues so low that newspapers disappeared from many local news markets. The second was that, by enabling virtually anyone to distribute news, the internet greatly increased competition within national news markets, forcing newspapers to substitute opinion-reporting for fact-reporting, fragmenting the industry, and polarizing American public discourse.

Newspapers' responses have been inadequate. Attempts to force social media companies to share revenues will not restore newspapers' lost profits because the sharing of news links is a small part of social-media activity. The Tech Giants will not pay enough for links to restore newspapers' lost revenues. Embrace of a small-is-beautiful ethic in newsgathering, in the mode of Substack authoring, will only increase opinion-reporting, industry fragmentation, and polarization.

One solution to the problem of ruinous competition between newspapers would be to restore some of the cost of communication. The postal service could reinterpret its letter-box monopoly to apply to virtual mailboxes, allowing the postal service to charge postage for internet posts that garner large numbers of views. That would reduce the number of players in news markets and so the opinion orientation, fragmentation, and political polarization that afflict the industry. A solution to competition from social-media companies would be for regulators to cap the number of advertising impressions that social media companies are permitted to distribute per year. Because advertising is a race to the bottom, such a cap would not reduce the amount of money spent on advertising, but it would drive advertising dollars back to newspapers.

Index